HISTORY OF LINC(

Volume III

ANGLO-SAXON LINCOLNSHIRE

PETER SAWYER

HISTORY OF LINCOLNSHIRE
III

Anglo-Saxon Lincolnshire

PETER SAWYER

Lincoln
HISTORY OF LINCOLNSHIRE COMMITTEE
for the Society for Lincolnshire History and Archaeology
1998

Published 1998 by
The History of Lincolnshire Committee, Jews' Court, Steep Hill, Lincoln

ISBN hardback 0 902668 02 1

ISBN paperback 0 902668 11 0

Cover design by Max Marschner, Ampersand Designs, Lincoln LN5 8PN

The Flixborough brooch used in the cover design is reproduced by kind permission of Sir Reginald Sheffield. The illustration and caption are by courtesy of Dr Chris Loveluck, Humber Archaeology. The photograph is by Rob White, Senior Conservator, City and County Museum Conservation Laboratory, Lincoln

Typeset and produced for the publisher by Yard Publishing Services, Sudbury, CO10 6AG

Printed by Interprint, Malta

British Cataloguing-in-publication Data
A catalogue record for this book is obtainable from the British Library

To Catherine

CONTENTS

LIST OF ILLUSTRATIONS

PREFACE AND ACKNOWLEDGEMENTS

In February 1978 I was invited to take over this volume in the History of Lincolnshire, but a year later was told that the Committee was considering making 1982 'the last year for the receipt of manuscripts'. That timetable proved unrealistic; my move to Sweden in 1980 and many irresistible commissions in Scandinavia and the U.S.A as well as in England have caused delays and I am glad that the Committee has shown forbearance and is prepared to accept this manuscript fifteen years late.

It is some compensation that, as a result, account can be taken of recent discoveries, notably at Flixborough, and of recent publications, such as *Change and Continuity,* the Fenland report and the Allecto edition of the Lincolnshire Domesday. I have also been able to include some important results based on coins and other objects found with the help of metal detectors – evidence that began to be registered systematically in 1984. My main regret is that I have not been able to incorporate the final results of the survey of stone sculpture by Paul Everson and David Stocker, although they have given much valuable advice as well as encouragement.

As is made clear in Chapter I, there is little evidence and much of it can be interpreted in very different ways. Some of the consequent disagreements, for example about the date of Lincoln's first church, are of crucial significance. A coherent account of Lincolnshire's early history requires decisions to be made on such topics, but to include all the necessary discussions in the main text would be both confusing and tedious. Some of the most contentious issues are, therefore, discussed in appendixes in which the reasons for choosing the interpretations presented in the first part of the book are explained. The result is, necessarily, a personal interpretation, but it is hoped that enough information is given to enable readers to make up their own minds. Current research, for example on place-names, stone sculpture, pottery, and bones, when it is completed, as well as unexpected discoveries will certainly render the interpretation offered here out of date, but it is put forward in the hope that it will stimulate interest and provide a framework for future study.

I should like to thank the many people who have in various ways made this book possible. I am especially grateful to Alan Vince who has not only given me encouragement and valuable advice over many years, but has also spent a great deal of time and effort gathering and preparing the illustrations. I will not attempt to specify my other debts, but will list those who have helped in alphabetical order. They are: Marion Archibald,

Malcolm Atkin, the late Maurice Barley, David Bates, Guy Beresford, Mark Blackburn, Anthea Boylston, Geoffrey Bryant, Kenneth Cameron, Christina Colyer, Wendy Davies, Tania Dickinson, David Dumville, Paul Everson, Christine Fell, Gillian Fellows-Jensen, Richard Gem, Brian Gilmour, Lauren Gilmour, James Greig, Peter Hayes, Hilary Healey, Joyce Hill, Michael Jones, Kenneth Jonsson, Simon Keynes, Chris Knowles, Tom Lane, Kevin Leahy, Chris Mahany, Michael Metcalf, Dennis Mills, Richard Morris, Terry O'Connor, Elisabeth Okasha, Arthur Owen, Dorothy Owen, Simon Pawley, George Peterken, Elizabeth Pirie, Graham Platts, Julian Richards, Dennis Robson, Warwick Rodwell, David Roffe, Richard Sharpe, Ian Shennan, Brian Simmons, Pauline Stafford, David Stocker, Leslie Webster, Ben Whitwell, Ian Wood, and Patrick Wormald.I am deeply grateful to all and hope that most will think their efforts worth while.

I am also indebted to Kungl. Vetenskaps- och Vitterhets-Samhället i Göteborg and to the Adlerbertska forskningsfond of Gothenburg University for grants that enabled me to complete this work.

Trondheim
November 1997

P.H.S.

NOTE ON TERMINOLOGY, REFERENCES, AND NAMES

Lincolnshire is here used to describe the area of the shire throughout the pre-Conquest period although the shire was not created until the eleventh century.

Conquest, pre-Conquest, and post-Conquest refer to the Norman Conquest.

References to the *Chronicle* are to the *Anglo-Saxon Chronicle.*

An asterisk placed before a word (e.g.**lindo* on p. 16) indicates that it is an inferred, not a recorded form.

Most references to texts are given in two ways; to the pages of the editions and translations named in the bibliography and, for readers who do not have access to those versions, to the conventional divisions in books and chapters. References to DB (Domesday Book) are both to folios, with a and b indicating recto and verso, and to *LD* (*The Lincolnshire Domesday and the Lindsey Survey*), using its enumeration of fiefs and entries. References to *EHD* I (*English Historical Documents* I) are to the pages of the second edition, and also to the numbers of the texts, for the convenience of readers who use the first edition. All abbreviations are expanded in full in the bibliography.

The forms of place-names are those used by the Ordnance Survey.

Sir Frank Stenton's method of standardizing personal names has been adopted:

> Old English names which still survive, such as Alfred, Athelstan, Edward, and Edgar, appear in their modern shape. The others are represented by the simplest or the best known of their genuine Old English variants. Scandinavian names, which often caused difficulty to English clerks, appear in the forms which are either most familiar or most easily intelligible (Stenton 1971, p. ix).

CHAPTER I
THE EVIDENCE

There is very little written evidence for the history of Lincolnshire before the Norman Conquest. Five authentic pre-Conquest charters or wills concerning Lincolnshire have survived, but only as copies. One, recording an agreement made in 1054 about Stow minster, is preserved in the late twelfth-century chartulary of Eynsham Abbey in Oxfordshire, which was united with the Stow community in 1091. The others are from the archives of the abbeys of Burton upon Trent and Peterborough. Only one of these charters, granting Barrow to Bishop Æthelwold for the endowment of Peterborough Abbey, includes a set of bounds defining the extent of the land granted. There are, in addition, a few notes or memoranda made after the Norman Conquest in the abbeys of Peterborough and Ramsey summarizing what appear to have been genuine documents, now lost, about grants of land in Lincolnshire.[1]

Chronicles compiled in other parts of England occasionally refer to Lincolnshire. The *Anglo-Saxon Chronicle* (here referred to as the *Chronicle*) is, in fact, a family of related texts in English based on a chronicle compiled in Wessex at the end of the ninth century.[2] This common core has little to offer concerning Lincolnshire, but the continuations made in various places, including York and Peterborough, are more rewarding, especially in the eleventh century. Several versions incorporate tenth-century annals known as the Mercian Register that are of particular interest for our subject. Valuable additional information is provided by two Latin chronicles that were based on lost versions of the *Chronicle*. One, by Æthelweard, was made towards the end of the tenth century, the other, by Florence of Worcester, who died in 1118, survives in the continuation produced later in the twelfth century by John of Worcester. Some post-Conquest chronicles incorporate annals from lost pre-Conquest chronicles compiled in Northumbria and perhaps elsewhere. The most important of these are the early twelfth-century *Historia Regum* (History of the Kings) attributed to Simeon of Durham, and the *Flores Historiarum* (Flowers of the Histories) gathered by Roger of Wendover in the thirteenth century. At least two twelfth-century historians were able to draw on personal knowledge of Lincolnshire. Orderic Vitalis spent some time in Crowland, probably in 1114, and included an account of that abbey in his *Ecclesiastical History*.[3] Henry, archdeacon of Huntingdon, was even better informed for he was a schoolboy in Lincoln at the end of the eleventh century, and his *Historia Anglorum* (History of the English) provides valuable information.

For the seventh century the most important source is the *Ecclesiastical History of the English People* that Bede completed in 731 in the monastery of Jarrow on the river Tyne. At least two of Bede's informants were from Lindsey. One of them was Cyneberht, its bishop, and Bede was, therefore, relatively well informed about that part of Lincolnshire.[4] In contrast, he gave no information about the southern part of the shire; he mentions neither St Guthlac nor his cell at Crowland. Fortunately the *Life of St Guthlac*, written by Felix in about 740 for an East Anglian king, has been preserved. It includes a description of the Fens and, more important, illuminates the role of that saint and his shrine in early eighth-century politics. Although no other saint's life is so directly concerned with Lincolnshire a little can be gleaned from the *Life of Gregory the Great* written early in the eighth century by a Whitby monk, the *Life of St Werburg*, written by Goscelin in 1095, and the *Liber Eliensis*, a history of Ely Abbey compiled about a century later on the basis of documents in the abbey's archives that have not survived.[5] A little extra light is cast on the religious history of the region by a list of saints' resting places that was originally compiled in the ninth century and enlarged later.[6]

For much of the period between the end of the seventh century and the beginning of the eleventh Lincolnshire was divided between two dioceses, Lindsey and Leicester; Leicester was transferred to Dorchester in Oxfordshire between 869 and 888. Most of the bishops are little more than names in lists of episcopal succession or among the subscriptions to royal charters or ecclesiastical councils. The dates of accession and death of many of them are, moreover, very uncertain.[7] Lindsey was also a kingdom in the seventh century, and probably in the eighth century too, but its rulers are even more obscure than its bishops. The name of only one king is known for certain, Aldfrið, but it is not known when he reigned.[8] Such evidence hardly makes it possible to reconstruct a coherent account of the political development of the area in the centuries between the collapse of Roman rule and the Norman Conquest. Even with the help of the more abundant evidence from neighbouring areas we can hardly hope to do more than recover the main outlines of Lincolnshire's early political history.

The surviving pre-Conquest texts are no more satisfactory as sources of knowledge about the economic and social history of the region or the way it was governed. The period of Mercian supremacy described in Chapter V is dimly illuminated by a text known as the Tribal Hidage, which is discussed in Appendix 2. Comparison with other parts of England for which there is

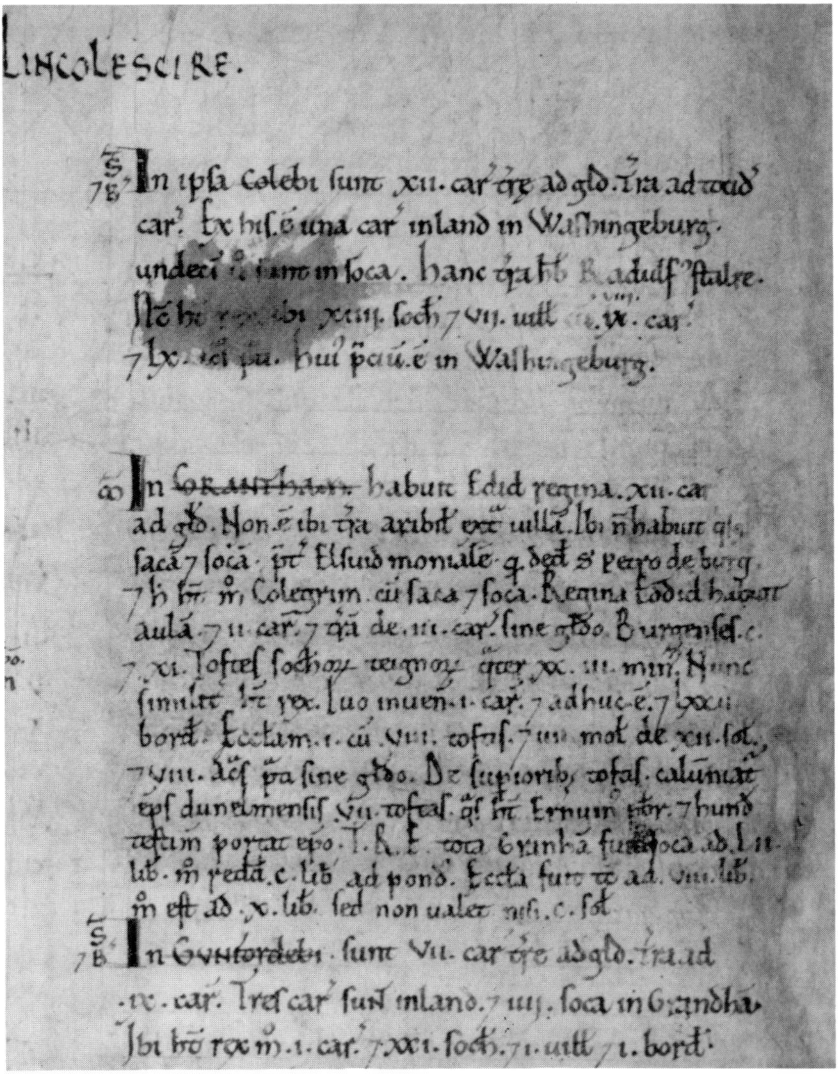

Fig. 1.1 Parts of the descriptions of the royal manors of Coleby and Grantham in DB i. 337b, col. 2. King William put Coleby, about seven miles south of Lincoln, under the royal manor of Washingborough, two miles east of the city, but there is no entry for Washingborough in Domesday Book. The compression of the Grantham entry (13 written lines over 10 ruled lines) shows that it was a late addition. It is followed by the description of the berewicks and sokelands of Grantham with normal spacing. The scribe apparently began work before the information about Grantham manor was ready, but left too little space for it.
Reproduced with permission from the Public Record Office.

better evidence can help us to understand what was happening in Lincolnshire, but as later evidence reveals significant regional differences it would be misleading to assume that Lincolnshire developed in the same way as other areas. The history of the shire cannot, however, be understood in isolation. In the seventh century, and again after the Viking conquest in the ninth century, Lindsey was part of the archiepiscopal province of York, and at the end of the tenth century Lincolnshire formed part of a large district known as the Five Boroughs, namely Lincoln, Stamford, Derby, Leicester and Nottingham. The first information about the operation of royal government in Lincolnshire is, indeed, provided by laws enacted for that district, probably in 997, by King Æthelred and his council.[9]

Domesday Book, discussed more fully in Appendix 3, is a survey of the greater part of England made in 1086 that, for the first time, makes possible a general description of the whole of Lincolnshire. It gives a great deal of information about landowners and their resources, the distribution and social status of the population, taxation assessments, and it includes descriptions of Lincoln, Stamford and Torksey. Any history of pre-Conquest Lincolnshire must be to a large extent an attempt to explain how the situation described in Domesday Book came about. The inadequacy of the surviving written evidence, however, means that any such explanation must be based largely on other sources of information.

ARCHAEOLOGICAL EVIDENCE

A little can be learned from the few surviving remains of pre-Conquest churches.[10] Even more revealing is the evidence unearthed by archaeologists or found with the help of metal detectors, which have in recent years yielded a rich harvest of ornaments and coins.[11] Archaeological evidence is particularly helpful in tracing social and economic development. Cemeteries, Christian as well as pagan, make it possible to draw conclusions about burial customs, and much else besides. As long as graves were furnished, the goods interred with the dead provide some indication of their wealth and status. Other information can be gleaned from the study of skeletons, such as the medical history of some individuals, the diseases from which they suffered, their stature, even diet, and occasionally the cause of death. Few studies of this skeletal evidence have yet been undertaken; a notable exception is the recent analysis of skeletons excavated in the Castledyke cemetery in Barton-upon-Humber which has cast unexpected light on the population of that area in the sixth and seventh centuries.[12]

The archaeological evidence does, however, have significant limitations that should be borne in mind when attempting to build conclusions on it. In the first place, graves and other remains of the pagan period cannot be closely dated. There are no coins or inscriptions to provide firm date limits;

Fig. 1.2 Cremation burials in the course of excavation at the Cleatham cemetery. This burial rite predominated during the 5th and 6th centuries, but during this period it was supplemented, and later replaced, by inhumation. The Cleatham cemetery contained more than 1100 cremations and at least 62 graves and was in use from the 5th to the 7th century. Photo and © Kevin Leahy.

Fig. 1.3 4th-century Germanic tutulus brooch from Kirmington and a supporting arm brooch from Hibaldstow. While these brooches suggest a very early German presence in Lincolnshire, this material is uncommon and there is little evidence for major Anglo-Saxon incursions before the mid 5th century. Photo and © by Kevin Leahy.

the chronology depends on the typological development of pottery, ornaments, weapons, and other objects. There were undoubtedly changes in design and technique and some objects are demonstrably earlier than others, but the main evidence from Lincolnshire consists of pottery, many types of which remained in fashion for a very long time and can, therefore, give no reliable indication of date. On the other hand, some datable objects may have been very old when they were buried or lost. A brooch found at Kirmington, for example, may well have been a type that was popular in the fourth century but that does not mean that it must have reached Kirmington then.[13] Similarly, the fifth-century bronze bowl found in a grave at Nettleton may well have been an heirloom.[14] Archaeological finds can be a more reliable guide to chronology when relatively large quantities are available. The chronology of the sixth century may therefore be determined with rather more confidence than the earliest phase of the English occupation.

A second problem is that few sites have been investigated with much care and a lot of the excavated material has been lost. No cremation urns survive, for example, from the cemeteries of Wold Newton and South Willingham. Until recently there was far more interest in decorated than in plain pots and many of the latter were discarded, often with no record kept of their shape or size. What is more, only a very small part of most cemeteries has been excavated; in only three Lincolnshire cemeteries, Cleatham, Elsham, and Loveden, has the whole area, or most of it, been explored, and none is fully published. Even the most careful excavation cannot make good the losses suffered through earlier disturbances. At Elsham, for example, only the bottoms of most urns were still in place, the upper parts having been broken by ploughing. We have no means of determining how many pots may have been completely destroyed. The broken pieces that are found in the top soil represent lost urns, but only the crudest estimates can be made of their number. Most of the material on which archaeological conclusions have been based has not been found in scientific excavations but by accident or with the help of metal detectors. The distribution of recorded finds therefore tends to reflect such non-archaeological factors as the activity of metal-detector enthusiasts or the extent of iron working, which helps to explain the relatively large number of finds from the Scunthorpe district.

Archaeological investigations of settlements, urban as well as rural, have greatly enlarged our knowledge of the circumstances in which people lived. Scientific methods of analysis can help the study of ecology, the crops that were cultivated, and the animals that were reared, while dendrochronology, based on the pattern of annual growth rings in timber, makes it possible to date some structures with great precision. It should, however, be emphasized that no settlement has been completely excavated, and that many excavations have not been published. However, even such partial excavations as have been made at, for example, Osbournby and Salmonby, make it possible to discover the size, methods of construction, and internal arrangement of houses.[15]

Guy Beresford's very skilful excavation of the site he identified as Goltho is a good illustration of some of the problems that can arise when interpreting the development of a site and its chronology. A complex sequence was discovered with a sizeable hall surrounded by defences, on the site of a Romano-British settlement, all under a motte of the twelfth century.[16] The nearby deserted village was apparently a post-Conquest development. Paul Everson has given convincing reasons for thinking that the place was in fact Bullington and that the last phases should be dated some decades later than proposed by the excavator.[17] More recent studies of the pottery of the region have reinforced doubts about the date of the first development of the site after the Roman period.[18] It seems more likely to have been in the tenth century than the ninth as proposed in the excavation report.

More attention has been paid to urban than rural archaeology in the county. Excavations in Lincoln, Stamford and Torksey, even though only tiny parts of these towns have been studied, have nevertheless made a very important contribution to our understanding of urban development and the occupations of townsfolk.

COINS AND NAMES

For historians coins are perhaps the most informative objects that are recovered in excavations or found in other ways.[19] Like other artefacts their fabric, style and methods of production can be studied, but many of them can also be dated, often within narrow limits. Most have legends that name the rulers or other authorities for whom they were produced. They can sometimes also reveal connections, as when coins minted in Lincoln were modelled on those of York. When relatively large numbers of coins are available for study it is possible to gain some impression of the total production of different mints and this can be a guide to their relative importance. The fact that Lincoln minted about 10 per cent of all English coins in the late tenth and early eleventh centuries confirms the importance of the city at that time.

Fig. 1.4 Penny of King Alfred the Great, struck in Canterbury, c. *871–5, found in the excavation of St Paul-in-the-Bail. See Appendix 9. (Blackburn, Colyer, and Dolley 1983, p. 11 and table 1, no. 2).*

The names of settlements, large and small, of natural features, fields and of districts are an exceptionally important source of information about Anglo-Saxon Lincolnshire. They give clues to early roads, fords, natural vegetation and to fortifications, although these were not necessarily Anglo-Saxon – some names refer to Roman or Iron Age forts. The historical value of this evidence has been greatly enhanced in recent decades by numerous specialist studies, but many problems remain. The earliest evidence for most names is Domesday Book, and there is uncertainty about when some were first coined. The many Scandinavian names cannot be older than the ninth century when the Scandinavians conquered the area and began to settle in it, but the settlements with Scandinavian names could be much older. Archaeological evidence proves that some certainly were. Some early types of non-Scandinavian name can be distinguished, but it is not always clear whether they refer to single settlements or to districts or estates that had many settlements. Names alone are, therefore, an uncertain guide to the history of settlement.

The margins of uncertainty in the interpretation of even major names is well illustrated by recent discussions of the meaning of the name Lindsey,

Fig. 1.5 Figure in the west wall of the late 11th-century tower of St Peter-at-Gowts, Lincoln. This has variously been interpreted as Christ in Majesty, St Peter, or Jupiter (Hill 1948, p. 139). David Stocker (1997) has suggested that it is a Roman sculpture. Photo P. Everson and D. A. Stocker. ©Department of Archaeology, Durham University.

the second part of which is an Old English word meaning 'island', *ēg* or *īg*.[20] It has been claimed that, as *ēg* (*īg*) was only used for small areas, Lindsey cannot have meant the same in the seventh century as it did later. The force of that argument is weakened by the fact that in the ninth century *ēg* was used to describe a district much larger than Lindsey; in the Old English version of Orosius what is now the Swedish province of Skåne is called *Sconeg*.[21] Steven Bassett has suggested that the original Lindsey was Wigford, south of the Witham, opposite the walled Roman city of Lincoln.[22] There is however no archaeological evidence for early occupation of that area after the Roman period. A solution has been offered by Margaret Gelling who is reported to have suggested that *ēg* could be used for a promontory, and could well refer to the ridge on which Lincoln stands.[23] The first known occurrence of the name is in the late ninth century when Asser called it *Lindesig*. The earlier name for the region, *Lindissi*, continued to be used until the twelfth century, but was then displaced by the increasingly popular 'island' form. The most satisfactory explanation, put forward by W. H. Stevenson in 1904, is that the last part of the earlier name *Lindissi* was 'wrongly connected' with the Old English word for island.[24] Before discussing the historical development of Lincolnshire, it may be helpful in the next chapter to comment on the main changes that have occurred in the landscape of the shire since the eleventh century, and to consider its resources. Another topic of general importance throughout the period, on which some preliminary comment may be welcome, is the system of communications by which people could travel, for peaceful or hostile purposes, to and from Lincolnshire, and within it.

NOTES TO CHAPTER I

1 The charters concerning Lincolnshire are listed in Appendix 5.

2 Editions and translations of the texts mentioned in this and the next paragraph are noted in the bibliography. A very helpful introduction to many of them is *EHD I*, pp. 109-29, with a select bibliography, pp. 139-41.

3 See below, p. 148.

4 *HE* preface and ii. 16, ed. Colgrave and Mynors 1969, pp. 6-7, 192-3.

5 Colgrave 1968; Goscelin; *Liber Eliensis*, ed. Blake.

6 Rollason 1978.

7 The bishops are listed in Appendix 6.

8 See p. 49.

9 See pp. 128–9.

10 See pp. 157–8.

11 The coins found in Lincolnshire by 1994 are listed in Appendix 9.

12 See p. 42.

13 Everson and Knowles 1978.

14 Meaney 1964, p. 160; Bruce-Mitford 1993, no. 4.
15 Mahany 1977; Everson 1973.
16 Beresford 1987.
17 Everson 1988.
18 Vince 1993c, pp. 158–60.
19 See Appendix 9.
20 *PNL* 2, pp. 2–7.
21 Lund 1984, p. 22.
22 Bassett 1989a.
23 Cited by Yorke 1993, p. 143.
24 Asser, p. 242.

CHAPTER II

THE SHIRE AND ITS RESOURCES

Since the eleventh century the landscape of Lincolnshire has been changed in many superficial ways by farmers and builders, but there have also been some major changes wrought either by nature or by drainage schemes along the coast, in the Fenland, and in the large inland areas that were, before the Norman Conquest, covered by freshwater marshes.[1] The most extensive coastal change has been in the Wash which was much larger in the eleventh century than it is now. It then extended to Wisbech, into Bicker Haven and almost as far as Spalding. There have also been significant changes along the Lindsey coast. In the north, silt deposited by currents flowing south along the coast of Holderness has enlarged the area of land, but in the south, from Mablethorpe to Skegness, there has been much erosion; since the early thirteenth century the sea may have encroached in places by almost a mile, and four medieval churches have been lost.[2]

FENS AND MARSHES

In the Anglo-Saxon centuries there was no well-defined coastline around the Wash or along the Lindsey Marsh, but rather a zone separating firm land from the normal low water level of the sea. This coastal zone was most extensive in the Fenland where the interaction of the sea and fresh water created a complex and changing environment. Around the Wash there was a wide band of silt and salt marsh that hindered the outflow of fresh water into the sea, and as a result freshwater fens, in which peat could develop, were formed. There is an eighth-century description of these fens in the *Life of St Guthlac.* [3]

> There is in the midland district of Britain a most dismal fen of immense size, which begins at the banks of the river Granta not far from the camp which is called Cambridge, and stretches from the south as far north as the sea. It is a very long tract, now consisting of marshes, now of bogs, sometimes of black waters overhung by fog, and traversed by the windings of tortuous streams.

Guthlac was taken in a fisherman's skiff (*piscatoria scafula*) 'through

Fig. 2.1 Spoil dumps from medieval salt working in Wainfleet Tofts on the sea-ward side of the early medieval sea bank (Everson and Hayes 1984, fig. 15). Photo by P. Everson and T. Hayes. Reproduced from Field and White, with permission.

trackless bogs within the confines of this dismal marsh' to Crowland, an island that was then uninhabited, 'untilled and known to very few'. Felix, the author of this *Life,* may have exaggerated the isolation not only because a desert was appropriate for the habitation of such a holy man, but also because he wrote for an East Anglian king, from whose territory Crowland was indeed remote. The fens between the settlements in Elloe wapentake and the Isle of Ely were a frontier region in which the boundary between Holland and Cambridgeshire was not finally settled until 1562.[4]

Long-term changes in the sea level affected the extent of the tidal marshes and as a result the boundary between the freshwater fens and the coastal salt marshes slowly moved.[5] When the Anglo-Saxons began to arrive the sea level was relatively high, but by the seventh century it was dropping and the limit of tidal water was then retreating east, allowing the freshwater fens to expand (Fig. 2.2). It is not known for certain when the silts were formed. There are indications that in the south of Holland, east of Crowland, they are pre-Roman and that further north, at Bicker Haven, they were perhaps deposited as late as the fifth century.[6] This probably explains why the freshwater fen and the peat was much more extensive in the south than in the north of Holland. In the nineteenth century peat

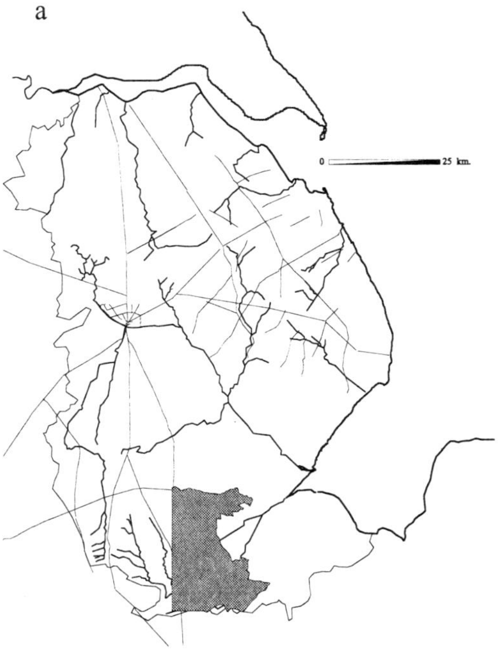

Fig. 2.2

Distribution of settlement in the Fenland Survey, showing environmental change:
(a) location of survey area;
(b) Romano-British period;
(c) early to mid Anglo-Saxon period.

Key:
dark grey = fen edge,
light grey = silt,
unshaded = freshwater fen,
dots = evidence for settlement.

Redrawn, with permission, by A. Vince and A. Oliver from Hayes and Lane 1992, figs. 126, 127.

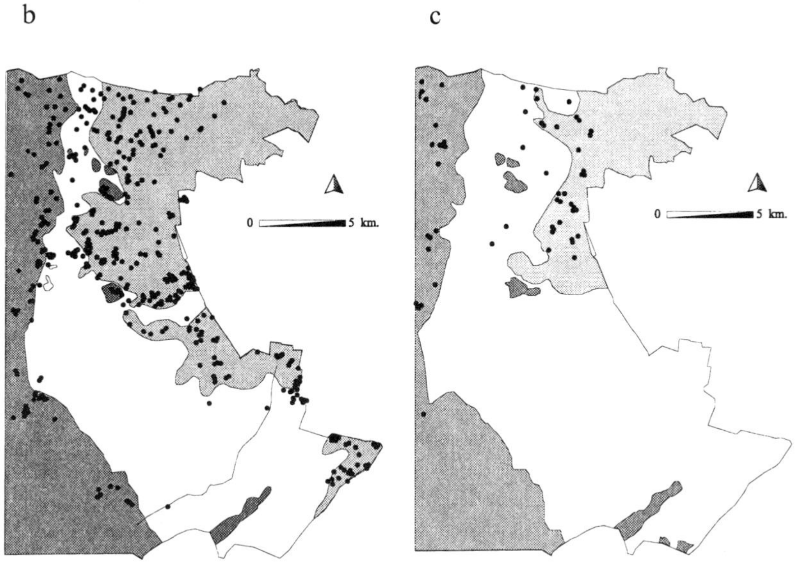

covered almost all of Deeping Fen, about six miles across, but it narrowed to about a mile in Billingborough Fen.[7]

Changes in the coastal zone were also caused by salt making. Domesday Book records over 260 salt-pans (*salinae*) in Lincolnshire, some of them as appurtenances of inland manors. No certain traces of Anglo-Saxon salt production have been found, but the method used was presumably the same as in later times, for which there is abundant evidence.[8] The best places were on gently sloping ground at the head of inlets or creeks below the highest limit of tides. During the summer, before the fortnightly spring tides, an area (which could be two acres or more) was prepared by raking or making shallow depressions in which pools could form. After the spring tides the impregnated sand was scraped up, stored, and later put into a filter bed, which could be a trough or a pit lined with clay and filled with peat. The sand was then washed and the resulting brine evaporated to form salt crystals. Fresh water produced the best result. The leached sand was then dumped above the tidal limit. When a site was worked in this way for a long time, the resulting heap, or salt-hill, could be very large, up to twenty feet high.

Salt-hills are found in many parts of the coastal zone with some remarkable concentrations, for example inside what used to be Bicker Haven. Arthur Owen has drawn attention to several on which churches have been built, including Tydd St Mary, and Gedney in South Holland, as well as Marshchapel, Grainthorpe, Conisholme and North Coates in Lindsey Marsh.[9] Domesday records a church in none of these places, but a piece of tenth-century sculpture found in Conisholme church confirms that there was already one on that site before the Conquest.[10] Many old salt-hills are less easily recognized, but Arthur Owen has pointed out that in some places 'the surface of a field or two, instead of being a natural dead level, or showing the regular undulations of old ridge-and-furrow, consists of irregular low hummocks'.[11] The case for identifying these as old saltern sites is strengthened when such fields adjoin a church which is itself on slightly raised ground, as at Skidbrook, Saltfleetby St Peter, Theddlethorpe All Saints, Croft, Thorpe St Peter and Friskney, only one of which, Thorpe St Peter, is mentioned in Domesday. The discovery of tenth-century sculpture in Theddlethorpe St Helen church strengthens the likelihood that the church at Theddlethorpe All Saints, about a mile inland, was also early. Some of these apparently Anglo-Saxon salt-hills were, after the Conquest, linked to form the earliest sea-banks, thus creating a better defined coast-line.[12] The best sites for permanent settlement in the Fenlands were on the coastal silts, or high-silts as they are sometimes called, on salt-hills, or on the bands of silt known as roddons deposited by creeks that once drained the region. Permanent settlement in the fresh-water fen was, however, only possible in a few places, Crowland being the most

Fig. 2.3 Aerial view of Croft church which is located on the remains of early salt working. Photo and © Paul Everson.

important.

There were large areas of marsh in other parts of Lincolnshire. North of Gainsborough the Trent flowed into a huge expanse of freshwater marshes that surrounded the Isle of Axholme and extended over twelve miles into Yorkshire. For much of its course the Ancholme was flanked by marshes that hindered communications between the wapentakes of Manley in the West Riding and Yarborough in the North Riding. The only crossing below West Rasen was at Glanford, now called Brigg thanks to the bridge, first mentioned in 1203, built across the river there.[13] West of the Lincoln Gap, the rivers Witham and Till combined to feed a large lake that survives, much reduced by drainage, as Brayford Pool. The name Lincoln preserves the memory of that lake, for its first element derives from a British word, **lindo*, meaning a pool or lake.

COMMUNICATIONS

Below Lincoln the Witham had a band of freshwater fen and peat on its right bank for about nineteen miles before it flowed into the main Fenland basin. The effectiveness of this barrier to early communication is demonstrated by the fact that it marked the boundary between the northern and midland dialects of medieval English.[14] In contrast, the Humber was not a serious barrier. The Lincolnshire Domesday reports ferries at

Grimsby, Barton-upon-Humber, South Ferriby, and Winteringham which was probably across the estuary of the Ancholme.[15] Only one ferry across the Trent is mentioned in the Lincolnshire Domesday, at Lea near Gainsborough.[16] There must have been several others, for example at Littleborough where the Roman road, now represented by Tillbridge Lane, reached the river. There was a ferry there in the fourteenth century. Other

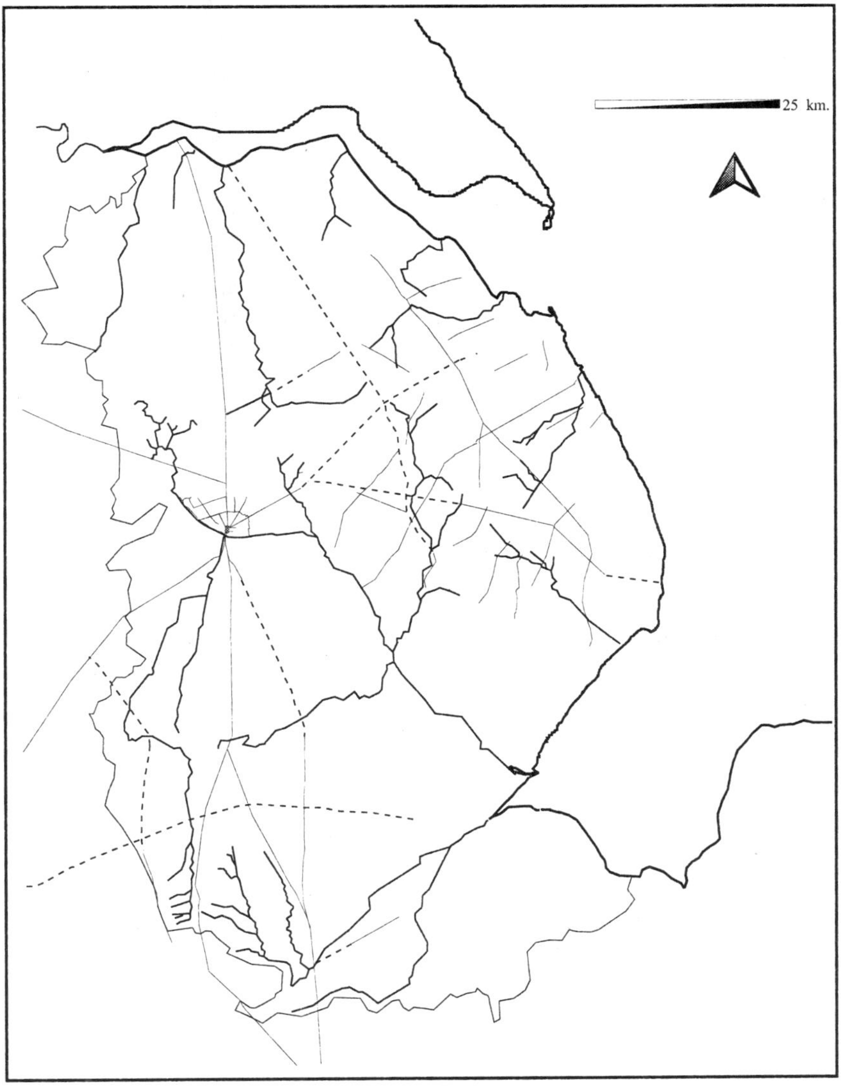

Fig. 2.4 Roman roads (solid line = certain, broken line = deduced) and major waterways in Lincolnshire. Compiled from data provided by A. Owen and J. B. Whitwell. © A. Vince and A. Oliver.

ferries to the west bank and to Axholme were certainly needed; the lowest ford across the Trent was at Spalford and the bridge at Newark was not built until the twelfth century. The ferry at Newton-on-Trent and Kinnard's Ferry (incorporating the Old English name *Cyneheard*), both mentioned in the twelfth century,[17] probably existed before the Norman Conquest, and others that first appear later may also have done so.[18]

Rivers were routeways as well as barriers. It was possible to travel up the Ouse as far as Boroughbridge, about fifteen miles above York, and the Trent was navigable at least as far as Nottingham. The Nottinghamshire Domesday in fact notes that anyone obstructing the passage of the Trent incurred a heavy penalty.[19] One of the main medieval routes from southern England to York was by road to Torksey and then by boat. This must already have been a well-established route in the eleventh century for, according to Domesday Book, the inhabitants of Torksey had the duty of taking royal messengers to York 'with their ships and their means of navigation'.[20] There is no good evidence for navigation on other rivers but the Witham must have been one of the main means of access to Lincoln. The Welland and Nene were used later to ship wool and other goods to Lynn; it seems reasonable to assume that they carried similar traffic earlier. The boats need not have been large and could have been very shallow, rather like modern punts.

The main obstacles to navigation, apart from natural falls and silting, were fishing weirs. The remains of such a weir of the ninth century or earlier have been found in the former bed of the Trent at Colwick near Nottingham.[21] Domesday records fisheries at 42 places in Lincolnshire, and this is certainly an incomplete list. The main concentration was around Axholme and there were several scattered through Holland, with as many as 30 at Bourne.[22] These are unlikely to have hampered navigation, but the eleven at Torksey and others along the Witham below Lincoln probably did.

By recording ferries and places named after river crossings Domesday Book provides some clues to the road system of eleventh-century Lincolnshire. In addition to such relatively obvious names as Ludford, Stamford, and Bracebridge, there are names such as Waithe and Langworth that contain a Scandinavian word for 'ford', *vað*. There is also Rasen, from the Old English *ræsn*, 'plank', used for a plank-bridge across the river that takes its name from this construction, a type of name-giving known as back-formation. Names of bridges and fords may, of course, indicate minor tracks of only local importance, but the ferries named in Domesday are more likely to have linked major routes, and the valuations give some impression of their relative importance. Thus the ferries at South Ferriby and Winteringham rendered 120s. and 13s. respectively, while that across the Trent at Lea only rendered 12d.[23]

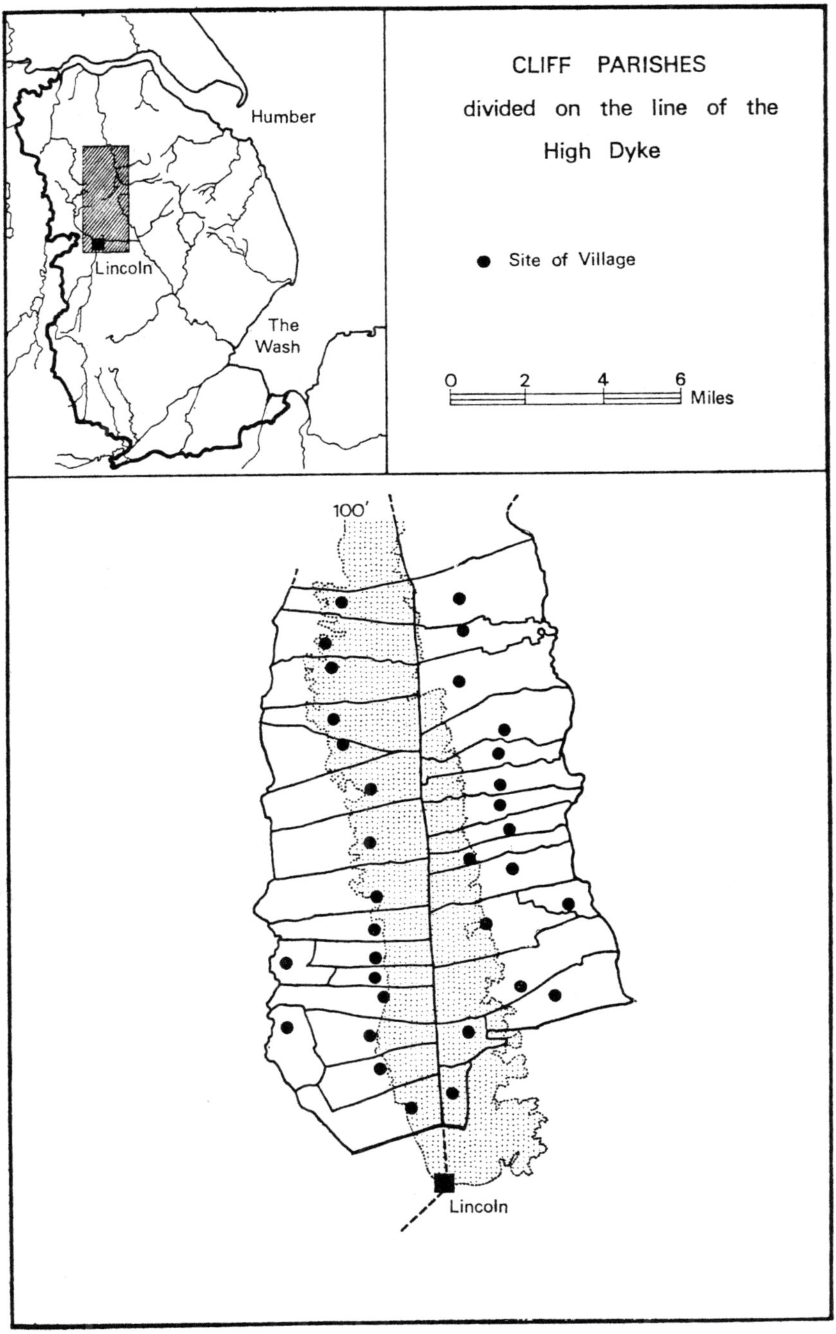

Fig. 2.5 Ermine Street and cliff parish bounds. Reprinted from D. Owen, Church and Society in Medieval Lincolnshire.

The Domesday survey of neighbouring shires is a little more informative and shows that some roads were under royal protection. In Yorkshire the king is said to have had 'three ways by land and a fourth by water', the latter presumably being the Ouse.[24] In Nottinghamshire, not only was the passage of the Trent protected as already mentioned, but so too was the road to York and, more relevant here, the Fosse Way. Both were described as king's roads and it can be assumed that in Lincolnshire the Fosse Way and other main roads, including Ermine Street, were similarly considered to be royal. An early twelfth-century text states that the king's highway should be wide enough for sixteen armed knights to ride abreast, or for two waggons to meet and pass, with a margin wide enough to allow the herdsmen to make contact 'with their goads at full stretch'.[25] Many tracks must have been as wide as this, or more, so that in bad weather heavily rutted sections could be avoided. Indeed, according to the Nottinghamshire Domesday, no obstruction was allowed within two perches, that is eleven yards, either side of the king's roads.[26] Several of the medieval roads of Lincolnshire, like the Fosse Way, were constructed or improved by the Romans, but even the main Roman roads were less than eleven yards wide and their medieval successors must have extended well beyond the paved surface laid by the Romans.

Roman roads were originally built for military and administrative purposes, to link forts, harbours, and major urban centres. A good example is Ermine Street. North of Lincoln it runs almost dead straight to the Humber crossing. It was, in effect, a by-pass running between the settlements that lay either side of it and were connected by much older tracks. The one to the west, along the top of the scarp face, the Jurassic way, was an important prehistoric route. After the Roman withdrawal the roads they had constructed were no longer well maintained and many stretches were abandoned. Even an abandoned Roman road was, however, a prominent feature and it is not surprising that some sections later served to mark parish boundaries. (See Fig. 2.5.) For about fifteen miles north of Lincoln Ermine Street served as a boundary for fourteen parishes that flanked it. In Kesteven the same road marked the boundaries of parishes for about 25 miles from Welbourne to Grantham.[27] It also served as the boundary between Flaxwell and Loveden wapentakes. Similar straight alignments of parish or wapentake boundaries elsewhere point to the existence of roads that were built or improved by the Romans even when no trace of the early road surface has been found. Several have been identified in this way linking the Wolds with the coastal marshes.[28]

Early place-names and medieval evidence show that many sections of Roman roads were not abandoned. Indeed, some modern roads have Roman foundations. That is not surprising when the route is determined by natural features such as the narrow strip of slightly raised ground (or chain of islands) between the East and West Fens south of Bolingbroke that the Anglo-Saxons called *Sticca*, 'the stick', or *Sticcan ēg*, 'the stick island', along which the main road A16 now runs.[29] This must have been a route into the coastal zone long before the English called one place on it Stickford.[30] The sections of Roman roads that were abandoned are, in some respects, more interesting, for they suggest that changing circumstances made them redundant even for local traffic. The survival, or revival, of several minor roads linking the Wolds with the coastal marshes of Lindsey is in marked contrast to the uncertainty that prevails about the alignment of sections of both the main Roman roads from Lincoln to the east. The abandonment of these 'trunk-routes' is consistent with the archaeological evidence that Lincoln and its neighbourhood had little contact with the coast between the fifth and ninth centuries. The distribution of pottery from the Continent and of the type produced at Ipswich suggests that although there was some traffic along the coast of Lindsey and its Humber shore in the seventh and eighth centuries, Kesteven and the inland parts of Lindsey were not affected by it.[31]

Ships travelling, for example, between Northumbria and southern England or the Continent, must occasionally, if not regularly, have visited Lincolnshire havens. Ships also came to Lincolnshire to collect its produce. In the eleventh century exports included wool, cloth and corn as well as salt. Before the tenth century salt was the main product of the region for which there was significant demand elsewhere, although the evidence of coins and pottery imports discussed below (pp. 173–7) suggests that traders came by sea to the Wolds already in the eighth century, presumably to obtain wool or cloth, and possibly food, as well as salt. Salt was extracted from the sea at many places on the coast of Britain, but in the eleventh century one of the main concentrations of salt-pans was around the Wash and in the Lindsey Marsh; almost half the *salinae* recorded in Domesday Book were on that stretch of coast.[32] Production then was, of course, not on the scale it reached by the early fourteenth century,[33] but the many salt-hills, some of which were certainly heaped up in the Anglo-Saxon period, suggest that more salt was being produced than was needed locally. Some was taken inland by packhorse or cart along roads that were later known as the Way, Lane or Gate of the Salters. These names are first recorded long after the eleventh century, but the fact that Salterford in Nottinghamshire, twelve miles west of Newark, is named in Domesday Book confirms that salt from the Lincolnshire coast was being distributed inland before the Norman Conquest.[34] A more convenient and cheaper means of distribution was by boat. According to the disputes section of the Lincolnshire Domesday, toll was taken from ships arriving at three places on the Lindsey coast, Saltfleet, Mare, and Swine, as it had not been before the Conquest.[35] The name Saltfleet suggests that boats were collecting

Lincolnshire salt there long before the Conquest. It means 'salt creek or stream'. As Arthur Owen has pointed out, Ekwall's explanation that the stream 'was no doubt salt at least at high tide' is unsatisfactory; that applied to all tidal streams.[36] A more likely explanation is that boats collected salt there.

RESOURCES

The first detailed information about the resources of Lincolnshire is provided by Domesday Book. In using that evidence it is important to bear in mind that the survey was not undertaken to record the total value of resources, but to discover what they were worth to the landlords. When details of stock, other than draught oxen, are given, for example in Norfolk, only the animals belonging to lords are noted; the sheep, dairy cattle, horses, pigs and goats belonging to their tenants are not recorded. This limited purpose explains why the Lincolnshire Domesday records little marsh or fen, for these were treated as common land, shared by the inhabitants of nearby communities and their lords. Woodland, in contrast, was scarce. Oliver Rackham has estimated that in 1086 only 3.5 per cent of Lincolnshire was woodland, about half the average for England as a whole.[37] It is, therefore, not surprising that woodland is carefully noted among manorial assets. Consequently, Domesday appears to be a fairly reliable guide to the distribution of woodland in the county.

The Lincolnshire Domesday generally distinguishes between *silva minuta,* 'coppice wood', and *silva pastilis* which is commonly, but mistakenly, translated as 'wood for pannage'; in fact it meant 'pasture wood'.[38] There are approximately equal amounts of each. Apart from the chalk and limestone uplands and the fens, there were coppice woods in most parts of the county. The pasture woods were mainly in south Kesteven, the eastern part of the South Riding of Lindsey (between Stainton, Tattershall, and Wood Enderby), along the Trent and on Axholme, where six entries describe a total of over 10,000 acres or some six square miles of *silva pastilis.* The wooded nature of Kesteven was commented on by Æthelweard in the tenth century.[39] The first element of the name Kesteven is, indeed, believed to derive from a British word meaning wood.

Much of the woodland described in Domesday Book survived until the nineteenth century, and some still exists today. One characteristic of this ancient wood is the presence of lime, a native tree. It is found in many parts of the county and gave its name to three places in Lincolnshire: Limber, west of Grimsby, and Linwood, near Market Rasen, that both appear in Domesday Book, and Linwood, near Tattershall, which is first recorded in the thirteenth century. Until recently there was a fine lime wood (called

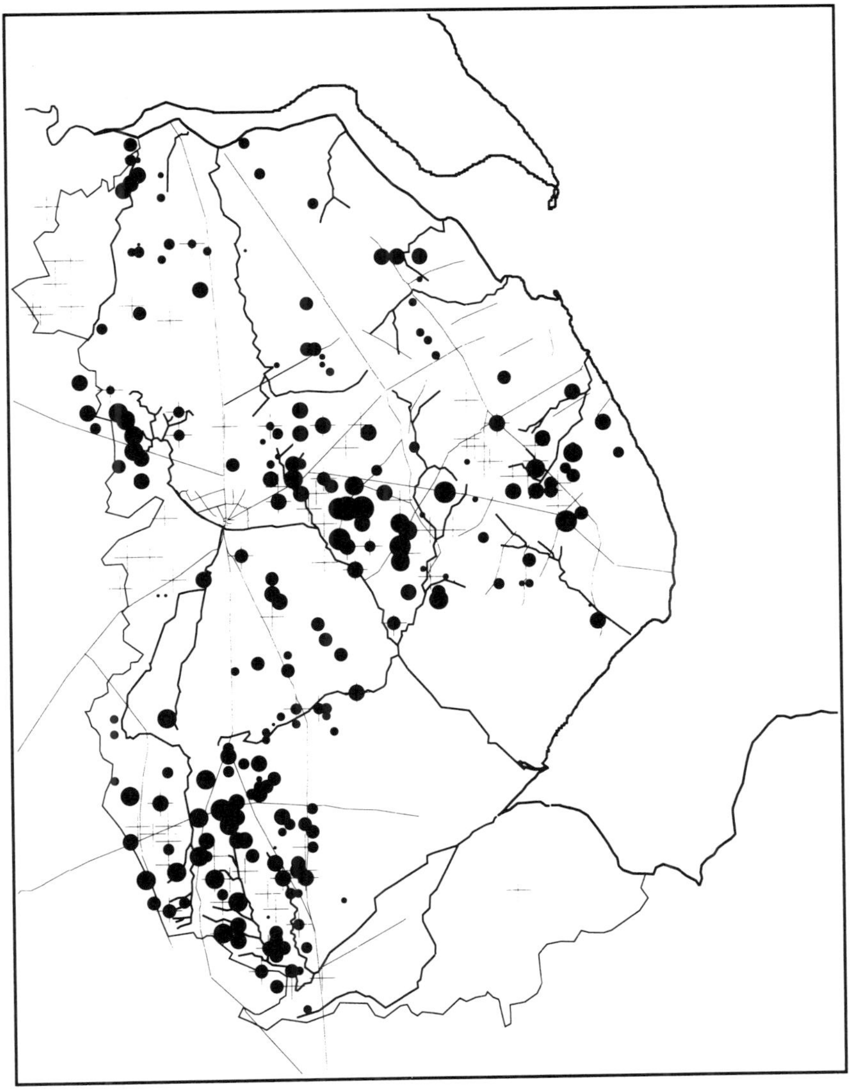

Fig. 2.6 Woodland in Domesday Lincolnshire. The area of the circles is proportional to the extent of the recorded woodland. Crosses indicate other mentions of woodland. Produced by A. Oliver and A. Vince.

Lynwode Wood) in the Domesday Linwood, now sadly replanted with conifers. George Peterken has pointed out (in a letter to me dated 2 June 1983) that 'parishes with woodland in 1086 either still have an ancient wood, did so recently, or have signs in field names and wood-relic hedges that they once had an ancient wood. Parishes without woods in 1086 have no sign of ancient woods now. Furthermore, the size of woods in

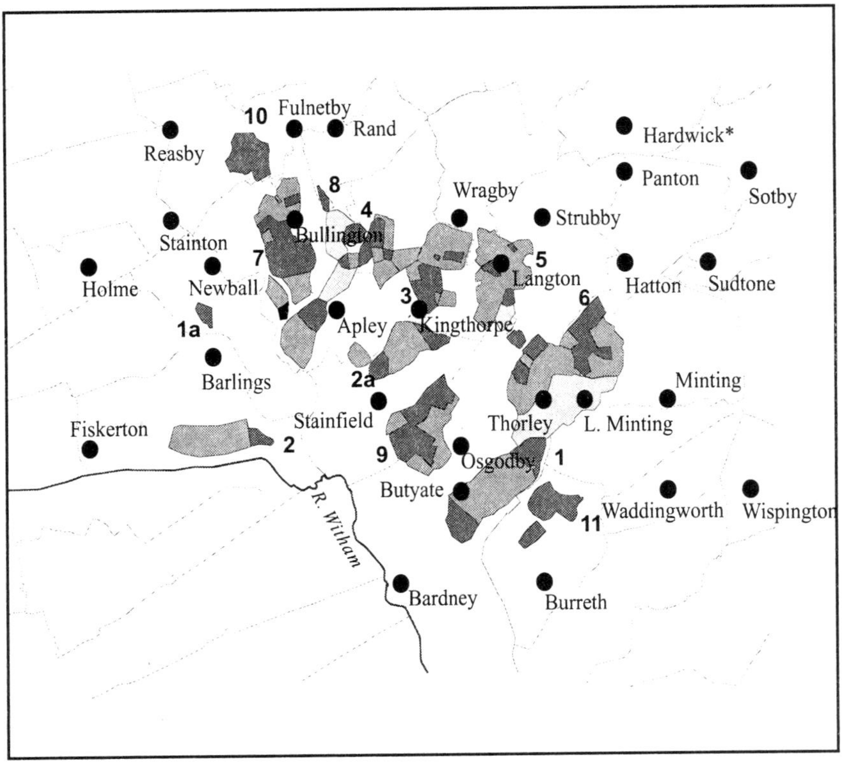

Fig. 2.7 Medieval woodland in south Lindsey

1. Austacre Wood; 1a. Barlings Park; 2. Fiskerton Long Wood; 2a. Foxhall Wood; 3. Glad Wood; 4. Great West Wood; 5. Langton Wood; 6. Minting Wood; 7. Newball Wood; 8. Short Wood; 9. Stainfield Wood; 10. Stainton Wood; 11. New Park Wood (probably medieval secondary woodland).

Extant ancient woods, *as determined by interpretation of cartographic, documentary, and archaeological sources, and reinforced by the presence of many flowering plant species which are rarely found in known secondary woods.*

Cleared ancient woods, *mostly cleared since 1850, identified on the basis of eye-witness accounts, wood-relict hedges, and interpretation of woodland earthworks, old maps, and documents.*

Probable ancient woods, *areas which may have been wooded in the Middle Ages, identified on the basis of woodland earthworks, wood-relict hedges, and records of extensive woodlands which have been lost.*

Based on map by G. F. Peterken, and reproduced with permission. Drawn by A. Vince and A. Oliver.

Domesday Book correlates reasonably well with the area of ancient woodland in the parish at later dates.'

Dr Peterken has put me further in his debt by allowing me to use in Fig. 2.7 the results of his detailed study of the evidence for medieval woodland between Wragby and Bardney, an area that in Domesday Book had over 6000 (modern) acres of wood, two-thirds of it pasture wood, a significantly larger proportion than in the county as a whole.

In Anglo-Saxon Lincolnshire farming was predominantly pastoral, but by the eleventh century, and probably long before, there was some arable in all parts, including the Fenland silts. Domesday Book indicates the relative importance of arable farming in different areas by recording the number of plough teams.[40] In large areas of Lindsey and along the Fen margin in Kesteven where there were, in general, two ploughs per square mile, no more than a third of the land was cultivated. Immediately north of Lincoln and on the flanks of the Wolds the proportion was about a half and in a small area at the southern extremity of the Wolds as much as three-quarters. In most of Kesteven about half the land was arable but south of Sleaford there was an small area where almost all the land (90 per cent)

Fig 2.8 Hatton Wood in April 1974. This is one of the ancient woods associated with Minting Park. In the late 19th century oak appears to have been planted into the coppice, which has been allowed to grow to high forest. The mixture of pedunculate oak, small-leaved lime and silver birch shown in the photograph almost certainly characterized this site throughout the last 5000 years. Photo and © G. F. Peterken.

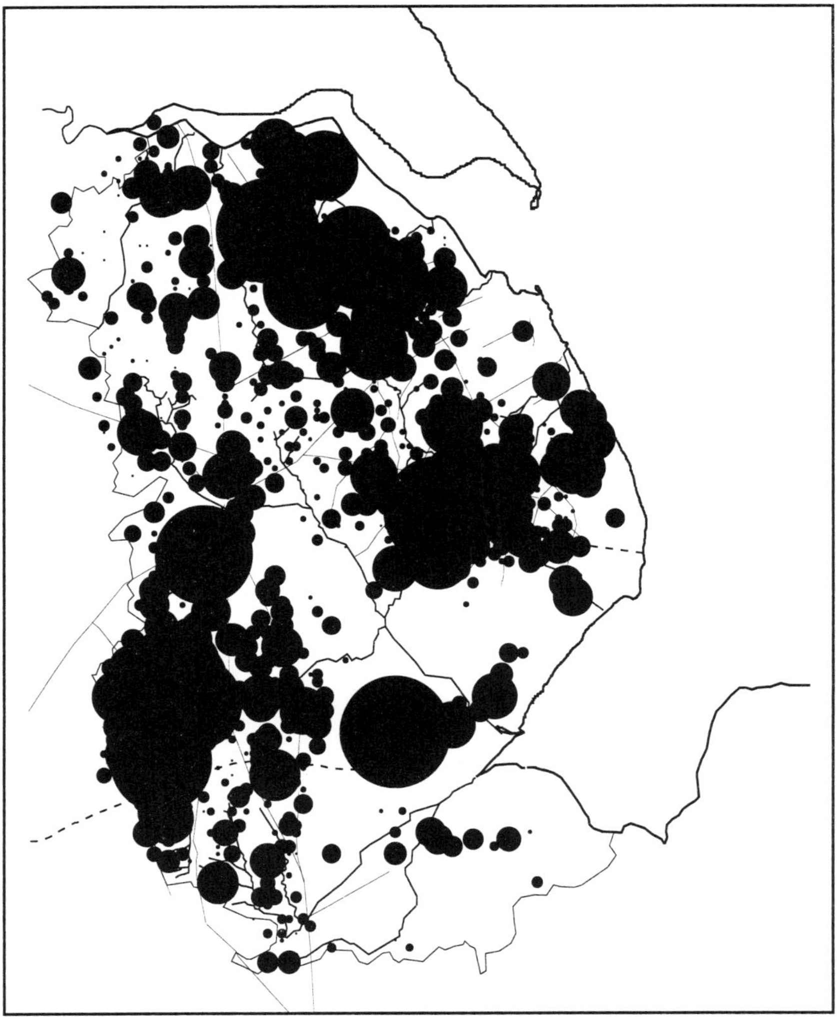

Fig. 2.9 Plough teams in Domesday Lincolnshire. The area of the circles is proportional to the number of recorded ploughteams. Produced by A. Oliver and A. Vince. © A. Vince.

was arable. The evidence for the relative importance of arable farming is consistent with the Domesday record of mills. Concentrations are recorded along the upper Witham and in the southern valleys of the Wolds. The importance of arable near Sleaford explains why there were eight mills there. Quarrington, near Sleaford, had four relatively valuable mills, and its name, meaning 'the *tūn* of the millers' suggests that arable farming was important in that part of Lincolnshire long before the Conquest.[41]

Meadows were needed to provide winter feed for plough oxen, and relatively large areas are recorded where arable farming was important. Similar amounts of meadow in areas with little arable, for example in north-east Lindsey, were presumably needed to feed dairy and breeding cattle. In areas with clay soils there was rough grazing in pasture woods. Far richer grazing was to be found in the salt marshes along the coast and in the chalk and limestone uplands, which later supported very large flocks of sheep that produced high quality wool. There are indications, discussed in Chapter IX, that sheep began to be an important element in the economy of Lincolnshire during the latter part of the tenth century and that in the eleventh century the prosperity of Lincoln and its region was in large measure based on the export of wool.

POPULATION AND SETTLEMENTS

Domesday Book makes it possible, for the first time, to gain some idea of the number of people in the shire, and where they lived. The Domesday Survey was, however, not a population census; it enumerated the people whose renders and services contributed to the value of the estates of the king's tenants-in-chief, or who paid tax. There were over 21,000 in Lincolnshire, most of whom must have had families. On the basis of later evidence suggesting that the average size of a rural household in medieval England was five persons,[42] the rural population of Lincolnshire represented in Domesday Book can be estimated at about 100,000. As the Domesday record is certainly incomplete the total was probably somewhat larger, but it is not possible to say by how much. In addition there were at least 10,000, possibly 20,000, town dwellers.

The rural population was widely spread. With the exception of the freshwater marshes there were settlements in all parts of the shire in the eleventh century. The evidence of pottery found in ploughed fields and of metal work (discovered with the help of metal detectors) suggests that, with the exception of the upper Ancholme valley where the earliest Anglo-Saxon pottery is of the ninth century, settlement was as extensive in the seventh and eighth centuries as in the eleventh, although it may well not have been so dense.

In describing the estates of Lincolnshire and their components, Domesday Book names some 790 places, almost all of which can be located, at least approximately.[43] By listing the component parts of estates Domesday appears to be a better guide to the pattern of settlement than in some other shires.[44] It is, nevertheless impossible to map the farms and villages of Lincolnshire on the basis of Domesday. Most of the places named in it can be identified in medieval or modern sources, but they did not necessarily then have the same location or form as they did in the eleventh century. Moreover, in some entries Domesday identifies settlements by the name of the hundred (a taxation unit of twelve carucates) in which they lay. In Holland, for example, some of the land tributary to the great manor of Drayton is described as being in the hundreds of *Reschintone* and *Riche,* places whose location is only approximately known.[45]

The pattern of settlement was not static; it was constantly changing as farms, hamlets and villages were established, abandoned, moved, or reorganized. This process can be traced in some detail after the eleventh century, but there was similar instability earlier. It is likely that in Lincolnshire, as in other parts of Anglo-Saxon England, one of the main changes was the replacement of many small and scattered farms by nucleated villages with common fields in which many villagers had a share. This was happening before the Norman Conquest and continued after it.[46] Charters of the twelfth and thirteenth centuries show that some places named in Domesday were by then nucleated villages, most with two common arable fields.[47] It is, however, uncertain when they were formed.

The most systematic study of the history of settlement in Lincolnshire, undertaken by the Royal Commission on the Historical Monuments of England in the north-west of the county, and published in 1991 as *Change and Continuity*, uncovered abundant evidence of both change and continuity. It also underlined how little is known about the development of settlement in Lincolnshire, especially before the Norman Conquest. Its authors comment that although 'there is abundant material available, including place-names, burials, and historical documentation, as well as a little occupation evidence...it is difficult, if not impossible to reconcile it all and to produce a satisfactory picture of settlement development.' They conclude that 'it is no longer possible to be certain that all of those places that were to be medieval villages were actually in existence by the 6th or 7th centuries', and that 'all that can be said is that by the late 11th century or early 12th century, most of the major later settlements of West Lindsey were in existence but these were not necessarily very old at that date, nor on the site nor in the form of the later medieval villages.'[48]

LORDSHIPS

In the eleventh century a large proportion of the wealth of Lincolnshire, gained by the skills and industry of its people, was paid either as tax to the king or as tribute to the hierarchy of lords who dominated the economic as well as the social and political life of the region. Most of the people enumerated in Domesday Book were, in varying degrees, under lordship and were obliged to render to their lords service and tribute, in cash or kind. Some lords were themselves subordinate to superior lords to whom, in their turn, they paid tribute.

Lordships, large and small, had central places, each normally with a hall at which tribute was delivered and in which courts were held by the lord or his agents. Such an estate centre was called by the English a *tūn*, and by the Normans a manor *(manerium)*, the term used in Domesday Book. Most manors had land that the lord kept in his own hands, later known as his demesne, from *dominium,* 'lordship'. Parts of the demesne that were separate from the manor were called berewicks. Demesnes were cultivated by customary tenants who had an obligation to work on their lord's land for a specified number of days each week. Many manors also had land that was not cultivated by the lord, but owed him tribute, described as 'soke' (Old English *socn*, Latin *soca*). A man rendered soke to his lord. By the twelfth century the meaning of the word soke was being limited to the right to exercise minor jurisdiction or to take its profits. Its earlier and more basic meaning, however, was service and tribute owed to a lord; jurisdictional rights were but one element in a more comprehensive form of lordship.[49] The same word could also be used to describe land that rendered soke. In the Lincolnshire Domesday the component parts of many estates are described as *soca.* By a natural extension of meaning the word came to be used for a whole estate. Folkingham, for example, with scattered soke in 25 places is often called the Soke of Folkingham. Most manors had some sokeland, but the description 'Soke' is generally reserved for the larger estates that were held under the king by lords who were specially privileged.

The Scandinavian word *soke* was first used in England in the tenth century, but estates of this kind were much older and had existed in many parts of Britain long before the Scandinavians invaded.[50] Whatever their origin, with the formation of the Anglo-Saxon kingdoms they were apparently treated as royal, although by the eleventh century many were held by laymen or churches.

Sokes were an archaic type of estate, but those described in Domesday Book were not necessarily old. New sokes could be created on the ancient pattern and old ones reshaped as sokelands were added or taken away. Inheritance could result in the division of sokes, and grants to laymen or churches, or usurpations, could also lead to their fragmentation. Some of the resulting smaller estates continued to be treated as part of the original soke from which they had come and paid tribute to its lord in recognition of his superiority. There was, however, a natural tendency for the lords of inferior sokes to claim independence and to stop paying tribute to the original soke-lord.

The pattern of lordships and obligations described in Domesday Book was the product of a long process. Any attempt to trace the early stages of that process must largely be conjectural. The widespread occurrence in Britain of estates similar to the Lincolnshire sokes suggests that their origin is to be sought in the period before the arrival of the English. To explore that possibility would be beyond the limits of this book and the competence of its author. There are, however, hints, discussed in the next chapter, that some of the major sokes of eleventh-century Lincolnshire can be traced back at least to the seventh century.

NOTES TO CHAPTER II

1 The geology and landscape of Lincolnshire have been briefly described in the first two volumes of this history of the county; May 1976, pp. 1–9 and Whitwell 1970, pp. 1–4. Bennet, S. and N. 1993 has good maps with helpful commentaries.

2 Owen, A. 1993

3 Felix, cc. xiv–xv, ed. Colgrave, pp. 86–9

4 Owen, A. 1992.

5 Hayes and Lane 1992 provide the most detailed and up-to-date study of this process. They summarize their results on pp. 205–17.

6 Hayes and Lane 1992, pp. 6, 110–11, 114.

7 Hayes and Lane 1992, p. 7.

8 Rudkin and Owen, D. 1960, pp. 80–3; Sturman 1984.

9 Owen, A. 1984, p. 46.

10 The church recorded as in Tydd St Mary in DB i. 351b = *LD* 14/97 was in fact in Long Sutton, see Roffe 1992, p. 9. I am indebted to David Stocker for information about the sculpture mentioned in this paragraph.

11 Owen, A. 1984, p. 46; cf. Everson and Hayes 1984, fig. 15.

12 Owen, A. 1975, modified by Owen, A. 1984.

13 *PNL* 2, p. 117.

14 Kristensson 1967, pp. 238–46.

15 Grimsby: DB i. 343a, 363a = *LD* 4/70, 36/1; Barton: DB i. 354b = *LD* 24/13; South Ferriby: DB i. 354ab = *LD* 23/1, 24/14, see also n. 23 below; Winteringham: DB i. 354b = *LD* 24/12.

16 DB i. 347a = *LD* 12/4.

17 *RA* i, no. 172, p. 109; Ekwall 1960, p. 278. Kinnard's Ferry was between East Ferry and Owston.

18 Barley 1936.

19 DB i. 280a.

20 DB i. 337a = *LD* p. 11.

21 *Med. Arch.* 26 (1982), p. 201.

22 Darby 1952, pp. 66–8.

23 A *passagium* at South Ferriby is recorded in two entries, each rendering £3 (DB i. 354a and b = *LD* 23/1, 24/14). This probably means that the ferry's render was £6, divided between two lords. It has been suggested that one crossed the Humber, the other the Ancholme (Eagles 1989, p. 205). The stated values make that unlikely. Similarly, two Grimsby entries record a ferry, DB i. 363a = *LD* 36/1 valued at 5s. and DB i. 343a = *LD* 4/70 valued, with the customs, at 40s.

24 DB i. 298b.

25 *Leges Henrici Primi* 80.3, ed. Downer, pp. 248–9.

26 DB i. 280a.

27 Ancaster parish, which straddles Ermine Street, appears to be an exception. Dennis Mills has pointed out that this is the result of a modern reorganization; formerly the road divided the parishes of Ancaster and Wilsford

28 Owen, A. 1984, pp. 48–9; Owen, A. 1997.

29 Ekwall 1960, p. 442, *s.n.* Stickford.

30 Owen, A. 1997.

31 Vince 1993b, p. 5. See also below, p. 174.

32 Bridbury 1955, pp. 19–20; Keene, L. 1988.

33 Bridbury 1955, pp. 20–1, 168–9.

34 DB i. 292a.

35 DB i. 375b = *LD* 69/39–40. For the location of these havens see Owen, A. 1954.

36 Ekwall 1960, p. 403 ; Owen, A. 1954, p. 90.

37 Rackham 1976, pp. 59, 61.

38 Rackham 1976, pp. 59–61.

39 Campbell, A. 1962, p. 51.

40 Fig. 2.9. For the interpretation of this evidence see Darby 1977, pp. 121–36.

41 For mills on the river Slea and their role in the development of the area, see Pawley 1988.

42 Moore 1992.

43 This is the number reckoned by Roffe 1992, p. 8. According to Darby 1952, p. 30, the total number of places named was approximately 755.

44 Sawyer 1976.

45 DB i. 348b = *LD* 12/72, 74.

46 Rowley 1981.

47 Fox 1981.

48 Everson, Taylor, and Dunn 1991, pp. 8–9. See also Everson 1993.

49 Davis 1954, pp. xl–xli. See below, pp. 107–8.

50 Barrow 1973, pp. 7–68.

CHAPTER III

BRITONS AND ANGLO-SAXONS

In A.D. 400 a large part of Britain lay within the Roman Empire. Two hundred years later most of what had been Roman Britain, including the region between the Humber and the Welland, was ruled by Germans, leaders of the numerous immigrants, conventionally known as Anglo-Saxons, who came from the coastlands north and east of the Rhine estuary. The way in which this happened is exceedingly obscure. The written sources are too slight to make possible more than a very general account of British history during those two hundred years and provide no information specifically about the area between the Humber and the Welland. The main native source, *The Ruin of Britain,* by Gildas, a sixth-century British deacon, is a diatribe against contemporary corruption with only vague indications of the chronology and location of the events he mentions; even the date and place of its composition are uncertain. Texts written in Gaul and elsewhere in the Empire, by men who knew something about the situation in fifth-century Britain, provide some additional information, but not about the area of Lincolnshire. For developments there we are almost entirely dependent on the evidence of place-names and archaeology. The interpretation of that evidence does, however, require some awareness of the general situation in Britain towards the end of the period of Roman rule, so far as it can be known.[1]

THE END OF ROMAN RULE

In the second half of the fourth century there were numerous attacks on Roman Britain by its traditional enemies, then known as the Picts, who lived north of the Forth and Clyde estuaries, and the western coasts were raided by Scots and Attacotti. In the last years of the century there were also raids by Saxons, a Germanic people who together with the Franks had earlier raided the coasts of Gaul.[2]

There were also internal disputes. Several revolts against emperors were planned in Britain during the century and in 350, and again in 383 the army in Britain supported usurpers who tried to seize imperial power. After the first attempt was crushed in 353 savage reprisals were taken on behalf of the emperor against officers and others in Britain suspected of complicity in the rebellion; in the process many innocent people were also victimized. This must have weakened respect for imperial authority, at least as wielded by Constantius II. There is, however, no hint of any movement to make Britain independent. There were undoubtedly many people in Britain with little cause to be loyal to the Empire, but for many Britons, especially those of high status, it offered great advantages. The Roman army provided the best hope of defence against barbarian invaders and protection from insurrections by the oppressed poor. Some gained advancement by service in the imperial bureaucracy and others, as *curiales*, local councillors, could by extortion compensate for the burdens of local government imposed on them. Wealthy Britons could display their riches in the form of luxuries from other parts of the Empire or by building and adorning villas and fine town houses. The largest villas, which bear comparison with great houses of modern times such as Grimsthorpe Castle, were probably owned not by Britons but by members of the senatorial aristocracy, some of whom had houses in other parts of the Empire, but some villas were undoubtedly the homes of Britons. Many British landowners must also have had houses in towns near their rural estates.

Fig. 3.1 The Roman town wall of Lincoln. This stretch lies between Cecil Street and Chapel Lane. The city ditch in front was still a sizable earthwork until Victorian housing encroached upon it. Photo and © H. N. Hawley.

In the fourth century Lincoln was the capital of one of the four provinces of Roman Britain, and it is therefore not surprising that the remains of several fine houses of that date have been found in the lower city.[3] It would have been convenient, even desirable, for landowners of the region, especially the more important of them, to have houses in the city where the provincial council and law courts met. The provincial governor and other officials presumably had their residences in the upper city, near the Forum. Lincoln was also an episcopal see in the fourth century and the first church was probably in the upper city too. It has been claimed that it was the apsidal church built in the courtyard of the Forum, later the site of St Paul-in-the-Bail. Reasons for doubting that are given in Appendix 4.

Late in the century there were major changes in Lincoln. There are clear indications that people were living in the city at least until the early fifth century, but in the late fourth century some buildings in the lower city were demolished and their sites covered by earth, apparently dumped deliberately for reasons that are unclear. The conditions of the bones and pottery sherds found in this newly made-up ground, known as 'dark earth',

Fig 3.2 A late-Roman masonry town house at Hungate, Lincoln. This building was systematically demolished in the late 4th century and buried beneath more than 1.5 metres of debris, presumably in order to create a terrace for further rebuilding. No traces of this latest Roman structure, if it ever existed, were found in the 1983–5 excavation. As suggested below, the space may have been used for temporary accommodation, perhaps in tents. The measuring rod is 2 metres long. Photo and © CLAU.

do not suggest that it was cultivated. Faint traces of what may have been timber buildings have been noticed in its surface.[4] The intention may have been to provide space for temporary accommodation, perhaps in tents, for people seeking shelter in disturbed times. Coins found in the rubble of one house, in Hungate, show that it was demolished in about 370. If the other demolitions occurred at the same time they may best be understood as a reaction to the exceptionally serious crisis of 367. In that year invasions by Picts, Scots, and Attacotti overwhelmed the defences and caused a breakdown of military discipline. There was also widespread disorder that can reasonably be described as civil war.[5] It took the imperial government over a year to regain control. After such a shock one priority may well have been to provide refuges in towns that were well protected by walls, some of which were strengthened at that time. The walls of Lincoln had been massively enlarged earlier in the fourth century, possibly for reasons of prestige after it was made a provincial capital. That could explain why instead of fortifying a part of the city, which was the common practice in Gaul, the whole circuit of the city walls was rebuilt, a total length of well over a mile. Whatever the reason, the walls provided a large and relatively safe refuge. Other fortified centres in the region were much smaller and may well have been primarily military, but they too could have served as refuges.

Unprotected villas in the open country, many of them built or improved in the first half of the fourth century, were obviously vulnerable to marauding bands, whether of barbarians, army deserters, or civilian rebels. Some were probably destroyed or abandoned towards the end of the century, but the date of destruction or abandonment can rarely be determined with any confidence. It is, for example, not possible to say when the villa at Scampton, north of Lincoln, or Norton Disney, ten miles south-west of the city, burnt down. Some villas were still occupied in the early fifth century, but by the middle of the previous century many of the richest owners had left Britain and those who remained did not long have the means to maintain the old Roman life-style.[6]

Towards the end of the fourth century the number of Roman troops in Britain began to be reduced. In 383 some of the best units of the army left Britain to support Magnus Maximus in his attempt to seize imperial power. They did not return. The army in Britain was further depleted in 401 when a legion was withdrawn to help defend Italy against the Goths. Six years later the effective troops still in Britain crossed to Gaul under the leadership of Constantine III, whom they had proclaimed emperor. For a while his authority was recognized in Gaul and Spain, but in 411 he was overthrown and executed.

In 407, therefore, the Britons were left to defend themselves with whatever help they could get from the soldiers who remained in Britain.

For a while they did so with success; in about 410 a Saxon invasion was repelled. According to Zosimus, the main source of information about imperial affairs in the early fifth century, the Britons then, literally, took the law into their own hands. They expelled the magistrates who had been appointed or were approved by Constantine and began to govern themselves.[7]

The departure of military garrisons and of Roman officials and their servants was, doubtless, a relief to many, but they had contributed to the prosperity of the localities in which they lived. Traders and craftsmen must have felt the pinch. To make matters worse, no coins were sent to Britain after the reign of Constantine III. After 326, apart from the period of Magnus Maximus's usurpation, there was no mint in Britain; all the coins needed to pay troops and officials were imported. These imports stopped in the first decade of the fifth century. The last bronze coins shipped to Britain were struck in 402. The supply of gold and silver coins continued a little longer, but ended with the reign of Constantine III. The coins that remained in circulation in Britain soon lost any value as currency. Until the reign of Constantine III the prohibition against clipping gold and silver coins was strictly enforced; hardly any of the coins found in hoards deposited before then were clipped. It was under Constantine that clipping began to be practised on a large scale, thus undermining the value of the coinage and illustrating the collapse of Roman order.[8]

Without coins as a readily available and universally respected means of exchange, payments of all kinds – rents, wages, bribes – had to be rendered in kind. Marketing had then to depend on barter, and inevitably the economy, which must also have been badly affected by the disappearance of many rich men, soon stagnated. The pottery industry in the Nene Valley and elsewhere in Britain collapsed in the early years of the fifth century and pottery imports seem to have stopped at much the same time.

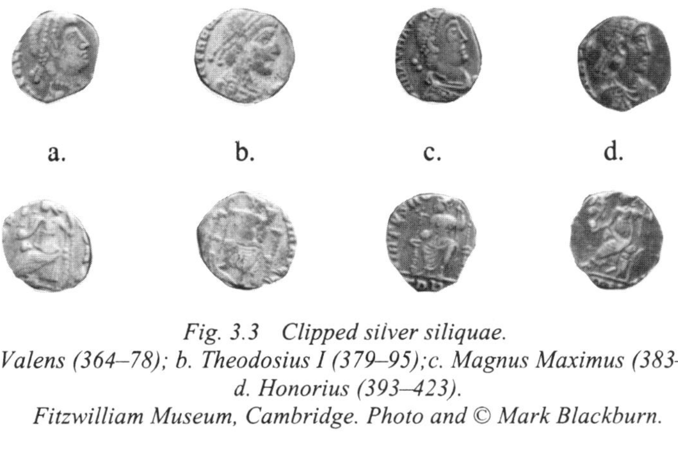

Fig. 3.3 Clipped silver siliquae.
a. Valens (364–78); b. Theodosius I (379–95); c. Magnus Maximus (383–8); d. Honorius (393–423).
Fitzwilliam Museum, Cambridge. Photo and © Mark Blackburn.

Despite these changes, there is no evidence that contemporaries thought that Roman Britain ended with Constantine's usurpation. No military reinforcements or imperial officials came to Britain after that, but contact with Gaul was maintained by churchmen. Germanus, bishop of Auxerre, and Lupus, bishop of Troyes, visited Britain in 429 to combat heresy, and Germanus returned sometime in the 430s.[9] Some British leaders still hoped, at least until the middle years of the century, that Roman troops would return to help protect them from barbarian attacks. Some of the councils that the Romans had established in Britain continued to function for a while, but corporate government was unlikely to be effective for very long in the absence of Roman officials, backed by Roman arms. Power naturally passed into the hands of military leaders. There is no reason to doubt the general reliability of Gildas when he described power in fifth-century Britain resting not so much with councils as with kings who were, in his view, tyrants. Many of the fifth-century warriors were natives, Britons or descendants of Roman soldiers who had made their home in Britain, but at least some British rulers recruited Germans. The Romans had done likewise and German soldiers could rise to high rank in the Roman army. The Romans also recruited, or impressed, groups from Germanic tribes to form ethnic units such as the detachment of Frisian cavalry stationed on the northern frontier in the third century. They do not however seem to have had any Saxon units of this kind.[10]

There were, doubtless, some Saxons in the Roman army serving as individuals, but there is no good evidence for the settlement of groups of Saxons in Britain before British rulers recruited some in the fifth century. According to Gildas this happened after Aëtius, the Roman commander in the western empire, failed to send help when it was requested by the Britons in, or soon after, 446.[11] Gildas then describes the decision of the British councillors together with a ruler described as 'the proud tyrant' to recruit Saxons to help resist the Picts. The first arrivals were soon joined by others and arrangements were made to provide them with supplies. Later, these Saxon allies, or mercenaries, revolted and caused widespread devastation before withdrawing to their own territory or bases. After that crisis the Britons gained temporary relief under the leadership of Ambrosius Aurelianus but the Saxons, now firmly established in the east, remained a threat. A period of varying fortunes ended with the siege of Badon Hill, an unidentified place. Gildas described this recent, but undatable, British victory as 'pretty well the last defeat of the villains, and certainly not the least'.

There are, however, grounds for suspecting that there were Saxon settlements in Britain earlier than that described by Gildas. According to a text that was probably compiled in Gaul and is known as the Chronicle of 452, between 440 and 446, that is before the appeal to Aëtius described by

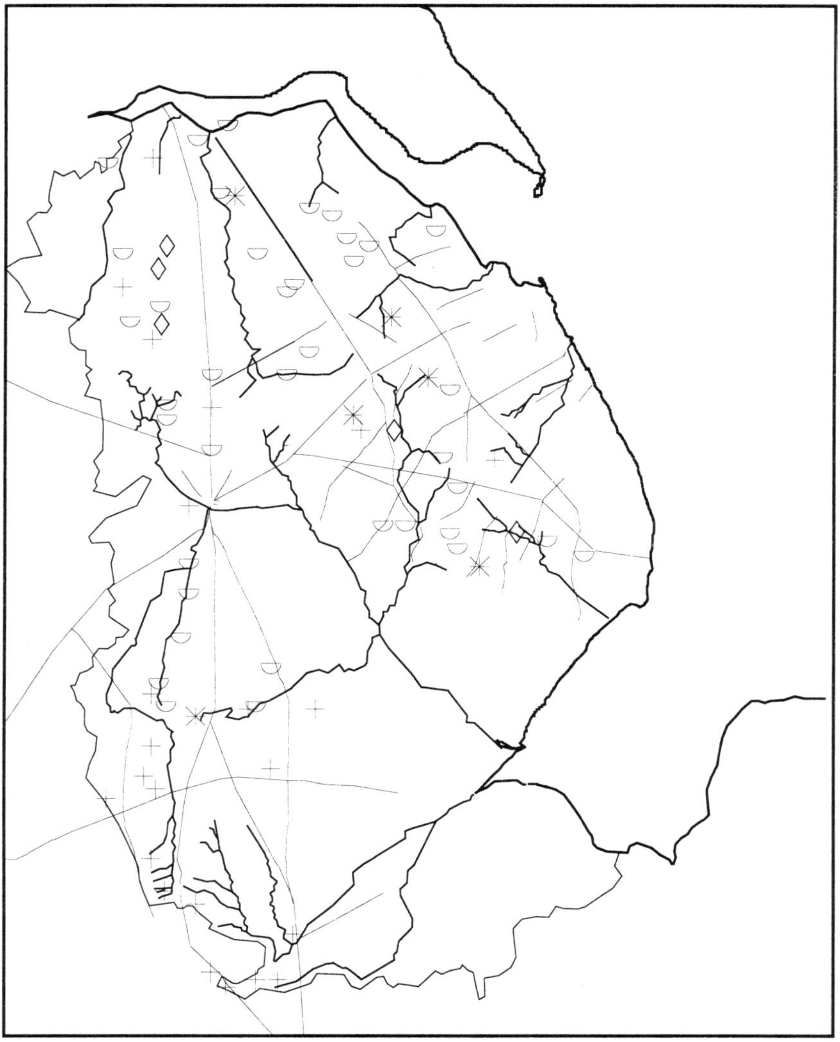

Fig. 3.4 Location of Anglo-Saxon burials in Lincolnshire.
Key: stars = cemeteries consisting mainly of cremations,
open hemispheres = cemeteries consisting mainly of inhumations,
lozenges = burial mounds, crosses = unknown.
Map produced by A. Oliver and A. Vince. © A. Vince.

Gildas, 'the Britons, having hitherto been overrun by various calamities and events, are subjected to Saxon authority'.[12] This conquest was probably in south-east Britain; archaeological evidence reveals a substantial Anglo-Saxon settlement in Kent, Essex, East Anglia, and the Thames valley already by the mid fifth century. If, as seems likely, Gildas lived in north Britain, the Saxon settlement that he described as in the east may have been north of the Humber. It is, indeed, possible that at least some of the Saxons he says were recruited against the Picts came from somewhere in south-east Britain.

The compiler of the Chronicle of 452, unlike Gildas, was probably best informed about events in southern Britain. He seems to have seen the Saxon conquest of the Britons as one element in the disintegration of Roman power in the west. Other entries in the same chronicle describe the surrender of parts of Gaul to the Alans and Burgundians, and the conquest of Africa by the Vandals. He exaggerated the completeness of the Saxon conquest at that time, although it is, of course, possible that even in the fifth century Anglo-Saxon leaders based in south-east Britain from time to time dominated areas well beyond the limits of the settlements of their followers.

In Lincolnshire there is little or no trace of the conquest described in the Chronicle of 452 or of the Saxon settlement reported by Gildas. There are a few fifth-century graves but none can be dated with any confidence earlier than about 450.[13] The earliest so far noted were in the cemeteries at Fonaby near Caistor, Cleatham, South Elkington, and West Keal. In each case very few graves can be so early. At Great Casterton, just outside the county, Anglo-Saxons seem to have lived alongside natives sometime during the fifth century. That is suggested by two groups of graves in the counterscarp of a ditch that was enlarged in the late fourth century. A dozen or so inhumations were found that may be part of a cemetery of the third and fourth centuries. The graves were described by the excavator as Late Roman but, as there is no means of telling how late Late Roman may be, they should perhaps be described as native. About 100 feet to the east there was a group of Anglo-Saxon graves, cremations as well as inhumations, including some of women and children. The most interesting feature of these burials is that the two groups appear to have been contemporary and that later Anglo-Saxons were prepared to disturb earlier Anglo-Saxon burials, but not the native ones.[14]

THE ANGLO-SAXON INVASIONS

The main influx of Anglo-Saxons into Lincolnshire began at the end of the fifth century or early in the sixth. The evidence from the cemeteries suggests that the invaders came in fairly small groups; Gildas may well have preserved a reliable tradition when he described the initial Saxon settlers coming in three ships – he here used the English word *cyul*, 'keel'. He did not name the leaders, nor did he give any details about what he called the 'second and larger group of satellite dogs' who arrived by ship to join the first group.[15] He described them all as Saxons, a general term used by both Romans and Britons for the German invaders whatever their tribal origin.

According to Bede, the invaders belonged to three 'very powerful German tribes, Saxons, Angles and Jutes'. He located the homeland of each tribe and claimed that each settled in a different part of Britain. The Jutes, who came from Jutland, settled in Kent, the Isle of Wight and south Hampshire; the Saxons, from Old Saxony, that is the area between the lower Elbe and the Weser, were represented by the East, South and West Saxons; while the rest, who settled along the east coast from East Anglia to Northumbria were Angles. According to Bede their homeland, called *Angulus*, lay between the Jutes and Saxons, in what is now South Jutland and Schleswig-Holstein, part of which is still called Angeln.[16]

Investigations of the graves of the immigrants have raised doubts about the reliability of Bede's account. In their homelands the Angles were culturally distinct from the Saxons, with different types of pottery and jewellery, but during their migration along the North Sea coastland of Frisia they passed through a cultural melting pot and when they settled in Britain could not be described as either Angles or Saxons.[17] The fifth-century Frisian cemetery at Issendorf certainly contained a mixture of 'Saxon' and 'Anglian' styles of pottery and jewellery, as did several Lincolnshire cemeteries, including Loveden, South Elkington, Fonaby, and Cleatham. The communities that used these cemeteries were mixed, although many individual families maintained their own Anglian, Saxon or other cultural traditions. Bede's classification of the invaders was justified not by the ethnic or tribal purity of the immigrants in any one area, but by the ancestry claimed for their leaders. The followers of a Saxon would naturally be considered Saxons, and Lincolnshire, together with East Anglia, Northumbria and most of Midland England was considered Anglian because the men who controlled those areas in the seventh and eighth centuries claimed to have Anglian ancestry.

Some of the Anglo-Saxon men were equipped as warriors and most must have been expected, and prepared, to fight, but very few graves of well-armed warriors have been found in Lincolnshire, a marked contrast to Kent. Swords are rarely found, shields and spears being more common. Age and sex can rarely be determined, but when that is possible many graves prove to be of women and children. In some cemeteries the proportion of women is high. Fonaby is in this respect remarkable: to judge by the grave furnishings there were at least 31 women buried there but only eight male graves could be recognized.[18]

In the fifth century the dead were normally cremated but after 500 the proportion of inhumations increased, probably reflecting the customs of newly arrived immigrants. Throughout the sixth century both cremation

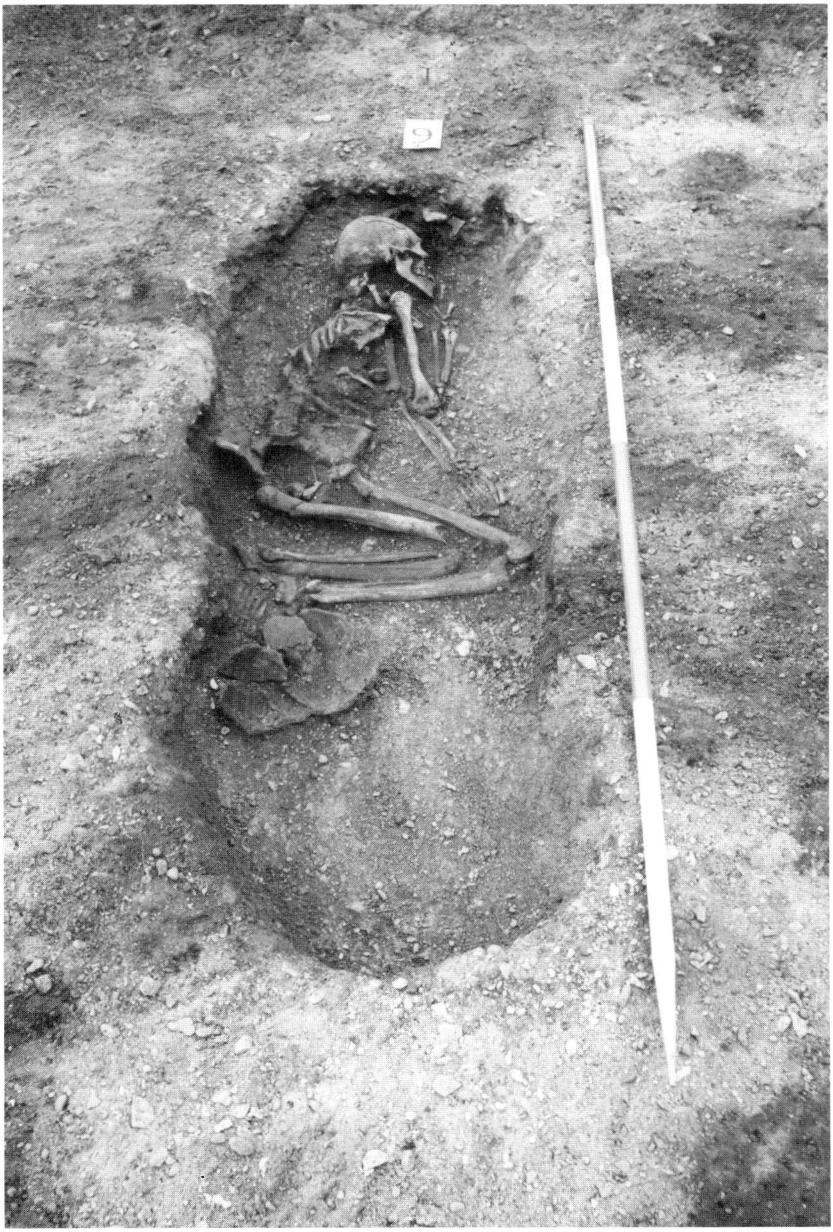

Fig 3.5 Grave 9 in the inhumation cemetery at Ruskington. A female over 50 years old with traces of osteo-arthritis was laid in the 'crouched' position common in this district. The burial was associated with a bronze pin, a necklace of amber beads with a silvered bronze pendant, an iron buckle, and a large vessel, broken in situ. Photo and © M. Atkin.

Fig. 3.6 The hanging bowl from St Paul-in-the-Bail, Lincoln. It was found buried behind the stone lining of an empty cist that was presumably originally a high-status grave from which the remains were removed at some stage. See Appendix 4. Photo and © CLAU.

and inhumation were practised, and although there are several mixed cemeteries others are predominantly of one type. At Elsham, for example, only four inhumations were found among 600 cremations. Cremation naturally destroyed much evidence, but the careful study of the fragments of bone and objects that survived the fire can yield useful information. People buried or cremated with valuable jewellery and equipment clearly belonged to wealthy families of high social status. The absence of such grave goods does not necessarily indicate poverty; it may reflect a different burial tradition. The bones themselves can be more revealing. The only Anglo-Saxon cemetery in Lincolnshire with a substantial number of relatively well-preserved skeletons that have been systematically studied is at Castledyke in Barton-upon-Humber.[19] About 200 graves of the sixth and seventh centuries have been excavated there, most of them between 1982 and 1990. The remains of 209 individuals, 169 of them adults, show that the population was reasonably healthy and adequately fed, with an unexpectedly large proportion of elderly people. A number of both men and women, including some who died as young adults (17–25 years old), suffered from back trouble probably caused by hard labour or carrying heavy weights. Similarly, a preliminary investigation of some of the cremated remains from Loveden suggests that many young men died after a life of hard manual labour.[20]

The archaeological evidence makes it possible to trace the progress of Anglo-Saxon colonization, at least in broad outline, but it provides virtually no information about the fate of the natives.[21] When Roman types of pottery were no longer made in Britain or imported, and Roman coins no longer reached the island, there is little material with which native graves or settlements can be dated. The possibility must therefore remain open that some apparently late Roman sites were in fact occupied by natives during and after the fifth century. The discovery of distinctive Germanic ornaments on such sites does not prove that natives had been replaced by Anglo-Saxons; such ornaments may well have been acquired by Britons.

It is usually argued that the virtual disappearance of the Britons is proved by the replacement of British by English speech, and by the rarity of

Fig. 3.7 Anglo-Saxon cruciform brooches from Cleatham (left and right) and a gilded square-headed brooch from Nettleton (centre). Cruciform brooches are relatively common finds in the graves of sixth-century women and represent an Anglian (as opposed to a Saxon) cultural tradition. Square-headed brooches were introduced into England in a second wave of continental influence during the later fifth century. These contacts also introduced the sleeve clasps which formed an important element of female dress in eastern England. The scale represents 2.5 cm. Photo and © K. Leahy.

British place-names. There are certainly very few British names in Lincolnshire. Lincoln and Lindsey both derive ultimately from a British word for a pool or lake, a word that recurs in the Norfolk name Lynn, and the first element in the district name Kesteven has been identified as a British word cognate with Welsh *coed*, meaning a wood. Most of the names with a possible British origin are of rivers, namely Glen, Lymn, Nene, Trent, Welland, and Witham, while the first part of the river-name Ancholme is a British word for marsh, *an*. Language is, however, a poor guide to the ethnic character of the people who speak it, and British speech was replaced even in areas where there were few immigrants. It is possible that a relatively large number of Britons did survive, and lived alongside or under the domination of the Anglo-Saxons. With the loss of their language they have disappeared almost without trace.

The fact that many farms and settlements flourished in the Roman period as well as in the seventh century or later does not prove continuous occupation. Anglo-Saxons or 'Anglo-Britons' may have reoccupied abandoned settlements after an interval, but continuity is also possible, whether the transfer was by force or peaceful agreement. We are similarly ignorant about the transfer of power from Britons to Anglo-Saxons. There are, however, several indications that Lincoln continued to be a centre of power after the departure of the Roman governor. This is suggested by the absence of early Anglo-Saxon cemeteries in its vicinity. The large cremation cemeteries form, in effect, a ring round, but at some distance from, the city (see Fig. 3.4). The nearest are Cleatham, about nineteen miles north, and Loveden about seventeen miles south-south-west.[22] This is in marked contrast to the other walled towns in Lincolnshire. Fonaby cemetery, with both cremations and interments, is under two miles from Caistor; there is a mixed cemetery just outside the walls of Ancaster, and the predominantly cremation cemetery at West Keal is only seven miles from Horncastle. As Kevin Leahy has pointed out, cremation cemeteries have been found very close to York, Leicester, and Caistor-by-Norwich. This led him to pose the question, 'Why should the cremation cemeteries avoid Lincoln?'[23] A plausible answer is that the Britons retained control of Lincoln and the surrounding area for most if not all of the fifth century. It is even possible that some of the Anglo-Saxons buried in the cremation cemeteries settled in the region with the agreement of those who controlled Lincoln.

The continued importance of Lincoln as a local centre is also implied by the fact that, unlike many other cities, its early English name, **Lindcolun* was derived, with little change, from its late British name, **Lindgolun*. What is more, the city gave its name to the seventh-century Anglo-Saxon kingdom, *Lindissi, Lindesse*, later known as Lindsey.[24] The city was clearly an important centre in the early seventh century when its *praefectus*

Blæcca was converted by Paulinus and a church was built there. It was, moreover, in that church that Honorius, the fifth archbishop of Canterbury, was consecrated.[25]

To judge by the places Bede mentions as *in provincia Lindissi* it was as extensive as Lindsey in Domesday Book, when the river Witham formed the southern boundary in the vicinity of Lincoln. The territory administered by Roman Lincoln, even before it became a provincial capital, must have extended south of the Witham. It is not known when Lincoln lost its claims south of the river, but it appears to have happened by the early seventh century, possibly in the process by which the kingdom was formed.

We are no better informed about the organization of sub-Roman Kesteven, but there is good evidence that in the seventh century it was divided among a number of separate territories or lordships under the hegemony of kings based in the upper Trent valley, in the region later known as Mercia. The first of these Mercian kings who is more than a name was Penda. He made himself overlord over a large part of Britain and went to his last battle and death in 655 at the head of an army with contingents brought by 30 subordinate rulers. According to the *Life of St Guthlac*, the Mercian royal dynasty descended from *Icles*, and in the Old English translation of that text they are called *Iclingas*, the implication being that *Icel* was the first of the family to win power in Britain.[26] In the Mercian royal genealogy, probably compiled in the eighth century, *Icil* appears as the great-grandfather of Creoda, Penda's grandfather, who ruled towards the end of the sixth century.[27] The earlier names in this genealogy include several that figure prominently in Scandinavian tradition; they also appear in the Old English poem Beowulf, including Offa, who was remembered as an early king of the continental Angles. Reckoning 25 years per generation would mean that Icel lived in the early sixth century. A similar date is given by an entry in the chronicle compiled in the early twelfth century by Henry of Huntingdon. Under 525 he reports: 'At that time many came from Germany, and on many occasions, and they occupied East Anglia and Mercia, but they were not yet brought under one king. Many leaders occupied these regions, whence innumerable wars arose. The names of the leaders, since they are so many, are unknown.' A very similar annal is also found in chronicles compiled later at St Albans. It has been persuasively argued that the source from which these annals came was compiled no later than the seventh century and that the intended date was 515.[28] Little weight can be put on the exact date, but the general period agrees well not only with the genealogical tradition but also with the archaeological evidence that the main immigration into this part of Britain began shortly before or after 500. It is therefore possible that during the fifth century the area remained under some form of British rule, as did the nearby British kingdom of Elmet, on the far side of Hatfield Waste, which preserved some degree of independence until the early seventh century.

In the early years of the sixth century the situation changed radically. The archaeological evidence suggests that Anglo-Saxons were then settling in most parts of Lincolnshire. The custom of inhumation had begun to be common, replacing cremation; inhumation cemeteries, smaller than the earlier cremation cemeteries, are more widely distributed (see Fig. 3.4). Scatters of pottery of the pagan period have been found in many parts of the county. Although some may come from destroyed cremation burials, much is likely to be debris from settlements. Substantial quantities of pottery fragments found at Cherry Willingham and Middle Carlton, each under four miles from the centre of Lincoln, suggest that by the sixth century immigrants had begun to settle close to the city.[29]

The claim in the annals that the new arrivals had many competing leaders seems entirely likely; the details of their conflicts are lost and only the names of the victors were remembered, the *Wuffingas* of East Anglia and the Mercian *Iclingas*. By the seventh century the *Iclingas* were based in the upper Trent valley, an area that had then only recently been occupied by Anglo-Saxons. A plausible reconstruction of events is that shortly before or after the year 500 a band of Germans under the leadership of Icel came to East Anglia or some area near the Wash. A century later his successors dominated the various groups of Anglo-Saxons, later known collectively as the Middle Angles, and in the early seventh century extended their power further west and south at the expense of both Britons and other Anglo-Saxon settlers.

Gildas gives a hint of this sixth-century Anglo-Saxon expansion when he complains that his contemporaries 'were deprived of' the shrines of St Alban at Verulamium, and of Aaron and Julius at *Legionum urbis* (presumably Caerleon) 'by the unhappy partition with the barbarians'.[30] If this can be trusted, and here Gildas is writing of his own time, it suggests that the power of the invaders extended well beyond the area in the east where archaeological evidence reveals substantial Anglo-Saxon settlement in the sixth century. We cannot exclude the possibility that during the sixth century, in Gildas's lifetime, Anglo-Saxon rulers established overlordships over Britons as well as other Anglo-Saxons, just as their seventh-century successors did.

THE TRIBAL HIDAGE

A remarkable monument to the Mercian overlordship is a text known as the Tribal Hidage, a list of 35 kingdoms or peoples with a number of hides, or assessment units, for each.[31] It was based on a list compiled some time before the ninth-century Viking conquests, probably in the late seventh or early eighth century, recording the assessments of the peoples or groups owing tribute to the Mercian king. Some entries, with assessments of thousands of hides, refer to kingdoms or sub-kingdoms that are well attested in the seventh century. These include Lindsey which, together with Hatfield, was assessed at 7000 hides. Many of the groups had much smaller assessments. One that certainly occupied part of south Lincolnshire was the *Gyrwe*, described as having two components, the North and South *Gyrwe*, each assessed at 600 hides. Bede described the site of *Medeshamstede* (the original name of Peterborough) as *in regione Gyruiorum* and according to a ninth-century list of saints' shrines Crowland lay in the middle of *Gyrwan fenne*.[32]

The *Gyrwe* did not give their name to any modern place. This may be because many places were renamed after the Scandinavian invasions. This could explain why so few of the Tribal Hidage groups have been located in Kesteven or Leicestershire. On the other hand, a few of the Tribal Hidage groups appear to have given their names to several places, some of them many miles apart. Thus the *Spalda* have been recognized in Spalding in Lincolnshire, Spaldwick in Huntingdonshire, Spalford in Nottinghamshire, and in both Spaldington and Spalding Moor in the East Riding of Yorkshire. Some direct connection between places with related names cannot be ruled out. Individuals or groups who left the original areas of settlement to find new homes elsewhere may well have been identified by their original name, just as in more recent times some people have been named after the place from which they or their families came. In the course of the Anglo-Saxon colonization some groups may have successively settled in different places, or split into two or more groups. That may explain why Bede used the same name, *Lindisfari*, a Latinization of Old English *Lindisfaran*, both for the inhabitants of the island of Lindisfarne, off the Northumbrian coast, and for the people of Lindsey. Ekwall concluded that Lindisfarne was either colonized from Lindsey or that its 'people have been or regularly go to Lindsey'.[33] That the two names are associated has been described as 'as certain as anything in place-name studies can be'.[34]

It is also possible that the same name was used for more than one tribe or group. There are, for example, place-names in many parts of England that appear to derive from a group named *Billingas*; Billing in Northamptonshire, Billingford in Norfolk, Billingham in Durham, Billingley in Yorkshire, a lost *Billingabyrig* in Sussex, Billington in Lancashire and three Lincolnshire names that will be discussed below.[35] It is possible that members of one group were scattered so widely but as the group name may itself derive from a word for sword, it is perhaps more likely that there were several groups with the same or a very similar name.

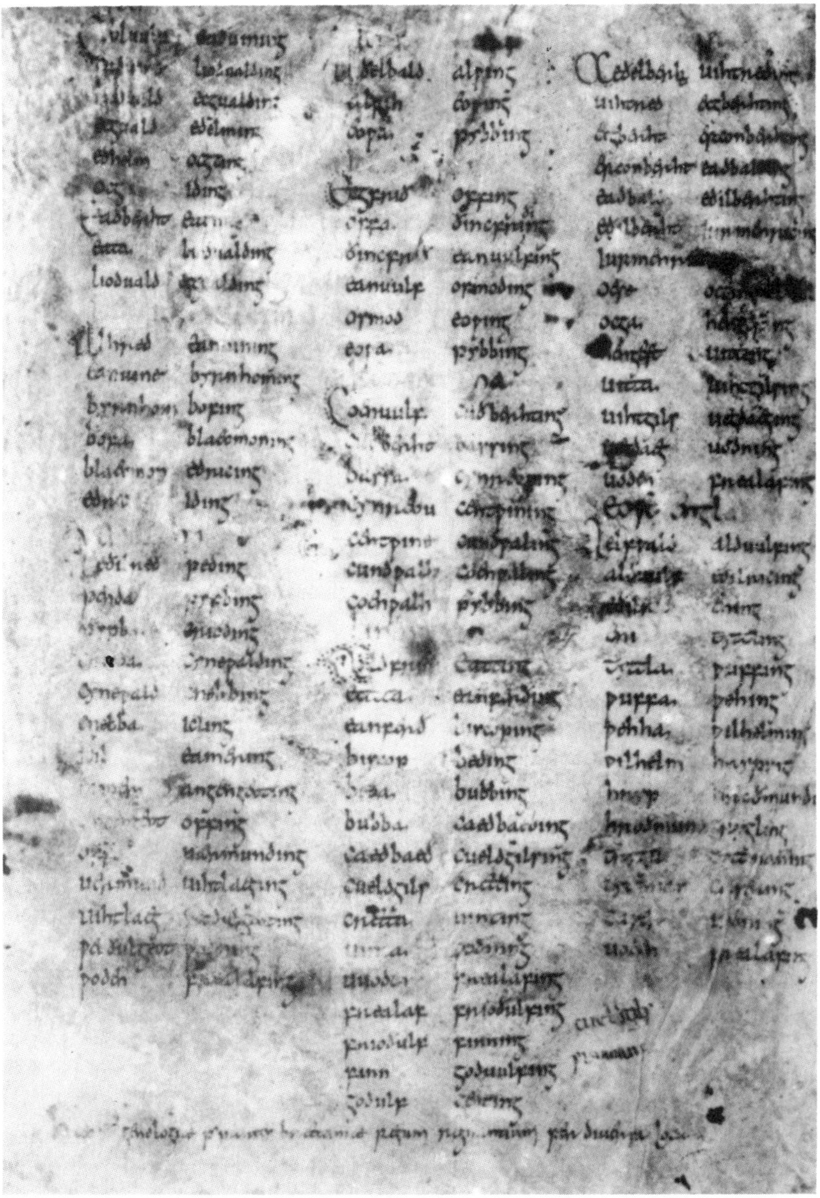

Fig 3.8 The Lindsey genealogy from British Library, Cotton Vespasian B.vi, fo. 109v. Reproduced with permission of the British Library.

Recent investigations in the Fenland have strengthened the case for associating the *Spalda*, a group assessed at 600 hides, with Spalding. Early and Middle Saxon pottery fragments found, in the course of the Fenland Project, west of Spalding show that Anglo-Saxons were living in the area from the sixth century.[36] It is unfortunate that Spalding itself lay outside the area investigated, but the silts on which it lies offered better opportunities for settlement than the Fens and it may well have been a centre of some local importance.[37]

The territory occupied by another early group, the *Billingas*, is indicated by a cluster of place-names in Kesteven; Billingborough and Billinghay, respectively 'the *burh* or fort' and 'the stream or island' of the *Billingas*, together with Horbling, 'the Mud-*Billingas*', or the '*Billingas* on muddy land', a suitable name for a settlement in the coastal zone of Kesteven.[38] It has been suggested that this group appears in the Tribal Hidage as the *Bilmiga*.[39] Reasons for doubting that identification are given in Appendix 2.

The Tribal Hidage may cast very little light on the early development of Kesteven but it does suggest that Lindsey, together with Hatfield, had much the same status as the Hwicce, a sub-kingdom of the Mercians for which the bishopric of Worcester was established; both were assessed at 7000 hides. Bede mentions Lindsey several times as a *provincia*, a word he frequently used for kingdoms that were subordinate to an overlord. Its distinctness was confirmed when a separate bishopric of Lindsey was established in 678, but it never appears in our sources as an independent kingdom. Only one king of Lindsey is known, Aldfrið, whose genealogy forms part of a collection of royal genealogies and king-lists compiled between 765 and 779.[40] Until recently it has been accepted that Aldfrið was the *Ealdfrid rex* who, according to the only edition of the text, witnessed a charter of the Mercian king Offa, dated between 772 and 786.[41] A re-examination of the fourteenth-century chartulary in which this charter is preserved has shown that the name is *Ealfrid.* As Simon Keynes has argued, this is almost certainly a misreading of *Ecgfrid rex*, Offa's son.[42] It is, therefore, uncertain when Aldfrið was king of Lindsey. The best that can be said is that it was before the genealogy was compiled. That text has several features that raise doubts about its value as a source for the early history of the kingdom, quite apart from the doubts that must attach to any royal genealogy. His ancestors are listed in reverse order as: *Eatta, Eanferth, Biscop, Beda, Bubba, Cædbæd, Cueldgils, Cretta, Uinta, Woden. Woden*'s ancestors are then traced back through five generations to *Geot*, but that extension appears to have been intended to apply to several genealogies and is only placed under Aldfrið's by chance. The alliterative groups and the names *Biscop* and *Beda* are suspicious features and this certainly cannot be regarded as a reliable list of the early kings of Lindsey

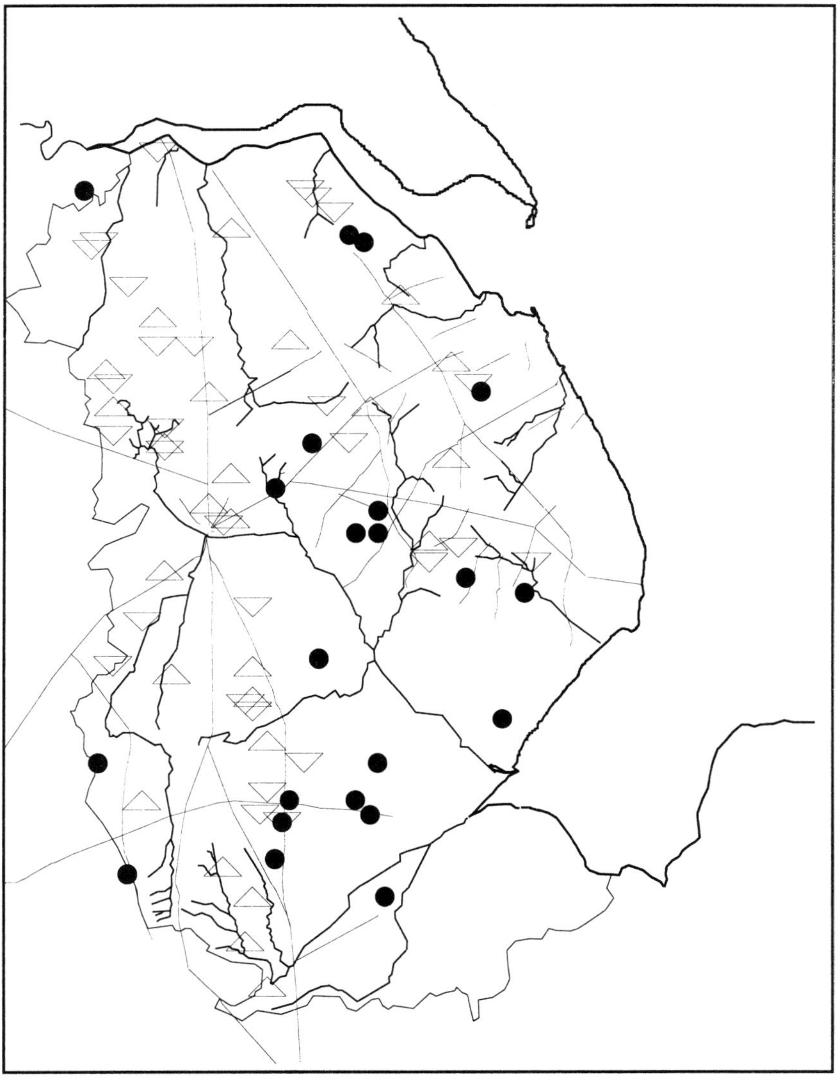

Fig. 3.9 Lincolnshire place-names ending in -hām, -ingahām, and -ingas.
Key: △ = *-hām;* ▽ = *-ingahām;* ● = *-ingas.*
Based on Cox 1973.
Drawn by and © A. Vince.

or even of Aldfrið's ancestors. Nor should too much be made of the name *Cædbæd*, in which the first element appears to be a British word, *cad* 'battle'. It is likely that the later rulers of Lindsey had some British ancestry but this genealogy cannot be taken as proof that they did.

The first person known to have had authority in Lindsey was Blæcca, described by Bede as *praefectus* of Lincoln, who welcomed the missionary Paulinus between 627 and 631.[43] Lindsey was at the time under Northumbrian overlordship and Blæcca may have been simply the local agent of Edwin, the Northumbrian king; *praefectus* can be translated 'reeve'. The word could, however, also have a more exalted meaning and was sometimes used as the equivalent of *dux* or *subregulus*, implying an authority that was not independent, but was nevertheless more exalted than that of a reeve. There are, therefore, indications that Lindsey was a separate lordship or kingdom, and it may at one stage have been independent, but from the seventh century, when it is first mentioned, it was always subordinate to one of its more powerful neighbours.

The Tribal Hidage treats Lindsey as a unit together with Hatfield, but there may have been some groups within it similar to the *Gyrwe*. One of these appears to be indicated by the place-names that incorporate the river-name Lud, including Louth. Several of the Tribal Hidage groups were named after rivers, and the facts that Ludford is on the river Bain, not the Lud, and that Ludborough is some five miles north of that river suggest that there may have been a group named after the river Lud, possibly with Louth as a centre.[44] Some of the later sokes may have originated in such groups, and it may be significant that several have early Anglo-Saxon cemeteries close to their centres. In Lindsey there was a major cremation cemetery at Cleatham, near Kirton, the centre of an important soke, and there were cemeteries at Nettleton and Fonaby, near the centre of the later soke of Caistor. A similar relationship can be observed in Kesteven at Ruskington and at Sleaford, while Loveden, the largest cemetery, was the meeting place of a later wapentake.[45]

Early groups or districts may also be indicated by place-names that end in *hām*.[46] These names were among the earliest given by the invaders and they indicate some of the areas in which the Anglo-Saxons first settled. As *hām* has a wide range of meanings, from 'homestead' to 'large estate', it cannot on its own help identify early estates or districts. It is, however, significant that the centres of several of the sokes described in Domesday Book have *hām* names, including Edenham, Grantham, Greetham and Waltham, as do two of the major early cemeteries, Cleatham and Elsham.[47] A slightly later phase of settlement is indicated by place-names ending in *-ingahām*, 'the *hām* of the followers or dependants of X'. The leader, X, is named in many cases; all but two or three of the 29 *-ingahām* names in Lincolnshire have a personal name as the first element. Barrie Cox has pointed out that in Lincolnshire these place-names 'appear occasionally in small groups, suggesting regions of expansion in the *-ingahām* phase'. He cites as an example the group comprising Metheringham, Leasingham, Helpringham, and Threekingham around Sleaford.[48] A third type of early name, ending *-ingas*, 'the followers or dependants of X', also apparently refers to groups of people. The *Spaldingas* are a good example. The distribution of these names in Lincolnshire, notably on the Fenland silts, suggests that they reflect a phase of settlement later than those indicated by names in *-hām* and *-ingahām* (see Fig. 3.9).

The complexity of the situation in sixth- and seventh-century Lincolnshire, and our ignorance, is underlined by the remarkable burial at Caenby.[49] It is a tragedy that this was excavated as early as 1850 (it took four days!) before modern methods of investigation and of conservation had been developed. It was in a large barrow or mound that, when it was excavated, had a larger diameter and was almost as high (340 x 8 feet) as that covering the ship-burial at Sutton Hoo. The contents bear comparison even with that spectacular find. The Caenby barrow appears to have been robbed at an early date but enough remained to show that the body had been in a sitting position. The report that fragments of wood, over an inch thick, and decorated with gilt-bronze ornaments of the highest quality, were found above the body may mean that there was an elaborately decorated burial chamber. They could, alternatively, have come from a coffin or from a piece of furniture. It has been suggested that it was a bed, but the sitting position of the body encourages the speculation that it could have been a richly decorated chair, a 'high-seat'. Many fragments of decorated silver foil were found, some perhaps from drinking vessels. Among these fragments designs very similar to some from Sutton Hoo have been recognized, including a helmeted figure with horns that end as birds' beaks.

The scale and magnificence of this burial suggests that it was for a ruler, perhaps of Lindsey, for it stands close to an important crossroad in the centre of the kingdom.[50] It cannot be dated more closely than to the first half of the seventh century. It therefore belongs to the period in which the overlordship of the southern English was successively held by at least four kings; Rædwald of East Anglia, Edwin and Oswald of Northumbria and Penda of Mercia. The first three had direct dealings with Lindsey. Rædwald led an army through it to battle against the Northumbrians on the bank of the river Idle in 616, Edwin's bishop Paulinus visited Lindsey and baptized many converts in the Trent in the presence of the king, and Oswald was remembered at Bardney as the conqueror of Lindsey. The man buried in Caenby barrow could possibly have seized the opportunity to claim or reassert Lindsey's independence when Edwin or Oswald was overthrown, but it is as likely that he was a *praefectus*, *dux*, or *subregulus* under a Northumbrian or Mercian overlord. These can be no more than speculations. The grave, however, remains; a reminder of how little is known about the early history of Lincolnshire.

Fig. 3.10 Gilded bronze plaques set with pearls and decorated with zoomorphic interlace; they were fixed on to a substantial oaken object, perhaps a chest, of which only fragments survive.
From the early 7th-century high-status barrow burial at Caenby.
Reproduced with the permission of the British Museum.

NOTES TO CHAPTER III

1 Salway 1981. Cleary 1989 is a useful, but selective, survey of the archaeological evidence.

2 The evidence for the Saxon raids, and for the so-called Saxon Shore forts is discussed by Wood, I. 1990. Bartholomew 1984, p. 176 shows that the one apparently contemporary reference to Saxon raids on Britain in the 360s, Ammianus Marcellinus xxvi.4.5, is the invention of a modern editor.

3 The most up-to-date accounts of Lincoln in the fourth and fifth centuries are Jones 1993, and Steane and Vince 1993.

4 Darling and Vince 1992; Steane and Vince 1993, pp. 71–2, 76–7.

5 Thompson 1990.

6 The evidence for villas in Lincolnshire is conveniently summarized by Whitwell 1970, ch. 6.

7 Zosimus vi. 5, ed. Paschoud, p. 9.

8 Burnett 1984.

9 Wood, I. 1984; 1987.

10 Frere 1967, pp. 181, 186.

11 Gildas, cc. 20, 23-6, trans. Winterbottom, pp. 23–4, 26–9.

12 Wood, I. 1984, pp. 18–19.

13 Pagan cemeteries and graves are listed in Appendix 1 and mapped in Fig. 3.4.

14 Fennell 1974, p. 384. I am indebted to Christine Mahany for information about these burials at Great Casterton.

15 Gildas, c. 10, trans. Winterbottom, p. 19.

16 HE i.15, ed. Colgrave and Mynors, pp. 50–1.

17 Hill, C. 1979, pp. 315–17.

18 Cook 1981, p. 76.

19 Rebecca Wiggins and Anthea Boylston generously sent me a copy of their 1992 report on the human skeletal remains from Castledyke which will appear in the forthcoming report on the excavation of that cemetery.

20 Wilkinson 1980.

21 The evidence of place-names for Anglo-Saxon settlement is discussed below, pp. 51–2.

22 South Willoughby is a little closer, about sixteen miles north-east, but its size is not known and none of the urns found there in 1856 survives, Meaney 1964, p. 165.

23 Leahy 1993, p. 36.

24 *PNL* 1, pp. 1–3; 2, pp. 2–7. It is possible, but improbable, that the first element in the name Lindsey referred to the pool from which the city was named.

25 HE ii. 16, ed. Colgrave and Mynors, pp. 354–5.

26 Felix, c. ii, ed. Colgrave 1956, p. 74.

27 Dumville 1976, pp. 30, 33, 36.

28 Davies 1977. Brooks 1989, pp. 162–3 is sceptical about this argument.

29 Everson 1979; Field 1981.

30 Gildas, c. 10, trans. Winterbottom, p. 19.

31 See Appendix 2.

32 *HE* iv. 6, ed. Colgrave and Mynors, pp. 354–5; Rollason 1978, p. 89. A charter dated 957, S 649, names *Gyruwan fen* in the bounds of Conington in Huntingdonshire.

33 Ekwall 1960, pp. 298–9.

34 Wallace-Hadrill 1988, p. 235.

35 Ekwall 1960, p. 43.

36 Hayes 1988, pp. 324–5.

37 Middle Saxon pottery has been found at several places on the Fenland silts, including Algarkirk, Burtoft, Fishtoft, Fleet, Frampton, and Gedney; Healey 1979.

38 Ekwall 1960, pp. 43, 249–50.

39 Hayes 1988, pp. 324–5.

40 Dumville 1976.

41 S 1183.

42 Reported by Foot 1993, p. 133.

43 *HE* ii. 16, ed. Colgrave and Mynors, pp. 190–3.

44 Arthur Owen 1997 has advanced good reasons for thinking that Louth was the site of a Roman fort.

45 For the district or 'shire' of Sleaford, *s*ee Pawley 1988.

46 Sawyer 1978, pp. 157–60; Gelling 1978, pp. 112–16.

47 Cox 1973, pp. 51–2.

48 *ibid*, pp. 48–9.

49 Jarvis 1850; East and Webster, forthcoming.

50 Everson 1993, pp. 94–8.

CHAPTER IV

THE SEVENTH CENTURY

The history of Lincolnshire in the seventh century is dominated by the conflict between Mercian and Northumbrian kings as they struggled to extend their authority and enlarge their resources.[1] By the end of the century the king of Mercia was the undisputed overlord of the whole area and it remained under Mercian control for 200 years. Kesteven, which was part of the territory of the Middle Angles, appears to have been under Mercian lordship throughout the seventh century apart from the short periods when Northumbrians were overlords south of the Humber. The seventh-century history of Lindsey was more complicated. For a while it formed part of a kingdom that included Deira, north of the Humber. Edwin, who was overlord of much of Britain for several years before his death in 633, regarded Lindsey and Deira as the heart of his kingdom. He was, indeed, described in one eighth-century text as king of the *Humbrenses*.[2] A kingdom spanning the Humber was a natural development in the course of the Anglo-Saxon conquests and settlement; that river was one of the main invasion routes and for those who settled near its shores it was a means of communication rather than a barrier. In the competition for power after Edwin's death the unity of this Humbrensian kingdom was broken, but its memory was preserved in the see of York, which was established by Edwin and originally included Lindsey. The claim that Lindsey was part of the ecclesiastical province of York was revived after the Danish conquest in the ninth century and was still an issue two centuries later.[3]

THE STRUGGLE FOR OVERLORDSHIP

Northumbria originally comprised two kingdoms that were created in the sixth century, Deira and Bernicia. Deira was immediately north of the Humber and by the beginning of the seventh century probably extended as far as the river Tees. Beyond that river was Bernicia, with its main stronghold at Bamburgh. For much of the seventh century they were separate kingdoms, even though the ruler of one of them normally had some form of superiority over the other. They were first united shortly before the end of the sixth century by a Bernician, Æthelfrith. During his reign Edwin, the son of the previous Deiran king, was in exile, 'wandering secretly as a fugitive for many years through many places and kingdoms until at last he came to Rædwald, king of the East Angles, and asked him for protection against the plots of his powerful persecutor'.[4] Æthelfrith unsuccessfully attempted to persuade Rædwald to kill his guest, and it was Rædwald who defeated and killed Æthelfrith in 616 in a battle fought by the river Idle, about twenty miles from Lincoln along the Roman road to Doncaster. Edwin then took Æthelfrith's place as ruler of both Deira and Bernicia, and Æthelfrith's sons fled into exile among the Picts and the Scots. By 625 Edwin had made himself overlord of most of the southern English kingdoms and of the British kingdom of Gwynedd.

By 625 he had also been converted and his later actions suggest that the core of his kingdom included Lindsey. He encouraged the Christian mission there as well as in Deira and Bernicia, but made no attempt to convert the English rulers who acknowledged him as overlord. It may be significant in this connection that in his time churches were built in York and Lincoln, but not in Bernicia.

In 633 the king of Gwynedd, Cadwallon, rebelled and in alliance with Penda, king of the Mercians, defeated and killed Edwin in a battle fought in the district known as *Hœthfeld*. The name survives in Hatfield Chase, but in the seventh century Hatfield was much larger and included Edwinstowe in Nottinghamshire which was possibly the site of the battle and of Edwin's first burial.[5]

The unity of Northumbria was broken. Deira passed to Edwin's cousin Osric, and Bernicia to Æthelfrith's eldest son, but within a year both had been killed by Cadwallon whose triumph was, however, short-lived; in 634 he was killed near Hexham by another of Æthelfrith's sons, Oswald who reunited Bernicia and Deira, and soon re-established Northumbrian overlordship south of the Humber; in Lindsey he was remembered as a conqueror.[6] When, in 642, Oswald was killed by Penda in a battle near Oswestry, Northumbria again broke up into its constituent kingdoms.

Penda quickly established his authority over a very large part of southern England, including Lindsey and Kesteven. Sometime before 653 he made his son Peada king of the Middle Angles. If, as seems most likely, Peada's kingdom had the same extent as the later bishopric of the Middle Angles with its see at Leicester, he was king of Kesteven, but not of Lindsey, which may have retained its separate status under Penda's overlordship. In 655 Penda attempted to conquer Northumbria. He succeeded in forcing Oswiu, Oswald's brother and successor as Northumbrian king, to retreat to the Firth of Forth and to pay a huge tribute. On the return journey, however, Penda's army was overtaken in the neighbourhood of Leeds and defeated in a battle fought on 15 November by an unidentified river called the *Winwœd*. Penda was killed together with most of the tributary rulers who had accompanied him.

Oswiu made Peada king of the southern Mercians instead of the Middle Angles, who were put under the authority of his own agents. Bede does not say how Lindsey was treated; it may have continued as a subordinate kingdom. Peada was murdered in 656 and two years later the Mercians rebelled, expelled Oswiu's agents and restored Mercian independence with Wulfhere, Penda's young son, as king. He re-established Mercian supremacy over the southern English and in 674 attempted to conquer Northumbria, then ruled by Oswiu's son, Ecgfrith. The Mercians were defeated and were themselves forced to pay tribute to Ecgfrith, who took the opportunity to annexe Lindsey, thus recovering what had once been an integral part of the Northumbrian kingdom. He did not have it long, for in 679 he was defeated in a battle described by Bede as at the Trent. The Mercians then regained control of Lindsey and it remained part of the Mercian Empire until the Scandinavian conquest in the ninth century.

CONVERSION AND EARLY CHURCH ORGANIZATION

Secular politics in Anglo-Saxon England were often closely reflected by the fortunes of the church, its leaders and, perhaps even more revealing, by the cults of saints. That is fortunate, for our knowledge of the internal history of Anglo-Saxon Lincolnshire largely depends on evidence concerning bishops, religious communities and the shrines of saints.

The first missionary who is known to have worked in Lincolnshire, Paulinus, did so under the protection of King Edwin who was converted following his marriage in or before 625 to Æthelburh, daughter of Æthelbert, king of Kent. Æthelbert had been converted by Augustine, a missionary sent by Pope Gregory in 597. Paulinus, one of Augustine's companions, was consecrated bishop in 625 in order to accompany the bride to Northumbria, and two years later Edwin was himself baptized. Paulinus made at least one journey into Bernicia but no churches were built there in Edwin's reign; the missionary effort was concentrated in Deira, where at least two churches were built, and in Lindsey. Bede reports that the first converts in Lindsey were Blæcca, the *praefectus* of Lincoln, and his household and that Paulinus built in Lincoln 'a stone church of remarkable workmanship', adding that 'its roof has now fallen either through long neglect or by the hand of the enemy, but its walls are still standing and every year miracles of healing are performed in this place'.[7]

It was in this church that Paulinus consecrated Honorius as archbishop of Canterbury in or before 631.[8] Bede was probably mistaken in thinking that it was built of stone. Lincoln is unlikely to have had a stone church before York where the church 'hastily built of wood' in which Edwin was baptized in 627 was replaced by 'a greater and more magnificent church of stone' that was unfinished when Edwin was killed in 633.[9] The building was completed by Oswald. Bede's description of the church in Lincoln need not be an obstacle to interpreting the apsidal building, traces of which were found on the site of St Paul-in-the-Bail, in the Forum courtyard, as the church built by, or for, Paulinus. The evidence from that site, discussed in Appendix 4, is consistent with this identification.

Bede reports one other incident in Paulinus's mission in Lindsey that he heard about from Deda, abbot of Partney. Deda had met an old man who told him 'that he had been baptized at noon by Bishop Paulinus, in the presence of King Edwin together with a great crowd of people, in the river Trent, near a city (*civitas*) which the English call *Tiouulfingacaestir*'.[10]

When Edwin was killed, Paulinus fled back to Kent with the king's widow and children, leaving his deacon James at York. The Roman mission to the northern English collapsed. The further extension of Christianity in that part of Britain was made possible by Oswald, who had been converted while in exile in Dál Riata, the Irish, or Scottish, kingdom in what is now Argyll. In response to a request from Oswald, Bishop Aidán was sent from Iona, the religious centre of Dál Riata, and he chose

Fig 4.1 The apsidal eastern end of the principal church structure on the site of St Paul-in-the-Bail, Lincoln. The line of the chancel screen with five post holes is right of centre. To its left (east) is the excavated foundation trench of the east wall of the succeeding structure (mausoleum?), which was probably associated with the hanging-bowl grave to the right. Photo and © H. N. Hawley.

Lindisfarne as the site of a new bishopric. Oswald's defeat by Penda must have hindered the missionary effort, for the Mercian king was a pagan. He was, however, not an implacable opponent of Christianity and tolerated the conversion of his son Peada. Peada's marriage with Oswiu's daughter was on condition that 'he and his nation accepted the Christian faith and baptism'. He was therefore baptized, probably in 653, by Bishop Finan, Aidán's successor at Lindisfarne, and returned to his kingdom of the Middle Angles with four priests. After Penda's death in 655, Finan consecrated one of these priests, Diuma, as bishop of the Middle Angles and the Mercians.[11] He died soon after his consecration and during the next 25 years there was a succession of seven bishops responsible for the same huge diocese which after Diuma's pontificate certainly included Lindsey.[12]

These bishops must often have stayed in royal residences and were probably given hospitality elsewhere, but they also acquired estates in which they could establish bases for their missionary efforts. One notable example is King Wulfhere's gift of 50 hides at Barrow-upon-Humber to Chad, who was bishop from 669 to 672. Chad founded a monastery there, the first church known to have been built in Lincolnshire outside Lincoln. Barrow was conveniently close to one of the main ferries across the Humber, and must have helped the bishop to keep in touch with Deira, where he had close connections, having been abbot of Lastingham and bishop of York. One of his predecessors as bishop of Lindsey and the Middle Angles, Trumhere, had even closer links with Deira, for he was a kinsman of King Edwin.

Diuma and his successor were Irish, and although the later bishops were all English, many had been trained in Ireland or Iona, and links with the Irish church continued to be very close throughout the century. For example, Æthelwine, who was bishop of Lindsey in the 680s, was educated in Ireland and in 664 his brother, Æthelhun died in the Irish monastery of *Rath Melsige*.[13] Traditions in the Irish church differed in some important respects from those that had developed in Rome. One particularly significant point of confusion was that they had different methods for calculating the date of Easter. Much of the Irish church decided to accept the Roman tradition by 633, but Iona preserved the old tradition until 716. Rome also put great emphasis on order and obedience to the church law as it was being defined in Rome. As the English church was increasingly exposed to the influence of Rome, tensions became acute. An important step in resolving these difficulties was taken at the Synod of Whitby in 664 when it was decided to follow Roman practice. In the five years after that synod there was, however, an almost complete breakdown of ecclesiastical order. When Jaruman, bishop of the Mercians, died, probably in 667, no successor was immediately appointed. At the request of King Wulfhere, Wilfrid frequently visited Mercia 'to fulfil various episcopal duties'. In 664 he had been chosen bishop of York and in order to ensure that his ordination was canonically correct he went to Gaul. When he returned in 666 he found that Chad had been intruded into York in his absence. Wilfrid then retired to the monastery that he had founded at Ripon. In 669, therefore, there was no regularly constituted bishop in Mercia and the Northumbrian see was occupied illegally.

Order was restored by Theodore, who was consecrated archbishop of Canterbury by Pope Vitalian and reached England at Easter 669. Later that year he visited Northumbria, removed Chad from York and put Wilfrid in his place. Chad, having been properly consecrated, was made bishop of the Mercian diocese and given Lichfield as his see.

A bishop was supposed to visit all parts of his diocese once a year and in this missionary phase was expected to preach, teach, baptize, and celebrate the holy mysteries, tasks that would later be done by assistant priests, as well as perform the functions that could only be done by a bishop; that is, to confirm baptized converts, ordain priests, and consecrate churches. No one man could possibly do that effectively in a diocese that stretched from the Humber to the Thames, and from the Severn to the Wash. Wilfrid's diocese was even larger.[14] Theodore well understood that these bishoprics were far too large but when, after Chad's death in 672, he attempted to divide them, he was unable to gain the agreement of the incumbent bishops. Chad's huge diocese remained intact with Winfrith as bishop. He was, however, deposed sometime before 676 by Theodore 'for disobedience'. Bede did not explain how Winfrith had disobeyed. It has been supposed that he opposed Theodore's plan to break up his diocese, but no other bishop was deposed for such obstinacy. He set out to appeal to Rome but apparently returned after having been badly assaulted while travelling in Gaul, and retired to the monastery at Barrow.

It was in 678, when Wilfrid quarrelled with the Northumbrian king and went into exile, that Theodore had an opportunity to divide the Northumbrian diocese to which Lindsey had recently been restored. Lindsey then became, for the first time, a separate see, with one of Chad's old companions, Eadhæd, as bishop. When the Mercians recovered Lindsey a year later Eadhæd withdrew to Ripon,[15] but it survived as a separate, Mercian, diocese until the ninth century.

At about the same time as the diocese of Lindsey was formed the remainder of the Mercian diocese was also divided into several sees. The details of this development are obscure and the dates uncertain. By 680 separate sees had been created at Worcester and Hereford. From 691 to 706 there was also a see at Leicester for the Middle Angles, with Wilfrid as bishop, but after that the Middle Angles, including the people of Kesteven, were once again part of the diocese of Lichfield until 737 when the regular succession of bishops of Leicester began. The early history of the Mercian dioceses illustrates very clearly the political significance of the church at that time. The missionary diocese of Diuma and his first three or four successors extended over the whole area of Mercian domination in which bishoprics had not already been established. Lindsey first became a separate see under a Northumbrian king, but was soon incorporated in Mercia. The sees of Worcester and Hereford were created for the Mercian sub-kingdoms of the *Hwicce* and the *Magonsæte*. The delay in creating a permanent see at Leicester not only underlines the close links between Mercia and the groups collectively known as the Middle Angles, it also suggests that the Middle Angles lacked the coherence of the *Hwicce* and the *Magonsæte*; that would not be surprising, for the Middle Anglian kingdom began and ended with Peada.

The first churches were built by or for bishops either in former Roman cities, such as York and Lincoln, or on royal estates and it is likely that by the end of the seventh century many royal *villae* had churches. Their development cannot be traced in detail in Lincolnshire, but there are enough later indications to show that the early church organization there was much the same as elsewhere. These early episcopal churches were the main centres for the evangelism of surrounding areas and most, if not all, of them were sooner or later served by communities of clerks or chaplains and are generally called minsters, an English word deriving from the Latin *monasterium*.[16] It has been objected that the distinction between episcopal minsters and other monasteries (discussed below) is not justified by contemporary evidence; all monasteries were, at least in theory, under episcopal authority and many had some responsibility for pastoral care.[17] There are, however, indications that although some churches on royal estates were royal chapels, they all had pastoral care as one of their main functions, while other monasteries cared for their own tenants and servants, not for the general population.[18] Each minster had its own territory or *parochia* from whose inhabitants various renders were demanded.[19] The earliest was church-scot which is described as a compulsory payment in West Saxon laws of about 700. It was later paid at Martinmas (11 November). It has been suggested that this was the 'ancient render' called Marycorn that Lincoln Cathedral claimed in the twelfth century from the parishioners of Lincolnshire. The fact that this render was to be paid throughout the shire and not just in Lindsey means that it cannot be accepted as good evidence for a traditional render in the see of Lindsey, although there is no reason to doubt that church-scot was an early exaction in all dioceses. Dorothy Owen regards the cathedral's claim as 'no more than a twelfth-century attempt to manufacture evidence'.[20] Other payments that may have been due from an early date, although the earliest evidence for them is tenth century, were plough-alms or plough-scot, later amounting to a penny from each plough-land, and the burial fee known as soul-scot. There were also tithes that were originally voluntary but had been made compulsory by the tenth century. These early dues rendered to the minsters were the spiritual counterpart of the secular dues rendered to the royal villas in which they had been established.

The Scandinavian raids and conquests and the subsequent activity of landowners in founding churches on their estates, described in Chapters VI and VIII, weakened the minsters and by the mid eleventh century there were traces of only a few in Lincolnshire. Grantham and Horncastle were both exceptionally large parishes in the twelfth century that presumably originated as *parochiae* of early minsters. In 1065 both were royal manors with numerous separate settlements.[21] Caistor was also a royal manor with dependent chapels in its soke. The names of the two places in Lincolnshire called Kirton suggest that they had important churches at the time of the Scandinavian conquest. Kirton in Lindsey was, moreover, a royal manor with a large soke, and Kirton in Holland gave its name to a wapentake.

When William the Conqueror granted Bishop Remigius the churches at Caistor, Kirton, and Wellingore he was probably restoring what the bishop's predecessors had held four hundred years earlier. Wellingore is particularly interesting; according to Domesday Book that church 'belonged to the church of St Peter in Lincoln', that is St Peter at Pleas.[22] If Wellingore was an episcopal minster its mother church in Lincoln is likely to have been the cathedral.

MONASTERIES

Episcopal minsters were not the only religious communities that began to be founded in the seventh century. There were also monasteries, communities of men or women, or sometimes both, dedicated to a life of prayer and worship, rather than to the work of evangelism and pastoral care. Charters granting land and privileges to such monastic communities in other parts of England explain that this was done for the sake of the souls of the benefactors and their kin. Donors hoped to gain divine favour in life and after death through the intercession of men and women who had been enabled to lead a life of spiritual purity by their generosity.

Churchmen were eager to encourage rulers, and others, to earn divine favour and had no difficulty in explaining failure as a result of disobedience to God's will as interpreted by his servants. According to Wilfrid's biographer, so long as King Ecgfrith favoured Wilfrid the Northumbrians prospered, for example by conquering Lindsey, but the king's abandonment of the bishop led directly to the loss of Lindsey and six years later to his defeat and death. With clerical advisers who interpreted events in this way, it is not surprising that King Oswiu was prepared to endow twelve monasteries as a thank offering for his victory over the heathen

Penda, or that he was ready to atone for his part in the 'foul murder' of the Deiran king Oswine by endowing a monastery 'in which prayers were to be offered daily to the Lord for the redemption of the souls of both kings, the murdered king and the one who ordered the murder'.[23]

Kings were not the only people to found religious communities. In 734 Bede complained to the archbishop of York that many laymen had founded so-called monasteries in Northumbria, especially in the preceding 30 years, and called themselves abbots without giving up their secular life as 'reeves, or thegns, or servants of the king'. As the members of these communities were not celibate the religious rituals that Bede admits were performed in them were, in his view, worthless; 'the very same men now are occupied with wives and the procreation of children, now rising from their beds perform with assiduous attention what should be done within the precincts of monasteries'.[24] He also complained about sham nunneries ruled by the wives of these 'lay-abbots'. There were, doubtless, communities of this kind in Lincolnshire as well as Northumbria in the early eighth century.

The five Lincolnshire monasteries that Bede refers to in his *Ecclesiastical History* were all in Lindsey: Bardney, Barrow, Partney, and an unnamed nunnery near Partney. He also mentioned a certain 'holy and abstemious man named Hygbald, who was abbot in the province of Lindsey'.[25] Hygbald's abbey was almost certainly at Hibaldstow. According to the list of saints' resting places *Higebold*"s remains were at *Cecesege* on the river *Oncel* or Ancholme.[26] The name *Cecesege* is otherwise unknown, but the place can safely be identified as Hibaldstow which is about a mile from the Ancholme. The only churches dedicated to St Hygbald are at Hibaldstow itself, in the neighbouring parishes of Manton and Scawby, and at Ashby de la Launde in Kesteven.

Bede only comments on the foundation of one of these monasteries, Barrow, which he explains was established by Chad shortly before he died on 50 hides of land given by King Wulfhere.[27] Bede's comment that 'traces of the monastic rule which he (Chad) established still survive' suggests that standards had declined. Wulfhere's loss of Lindsey soon after Barrow's foundation probably affected it badly, and Bede's attitude may also have been influenced by the fact that the 'disobedient' bishop Winfrith retired there. Despite this decline, and the disruption caused by the Scandinavians in the ninth century, the Barrow estate survived as a unit and was acquired by Peterborough Abbey some 300 years after the original foundation.[28]

Bede said little about the religious life in the other houses. Partney is only mentioned because its abbot Deda, 'a most truthful man', had told Bede what he had learned from one of the men baptized by Paulinus. Bardney was described as 'a famous monastery' because it held the shrine of St Oswald. In 704 when King Æthelred abdicated, he retired to Bardney, and died there as its abbot in 716. Both Æthelred and his queen, Osthryth, were enshrined at Bardney as saints. This close association has led to the suggestion that Æthelred founded Bardney but, as Plummer pointed out, 'Bede would hardly have omitted this had it been the fact'.[29] There are grounds for thinking that Bardney was, in fact, founded as a daughter house of *Medeshamstede*. That abbey was not a royal foundation but it was greatly favoured by Mercian kings, including Æthelred, and quickly acquired a monastic empire that reflected the hegemony of those kings, with daughter houses not only in Mercia, at Breedon and Repton, but also in Surrey, at Woking and Bermondsey.[30] Bardney seems originally to have been part of this constellation and was presumably founded after the Mercians recovered Lindsey in 679. At a very early stage it became a royal house and played a central role in the religious politics of the Mercian Empire.

It has been claimed that Bardney was one of the double monasteries that were a prominent feature of the early English church. These were communities of monks and nuns that were presided over by abbesses, most of whom were members of royal families. Bardney was, however, ruled by an abbot, and therefore cannot have been a double monastery. A better, if weak, case can be made for the unnamed monastery near Partney. Its abbess, Æthelhild, who was alive when Bede wrote, belonged to a family that was very prominent in the early history of the church in Lindsey. Bede does not say that he met her, but she appears to have been the ultimate source of his account of the reception of Oswald's remains at Bardney, an episode that is discussed below. The account of a miracle wrought by Oswald in her monastery provides some details about the organization of that community.[31] A guest was taken ill, he apparently had a fit. 'As he could neither be held down nor bound, a servant ran and knocked at the abbess's gate and told her. She opened the monastery door and went out with one of the nuns to the men's dwelling (*ad locum uirorum*) where she called a priest (or the priest) and asked him to come with her to the patient'; the priest unsuccessfully attempted to exorcise the devil. Æthelhild then remembered that she had been given, at Bardney, some soil on which water used for washing Oswald's bones had fallen. A woman servant was sent to fetch the casket in which this soil was kept, and when it was brought into the porch of the house in which the demoniac was lying, he was suddenly cured. The guest was not in the men's dwelling, where the priest slept, he was presumably staying in the abbey's guest-house. What Bede described as the men's dwelling may have housed male members of the community, although it must be admitted that in describing Barking, Ely, and Coldingham, he explicitly mentioned brothers, and named five bishops who came from Whitby.[32] If Æthelhild's monastery was a community of monks and nuns, it is likely that she belonged to a royal family of Lindsey.

According to the twelfth-century *Liber Eliensis* Æthelthryth, who founded Ely Abbey, also founded two monasteries in Lincolnshire.[33] One was near Winteringham on an island called *Alftham*, the other was named *Ædeldreðestowe* after her. This narrative was dismissed by Plummer as 'quite mythical',[34] but there is no reason to doubt that she did found two communities in Lincolnshire, and that one of them was at Threekingham. The only other references to this monastery are in connection with St Werburg. In her *Life*, by Goscelin, Threekingham is said to have been one of the Mercian houses that she was put in charge of by her uncle, King Æthelred. She died there but her body was soon taken to another of her houses at Hanbury in Staffordshire where the Mercian king Ceolred (709–16) built a shrine. David Roffe has argued that this monastery was in fact at Stow Green, about two miles south of Threekingham, where there was, in the twelfth century, a church dedicated to Æthelthryth and in the thirteenth century a fair was held there on her festival, 23 June. This fair is recorded in Domesday Book as being at Threekingham, presumably because that was the name of the estate or district in which Stowe lay.[35]

It has been suggested that the other foundation was at West Halton, where the church is dedicated to St Æthelthryth. It was apparently an exceptionally large church building. Abraham de la Pryme, the curate of Broughton nearby, described it in the late seventeenth century as 'all now faln to ruins, but appears to have been very stately, magnificent, and larger than any one for a great many miles round about it'.[36] That identification means rejecting the description of *Alftham* in the *Liber Eliensis* as an island surrounded by marshes about a mile from Winteringham. That need not be a serious obstacle. Such details in a twelfth-century account of an episode in the seventh century are more likely to reflect knowledge of the landscape near Winteringham, where Æthelthryth is said to have landed after crossing the Humber, than a reliable tradition.

Another possibility is that Æthelthryth's monastery was at Flixborough, about six miles south of West Halton. Excavations there have revealed remains of what appears to have been a religious community that flourished in the eighth and ninth centuries. It will be some time before the final report on this excavation is published, but it is already clear that there were numerous buildings, up to 18 yards long, that were rebuilt at least twice, with cobbled paths between them. The high status of the community is indicated by the quality of the finds and the range of imports which included quern stones from the Rhineland, pottery from Frankia and Frisian coins. Numerous styli used in writing on wax or clay tablets suggest that it was a literate community in which people learned to write. The many objects found are very similar to those found at Whitby abbey and near Beverley minster, and also recently at Barking and Brandon. A unique find (Fig. 4.3) is a lead plate that may once have been attached to a surface,

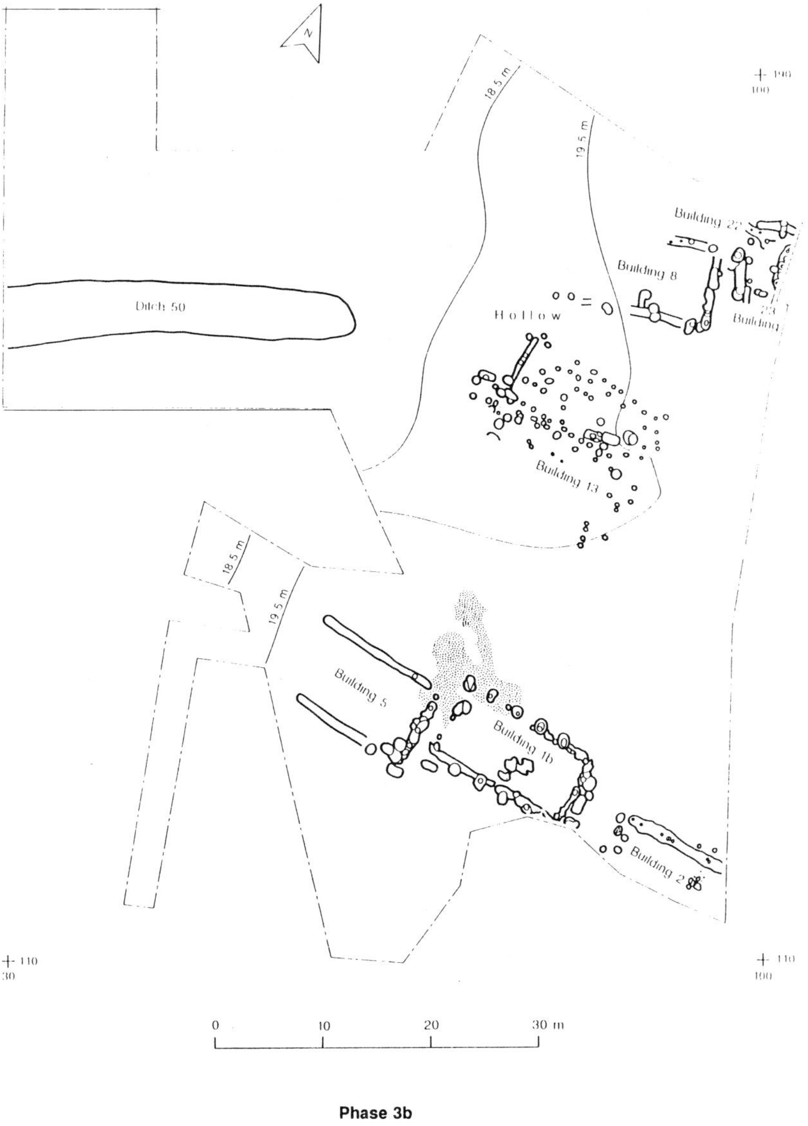

Fig. 4.2 The Flixborough Anglo-Saxon settlement in its mid 8th- to early 9th-century phase, when it may have been a monastery. Illustration reproduced with permission and by courtesy of the Humber Archaeology Partnership, in advance of publication.

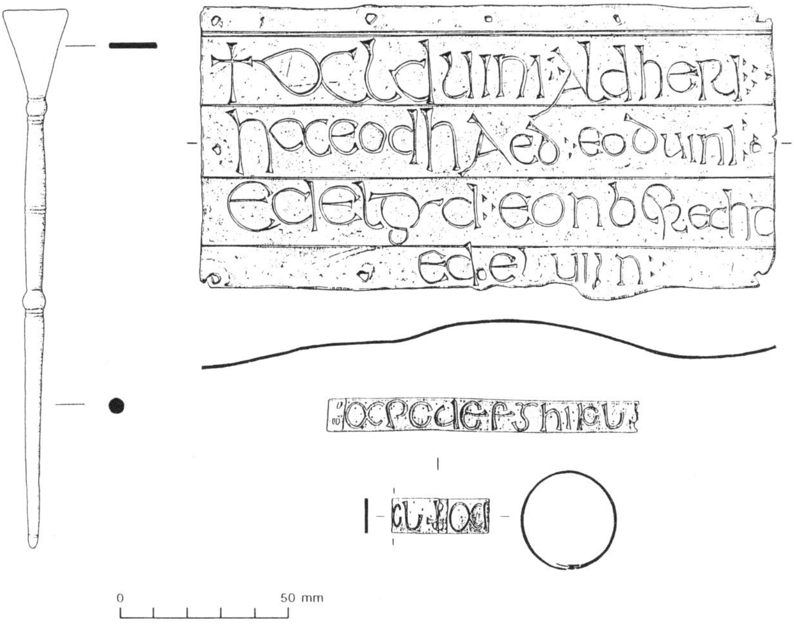

Fig. 4.3 Inscribed lead plaque, alphabet ring, and a silver stylus from Flixborough. The lead plate was found in the occupation layer over the foundation of building 1 (see Fig. 4.2). The text consists of seven Old English personal names: Alduini, Aldh̃eri, Haeodhaed, Eoduini, Edelgyd, Eonberecht, Edeluiin. These are forms of the recorded names: Ealdwine, Ealdhere, Eadhæð (probably), Eadwine, Æðelgyð (feminine), Eanbeorht, and Æðelwine (probably, with the last two letters transposed). Apart from the fifth name all are masculine, although the last could be the woman's name Æðelwyn. The script and form of the names shows that it was made in the 8th or 9th centuries. It may have commemorated members of the community or benefactors.
The ring has the first eleven letters of the alphabet, with B upside down, in a script earlier than the 10th century (see Okasha 1992, pp. 45–7).
After Loveluck 1988; illustration courtesy of the Humber Archaeology Partnership.

probably wood, with an inscription naming seven people, at least one of them a woman, written in very good letters of the late eighth or early ninth century. Michelle Brown has suggested that its function may have been to commemorate people who were important in the history of a religious community or to list those whose relics were contained in a reliquary to which it was once attached.[37]

Some seventh-century communities were highly regarded because of the reputations of their founders or early leaders. Many of the Irish missionaries, and the men they trained, led austere lives and by ostentatiously rejecting the commonly accepted social norms they

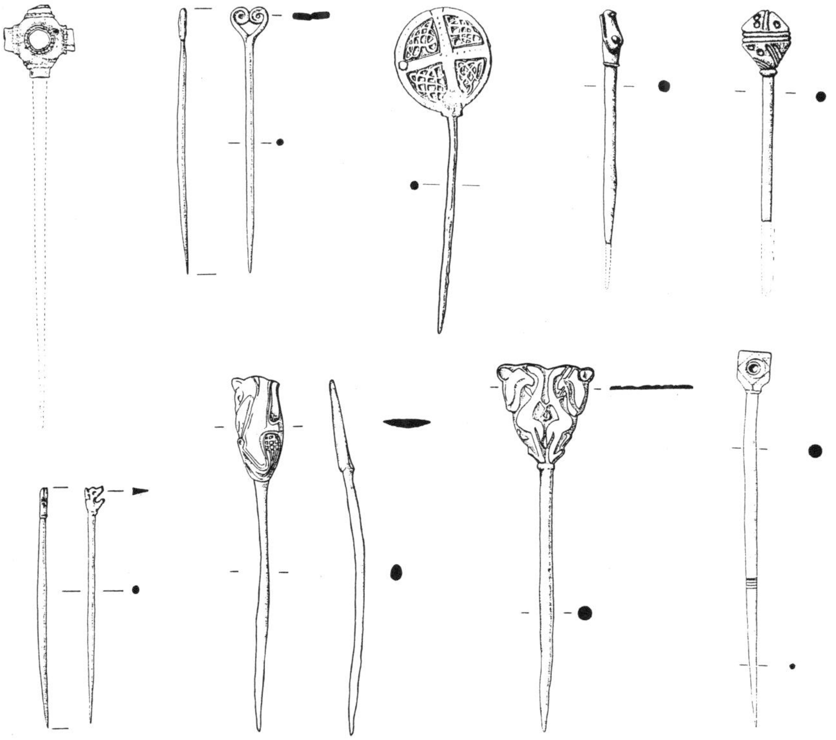

Fig. 4.4 A selection of 7th- to 9th-century copper alloy and silver pins from Flixborough. Scale 64%. After Loveluck 1997; illustration courtesy of Humber Archaeology Partnership.

demonstrated a special power. Aidán for example was reluctant to accept hospitality, and only gave money to the poor, not the rich. 'Neither respect nor fear made him keep silence about the sins of the rich, but he would correct them with stern rebuke.' He rarely travelled on horseback and when King Oswine of Deira gave him a 'royal horse', he promptly gave it away to a beggar.[37] His pupil Chad also preferred, 'as a religious exercise', to go on foot rather than ride. He was unwilling to obey Archbishop Theodore's order to ride when making long journeys, 'so the archbishop lifted him on to the horse with his own hands since he knew him to be a man of great sanctity and he determined to compel him to ride a horse when necessity arose'.[38]

Others were brought up in the very different tradition of the church in Gaul where bishops were expected to be rich, powerful and to preside over their dioceses with great splendour. Wilfrid, as a young man, spent three years in the household of the bishop of Lyons and for his own episcopal consecration went to Gaul with 'a force of men as well as a large sum of money, so as to enable him to enter Gaul in great state'.[40] One of the reasons for his exile in 678 was the jealousy that he aroused by 'his riches, the number of his monasteries, the greatness of his buildings, his countless army of followers arrayed in royal vestments and arms'.[41] Shortly before his death he divided up his treasure of gold and silver and precious stones into four. The best part was assigned to churches in Rome, the rest was divided among the poor, his household and, most revealingly, to the abbots of his monasteries of Hexham and Ripon 'so that they may be able to purchase the friendship of kings and bishops'.[42]

SAINTS

The reputation of many of these men lived after them whether, like Chad they prized austerity, or behaved like princes, as Wilfrid; their mortal remains were believed to be sources of power capable of working miracles. Places where saints died, or where their bodies once rested, were often believed to have miraculous power; when Oundle monastery was attacked and destroyed by some rebels the only part that survived was the house in which Wilfrid died. The same power was also believed to lie in places and objects associated with them, even if the association was remote, as in the miraculous cure reported in Æthelhild's nunnery.

There were also royal saints, two of whom, Oswald and Edwin, figure prominently in the early history of Lindsey and illustrate the political significance of cults. Oswald had long been revered as a saint in Northumbria, especially Bernicia, and his head and arms had been recovered soon after his death by his brother and enshrined in the Bernician centres of Lindisfarne and Bamburgh. The rest of his body was buried near the site of his death, near Oswestry. Soon after King Æthelred recovered Lindsey in 679, his queen Osthryth, who was Oswald's niece, transferred the saint's remains from Oswestry to Bardney Abbey. The monks were reluctant to admit the relics of a conqueror, but were persuaded to change their minds by a miracle.

> The relics remained outside all night with only a large tent erected over the carriage in which the bones rested. But a sign from heaven revealed to them how reverently the relics should have been received by all the faithful. All through the night a column of light stretched from the carriage right up to heaven and was visible in almost every part of the kingdom of Lindsey. In the morning, the brothers in the monastery who had refused the relics of God's beloved saint the day before, now began to pray earnestly that the relics might be lodged with them.[43]

Osthryth was murdered in 697 and when, seven years later, Æthelred abdicated, he retired to Bardney where he died in 716 as abbot. The adoption of the great Bernician saint in Lindsey under pressure from the Mercian royal family appears at first sight to be an extraordinary development, but it makes more sense in the light of Lindsey's history, and in particular Lindsey's early links with Deira, an association symbolised by the other great Northumbrian royal saint, Edwin.

The recovery of Oswald's remains and their removal to Bardney is closely paralleled by the transfer of Edwin's remains to Whitby, a double monastery over which Edwin's daughter Eanflæd and granddaughter Ælfflæd had jointly presided as abbesses. Bede, whose loyalties were Bernician rather than Deiran, says nothing about the translation of Edwin's relics; we only know about it thanks to the *Life of Gregory the Great* written early in the eighth century by a monk at *Streoneshealh* (later called Whitby).[44] He reported that during the reign of the Mercian king Æthelred (675–704), Edwin's remains were recovered by Trimma, a priest in an unnamed monastery of the South English. He was a Deiran and had a relative in the monastery of *Streoneshealh*. He was persuaded by a thrice repeated dream to go to a certain village in Lindsey, the author's informant

Fig. 4.5 Fragments of an 8th-century shrine at South Kyme. Photo P. Everson and D. Stocker.
© Department of Archaeology, Durham University.

could not remember its name, and ask a man called Teoful to show where in Hatfield Edwin was buried. After an initial failure he discovered the bones which he took, as bidden, to Whitby where they were 'honourably laid with other of our kings'. Trimma lived for a while at the place of Edwin's first burial and would have liked to build a monastery there. He claimed that he 'often saw the spirits of four of the slain, and certainly baptized, persons coming in splendour to visit their bodies'. As Edwin's remains had been removed these must have been his companions in the battle of Hatfield. The implication is that Trimma hoped to establish a Deiran cult centre near the place where Edwin was killed.

It would not have been surprising if Edwin had been a focus for local devotion – he had after all converted Lindsey – but the Mercian Æthelred was unlikely to have encouraged the cult of Edwin or any other Deiran 'martyrs' south of the Humber after he had regained control of the area in 679. As Alan Thacker has suggested, Osthryth's action in translating Oswald's relics to Bardney can best be understood as a deliberate attempt to counter residual Humbrian loyalties to Edwin.[45] Bardney's role as a shrine to the Mercian lordship of Lindsey was further reinforced by the development there of cults of both Osthryth, who was murdered in 697, and of Æthelred. It is, moreover, significant that Offa lavishly enriched Oswald's shrine, possibly in 792 when his daughter married the king of Northumbria, who was by coincidence also called Æthelred.[46]

NOTES TO CHAPTER IV

1 The classic history of Anglo-Saxon England is Stenton 1971. Campbell, John, and Wormald 1982 is a very stimulating and lavishly illustrated account of the period.

2 Colgrave 1968, pp. 94–5.

3 See below, pp. 115–16.

4 *HE* ii. 12, ed. Colgrave and Mynors, pp. 176–7.

5 Below, p. 72; Parker 1992.

6 See below, p. 70.

7 *HE* ii. 16, ed. Colgrave and Mynors, pp. 190–3.

8 Plummer 1896a ii. 106, 110

9 *HE* ii. 14, ed. Colgrave and Mynors, pp. 186–7.

10 *HE* ii. 16, ed. Colgrave and Mynors, pp. 192–3. The identification of *Tiouulfingacaestir* with Littleborough in Nottinghamshire (Plummer 1896a ii. 109) is possible, but unproven. It has been objected that Bede describes the baptism as happening in the kingdom (*prouincia*) of Lindsey. If, as the Tribal Hidage implies,

the kingdom included Hatfield, the plausibility of the identification is strengthened; see above, pp. 49, 57.

11 *HE* iii. 21, ed. Colgrave and Mynors, pp. 278–81.

12 Appendix 6.

13 *HE* iii. 27, ed. Colgrave and Mynors, pp. 312–13.

14 *HE* iv. 3, ed. Colgrave and Mynors, pp. 336–7.

15 Plummer 1896a ii. 224.

16 Blair 1988, p. 1. This interpretation of the evidence has been challenged by Cambridge and Rollason 1995, and defended by Blair 1995 and Palliser 1996.

17 Thacker 1992.

18 Thacker 1992, p. 142; Morris, R. 1989, p. 132.

19 The word *parochia* is used here for the district subject to a minster for church purposes; Blair 1992, p. 1. Most were later divided into several parishes, see below, pp. 155–7.

20 Owen, D. 1994, p. 12.

21 DB i fos 337b–338a, 339a = *LD* 1/8–25, 91–106. The medieval chapels in these, and other parishes, are listed in Owen, D. 1975.

22 DB i fo. 337b = *LD* 1/6. For the identification of the church, see Hill, F. 1948, p. 131.

23 *HE* i. 14, ed. Colgrave and Mynors, pp. 256–7.

24 Plummer 1896a i. 415–6, trans. *EHD* I, pp. 805–6.

25 *HE* iv. 3, ed. Colgrave and Mynors, pp. 344–5.

26 Liebermann 1889, pp. 12–13, no. 7.

27 *HE* iv. 3, ed. Colgrave and Mynors, pp. 336–7.

28 *HE* iv. 6, ed. Colgrave and Mynors, pp. 354–5; S 782.

29 Plummer 1896a ii. 155.

30 Stenton 1970, pp. 179–92.

31 *HE* iii. 11, ed. Colgrave and Mynors, pp. 246–51.

32 *HE* iv. 7, 19, 25, 23, ed. Colgrave and Mynors, pp. 356–7, 394–5. 422–5, 408–11.

33 *Liber Eliensis* i. 13, ed. Blake, pp. 29–30.

34 Plummer 1896a ii. 237.

35 Roffe 1986. Cox 1994b, p. 49 assumes that *Ædeldreðestowe* is Stow St Mary without referring to the evidence discussed here.

36 *Abraham de la Pryme, Diary of*, p. 140. Traces of a substantial defensive bank and ditch dated 600–800, have been found north of the church, *Med. Arch.* 27 (1983), p. 186.

37 Webster and Backhouse 1991, no 69a; Okasha 1992, pp. 46–7. I am indebted to Christine Fell for advice on this inscription.

38 *HE* iii. 5, 14, ed. Colgrave and Mynors, pp. 226–7, 258–9.

39 *HE* iv. 3, ed. Colgrave and Mynors, pp. 336–7.

40 Eddius Stephanus, c. 12, ed. Colgrave, pp. 26–7.

41 Eddius Stephanus c. 24, ed. Colgrave, pp. 48–9.

42 Eddius Stephanus c. 63, ed. Colgrave, pp. 136–7.

43 *HE* iii. 11, ed. Colgrave and Mynors, pp. 246–7.

44 Colgrave, pp. 100–4.

45 Thacker 1985, pp. 2–4.

46 Godman 1982, pp. xlvi–xlvii, 34.

CHAPTER V

THE MERCIAN EMPIRE

The heart of the Mercian empire, the Mercian kingdom itself, lay south of the Pennines on both sides of the river Trent, with two of its most important centres, the royal vill at Tamworth and the bishop's see at Lichfield, south of the river. The full extent of the kingdom is not known, but there is little doubt that its eastern boundary was the same as that between the dioceses of Lichfield and Leicester, the see of the Middle Angles.[1]

From this base Penda established a large empire and by the end of his life he was recognized as overlord by many English rulers. Subject rulers were expected to render to their overlord tribute and service, especially military service, and in his last campaign Penda was supported by thirty royal *duces*, each with his own contingent. Bede only named one, Æthelhere, king of the East Angles, thus showing that a man who was a king in his own right could be regarded by his overlord as a *dux*, a word meaning a military leader who could be described in English as an 'ealdorman'.[2] Other royal *duces* who fought and died in Penda's last battle may well have included the king of Lindsey and rulers of the *Gyrwe*, the *Spalda,* and of any other Middle Anglian groups that may also have occupied part of south Lincolnshire.

Overlordships like Penda's were inherently unstable; few outlived the death of their creator. When an overlord was killed in battle, the victor normally created a new overlordship, as happened after Penda's defeat. For about 200 years, however, most of Penda's successors as kings of Mercia succeeded in making themselves overlords of a large part of central and southern England, but not always over the same territory. In 731 Bede reported that all the 'southern kingdoms which reach right up to the Humber together with their various kings are subject to Æthelbald, king of the Mercians'.[3] Æthelbald was murdered in 757 and by the end of that year Offa, who was at best a distant kinsman of Æthelbald, was recognized as king by the Mercians. He faced determined resistance in East Anglia and Kent but in the ten years before his death in 796 his authority was probably as extensive as Æthelbald's had been. None of his successors could claim so much, but Mercian domination of the northern and central parts of England south of the Humber was sufficiently continuous for almost 200 years after 679 for the whole area to be thought of as Mercian. It was in this sense that Bede anachronistically described the battle fought by the River Idle in 616 as being within the bounds of the Mercians.[4]

The assessments in the Tribal Hidage give some indication of the relative importance of the various groups it names.[5] The *Gyrwe* were assessed at 1200 hides, twice as much as the *Spalda*. Lindsey with Hatfield was one of six groups or kingdoms assessed at 7000 hides, a symbolic figure.[6] Lindsey thus had the same status as the East and South Saxons. The other three groups were closer to the Mercian kingdom. The Hwicce, whose territory became the bishopric of Worcester, are well documented, but the others are more obscure; the *W(r)ocensætna* apparently occupied the area round the Wrekin in Shropshire, and the *Westena* may have been north of the Wrekin-dwellers in what is now Cheshire, although they have usually been identified with the *Magonsætan*, a late name for the kingdom for which the bishopric of Hereford was formed.

There are several indications that Lindsey retained a greater degree of independence than some of these groups with comparable status. In the first place the collection of royal genealogies compiled in Northumbria or Mercia in the late eighth century included one for Lindsey, but not for any of the others, although rulers of the South Saxons, often called *duces*, occur in eighth-century charters, and the East Saxon royal dynasty survived in subordination to the Mercians until 825. Two of the Tribal Hidage groups in question, the *Wrocensætna* and *Westena*, are even more obscure than Lindsey. Thanks to charters preserved at Worcester much more is known about the Hwicce and the way in which their ruling family was affected by subordination to the Mercians. Oshere issued charters as their king (*rex*) at the end of the seventh century, but his son is described as 'sub-king and companion (*subregulus atque comes*) of the most glorious king Æthelbald' in 736 and his successors are described as *reguli* or *subreguli*. One of them, Ealdred, is described in a charter of Offa as 'my underking, that is to say ealdorman (*dux*) of his own people the Hwicce'.[7]

Mercian kings, like other rulers in Dark Age Britain, spent much of their time travelling through their territory. They had to be itinerant in order to feed their household, retainers, and servants. Kings sometimes demanded hospitality from magnates or monasteries, but commonly they stayed on royal estates in which the food-rent that their subjects were obliged to render could be collected.[8] Such royal circuits enabled kings not only to feed their companions, but also to display their power and maintain links with powerful families in different regions. Mercian kings also held assemblies that were attended by leading churchmen and lay magnates. Charters recording grants of land or privileges made in such assemblies provide the main evidence for these occasions and sometimes state where they took place.[9] They were often held in or near London, or at Tamworth,

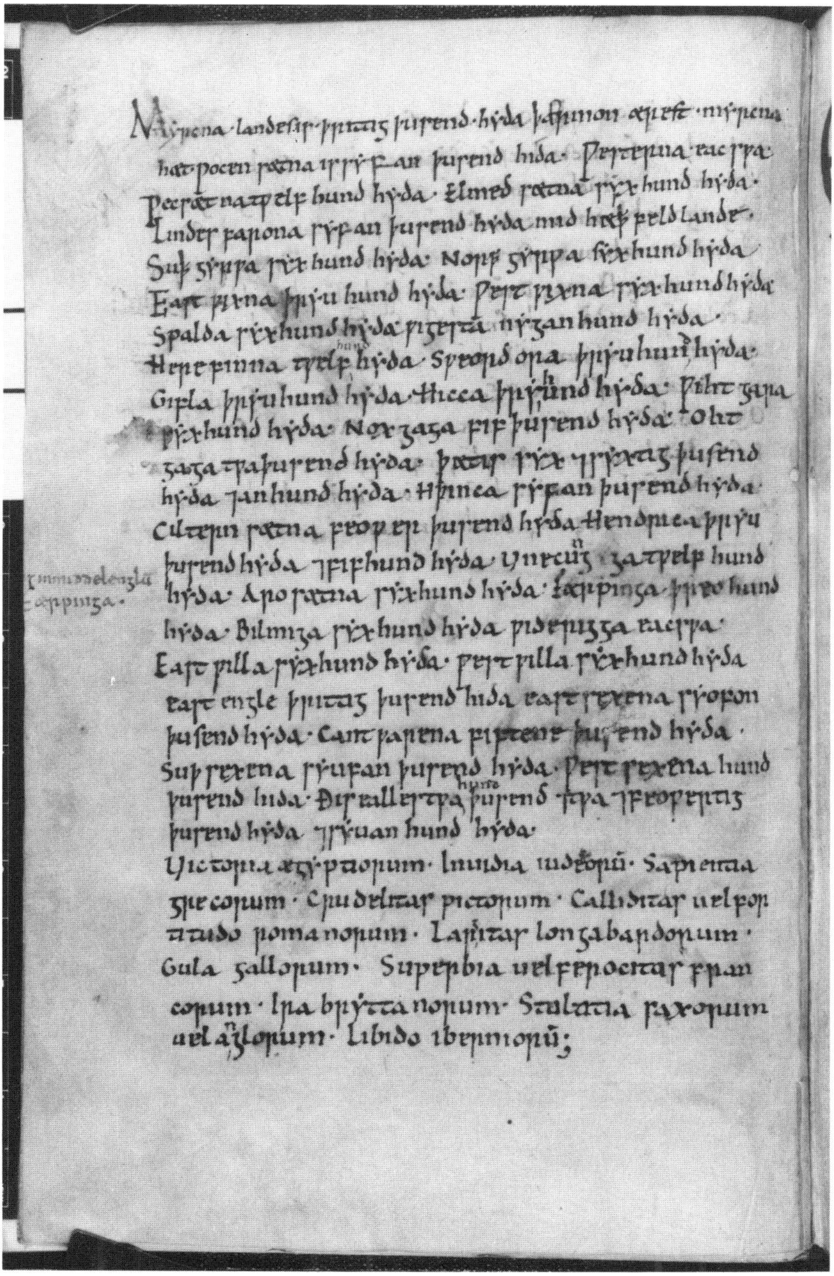

Fig. 5.1 The Tribal Hidage.
Recension A, from British Library, MS Harley 3271, fo. 6v.
Reproduced with permission from the British Library.

but on other occasions at places widely scattered in Mercian territory. Kings also took part in church councils, many of which were held at an unidentified place called *Clofesho.*[10] During the period of Mercian supremacy no royal or church council is known to have been held in Lincolnshire. It has been claimed that the royal vill of *Bearuwe* at which assemblies were held in 743 and 814 was Barrow-upon-Humber, but that is unlikely.[11] Other references to it give no hint that it was a royal vill and it is a long way from any other place of assembly. A more plausible identification is Barrow in Leicestershire, which was held by Earl Harold in 1065 and is fairly close to other places in which assemblies were held.

Subject rulers appear as witnesses in a few Mercian charters. Thanks to the relatively well-preserved Worcester archive the rulers of the Hwicce occur more often than any others. Only two rulers of the East Saxons witnessed Mercian charters before 800 and although a number of charters issued by rulers of the South Saxons have been preserved at Selsey, none witnessed a charter issued by a Mercian king. It is therefore not surprising that the only known king of Lindsey never attests a charter. It is possible that some rulers of Lindsey, like those of other kingdoms subject to the Mercians, were treated by their overlords, or by those who drafted the charters, as *duces* and appear, unrecognized, with that title in witness lists.

BISHOPS AND RELIGIOUS COMMUNITIES

The regular attendance of rulers of Lindsey in Mercian royal assemblies is rendered less likely by the infrequent appearance of bishops of Lindsey as witnesses in Mercian charters before the reign of Offa or, more accurately, before about 770.[12] After that date and until the Scandinavian conquest in the ninth century Lindsey bishops witness many Mercian charters. The first bishop of Lindsey to attest a charter was Edgar who appears as *electus* in 693. His successor, Cyneberht, witnessed no surviving document and until about 770 his successors mostly appear as witnesses in records of church councils. The same is largely true of the bishops of Leicester after that see was firmly established in 737. This is in marked contrast to the appearance of bishops of Worcester as witnesses in many charters from the foundation of the see.[13]

These witness lists, combined with early episcopal lists and occasional references in chronicles make it possible to discover the dates of almost all the bishops of Lindsey and Leicester. Virtually nothing is known about most of them, but Bede provides a little information about the early bishops of Lindsey. The first after 679, Æthelwine, seems to have been a member of an important Lindsey family. That is implied by the fact that one of his brothers was abbot of Partney and his sister was abbess of an unnamed community nearby.[14]

Æthelwine and his successor Edgar probably had no permanent see. Bede described them as bishops *in prouincia Lindissi* or *in prouinciam Lindisfarorum*.[15] A cathedral was built by the fourth bishop, Cyneberht, who was one of Bede's sources and who died in 732. Bede composed an epigraph to be placed in the apse of the cathedral, dedicated to an apostle, that Cyneberht had built in an unnamed city (*in urbe*).[16]

There is no agreement about the location of this cathedral. There were several places in Lindsey that could have been the *urbs* of Bede's verse. Although Bede tended in his prose to use the word *urbs* for places that were fortified, but not by the Romans, he did sometimes use it for especially important Roman cities.[17] There is only one text in which the bishop is associated with a particular place; the record of a church council held in 803 which Eadwulf, who was bishop from 796, subscribed as *Syddensis civitatis episcopus*.[18] The document is authentic and as the original survives there is no question of mistranscription by a later copyist. After the Norman Conquest some historians produced variants of the name, such as William of Malmesbury's *Sidnacestrensis*, but these all appear to derive from the text of 803. The meaning of *Syddensis civitas* has often been discussed; suggested identifications include Caistor, Horncastle, Louth, and Stow, as well as Lincoln. Of the thirteen episcopal subscriptions to this document, eight are in the form *N civitatis episcopus* and six of these *civitates* can be readily identified: Canterbury, Leicester, Worcester, Winchester, London and Rochester, all of them Roman cities. It therefore seems likely that *Syddensis* referred to Lincoln, but why the scribe of the 803 document chose to call it that is a mystery.[19] It was certainly the most likely site for the cathedral of Lindsey. Very few of Lincoln's churches were founded before the tenth century and there is no clear evidence to identify which, if any of them, was Cyneberht's cathedral. As Bede's epigraph shows that it was dedicated to an apostle, St Martin's and St Mary's must be excluded. The most likely candidate is St Peter at Pleas in the lower city.[20]

There is good evidence that Eadwulf's successor as bishop of Lindsey was especially associated with two churches. When, in 839, Beorhtræd, bishop of Lindsey, professed obedience to the archbishop of Canterbury, he did so as: 'Bishop of the people of Lindsey, together with both the congregations of the churches of those under vows, likewise together with the abbots, abbesses, and all the servants of Christ over whom I preside.'[21] Richard Gem has, in this connection, drawn attention to the fact that in the attestations to the 803 council Bishop Eadwulf is followed by Eadred and Daeghelm, both styled *presbyter abbas*.[22] It is tempting to think that they presided over the two episcopal communities mentioned in Beorhtræd's profession of obedience, but that cannot be proved. The location of these two regular congregations is unknown. One is likely to have served the cathedral. Comparison with similar twin episcopal churches at York,

Fig. 5.2 One of two mid 9th-century roundels that form part of a string course in the main south wall of the nave of Edenham church, above a 13th-century arcade. This evidence for the existence of an early and relatively large stone church in Edenham, together with the -hām *name, shows that it was an important centre before the Viking invasions, as it still was in 1066 when it was the head of an extensive soke (Taylor and Taylor 1965, i, p. 227; Roffe 1977b). Photo P. Everson and D. A. Stocker. © Department of Archaeology, Durham University.*

Canterbury and London, suggests that the second community was outside the walls of Lincoln; David Stocker has suggested Bardney but it could possibly have been Stow St Mary.[23]

Bardney is the only Lincolnshire monastery named by Bede that is mentioned in later sources: in the poem by Alcuin describing the adornment of Oswald's shrine by Offa, and in the list of saints' resting places recording that it housed the shrines of King Æthelred and his queen,

Osthryth.[24] If, as suggested above, Offa visited Bardney in 792 it is likely that he had other business in Lindsey, for it was in that year that Æthelheard, abbot of Louth, was chosen as archbishop of Canterbury, presumably by the king himself. Although that is the only reference to a monastery at Louth, the importance of that place as a religious centre is confirmed by later evidence that the cult of St Herefrith was celebrated there.[25]

Further evidence of the political significance of saints, discussed in the previous chapter, is provided by the *Life of St Guthlac*. Guthlac was a member of the Mercian royal family. After a youthful career as a warrior he renounced the world, became a monk at Repton and then, in about 699, withdrew to Crowland where he lived as a hermit until his death in 715. He had many visitors, including Æthelbald who, as an exile during Ceolred's reign (709–716) sought comfort and assurance from the holy man. After Guthlac's death Æthelbald visited his grave and was rewarded by a vision of the saint 'robed in angelic splendour' prophesying that within 12 months he would be king. After this prophecy was fulfilled Æthelbald put up 'wonderful structures and ornamentations' round the grave 'in honour of the divine power', and as a thank-offering for the support he believed his saintly kinsman had given him in his effort to win the Mercian kingship.[26] Æthelbald's success proved Guthlac's power just as Guthlac's support gave some supernatural legitimacy to Æthelbald's claim. Support was needed, for Æthelbald was the grandson of Penda's brother and was therefore not closely related to his immediate predecessors. His kinship with Guthlac was even more remote; their only common ancestor was Icel, the founder of the dynasty.

Felix gives no hint that the shrine was served by a religious community, he only reports that Guthlac was succeeded by Cissa, who was still alive when the *Life* was written.[27] It is, however, likely that there was some form of community at Crowland in the eighth century, although no reliable traditions about it have been preserved. The account of the early monastery written by Ordericus Vitalis in the early twelfth century does not inspire confidence.[28]

Despite the uncertainty about the status of Crowland before the tenth century, David Stocker has used it as the best example of an early monastic site in his discussion of the archaeological, topographical and documentary evidence for early religious communities in Lincolnshire.[29] There is, however, no reason to doubt his conclusion that Bardney, Partney, and perhaps other early monastic communities were, as in other parts of England, complexes, many of them on islands or peninsulas, with several chapels, cells and other buildings scattered in extensive enclosures with well-defined bounds.

Apart from the 50 hides with which Barrow was endowed, nothing is known about the land held by the religious communities of Lincolnshire before the tenth century. There is, however, evidence that between 787 and 796 *Medeshamstede* abbey leased land in Swineshead to Cuthbert *princeps* and that in 852 it leased land in Sempringham, Cheal in Gosberton, and apparently at Sleaford, as well as in *Forde* (possibly Greatford) and *Lehcotum* to Wulfred.[30] *Medeshamstede* also had land in other places that have been identified, with varying degrees of confidence, with places in Lincolnshire, but these identifications are very doubtful.[31]

MERCIAN GOVERNMENT

Very little is known about the working of royal government in our part of Mercia. There is, however, no doubt that as elsewhere Mercian kings depended on local agents to look after their interests, to collect the food-rents, and to muster warriors and gather the supplies that were needed for the military campaigns with which the Mercian rulers endeavoured to maintain, or enlarge, their empire. There was a hierarchy of such agents, the highest in rank being the ealdormen, normally called *duces* or *principes* in Latin. The ealdormen of Lindsey were probably, like those of the Hwicce, its kings or their descendants. Ealdormen seem to have been responsible for districts that corresponded to one or more of the early tribal groups or lordships of the kind listed in the Tribal Hidage. Some may, indeed, have been descendants of men who had once ruled such groups. The ealdormen who witnessed Mercian charters in the eighth and ninth centuries probably included some whose areas included part of Lincolnshire, but they cannot be identified. The only one known to have had an interest in Lincolnshire is the Cuthbert who leased Swineshead from *Medeshamstede*, although that does not prove that he was responsible for Lincolnshire. He witnessed, as *dux* or *princeps*, a number of charters of Offa and his son Ecgfrith between 792 and 796, but does not appear with or without a title before or after this period.[32]

Some indication of the variety of officials acting on behalf of Mercian kings is provided by a charter of King Ceolwulf, dated 822, granting land in Kent to the archbishop of Canterbury, and freeing it 'from all servitude in secular affairs, from entertainment of king, bishop, ealdormen, or of reeves, tax-gatherers, keepers of dogs, or horses, or hawks; from the feeding or support of all those who are called *fæstingmen*.'[33] The immunity was not complete, for the king reserved the universal obligations of military service and help in constructing bridges and fortifications, but it was freed from what was perhaps the greatest burden of all, the royal food-rent. This was levied on the basis of an assessment that was in most English kingdoms expressed in terms of hides. According to the law of the

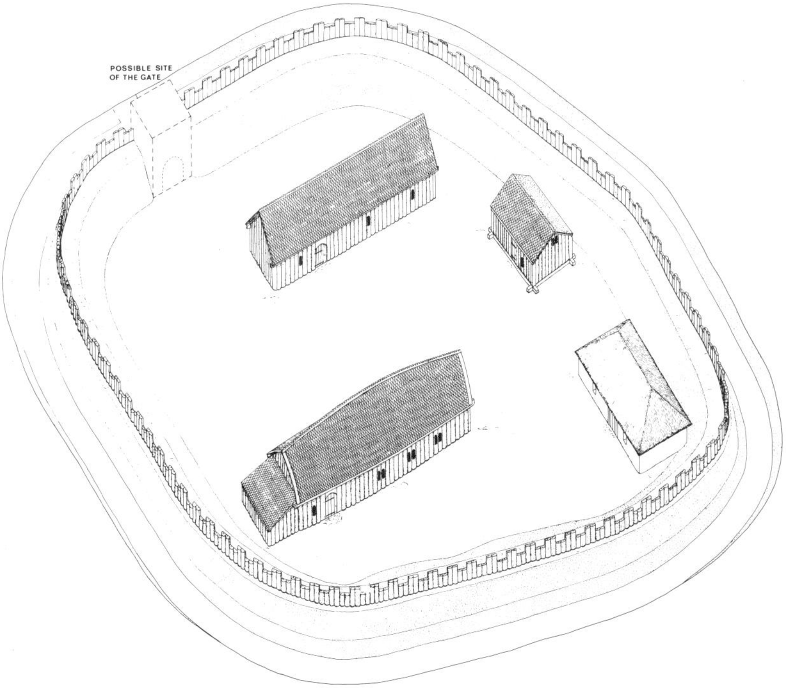

Fig. 5.3 Reconstruction of the 10th-century fort at 'Goltho'.
© G. Beresford.

West Saxon king Ine, compiled in about AD 690, a ten-hide estate was due to pay a food-rent consisting of: 'ten vats of honey, 300 loaves, 12 "ambers" of Welsh ale, 30 of clear ale, two full-grown cows or ten wethers, ten geese, 20 hens, ten cheeses, an "amber" full of butter, five salmon, 20 pounds of fodder and 100 eels.'[34]

The estate that Cuthbert leased at Swineshead was assessed at ten hides (*manentes*). As property of one of the most important monasteries in Mercia, it was probably free of the obligation to pay food-rent, but Cuthbert agreed to pay the abbey each year 1000 shillings and one day's food rent, the amount of which was unspecified. The expression of the rent in terms of shillings, a unit of account that in Mercia was the equivalent of five silver pennies, does not mean that it was paid in coin. Goods of equivalent value could be given instead.[35]

The immunity quoted above shows that royal agents could normally demand hospitality, but they also needed permanent bases from which to operate, and in particular to collect and store the food-rents. Some of this produce may have been sent to royal residences elsewhere, but much must have been consumed by the king's agents and their servants, or distributed by gift or sale. The centres of the major sokes described in Domesday Book, many of which were in 1066 held by the queen or the earls, were probably the bases from which ealdormen and other agents operated in the period of Mercian rule. Many royal estates had been alienated in whole or in part and some were new creations, but the overall framework seems to have survived.

Another ancient pattern was that of the wapentakes. That word was a Scandinavian innovation, but the institution was well established when the Scandinavians came; many wapentakes have English names.[36] The pattern was not fixed; districts could be divided or joined, but there is no reason to doubt that in the eighth and ninth centuries, as in the eleventh, there were districts in each of which the freemen gathered regularly at a convenient and traditional place to deal with local affairs. One of their most important functions must have been to recognize heirs and so legitimize their inheritance. These assemblies had a crucially important role in the extension of royal authority as kings imposed new burdens on them and royal agents began to attend, even to supervise, their proceedings. This may already have begun to happen under Mercian kings.

There is no record of any conflict involving Lincolnshire between 679 and the Viking attacks in the ninth century. The Mercians had to suppress rebellions in many other parts of their empire but not, so far as is known, in either Lindsey or Kesteven. There may well have been local disturbances of the kind that are rarely reported in the surviving sources. Our ignorance about such disorders is illustrated by an episode reported by Wilfrid's biographer. Within a decade of Wilfrid's death at Oundle in 709, the monastery there was almost entirely destroyed by 'certain exiles of noble birth who were ravaging with an army because of some wrong done to them'.[37] Neither Bede nor any other source mentions such a disturbance. The fact that we have no evidence for similar episodes in Lincolnshire does not mean that there was none; there is no reason to suppose that Lincolnshire was immune from the violence that was commonplace in other parts of England.

Churches and monasteries could provide sanctuary, even though it was sometimes violated, but kings and lay magnates needed physical defences against their enemies. Traces of extensive ditches and palisades built before the year 900 that presumably protected important residences have been found immediately east of St Peter's church at Barton-upon-Humber and on the site of Stamford Castle, and a tenth-century fortified residence has been excavated at Bullington.[38] Other early forts are indicated by place-names incorporating the Old English word *burh*, 'a fortified place'.

Some of these names refer to prehistoric or Roman forts – the best example in Lincolnshire is Yarborough, the name of a small, possibly Iron-age fort in Croxton.[39] Other *burh* names certainly commemorate fortified residences of the kind that has been found at Bullington. These names have recently been discussed by Barrie Cox, who has drawn attention to the contrast between Lindsey where there are at least twelve such names, and Kesteven with only four.[40] Two of the Kesteven names, Burton Coggles, and Burton Pedwardine, are examples of a common name with a range of meanings that make it an unsatisfactory guide to the location of the fort in question; *burh-tūn* could mean a fortified *tūn*, or a *tūn* near a *burh* or a *tūn* belonging to (but not necessarily close to) a *burh*.[41] One of the other Kesteven names, Billingborough, is clearly related to an early group known as the *Billingas*, but there is nothing to suggest a similar association for the other Kesteven name, Braceborough 'the strong fort'. Cox argues that the names in Lindsey are evidence of a system of forts constructed to defend Lindsey in the conflicts between Mercia and Northumbria in the seventh century. That is unlikely. The line of forts in the Wolds – Habrough, Stallingbrough, Ludborough, Burgh on Bain, Burwell and Burgh le Marsh – can hardly have been intended to resist Northumbrian invaders; some are more likely to have been made by early immigrants to hinder later arrivals and others may have been constructed later against Viking raiders. Some of these names are apparently early, but that does not mean that all were of the same date, or that they were all part of a unified system created by a king of Lindsey. There must have been some royal forts, and Cox has suggested that Coningsby in the south and Conesby near Flixborough are each Scandinavian modifications of an earlier English *cyninges-burh*, 'the king's stronghold'.[42] If they were in origin royal forts, the implication is that the other *burhs* were not. Some names, in particular Burton upon Stather, Flixborough, Gainsborough, and Gate Burton may well indicate forts intended to control landing places on the Trent, and

Fig. 5.4 A penny of Offa struck in Canterbury c. 792–6 found in the Fossdyke at Torksey before 1842 (Blackburn, Colyer, and Dolley 1983, p. 5 and table 2, no. 1).

Fig. 5.5 A penny of Æthelheard, archbishop of Canterbury, struck in Canterbury 793–6, found near Grantham in 1929 (Blackburn, Colyer, and Dolley 1983, pp. 5–6 and table 2, no. 2).

Fig. 5.6 8th- and 9th-century metalwork from Lincolnshire. Pins are common finds in the county and are represented here by the two copper-alloy examples (left) and the silver gilt pinhead (top right) decorated with animal interlace characteristic of the 8th century. The gilded copper-alloy brooch from Bigby (centre) is a poorer version of this sophisticated art. This object originally formed the central element of a set of three pins. The strap-end (bottom right) has an animal head terminal and is typical of the 9th century. Scale = 2.5 cm.
Photo and © by Kevin Leahy.

Washingborough was well placed to control access to Lincoln up the Witham, but others are more likely to commemorate residences of magnates fortified for their own protection as much as to control territory. West Saxon laws of the seventh and ninth centuries imply that the residences of important people were normally fortified; forcible entry into the residence of the king, a bishop, an ealdorman, a king's thegn or a noble was called *burgbryce*.[43]

Offa, who in the last ten years of his reign was overlord of most of England south of the Humber, died in 796. He was succeeded by his son who died before the year was out. The Mercian kingship was then held in succession by two brothers, Cenwulf and Ceolwulf, who claimed descent from Penda's father. They retained control of south-east England, with difficulty, but soon after Ceolwulf was expelled from Kent in 823 Mercian overlordship of that part of England was finally brought to an end, largely thanks to the West Saxons under their king Egbert. In 829 Egbert was briefly acknowledged as king of the Mercians. Cenwulf and Cuthwulf were the last Mercian kings who were believed to be descendants of Penda or his father. The parentage of the seven kings who ruled Mercia between 823 and 911 is not known, but five of them appear in earlier witness lists as ealdormen. Simon Keynes has suggested that 'it was not so much a matter of one dynasty, or branch of a dynasty, competing with another, as a matter of power residing in the collective body of the ealdormen, and every now and then a king being raised from the general gloom.... It seems that the Mercian ealdormen were princes over local peoples who set kings up over themselves'.[44] Mercian power was clearly in decline. It was, however, finally broken, not by civil war or by other English rulers, but by the Vikings whose raids and conquests in the ninth century made Lincolnshire once again an important centre of military and political developments.

NOTES TO CHAPTER V

1 Hart 1977.
2 *HE* iii. 24, ed. Colgrave and Mynors, pp. 290–1.
3 *HE* v. 23, ed. Colgrave and Mynors, pp. 558–9.
4 *HE* ii. 12, ed. Colgrave and Mynors, pp. 180–1. *in finibus gentis Merciorum* is incorrectly translated there as 'on the Mercian border'.
5 See Appendix 2.
6 Sawyer 1978, pp. 110–11.
7 S 57, 113. Sims-Williams 1990, p. 33, points out that 'the Hwiccian kings may have gained more than they lost from Mercian overlordship' and that 'their changing royal styles do not necessarily indicate a dramatic loss of real power'.
8 See below, pp. 82–3.
9 Sawyer 1983.
10 Keynes 1994b.
11 S 99, 177.
12 For the bishops, see Appendix 6.
13 The evidence of witness lists is clearly displayed in Keynes 1993.
14 The possibility that they were members of a royal family is discussed above, p. 65.
15 *HE* iii. 27, iv. 12, ed. Colgrave and Mynors, pp. 312–13, 370–1.
16 Wallach 1975, p. 144.
17 Campbell, J. 1979, esp. pp. 36–7 = Campbell, J. 1986, pp. 99–119, esp. pp. 101–2.
18 BCS, no. 312.
19 Bassett 1989a, pp. 4-6, reviews the discussions of the meaning and identification of *civitas Syddensis*. It has been suggested, most recently by Stocker 1993, p. 118, that it derives from Old English *suð* 'south'. ð is often rendered as *d*, but the *-dd-* and *-y-*

of *Syddensis* render that derivation improbable. Moreover, there seems to be no other example of a name formed by adding the suffix *-ensis* to *suð* or any other cardinal point. I am grateful to Joyce Hill for advice on this question.

20 See above, p. 63.

21 Richter 1973, no 19.

22 Gem 1993, p. 124.

23 Gem 1993, p. 124; Stocker 1993. See also Appendix 8.

24 Above, p. 50; Liebermann 1998, pp. 12-13, no. 8, the body of Oswald had been removed to Gloucester in 909.

25 Owen, A. 1980, 1997.

26 Felix cc. li–lii, ed. Colgrave, pp. 162–7.

27 Felix c. xvlii, ed. Colgrave, pp. 148–9.

28 See below. p. 148.

29 Stocker 1993.

30 S 1412, 1440.

31 See Appendix 7.

32 S 132, 136, 138, 150–1.

33 S 186, trans. *EHD* I, no. 83, p. 515.

34 Ine c. 70.1, text and trans. Attenborough 1922, pp. 58–9, trans. *EHD* I, no. 32, p. 406.

35 See below, p. 173.

36 See below, p. 134.

37 Eddius Stephanus c. 67, ed. Colgrave pp. 144–7.

38 Barton: Rodwell and Rodwell 1982, pp. 289–90, 307–8; Stamford: below, pp. 194–5; Bullington: above, pp. 7-8.

39 *PNL* 3 p. 100.

40 Cox 1994b.

41 Cox 1994b, p. 37.

42 Cox 1994b, pp. 41, 49–50.

43 Ine c. 45, Alfred c. 40, text and trans. Attenborough 1922, pp. 50–1, 82–3, trans., *EHD* I, nos 32–3, pp. 404, 414–15. Breach of an ordinary freeman's property was called 'fence-breaking', *edorbryce* in Alfred's laws, c. 40.1.

44 Personal communication. See now Keynes 1998, p. 5.

CHAPTER VI

THE FIRST DANISH CONQUEST

In June 793 the island monastery of Lindisfarne, off the Northumbrian coast, was raided by Scandinavian pirates, commonly called Vikings. For the next 250 years Vikings loom large in the history of the British Isles, as conquerors and settlers as well as raiders. They came from many parts of Scandinavia but the majority of those who were active in eastern England in the ninth century were Danes. That is what the contemporary *Chronicle* called them, and the place-names given by those who settled in Lincolnshire and other parts of eastern Mercia confirm that most were Danes, not Norwegians. The area they occupied was later known as the Danelaw.[1]

VIKING RAIDS, CONQUESTS, AND SETTLEMENTS

The raid on Lindisfarne in 793 may have been the first Viking attack on Northumbria, but a charter of 792 that refers to the obligation to defend Kent against pagan seamen shows that there had been earlier raids on south-east England, presumably by Vikings. In the next decade other Northumbrian monasteries, Tynemouth and Hartness, were raided as well as Iona, isolated island monasteries off the Irish coast, and the Frankish abbey of Noirmoutier near the mouth of the Loire. In 797 Alcuin, a Northumbrian who then lived in Frankia, commented in a letter to the people of Kent that 'a pagan people habitually makes pirate raids on our shore, a thing never heard of before' and by 800 the threat had become so serious that Charlemagne ordered the construction of defences along the coast north of the Seine estuary, probably as far as the Rhine.

These early raids were on a small scale and directed against targets that were easily accessible from the sea, but in the 830s the scale and range of Viking attacks grew. This was partly a direct result of Frankish political disputes that led to the temporary deposition of the emperor Louis by his sons. This naturally weakened the defences of the empire but, to make matters worse, Louis's eldest son actually encouraged Vikings to attack his father's territory. In Britain, too, Vikings were able to take advantage of internal disputes. The Britons who still preserved their independence in Cornwall and Devon allied with Vikings against their English enemies, and in 844 Vikings were apparently called in by a deposed Northumbrian king to help him recover his throne. One sign of the growing seriousness of the Viking threat was the removal of St Cuthbert's relics from the island of Lindisfarne to the relative safety of Norham on the river Tweed sometime in the years 830–45.

The raiders' intention was to gather plunder, extort tribute, and take captives who could be ransomed or sold as slaves. Trading places were probably attacked from the outset but most of the early raids mentioned in the sources were on religious communities. These were promising targets for, apart from the treasure accumulated in them, many monks and nuns were of high rank and had rich relatives who might be prepared to pay large sums for the release of captive kinsfolk. In 858 the abbot of St Denis, near Paris, and his brother were ransomed for over 600 pounds of gold and 3000 pounds of silver. Even objects could be ransomed; an elaborately ornamented Gospel book known as the *Codex Aureus* was bought back from the Vikings by the ealdorman of Surrey and given to Christ Church, Canterbury.

The *Chronicle*, compiled in the last decade of the ninth century, only mentions one raid on Lincolnshire. In 841 'Ealdorman Hereberht was killed by heathen men and many men with him in the Marsh and later in the same year many men in Lindsey, East Anglia and Kent, were killed by the enemy.' It has been suggested that 'the Marsh' may also refer to Lincolnshire, but as Hereberht only appears as a witness in Kentish charters it seems more reasonable to accept the general interpretation that it was Romney Marsh.[2] It is possible that one of the earliest recorded raids was in the Humber region. In 794 a monastery at *Donemuthan* was attacked. This has been identified as Jarrow, but it may have been in Hatfield by the Yorkshire Don.[3] There were probably unrecorded raids; the *Chronicle* certainly omits some Viking attacks, including one on Southampton in 842 and a major battle in Northumbria in 844. The Vikings' ships had very shallow draught and could have landed at many places along the Lincolnshire coast, or penetrated far inland along the rivers that flow into the Humber and the Wash. The monasteries and shrines of Lincolnshire were therefore vulnerable. Bardney, which had recently been enriched by Offa, was close to the Witham, and Viking ships would have had no difficulty in negotiating the route to the rich shrine at Crowland. These and other places in Lincolnshire may well have been attacked in the first half of the ninth century. That does not necessarily mean that the monasteries were destroyed; the community at Lindisfarne survived despite the attack in 793, and some communities may have escaped violence by paying 'protection money'.

There were, however, far more tempting opportunities in Frankia. In 841 towns along the Seine paid large sums to Viking raiders and in the next year, when the market of Quentovic, near Boulogne, was raided, some

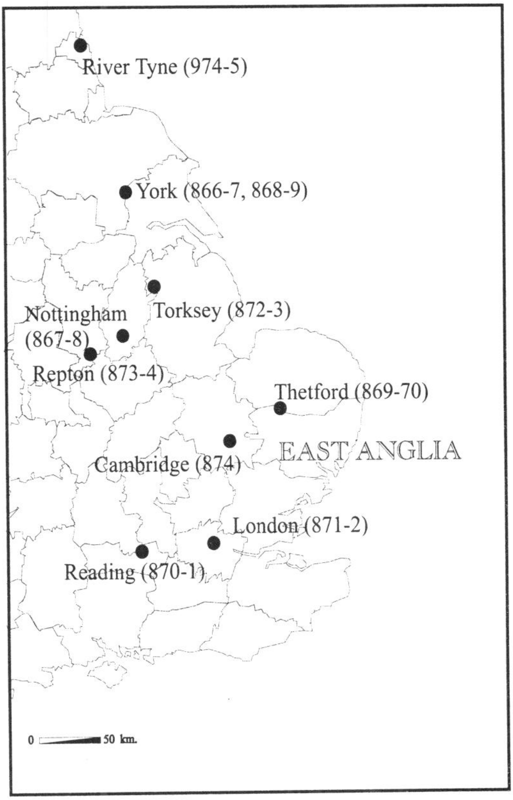

Fig. 6.1
A map illustrating the movements of the 'Great Army' of Vikings from its arrival in East Anglia in 865 to 874. The places named were its winter bases in the years indicated.

Drawn by A. Vince.

buildings were spared in return for money. In 845 an attack on Paris was averted by the payment of 7000 pounds of silver. It is hardly surprising that the Vikings then concentrated on West Frankia. For twenty years the Seine, Loire and other major rivers were exploited by Viking fleets and even the Rhône valley was plundered. The Franks were slow to organize defences, but in 862 they began to make a determined effort to protect at least the heart of the kingdom by a ring of forts and bridges, and by constructing walls round towns and abbeys. By 866 these arrangements were good enough to shelter Paris from attack for almost twenty years.

The improved Frankish defences made England more attractive to many Viking leaders, some of whom apparently hoped to establish themselves permanently there or in neighbouring parts of the British Isles. That is certainly what happened. In the autumn of 865 what the *Chronicle* described as 'a great heathen army' landed in East Anglia. In the next 15 years that army, reinforced by other bands of Vikings, transformed the political and ecclesiastical map of England by seizing control of East Anglia, southern Northumbria, and the eastern part of Mercia; they also disrupted church organization, causing a break in the episcopal succession in Lindsey, and forcing the bishops of Leicester to remove their see to Dorchester-on-Thames.

Lincolnshire was at the centre of these Viking conquests but almost nothing is known about Viking activity there. Viking ships navigated the Humber and Trent, mounted Vikings probably travelled through Lincolnshire more than once, and in 872 the 'great army' wintered at Torksey. It would not be appropriate here to trace the operations of these Vikings in detail, but the silence of our sources about Lincolnshire means that a brief account of their activity, especially in Mercia and Northumbria, may be useful, not least in providing some indication of their aims and methods, and the reactions they provoked.

The Vikings who arrived in 865 wintered in East Anglia. The *Chronicle* adds 'and there they were supplied with horses, and the East Angles made peace with them'. They were probably reinforced during the summer of 866 by others, including perhaps some of the Vikings who are said to have sailed away from the Seine in July. In the autumn the army went to Northumbria where there was civil war following the deposition of Osbert in 862 or 863 by Ælle, described as 'a king without hereditary right'. The fact that Ælle was the name of the founder of the Deiran dynasty, while names beginning Os- were favoured by the Bernician royal family, suggests that the dispute was between Deiran and Bernician factions, a tension that, as we have seen, played a major role in the seventh century, and was still a factor in Northumbrian politics 400 years later. The Viking leaders were certainly well aware of this conflict and the opportunity it offered. They had intervened in a similar dispute in 844. In 866, however, their intention was not to aid one party but to take control themselves. They made a surprise move late in the year and occupied York on 1 November. The required speed was apparently achieved using a combination of ships and horses, supplied by the East Angles. The *Chronicle* states that the army reached York by crossing the Humber estuary. No doubt the ships in which the Vikings had arrived in East Anglia were taken north – it would hardly have been safe to leave them – but the *Chronicle*'s words imply that a significant part of the army was ferried across the Humber from the Lincolnshire shore. Mounted men could then have covered the 30 miles between North Ferriby and York in a few hours at most; ships would have been slower and given more time for opposition to be organized.

After the Vikings seized York Osbert and Ælle agreed to cooperate. In March 867 they attacked the Vikings in York, but having forced their way into the city they were trapped and both kings were killed, together with eight ealdormen. The Vikings then established a puppet regime with an English king, Egbert. Once the outcome was clear, the archbishop of York, Wulfhere, who had retreated to the safety of his estate at Addingham in the Wharfe valley, returned and continued to perform his duties. Egbert and

Wulfhere show that some English leaders were willing to collaborate with the Vikings, and even to serve under them. There are other examples of alliances between the Vikings and English leaders. When King Alfred of Wessex died in 899, his nephew, Æthelwold, disappointed at not being chosen to succeed him, joined the Vikings and was accepted by the Danish army in Northumbria as their king. At about the same time Brihtsige, son of the ætheling (that is a royal prince) Beornoth, who is thought to have been a kinsman of the Mercian king Burgred, also joined forces with the Danes, and both he and Æthelwold were killed in battle in 902.

Later in 867 the 'great army' moved to Nottingham for the winter. Burgred, the Mercian king, appealed for help from the West Saxons and a combined force besieged the Vikings but made no attempt to storm the Danish fortifications; perhaps they were mindful of the disaster at York. The West Saxons returned home and the Mercians 'made peace with the enemy', meaning that they paid tribute. The Viking army returned to spend a year at York and the Mercians were able to regain control of Nottingham, but not Lindsey. In 869 the *Chronicle* says that the Viking army rode across Mercia from York to Thetford. The route is not described but, as in 866, they may have been ferried across the Humber and travelled through Lincolnshire.

Late in the year the East Anglian king, Edmund, fought against the Vikings but was defeated. He survived the battle but was killed soon afterwards on 20 November, and was before long widely revered as a martyr. A year later the army made Reading its base for attacks on Wessex. The *Chronicle* has a very detailed account of several engagements, including a famous victory over the invaders at Ashdown. But in the spring of 871 the Vikings were reinforced by 'a great summer army', and the West Saxons, now ruled by Alfred, were forced to 'make peace'. The army withdrew to winter in London and in 872 the Mercians were once again forced to 'make peace'. In that year the army returned to Northumbria, apparently because of a rebellion. Egbert, their Northumbrian ally, together with the archbishop of York, went into exile in Mercia, where they were welcomed by King Burgred. One interpretation of this obscure episode is that a Northumbrian faction, opposed to the Danes and their king, rose in revolt. It is, however, possible that Egbert and the archbishop were the rebels; their reception in Mercia, which the Danes were attempting to conquer, would make more sense if they too opposed the invaders. Egbert died in 873, and nothing is said about his restoration as king in Northumbria. In the same year Wulfhere returned to his see. The Danes seem to have had no difficulty in reasserting their authority in 872. They did not stay long in York but moved to Torksey where they spent the winter. Once again the Mercians were forced to 'make peace'. The following winter the Viking base was closer to the heart of Mercia, at

Repton. King Burgred then abdicated and went into exile at Rome. The Vikings established another puppet regime. In the words of the *Chronicle*:

> And the same year (874) they gave the kingdom of the Mercians to be held by Ceolwulf, a foolish king's thegn, and he swore oaths to them and gave hostages, that it [i.e. the kingdom] should be ready for them on whatever day they wished to have it, and he would be ready, himself and all who would follow him, at the enemy's service.

In nine years the Scandinavians had conquered East Anglia, Mercia, and Deira; only Wessex and Bernicia remained independent. The army then divided in an attempt to complete the conquest of the English kingdoms. One group, led by Halfdan, went north to winter on the Tyne and plunder what is now southern Scotland. The *Chronicle* implies that he conquered Bernicia but he did not attempt to consolidate his hold on the area. According to the *Chronicle*, in 876 he 'shared out the land of the Northumbrians, and they proceeded to plough and to support themselves'. Place-name evidence shows that this settlement was in Deira, in what later became Yorkshire, especially in the North and East Ridings. Roger of Wendover in his *Flores Historiarum* reports that 'the king of the same province, Ricsige, struck to the very heart with grief, ended his last day, and Egbert succeeded him'. Halfdan himself did not stay long; his death in Ireland in 877 is reported by an Irish chronicle.

The other part of the great army, under the leadership of three kings, went from Repton in 874 to Cambridge to prepare for a renewed assault on Wessex in the following year. After suffering several set-backs they withdrew into Mercia in 877 and split up. One group, under Guthrum, remained at Gloucester and early in January attempted to capture Alfred. He escaped and went into hiding. Some West Saxons submitted to the Vikings, but in the summer Alfred rallied his forces, defeated Guthrum, and forced him to submit and convert to Christianity. Two years later Guthrum's army settled in East Anglia 'and shared out the land'. In August 877 the Vikings who did not stay with Guthrum divided Mercia with their tributary king Ceolwulf. He retained part, but another part, not specified in the *Chronicle*, was shared out among the army. It has been assumed that this was when Scandinavians began to settle in Lincolnshire and elsewhere in the East Midlands.

Before considering the ways in which this Scandinavian invasion may have affected Lincolnshire, some general comments may be helpful. The first concerns the size and organization of the Scandinavian armies. The force that landed in 865 was unusually large. The *Chronicle* was probably justified in describing it as a 'great heathen army'. It appears to have comprised several Viking fleets that joined forces to campaign in England.

Fig. 6.2 The disarticulated remains of at least 250 people (mostly men in their prime but including a few women) from a burial mound excavated at Repton in Derbyshire where the 'Great Army' wintered 873–4. It is likely that this was a ritual burial (or reburial) of members of the army and their followers, most of whom died from an epidemic of some kind. Photo Martin Biddle. © The Repton Project.

A fleet can rarely have been much larger than a thousand men, but the combination of several such fleets could be a very formidable force indeed.

The leaders are called either kings or earls, the latter apparently being independent leaders of Viking fleets who accepted the authority of the kings. Two 'heathen kings' are named in the *Chronicle*'s account of the Battle of Ashdown in 871, *Bacsecg*, who was killed in the battle, and Halfdan, who later distributed land in Northumbria to his followers. Five earls who were killed in the same battle are also named. The army that wintered at Repton in 873 had four kings: Halfdan, Guthrum, and two others about whom nothing is known apart from their names, Oscetel and Anwend. In this invasion of England Viking leaders showed that, although they were not natural allies and often fought against each other, they could collaborate. Some joined forces for a campaigning season, forming what was called 'a summer army', but the 'great army' did not disperse each autumn; many of its operations were in the winter, and the 'great summer army' that arrived in 871 did not disperse for several years.

To many contemporaries the 'great army' must have appeared invincible. Small scouting parties might be attacked, but there is no record of any serious effort to oppose the 'great army' as it moved from base to base and attempts to dislodge it from those bases were unsuccessful. In most years the *Chronicle* simply remarks that one English king or another agreed to make peace with the enemy. The writer was naturally reluctant to give details of such submissions, especially when they were made by the West Saxons, but the implications were spelled out in the annal for 874, quoted above, when the Mercian king Ceolwulf submitted.

Many of the Vikings probably planned from the outset to settle in England, but at first the aim of their leaders was rather to force English rulers to submit; Edmund of East Anglia apparently did so for a while. If necessary, puppet regimes willing to accept such subordination were established. This happened in both Mercia and Northumbria.

Virtually nothing is known about the Scandinavian conquest of Lincolnshire. The Mercians probably lost control of most of the area soon after the arrival of the 'great army'. By the end of 869, when the Scandinavians had conquered both East Anglia and Deira, they must also have been effectively in control of at least Lindsey. It was at about this time that the bishoprics of Leicester and Lindsey were disrupted, but the details are too uncertain to provide a precise chronology of the conquest. Mercian episcopal lists are incomplete at the end of the ninth century – a consequence of the disruption – and there are few reliable Mercian charters with which the dates of the known bishops can be determined. The last attestation by Ceolred, bishop of Leicester, was in 869 and his successor did not subscribe until 888; by then that see had been removed to Dorchester-on-Thames.[4]

No bishop of Lindsey is named in the episcopal lists between Beorhtræd, who regularly attested charters until 862, and Leofwine, whose first attestation was in 953. Mary Anne O'Donovan's suggestion that Eadbald and Burgheard, who attested Mercian charters in 866 and 869 respectively, were bishops of Lindsey, is probably right, despite her doubting 'whether it is wise to make any assignation of bishops to particular sees in this period of confusion, for it ignores the possibility of *chorepiscopi*', that is, assistant bishops.[5] They both appear in the middle of their witness lists, while *chorepiscopi* would be expected at the end. In the charter of 866 Eadbald is the second episcopal witness, between Wulfsige, probably of Lichfield, and Ceolred, who was certainly bishop of Leicester. In 869 Burgheard precedes Deorlaf of Hereford. Ceolred's last appearance is in the charter witnessed by Burgheard. They could both have been in exile from their sees, but that is unlikely, for Burgheard seems to have been succeeded by a bishop Herefrith who was buried at Louth, and locally commemorated as a saint. The date of his death is not known but it is a reasonable conjecture that he was the last ninth-century bishop of Lindsey and that he was a martyr, dying violently at the hands of the Danes.[6] The fact that his feast was celebrated on 27 February is no objection for, as has been noted, the 'great army' did not hibernate.

The Scandinavians probably began to settle permanently in Lincolnshire in 877 when, according to the *Chronicle*, some sections of the 'great army' shared out part of Mercia. The area remained under Scandinavian control for about 50 years and in that time the original settlers may have been joined by others, although new arrivals were not necessarily welcome. What little is known about later Scandinavian immigrants suggests that many of them found their new homes in other parts of England. The land distributed by Ragnald in 914 was north of the river Tees, while the land occupied by Halfdan and his followers was south of that river. There was also some settlement of Scandinavians in the north-west along the coast between Cheshire and Dumfries, well away from the areas occupied by the first arrivals.

The *Chronicle*'s account of the settlements is certainly incomplete; it does not refer to either Ragnald's distribution of land or the Scandinavian settlers in the north-west. The one later settlement it does mention happened in 896, when another 'great army' that had invaded England in 892 broke up. It tried to conquer Wessex and the part of Mercia that was not under Scandinavian control but after three years had to admit failure. The army divided; the words of the *Chronicle*, 'One part went to Northumbria, the other to East Anglia, while those who were moneyless got themselves ships and went across the sea to the Seine', clearly imply that only those with money could settle in areas already controlled by Scandinavians.

It is difficult to believe that no one settled in Lincolnshire or other parts of Scandinavian Mercia in 896. The *Chronicle*'s omission of Mercia here may have been deliberate. In the next few years there are several references to the Danes who ruled East Anglia and Northumbria but none to the Danes who controlled eastern Mercia. Even in 909 when Edward invaded Lindsey, the Danes are described as 'the northern army'. The West Saxon chronicler may have been reluctant to draw attention to the Danish control of part of Mercia, a kingdom that was allied to the West Saxons, and was ruled by Alfred's children after 911. There probably was, therefore, some Scandinavian immigration into Lincolnshire after the original settlement of 877. Some may have come to live in England even after the whole country was ruled by English kings; they certainly did so in the reigns of Cnut and his sons, and in 1066 at least one notable Lincolnshire landowner, Ulf *Fenisc*, appears to have been a recent arrival.[7]

Apart from the annal for 877 there is no direct evidence for the original settlement of Lincolnshire or any other part of Mercia. The *Chronicle*'s phrase, 'share out part of Mercia', implies that it was not a haphazard affair with individuals seizing land in a general free-for-all, but was organized, presumably by the leaders of the army. That is what had happened a year earlier in Northumbria, a settlement about which we are a little better informed. The *Chronicle*'s description of Halfdan's distribution of land to his followers has been quoted above. There is a variant version of that annal in Roger of Wendover's *Flores Historiarum*: 'Halfdan occupied Northumbria and divided it between himself and his thegns (*ministri*) and had it cultivated by his army'.[8] Confidence in Roger of Wendover's version is increased by an account, written in the mid tenth century, of the distribution of land in Bernicia by Ragnald after he had defeated Ealdred, lord of Bamburgh, in 914: 'When the whole land was conquered, he divided the estates of St Cuthbert, and he gave the one part, towards the south, from the estate which is called Eden as far as Billingham, to a certain powerful thegn of his who was called Scula; and the other part, from Eden as far as the river Wear, to one called Olaf Ball.'[9]

LINCOLNSHIRE UNDER SCANDINAVIAN CONTROL

Much of the land occupied by Scandinavian settlers in Lincolnshire must have been taken from monastic communities. This threatened their survival more than physical destruction wrought by raiders or armies on the march. A monastic community could survive attacks, as Lindisfarne did, but not the loss of its land. I have previously suggested that one Lincolnshire monastery, Bardney, may have survived, if in a much reduced state.[10] This claim was based on the fact that there are relatively few Scandinavian place-names in the vicinity of Bardney which I interpreted as an indication that the community not only survived but retained control of its property better than, for example, Partney, which lies in the middle of the densest concentration of Scandinavian place-names in Lincolnshire. That

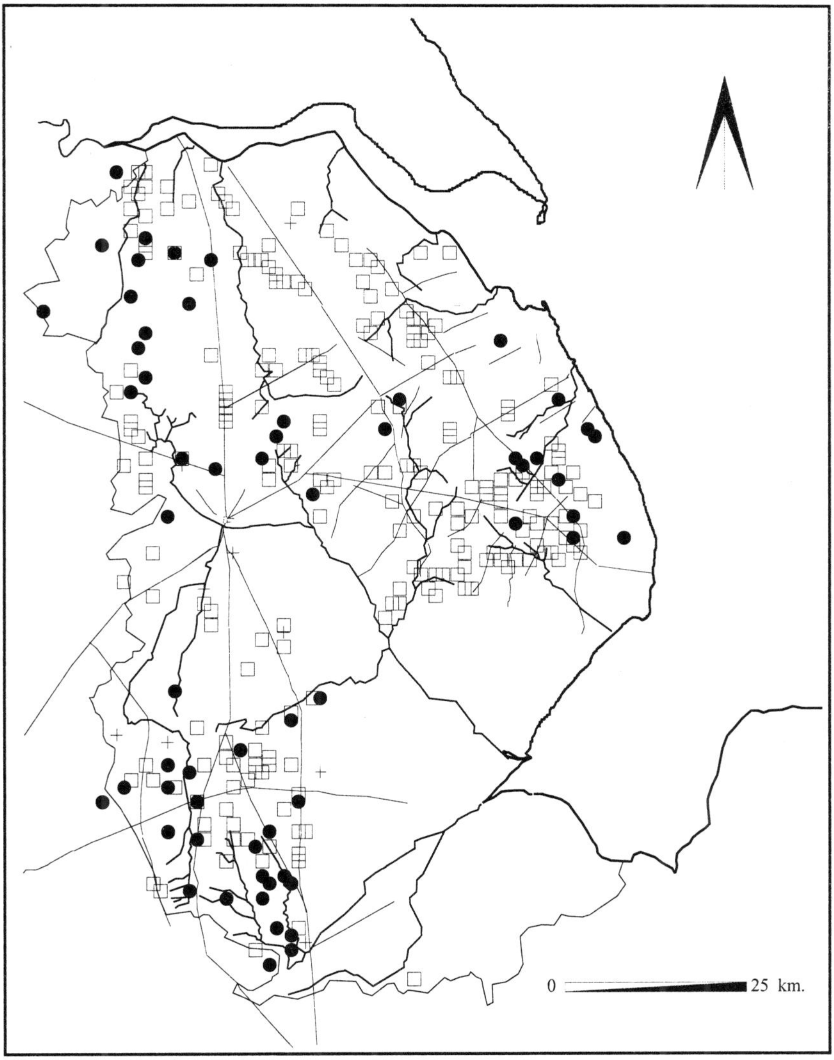

Fig. 6.3 The main Scandinavian settlement names in Lincolnshire, based on a map made by Gillian Fellows-Jensen. Key: □ = *names with* -by, ● = *names with* (-)thorp, + = *hybrid names with OE* tun.
© *Oxford University Press.*

argument was unsound. The place-names do suggest that the Bardney estate was not broken up, but it is more likely to have been kept intact by a powerful layman than by a church. Religious communities were ill equipped to protect their land and depended on the support of lay patrons. With the disappearance of the native English aristocracy they lost that protection. The Danes, although not hostile to Christianity, certainly had no respect for monastic property. Another early monastery with few Scandinavian place-names in its neighbourhood is Barrow. It is, however, doubtful whether it survived as a recognizable monastic community after the eighth century. Bede's comment that in his day only traces remained of the monastic rule established by Chad suggests that religious life was already in decline then. When the site of Barrow was given to Bishop Æthelwold in 971, the charter casts no light on its earlier history beyond stating that before the pagan devastation Barrow had been held by St Chad, information that is more likely to have been drawn from Bede than from local tradition. Whatever its religious status, at least the heart of the estate of Barrow appears to have been preserved intact after it was taken over by the Danes.[11]

The Vikings had lived for some years on the tribute of food, horses and other necessities, as well as treasure, supplied by puppet rulers or kings who had been forced to submit. When they began to settle in permanent homes they did not, of course, live in peace; many of those who were young and fit were doubtless eager to join 'summer armies' for plundering expeditions. Their leaders, who had organized the settlement, naturally took a large share of any booty gathered in this way, but they also expected to receive renders and services from their new lordships, just as their English predecessors had done. Ragnald's thegns Scula and Olaf Ball took the place of the community of St Cuthbert and must have expected to receive whatever had formerly been paid to the saint. Their followers would also have been expected to pay rent and render services to their lords. The burdens may not have been heavy, but the rank and file of the army could not expect to be freed from all obligations to the lords under whom they had won their new homes.

Nothing is known about the men who organized the settlement of Lincolnshire or the Scandinavians who ruled the area for the next fifty years. The names of the leaders, whether they were considered kings or jarls, and of their leading followers are unknown, although it is likely that some of the Danes whose deaths are reported in the early tenth century may have come from Lincolnshire. The *Chronicle* shows that, at least in the second decade of the tenth century, there were independent groups of Danish settlers based on fortified centres, or boroughs, such as Huntingdon. Most of these groups were led by earls, and their leading followers were called *holds*, a Scandinavian word, or title, which seems to have been regarded as the equivalent of the English thegn. Some kings are also mentioned, but their kingdoms are not. There is no evidence to connect any of these men with Lincolnshire; the *Chronicle* does not even name a leader when describing the submission of Stamford in 918.

The Danish conquest meant that the Humber was less significant as a frontier; indeed, the Humbrensian kingdom may have been revived. The Danes living either side of the Humber had a common interest, especially after 910 when the English began to force the Danes who had settled in Mercia and East Anglia to submit. There is some evidence to suggest that the Danes of York controlled a large part of Lincolnshire at the end of the ninth century. Æthelweard reports that in 894 a West Saxon ealdorman visited York, where he encountered 'the enemy, who possessed large territories in the kingdom of the Mercians, on the western side of the place called Stamford. This is to say, between the streams of the river Welland and the thickets of the wood called Kesteven (*Ceostefne*) by the common people.'[12] The word here translated as 'possessed' is *pandunt* which literally means 'opened out', possibly in the sense of 'taking control of'. The area in question appears to be Rutland, and the implication is that the Danes of York then controlled at least the adjacent parts of Lincolnshire, probably all of it.[13] To judge by the evidence of place-names, few Danes settled in Rutland but that does not mean that it remained under English control; an English enclave surrounded by Danish conquests seems unlikely. It was probably an English estate that was taken over as a whole.

The evidence of place-names and the structure of estates in the eleventh century, discussed below, makes it possible to identify some royal estates in Lincolnshire that were taken over by the Danes, presumably by their leaders. Parts of these estates may have been distributed to, or usurped by, other landowners but some of them survived both Danish rule and English conquest sufficiently well to be recognizable in 1066, when they were still held by the royal family or by the king's main agents, the earls. This suggests that at least some royal estates of the pre-Viking period remained in the hands of rulers despite successive conquests.

Fig. 6.4 This incomplete coin from a hoard found at Ashdon, Essex, deposited c. *895, was apparently issued for Guthfrith (all that remains of the name is GVDEF) who was king in York 883–95. The style is closely connected with that of other imitations of Alfred's coins produced in the Five Boroughs region. It is, therefore, likely to have been made in Lincolnshire or Rutland which were controlled by the Danes of York in the 890s; the mint was possibly at Stamford (British Museum, CM 1984, 4-14-3; Blackburn 1989, pp. 18–20);* *see above.*

Lincoln is never mentioned in the *Chronicle* or other contemporary texts during the period of Danish rule but, as coins were struck there soon after 880, it is reasonable to assume that it was a centre of authority from the beginning of the Danish conquest, similar to York if not so large.[14] Stamford was regarded as a centre for the settlers in Kesteven in 918 but that may have been a relatively recent development. Before 913 the *Chronicle* normally described the Danes in terms of kingdoms, such as 'the army in East Anglia' or 'the army in Northumbria'. In 913 they began to be associated with boroughs or fortified centres and were described, for example, as 'the army of Northampton and Leicester' or 'the army of Cambridge'. It is, therefore, possible that the Danes began to develop such fortified centres as Stamford when they began to be seriously threatened by the English. The lack of Scandinavian place-names in the vicinity of Lincoln and Stamford (and other boroughs that were Scandinavian centres) may be because few Scandinavians settled near these places. It is, however, possible that the lords who controlled Lincoln and Stamford, like those who held Bardney and Barrow, retained the surrounding districts in their own hands.

NAMES AND THEIR SIGNIFICANCE

Any attempt to estimate the scale of Scandinavian immigration into Lincolnshire, or to discover where they settled depends on the evidence of place-names, many of which contain Scandinavian personal-names or words, or show other signs of Scandinavian influence.[15] The Scandinavian word most commonly used in Lincolnshire place-names was *by*, meaning 'farm or village'. There are 218 in Domesday Book and at least 26 others in later medieval texts. *Thorp*, 'outlying or dependent settlement', is also common but is less certainly Scandinavian, for the English used the closely related *throp* in the same sense. Among the many other words used to name places there were several topographical terms such as *holmr*, 'island', as in Axholme, *lundr*, 'wood' which is combined with the personal name *Afi* in

Fig. 6.5 This coin, produced when the Danes controlled Lincolnshire, may well be one of the earliest struck in Lincoln. The monogram LINCOLLA is based on the London monogram that was widely copied by the Danish conquerors. It has traditionally been associated with Alfred's 'reoccupation' of the city in 886, but it is now believed to be earlier, c. 880 (SCBI 27, no. 2; Blackburn 1998, pp. 120–2).

the wapentake name Aveland, and *vað*, 'ford', from which Waithe and Langworth, 'long ford', derive. Scandinavians also had a distinctive stock of personal names, many of which were used in naming places, for example Hawerby and Hawthorpe which both contain the man's name *Hávarðr*.

The interpretation of these names poses many problems. In the first place hardly any of them are recorded before they appear in Domesday Book, and there are only 13 Lincolnshire settlement names in texts earlier than 900. There is, consequently, little direct evidence for the place-names that existed when the Scandinavians began to settle. Many English names that first appear later can be recognized as early types that must have been given long before the ninth century but many others, especially those ending in the common element *tūn*, could as well belong to the tenth century as to the eighth. It is, therefore, not possible to determine how many English place-names were given after the Scandinavian conquest. Ignorance about early place-names also makes it difficult to decide which are adaptations of English names, a problem that will be discussed more fully below.

The paucity of records before the Norman Conquest means that most Scandinavian names can only be dated within the broad limits 865, when the 'great army' arrived, and 1065. Some of them may have been given before 900, but there is no certain method of recognizing which, if any, are so early. Another difficulty is that many Scandinavian words used in naming places were very similar to cognate English words; Scandinavian *berg*, 'hill', means much the same as, and is difficult to distinguish from, Old English *beorg*. Other similar pairs are *ey* and *ēg*, 'island', *langr* and *lang*. Many of the Scandinavian personal names used in place-names can be recognized without difficulty but there are some uncertainties. Caenby, for example, probably contains a personal name but it could be either English or Scandinavian. It is, therefore, difficult to classify many place-names. The strength of Scandinavian influence in general has encouraged a preference for the Scandinavian alternatives. *Thorp* names, for example, are normally assumed to be Scandinavian even though some may originally have been English. Such an approach naturally tends to exaggerate Scandinavian influence, and can even dispel all doubts about the Scandinavian character of the words in question.

A related problem that has already been briefly mentioned, is the possibility that many apparently Scandinavian place-names were originally English names that were modified after the Scandinavian conquest. Some cases of such 'Scandinavianization' are easily recognized, especially those in which an English sound has been replaced by a Scandinavian one. Thus the Scandinavians were unfamiliar with the initial sound in *shilling* and tended to replace it by *sk-*. This happened in the name Scopwick, which was originally an English name meaning 'sheep-farm'. A similar change is apparent in Skidbrook, which was originally an Old English place-name *scite-brōc*, 'dirty brook', as well as in Skillington, Skellingthorpe and Ruskington, the first element of which was probably the English adjective 'rushy'. In some other names there is little doubt that a Scandinavian word has replaced an English one and there are grounds for suspecting that *by* has sometimes replaced *tūn*.

Changes of this kind cannot be taken to indicate places in which Scandinavians settled; they are rather evidence for the effect the Danes had on the dialect of Lincolnshire and other areas they occupied. Eventually these dialects influenced the English language in general; many words in common use today, including *bread, die, egg, happy, husband, law, low, sky, ugly, window*, as well as *hence* and *though*, were initially introduced into English speech by Scandinavians in the ninth and tenth centuries. This effect on the language means that there must have been a substantial immigration but there is no means of telling how many settlers there were. As already noted in the discussion of the replacement of British by English, language is an unsatisfactory guide to the ethnic character of the people who speak it. Many factors affect the interchange of languages: their relative status, their similarity, the length of time they are in contact, and the number of people who know both.

There is no doubt about the status of Danish. The Danes came as conquerors and their language had prestige. What is more, men of Scandinavian descent continued to dominate local affairs even after the authority of West Saxon kings was recognized throughout England. On the eve of the Norman Conquest most of the local aristocracy in Lincolnshire had Scandinavian ancestors. There was, however, a significant difference between these Danish conquerors and their Norman successors. Few Normans settled in Lincolnshire; they were rather landowners whose revenues were gathered from tenants by agents, most of whom were members of what was by then an Anglo-Danish local aristocracy or 'squirearchy'. The Normans therefore had much less influence than their Danish predecessors who settled in England. Another fundamental difference between the Danish and Norman conquests was that many of the Danes were farmers. The *Chronicle* emphasized that they 'ploughed and supported themselves', and this is confirmed by their influence on the farming vocabulary, especially on field-names.[16] French field-names are exceedingly rare in England but very many of the medieval field-names of Lincolnshire incorporate Scandinavian words. Some, such as *vangr*, 'field', and *eng*, 'meadow', were fairly common, but even those that were less frequently used, such as *stakkr*, 'stack', *flat*, 'piece of level ground', *kjarr*, 'brushwood' and later 'marsh, bog' are good evidence for the presence of Scandinavians who worked the land.

The wide social range of the Scandinavian settlers must itself have contributed to the survival of Scandinavian speech; colonists of all social levels could speak their own language and be understood by many of their neighbours. It is also likely that there were many Danish-speaking mothers as well as fathers, even though very few Scandinavian women's names are recorded in England. The extent and depth of the influence of Scandinavian implies that it was spoken alongside English for more than one generation. Children tend to learn their language in the first place from their mothers, and if most of the second generation after the settlement had had English-speaking mothers, the survival of Danish speech would have depended on newly arrived immigrants.

The permanent presence of people who spoke Danish provided many opportunities for contact with the native English. They cannot have understood each other at first without difficulty, even though their languages were very closely related with many similar words and much the same syntax. One authority on this topic is reported as doubting 'whether the English and the Vikings really could have communicated with each other except by means of ribald gestures and uncouth noises'.[17] Communication depended on people who knew something of both languages. Eventually Danish disappeared as the descendants of the settlers used English inflections instead of Danish, and began to use English words alongside, or instead of, Danish ones. They did not, however, forget all their words, and their English neighbours in time began to use them. The language of Lincolnshire remained English, but it was greatly changed. The stages of this process cannot be traced. We do not even know how far it had proceeded by 1066. The few texts that might have provided clues, including Domesday Book, were produced by outsiders. Even in the twelfth century, when texts begin to cast some light on the local language, the assimilation may not have been complete. There can, however, be little doubt that in the early stages, in the late ninth and early tenth centuries, there were some areas in which Scandinavian speech dominated, and other much larger areas where English continued to be the language of the majority, despite the presence of Scandinavian landowners in all parts of the shire. Gradually the Anglo-Danish speech of the areas of relatively dense Scandinavian settlement influenced the language of the people living nearby, just as later, the speech of Lincolnshire and other parts of the Danelaw influenced the speech of London, and consequently of the whole country.

These considerations suggest that we do not have to assume Scandinavian immigration on a massive scale in order to explain the changes in the language. There may well have been some areas in which Danes outnumbered natives but they can never have been in a majority in Lincolnshire as a whole. There can, though, be no doubt that there was a substantial influx of Scandinavians, probably spread over several decades. This is confirmed by the large number of distinctive personal names they introduced, many of which continued to be used long after the Norman Conquest.[18] To judge by the names of the pre-Conquest tenants in Domesday Book, there were more Scandinavian names in use in Lincolnshire in the eleventh century than English; over 100 compared with about 70. Some were only borne by one man, but others were very popular. Many of these names were introduced by the original settlers, and some younger types may have been brought by later immigrants, but several probably originated in England. The name of Merleswein, one of the major landowners in 1065, is a good example; the first part is probably English but the second is a common Scandinavian name. Many place-names contain personal names that were probably coined in England, including a number of the bynames or nicknames that were originally used to distinguish individuals by some recognizable characteristic. Many bynames, such as *Dúsi*, 'calm', in Dowsby, *Haddr*, 'hairy', in Haceby, *Lútr*, 'the stooping one', in Lusby and *Stígandi*, 'one who takes long strides, quick-footed', in Stainby, may have been brought by immigrants, but some were produced in England. This large, varied, and developing stock of personal names demonstrates the vitality of name-giving traditions among the settlers.[19]

It is likely that most of the men with Scandinavian names in the Lincolnshire Domesday were descendants of Scandinavian settlers. That cannot be proved because the only people whose ancestry can be traced back more than a generation were the high aristocracy, and the origin of some of those families is very obscure. In the 29 cases where the Lincolnshire Domesday names both a parent (four of them mothers: *Ulflet, Eddeua, Sceldeware, Sualeua*) and one or more sons, there are eleven in which both generations had Scandinavian names and only six in which both had English names. There are also five fathers with Scandinavian names who had sons with English names and one example of the opposite. In the one entry that names three generations, all had Scandinavian names; Svartbrand, son of Ulf, son of Svartbrand.[20] This suggests that in the eleventh century most men with Scandinavian names had fathers or mothers who also had Scandinavian names, and were probably of Scandinavian descent.

On the eve of the Norman Conquest almost all the leading landowners in Lincolnshire had Scandinavian names. The Lincolnshire Domesday lists 26 laymen, other than earls, who had full privileges as landowners in 1065.[21] Only five of them had English names – *Godric, Lewine, Ailric, Adestan, Wlward* – and one of these was the son of a man with a Scandinavian name, *Godric* son of *Toruert*. There is one example of the reverse, *Toli* son of *Alsi*. It seems safe to assume that most of these leading

Fig. 6.6 Viking metalwork from Lincolnshire. In recent years metal detecting has revolutionized our knowledge of the Vikings in Lincolnshire. Objects like the equal-armed brooch from South Kyme (left) and the trefoil brooch from Keelby (bottom right) represent direct links with Scandinavia, while the trefoil mount from Cranwell (centre) is an English copy of a Viking object. The tongue-shaped strap end (top right) can be linked with finds from the Irish Sea province. The large numbers of Viking objects from Lincolnshire support the historical and place-name evidence and point to large-scale Danish incursion into Lincolnshire during the late 9th and 10th centuries.
Photo and © K. Leahy.

landowners were descendants of Scandinavian settlers. A hundred and fifty years earlier, after the conquest, the local aristocracy must have been almost entirely Scandinavian; most English landowners who survived the conquest must have been subordinate to the invaders.

It is not surprising that the Scandinavian conquerors and their descendants, who continued to rule Lincolnshire long after the authority of the West Saxon kings was recognized there, have left their mark on local

Fig. 6.7 10th-century metalwork from Lincolnshire. Two strap ends (top left and bottom right) and the open-work mount (bottom left) bear a devolved leaf decoration and the strap end (top right) shows two intertwined animals. Both the disc brooch (centre) and the strapend (top left) are made from lead, which was commonly used for dress fittings during the 10th century. The other objects are made from copper alloy (scale bar at bottom of photograph). Photo and © K. Leahy.

administrative nomenclature. They used a word of their own to describe the estates or lordships that they took over; it first appears in England as *socn* and survives in the modern word 'soke'.[22] In Scandinavia the same word was later used to describe a parish, *sogn* in Danish, *socken* in Swedish. The administrative divisions were called wapentakes, a word of Scandinavian origin that comes from an Old Norse word, *vápnatac*, meaning the flourishing of weapons at an assembly, implying that it was an assembly of free men. The word riding, used for the major divisions of Lindsey, also derives from a Scandinavian word *thriðjung*, 'a third part'. After the Norman Conquest the initial *th-* was absorbed by the ending of the preceding 'North', 'South' and 'West', to give the form that is now familiar. Some Scandinavian legal terms were also adopted. Sureties for land transfers were called *festermen*, a Scandinavian word, in a tenth-century memorandum from Peterborough Abbey and in other texts.[23] The unit of assessment for tribute and the rendering of services, was locally given a Scandinavian name *plogesland*, 'ploughland', which was translated into Latin as *carucata*, whence the modern term 'carucate'. The conventional plough-team had eight oxen and the natural subdivision of the ploughland was the *oxgang*, another Scandinavian word, in Latin *bovata*.[24]

The conquest and the first stage of the subsequent settlement meant that there were Scandinavian landowners in all parts of the shire. It is therefore not surprising that the few Scandinavian place-names that can be shown to be relatively early are widely scattered. Spellings in Domesday Book and other early texts suggest that in 27 place-names the first element had a Scandinavian genitival inflection; two in *-ar*, namely Fotherby and Londonthorpe, the others in *-s*, for example Bransby, Roxby, and Lusby. These names must have been formed when Scandinavian was still spoken in Lincolnshire, but that does not mean that they are earlier than 900; as already noted Scandinavian was probably spoken in at least parts of Lincolnshire well into the tenth century.

Most of the Scandinavians, the men who did the ploughing, were not so widely scattered. The areas they settled in are probably indicated by the main concentrations of Scandinavian place-names, especially those containing the word *by*, that is in the Wolds, and in the central part of Kesteven. This is confirmed by the fact that almost all brooches and other objects decorated in Scandinavian styles that have been discovered in Lincolnshire with the help of metal detectors have been found in areas with the main concentrations of Scandinavian place-names. Many of the *by*-names may also have been produced relatively early. Only fifteen are first recorded after 1150, while 229 appear in earlier texts, most of them in Domesday Book. This suggests that most were formed well before the Norman Conquest, a conclusion reinforced by the fact that there is only one containing a Norman name, Grimoldby. Even the fifteen names that are not recorded before 1150 may well have been formed before 1066. Another indication that *by*-names tend to be early is provided by those that include personal names based on *Thor*. There are seven in Lincolnshire, all containing compound personal names such as *Thorgrimr* in Thorganby and *Thorulfr* in Thurlby. During the Viking Age short forms of Thor names, for example Toli, Toki, and Tope, became very popular in England as well as in Scandinavia and several pre-Conquest landowners in Lincolnshire had these names. The fact that such short forms were never used in *by*-names, although they were commonly used in compounds with *-thorp*, and later in field names, confirms that *by* was being used to form names early rather than late.

As already mentioned, many of these *by*-names are adaptations of earlier English names. Most instances of such 'Scandinavianization' are naturally in the areas of densest settlement, but as Scandinavian speech gradually influenced the whole shire, names in all parts were similarly affected. This process continued long after the Norman Conquest. As Gillian Fellows-Jensen has remarked:

> Scandinavianization of English place-names, both by the local people who used them and by scribes, can be shown to have been quite common in the twelfth century and to have continued to take place as late even as the sixteenth century. This means that caution must be shown when assessing the value of Scandinavianized names as evidence for Viking colonization in the early years of the settlement. They can only show that the local dialect had been strongly influenced by Scandinavian.[25]

This applies particularly to field names which reflect the dialect of later times; they cannot be used to assess the scale or extent of the original settlement.

The later 'Scandinavianization' tended to be less thorough than it was earlier; the conversion of place-names to *by*-names had slowed down even before the Norman Conquest. Nevertheless this prolonged period of Scandinavianization has changed many of the place-names of Lincolnshire, and the result can give a misleading impression of both the scale and extent of Scandinavian settlement. Even original names coined by Scandinavians do not necessarily refer to Scandinavian settlements, for a place tends to be named by neighbours not by its inhabitants.

The best direct evidence for Scandinavian occupation is provided by the places that are named after Scandinavians, in particular those that combine a Scandinavian personal name with either *by* or *tūn*. Medieval records from Lincolnshire contain at least 82 of the former but only seven of the latter. It has been argued that the people who gave their names to these places were

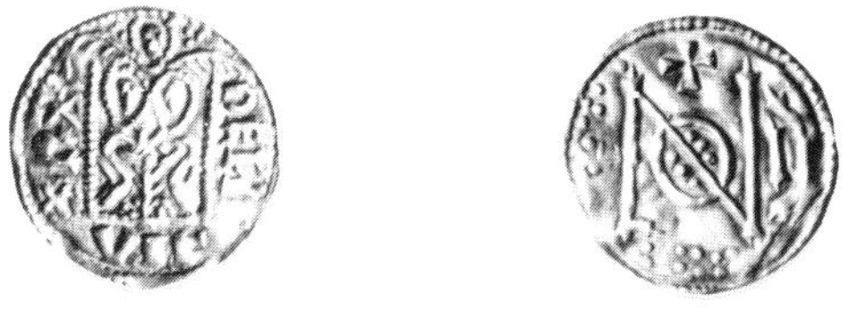

Fig. 6.8 This penny of a Danish king Halfdan was probably struck in the East Midlands, possibly in Lincolnshire. It copies two coins of Alfred, one of which was the London monogram type issued c. 880 (see Fig. 6.4; British Museum, CM 1896, 4-4-53; Webster and Backhouse 1992, no. 278).

the original settlers, and there has been a wide measure of agreement that the earliest Scandinavian settlements are represented by the place-names in which a Scandinavian personal name is combined with an English element, in particular *tūn*. These places are generally on good settlement sites that the English are most unlikely to have left unoccupied. According to this interpretation, these were among the first places taken over by the invaders, and their names commemorate the individuals who were responsible. The *by*-names, on the other hand, have been supposed to reflect a slightly later stage of colonization as the Scandinavians established themselves in less attractive areas that had not previously been so fully settled; in such circumstances the Scandinavians would naturally use their own word *by* to name their new settlements.

This interpretation is open to several objections. In the first place, as already explained, there is no reason to suppose that there was much vacant land suitable for settlement when the Scandinavians arrived. Large expanses of marsh and fen were, of course, devoid of permanent settlement and remained so, but there were few other areas of Lincolnshire that were not fully exploited and colonized. Three names, Aunsby and Owmby (two examples), have been interpreted as indicating farms that were deserted when the Danes began to settle in Lincolnshire. If so, they imply that other settlements were not deserted.

In parts of England that were occupied by the Scandinavians in the ninth century but soon recovered by the English, Scandinavian settlement names are exceedingly rare. In Cambridgeshire, for example, the Danes occupied an extensive area but they were driven from it in 903 and have left little trace in the place-names. It is possible that in such areas names that had been given by the Scandinavians were soon forgotten, but that seems unlikely. Even in areas like Lincolnshire that remained under Scandinavian control for a relatively long period there are few, if any, names that can be shown to be so early. The indications of early date that have already been discussed do not allow a narrower dating than the first century after the conquest. Indeed, if a significant number of names had been given in the ninth century, when Scandinavian speech was still vigorous, many more examples of the use of Scandinavian inflections might have been expected, despite the fact that almost all names were first recorded in late texts written by scribes who naturally tended to 'modernize' them.

It may also be doubted whether the Scandinavian settlers named places after individuals in the early days of their colonization. Such names were almost unknown in Denmark at that time; the Danes cannot have imported this habit of name-formation.[26] Place-names combining a personal name with *tūn* are, however, fairly common in many parts of England that were never under Scandinavian control.[27] These names were once thought to commemorate the founders of those settlements but it can be shown that in some cases the person named in this way was the first to have full rights of ownership.[28] These places were not new settlements, but the men who had formerly held them, although free, were not free to dispose of them by gift or sale. They were part of larger estates and owed tribute and services to the lords of those estates. In the tenth century, and earlier, kings gave some individuals the right to sell, lease, give or bequeath their land. Some places that were granted in this way were then named after the man or woman who was given the privilege, the first 'owner'. Woolstone in Berkshire, for example, is the '*tūn* of Wulfric', who was granted full rights over it in the tenth century, and Alverstoke in Hampshire was called *Stoce* in 948, while its present name incorporates that of Ælfwaru, who owned it a few years later, and was able to give it to Winchester Cathedral. Wulfric and Ælfwaru acquired their rights of ownership by royal grants, others did so by usurpation. In the process, some of the great estates that had once been the dominant form of land exploitation throughout England, were broken up.

The same thing happened in Lincolnshire after the Danish conquest, but not immediately. When the Danes arrived there were many great estates of this kind in all parts of the shire. The most important were probably royal, the bishops and monasteries certainly had some and laymen held others. The leaders of the Danes replaced these English lords, most of whom must have been either dead or in exile. The tenants of the estates, the farmers, could not flee so easily even if they wanted to, and most continued to render tribute and services to their new masters; the survival of the English language shows that many natives remained. Despite the scale of Scandinavian influence on the language, it is significant that the boundary between the Northumbrian and Midland dialects of Middle English followed the lower course of the river Witham which, to judge by the evidence of the place-names, ran between two of the largest and densest concentrations of Danish settlement in England.[29]

The survival of many estates, called sokes by the Danes, until the Norman Conquest shows that however the land was distributed, many seigneurial rights were retained by the Danish landowners. By 1065 some of these estates had been completely broken up, and others had lost some land. Some of this 'manorialization' may have happened before the Danes arrived, but the main fragmentation of estates happened after the Danish conquest, and is reflected in many of the place-names that include Scandinavian personal names. Some of these transfers into private ownership may have been with the consent of the Danes who had authority, but it is more likely that most happened as a result of conflicts in the early tenth century.

The death of Danish leaders in the campaigns that are discussed in the next chapter must have made it difficult for their successors to retain control of their estates, and to exact the services and renders that were due.

At least some of the Scandinavian personal names in Lincolnshire place-names may commemorate men who took advantage of this weakened lordship to claim that they owned their property.

The English conquest of Lincolnshire that began in 918 and was complete by 927 probably had a similar effect. Evidence from Ely Abbey concerning Huntingdonshire shows that Danes who submitted to the English king were able to retain their land; otherwise it was confiscated and either kept by the king or redistributed.[30] Retainers of the English king could naturally hope to benefit and it is possible that some Englishmen acquired land in Lincolnshire in this way. The place-names containing an English personal-name may have been one result. There is, however, no indication that there were many English landowners in Lincolnshire in the tenth century and it seems likely that the beneficiaries of any such land redistributions in the shire were of Danish descent. The English conquest would also have provided an opportunity to legitimize earlier usurpations.

As in other parts of England, many of the 'manors' as they would later be called, were named after the men who were first regarded as their owners. In areas in which Scandinavian speech was most vigorous, these personal names were combined with *by*. In other parts of Lincolnshire where Scandinavian speech at this time was less influential, the English word *tūn* continued to be used. There are, in fact, only seven place-names combining a Scandinavian personal name with *tūn*, and they are all in areas in which Scandinavian influence on place-names was slight: Baston, Blyton, Branston, Foston, Frampton, Gelston, and Harmston.[31] This is most clearly seen in the case of Frampton, named after a man with the Scandinavian name *Frani*; it is in Holland, an area in which there is not a single *by*-name and very few other signs of Scandinavian influence.

Hybrids like Frampton are not necessarily earlier than names like Thurlby. The difference between them is better explained by differences in the degree to which speech in various localities had been affected by the Scandinavians in the early tenth century when these names were probably produced. The places called Kirton, with the Scandinavian form of the word 'church', are similarly in areas with relatively few Scandinavian names – one of them is indeed near Frampton – while the Kirkbys are in areas with denser concentrations of Scandinavian names. These names illustrate the uneven effect of Scandinavian speech. They are also a reminder that in areas of relatively dense settlement many of the apparently Scandinavian names were adaptations or even translations of English names.

The earliest evidence for the structure and extent of the Lincolnshire sokes is provided by Domesday Book. Some appear to be relatively new creations, and the composition of the old sokes was certainly not the same as it had been two centuries earlier; but despite these changes, the pattern of place-names in many sokes is revealing. Those in the Wolds naturally tend to have a large proportion of Scandinavian names. Caistor, for example, had land in sixteen places, seven of which had *by*-names. In Waltham the proportion of *by*-names was even higher, nine out of fourteen, and one of the others was Waithe, from the Danish word *vað*, 'ford'. Horncastle also had land in fourteen places, and eight of them had *by*-names. With this degree of Scandinavian influence it is remarkable that in Caistor soke there was not one place-name incorporating a personal name, and in Horncastle there were only two, Scrivelsby and Wilksby, although overall a third of the *by*-names in the Lincolnshire Domesday were of this type. In some other sokes the proportion of such place-names is significantly higher; there were five in Waltham, and six or seven among the seventeen places in which Bolingbroke had land.[32]

Both Caistor and Horncastle were royal sokes, and Horncastle included Coningsby which is possibly an adaptation of an English name, 'the king's stronghold'.[33] These sokes may have been better preserved than many others. There is some support for this in the case of Horncastle. If the interpretation put forward here of place-names combining a personal name with *by* is correct, the names Scrivelsby and Wilksby imply that they were at some stage in private ownership, the only examples in Horncastle soke. It is perhaps no coincidence that land in both places also formed part of the small soke of Scrivelsby that appears to have been carved out of Horncastle.[34]

Another soke with no land in places named after individuals was Wragby which had remarkably few Scandinavian names, only two *by*-names among twelve places. This was not in royal hands in 1065, but it may have been earlier for one of its components was in Kingthorpe, a name that appears originally to have been English, 'the royal thorp'. Grantham, which was a royal soke in 1065, is a remarkable contrast, for seven of the sixteen places in which it had land were named after individuals.[35] If the interpretation of such names suggested here is correct, the implication is that Grantham soke retained land in several places that had been partly alienated and were consequently renamed.

The relatively large number of *thorp*-names is in accord with this interpretation. *Thorp* was a word used by both the English and the Scandinavians for an outlying component of a larger estate. The hundred names of this type in Lincolnshire are peripheral to the main settlement. In Lindsey most of them are in or on the edge of the Lindsey Marsh or are in the marshes bordering the Trent and Witham. The nineteen *thorps* in Domesday Book that were named after individuals may have been privately owned at some time before 1065, while the others continued to be associated with a nearby settlement or remained part of a soke.

The paradoxical conclusion to be drawn from the argument offered here is that the collapse of Scandinavian rule had a greater effect on the social and economic structure of rural Lincolnshire than the Scandinavian conquest. That conquest did however have an immediate effect on the church and on the economy, topics discussed in Chapters VIII and IX.

NOTES TO CHAPTER VI

1 There are general accounts of ninth-century Viking activity in the works listed in Loyn 1977, Sawyer 1982, and Keynes 1997. There are useful maps of the raids and campaigns in Hill, D. 1981, pp. 36–42, and in Hooper and Bennet 1996, pp. 18–25.

2 Dolley 1983; S 280, 286 dated 838; S 287 dated 839. S 189 dated 833 is a Crowland forgery and S 320 is certainly not trustworthy.

3 Parker 1985.

4 For the bishops, see Appendix 6.

5 O'Donovan 1973, p. 94.

6 Owen, A. 1980.

7 For Ulf, see p. 132.

8 *EHD* I, no. 4, p. 283.

9 *EHD* I, no. 6, p. 288.

10 Sawyer 1982, p. 104.

11 S 782; Everson and Knowles 1993.

12 Campbell, A. 1962, p. 51.

13 Keynes and Lapidge 1983, p. 337, treat *pandunt* as a mistake for *praedantur* because, in their view, the translation by Alistair Campbell quoted here is impossible: '*pando* is intransitive and cannot govern the accusative *territoria*', they say. But *pando* is transitive and in Classical Latin was used in very much this sense. See also Cox 1994a, p. lxiv.

14 The Lincoln monogram on these coins (Fig. 6.4) is based on the London monogram on coins struck for Alfred in the early 880s, Blackburn 1998, pp. 120–2.

15 Discussions of this evidence are reviewed in Fellows-Jensen 1975. The Scandinavian place-names in Lincolnshire are systematically discussed by Fellows-Jensen 1978.

16 Fellows-Jensen 1974.

17 Olof von Feilitzen, quoted by Fellows-Jensen 1980, p. 197.

18 Fellows-Jensen 1968.

19 Fellows-Jensen 1968, pp. lxiv–lxvi.

20 DB i. 336a = *LD* pp.3, no. 2 and p. 5, no. 12.

21 DB i. 337a = *LD* p. 13.

22 See above, p. 29.

23 Robertson 1939, pp. 74–83.

24 See below, p. 137.

25 Fellows-Jensen 1980, p. 201.

26 Pedersen 1960.

27 Fellows-Jensen 1978, p. 284.

28 Gelling 1978, pp. 180–5; Sawyer 1978, pp. 151–6.

29 Kristensson 1967, p. 241 and map 17 (p. 283).

30 See below, pp. 118–19.

31 Fellows-Jensen 1978, pp. 187–96.

32 Caistor: DB i. 338b = *LD* 1/65–80.; Waltham: DB i. 347a-b = *LD* 12/21–28, 32–6, 38–9; Horncastle: DB i. 339a = *LD* 1/91–106.

33 Cox 1994b, p. 41.

34 All the components of Scrivelsby soke (DB i. 363b = *LD* 38/3–7) were in places in which Horncastle had sokeland.

35 Wragby: DB i. 362ab, 354a, cf. 365b = *LD* 34/12–23, 22/37, cf. 47/8–9. Grantham: DB i. 337b–338a = *LD* 1/9–25.

CHAPTER VII

FROM EDWARD THE ELDER TO EDWARD THE CONFESSOR

When King Alfred died in 899 a large part of eastern England, from the Tees to the Thames estuary, was controlled by the heirs of the Danes who conquered that territory in the decade after 865. The main responsibility for resisting further Danish expansion lay with Edward, Alfred's son and successor as king of the West Saxons, and Æthelred, ruler of English Mercia. Æthelred shared power with his wife, Alfred's daughter, Æthelflæd who, after his death in 911, continued to rule the Mercians as their 'Lady', *domina Merciorum.*

The first recorded confrontation of the century was in 902 when the army in East Anglia raided Mercia.[1] According to the *Chronicle* they were induced to do this by Æthelwold, Edward's cousin who had failed to gain recognition as Alfred's successor, and may have hoped to make good his claim with Danish help. In reprisal Edward harried Danish territory in Cambridgeshire but when he withdrew one contingent of his army, from Kent, 'lingered behind there against his command' and was defeated in a battle in which Æthelwold was killed. In 906 Edward made peace with the Danish armies of East Anglia and Northumbria (some reports say he did so 'from necessity') at Tiddingford near Leighton Buzzard, which must then have been on the boundary between English and Danish territory.

THE WEST SAXON CONQUEST OF THE DANELAW

In 909 the English went on the offensive. The *Chronicle* reports that 'King Edward sent an army both from the West Saxons and from the Mercians, and it ravaged very severely the territory of the northern army, both men and all kinds of cattle and they killed many men of those Danes, and were five weeks there'. Lindsey was certainly affected, for the one specific achievement of this raid was the removal of St Oswald's body from Bardney to Mercia. It was reburied in the royal minster at Gloucester, where both Æthelred and Æthelflæd were buried. Æthelflæd may also have been responsible for introducing the cult of St Oswald to Chester.[2] The *Chronicle* represents Edward as the leader of this 909 campaign, but it seems to have been as much a Mercian as a West Saxon enterprise, and the Danes responded in 910 by raiding deeply into Mercia. On this occasion the English army overtook the invaders before they reached the relative safety of their own territory, and inflicted a crushing defeat on them in a battle fought near Tettenhall in Staffordshire.

For several years after that battle very little is known about the situation in Deira. The first known successor to the kings killed in 910 was Ragnald, whose reign began in 919.[3] If there were any kings in the intervening years they do not appear to have struck any coins, as Ragnald did.[4] The only coins produced in York between about 905 and 919 were the so-called St Peter's pence, apparently struck for the archbishop, which suggests that he was one of the main beneficiaries of the Danish defeat.[5] It may be significant that the *Chronicle*, which frequently referred to the armies of East Anglia and of Northumbria before 910, only mentions the former after that date. The Scandinavians settled in Northumbria no longer played such a significant role south of the Humber as they had done previously and it is likely that for a few years the Danes – and natives – in Lindsey were not subject to overlords based in York.

After the battle of Tettenhall the Danes in other parts of the former Mercian empire could no longer hope for support from the 'northern army'. The *Chronicle* describes them as belonging to independent groups or armies under the leadership of earls. Some of these local armies cooperated but in general the English were able to deal with them piecemeal. The English offensive began in 912, but some years earlier, while Æthelred was still alive, he and Edward began to encroach on territory under Danish control by encouraging their men to buy land from the pagans; charters show this being done in Derbyshire and Bedfordshire.[6] It was, though, after Æthelred's death that Edward and his sister began to strengthen the frontier region by building forts or 'boroughs' as a prelude to advancing into Danish territory. They secured their conquests by building, or gaining control of, similar forts that the Danes had built or taken over. By the end of 917 Edward had completed the conquest of East Anglia and had also extended his authority as far north as the river Welland. In the words of the *Chronicle,* 'Earl Thurferth and the *holds* submitted to him and so too did all the army which belonged to Northampton, as far north as the Welland, and sought to have him as their lord and protector'. Edward's forces then seized Huntingdon, restored the borough and 'all the people of that district who had survived submitted to King Edward and asked for his peace and protection'. In the following summer Edward led his army to Stamford and ordered a borough to be built south of the river. This led 'all the people who belonged to the more northern borough' to submit and accept Edward as their lord. In other words, he conquered Kesteven. Some light is cast on what submission meant by the *Liber Eliensis*. It reports a dispute over land at Bluntisham in Huntingdonshire.[7] This had been sold by a certain Wulfnoth to Bishop Æthelwold of Winchester, the refounder of Ely. In 975 the sons of a man called Boga claimed that Bluntisham ought to have belonged to their uncle Topi, because his grandmother had submitted to Edward at Cambridge. This implies that those Danes who submitted promptly were allowed to keep their land. The claim failed because witnesses remembered that Huntingdon submitted before Cambridge. Topi's grandmother's submission was therefore too late to save her land in Huntingdonshire.

While Edward advanced north into Lincolnshire his sister was mastering the Danes who had settled further west. In 917 her forces seized Derby and early in 918 she gained control of Leicester without a fight. According to a tenth-century chronicle known as the Mercian Register, 'the people of York promised her – and some had given pledges, some had confirmed it with oaths – that they would be under her direction'. What prompted this move is not known. The men of York may have hoped that by submitting to the Mercians they could avoid submitting to the West Saxons. It has alternatively been suggested that the invitation was made by a faction in York that was opposed to Ragnald.[8] Whatever the motive, it came to nothing because Æthelflæd died on 12 June. When news of this reached Edward at Stamford he immediately went to Tamworth and gained recognition as king of Mercia. He then attacked Nottingham, which was still under Danish control, captured the borough and, according to the *Chronicle*, 'all the people who had settled in Mercia, both Danish and English submitted to him'. That was probably an exaggeration; the Danes still had control of the lower Trent, and two years later Edward thought it necessary to build a fortified bridge across the Trent at Nottingham. Lindsey, about which nothing is said in the *Chronicle*'s account of these campaigns, was probably still under Danish control until 920, and it may be that Ragnald, who then ruled York, claimed some authority there.

Fig. 7.1 One of the rare St Martin's coins from Lincoln. These were modelled on, and are probably contemporary with, the Sword St Peter's coins of York that are now dated c. 921–7 (SCBI 27, no. 5; Stewart 1967; Grierson and Blackburn 1986, p. 323).

Fig. 7.2 The nine known coins of Sihtric, king of York 921–7, are, like the St Martin's coins, closely linked with the Sword St Peter's of York. There are, however, good reasons for thinking that they were struck south of the Humber, almost certainly in Lindsey which was under Sihtric's rule. Ian Stewart (1982) has suggested that they may have replaced the St Martin's issue. The retrograde inscription on the reverse of this one apparently contains the word Castra *followed by EQ(?)RT, presumably a place-name. (British Museum* ex *Lockett 439; Blunt, Lyon, and Stewart 1989, p. 107)*

Numismatic evidence suggests that Sihtric, who succeeded Ragnald as king in York in 920, did control Lindsey. Coins in his name seem to have been struck in Lincoln, not York. Links between the two cities after the submission of Stamford are confirmed by the St Martin's coins that were struck at Lincoln in the early 920s (see Fig. 7.1).[9] Like the St Peter's pence of York, on which they were modelled, they were a non-royal coinage, and may have been struck for the archbishop.

According to the *Chronicle* some rulers who had not already acknowledged Edward as overlord, did so in 920. One of them was Ragnald, but any claim that Edward could consequently make to overlordship of Lindsey was shortlived. Ragnald died in the same year and was succeeded by his brother Sihtric, who had been king of Dublin since 917. There is no hint that Sihtric ever submitted to Edward. He did however come to terms with Edward's son and successor Athelstan. Athelstan was brought up at the court of Ealdorman Æthelred and Æthelflæd, and the Mercians apparently accepted him with little delay as their king after Edward's death in 924. It was in Wessex that he faced opposition and his inauguration as king of the West Saxons was delayed until September 925. In the following January Sihtric married Athelstan's sister but died before the end of the year. Athelstan then determined to take control of Northumbria himself. Sihtric's brother, Guthfrith, and his son, Olaf, returned to Ireland and the Danish fort of York was destroyed. In the words of the *Chronicle*, Athelstan 'succeeded to the kingdom of the Northumbrians' and was therefore the first southern English king to rule Lindsey directly. He was also recognized as overlord by the kings of the Scots and of the Britons of Strathclyde.

Athelstan's charters illustrate the reality of his overlordship. The witness lists show that between 930 and 934 his court was attended by a total of 30 *duces,* many of whom had Scandinavian or Celtic names. The largest number in any one charter is fifteen. Some can be identified as ealdormen of provinces in Wessex and English Mercia, but the thirteen with Scandinavian names presumably had authority in the Danish areas that Athelstan then ruled.[10] These lists confirm that men of Scandinavian descent retained authority in Danish areas after submission to the English king, and that they sometimes attended his court. Sorne of these witnesses presumably came from Lincolnshire, but it is not possible to identify which.

Athelstan's achievement is also reflected in his coinage.[11] After 927 mints in many parts of England, including York, issued coins with an abbreviated form of the title *Rex totius Britanniæ*. Athelstan made some effort to control the coinage, one means being to require moneyers to put their names on their products. Mints are also named on coins from most parts of the country but none of his coins name a mint in Lincolnshire; the nearest mints named were Nottingham, Leicester, and Hertford. There is, however, no doubt that Athelstan had a mint in Lincoln, and probably in Stamford too. Coins were struck in Lincoln when it was under Danish control, two of them by moneyers who also produced coins for Athelstan, Lincoln is named as a mint on a coin of Eadred, and after 973, when all mints were indicated, Lincoln and Stamford were among the most productive. It is perhaps significant that Athelstan's coins from the unnamed mints do not have the *Rex totius Britanniæ* title. The conclusion reached by Christopher Blunt in his survey of Athelstan's coinage was that 'in those parts of England that had been under Viking control, a considerable latitude was allowed to the operation of mints; some peculiarly unkempt coins are to be associated with them'.[12] This is what might be expected from mints in Lincolnshire, that were under the control of men who recognized Athelstan as king and occasionally attended his court, but retained a great deal of independence.

This great extension of English power naturally provoked opposition and in 934 the Scots rebelled. Athelstan led a military expedition into Scotland, but the Scots refused to give battle and remained defiant. Three years later they joined forces with other opponents of Athelstan in a confederacy led by Olaf, son of the Guthfrith who had been expelled by Athelstan in 927. The northern army was beaten in a hard-fought battle at *Brunanburh*. This famous place is unidentified or, rather, many different identifications have been proposed. It was certainly inside Mercia and is likely to have been on the main road south from York, possibly near Doncaster, close to the site of many other battles between the Northumbrians and the southern English.[13] That was the route taken by Olaf Guthfrithsson when he invaded Mercia after Athelstan's death, and it was also followed by an English army making a punitive raid in Northumbria about ten years later. Athelstan's victory was celebrated in a long annal in the *Chronicle*, and was widely reported in the British Isles; it even found a place in Icelandic tradition. After it, Athelstan proudly claimed in a charter that he was *rex Angulsexna* and *Northhymbra imperator paganorum gubernator Brittanorumque propugnator.*[14] In making this boast he was perhaps guilty of some exaggeration, for the evidence of both charters and coins suggests that after 934 he did not have the same authority in Northumbria and in other Danish areas that he had enjoyed earlier. Many of the *duces* with Scandinavian names who witnessed charters between 930 and 934, do not appear in later charters. The absence of the archbishop of York from the witness lists from 935 until the end of Athelstan's reign suggests that the king's authority in Danish areas declined after 934. There are, moreover, signs that the York mint was less productive towards the end of Athelstan's reign.

When Athelstan died in October 939 his brother Edmund, then eighteen years old, was chosen in his place. Olaf Guthfrithsson seized the opportunity to return, and this time had more success. According to the annal for 939 in the *Historia Regum*, apparently drawing on a tenth-century northern chronicle, Olaf's army besieged Northampton, an important royal centre, but failed to take it. Then, after plundering Tamworth, they went to Leicester where the English army confronted them. There was a siege but no 'severe fighting' and Edmund was persuaded to agree to a treaty conceding to Olaf the lands north of Watling Street. A more reliable and specific indication of the area in question is given by the *Chronicle* when describing its recovery in 942; it was then said to consist of the five boroughs, Derby, Lincoln, Leicester, Nottingham, and Stamford. The chronology of this invasion is obscure. Alfred Smyth has argued that Olaf moved very quickly indeed after Athelstan's death but it must have taken some time to make the necessary preparations – he would not have wanted to risk a repetition of the disaster of *Brunanburh.*[15] According to the *Historia Regum* the agreement was due to the intervention of the two archbishops, Wulfstan of York, who apparently supported Olaf, and Oda of Canterbury, but Oda did not become archbishop until after the death of his predecessor on 12 February 941. It appears that either the negotiations were protracted, or that the campaign was in the winter of 940–41, which is not unlikely; many Viking attacks were made at that time of year. Coins provide independent evidence of Olaf's success. The mints at York, Derby and probably Lincoln and Stamford all produced coins for Olaf much as they had done for Athelstan. At Derby two of Athelstan's moneyers continued to strike coins for Olaf and at least one reverse die was used for both kings.[16]

Olaf Guthfrithsson was killed during a raid in Lothian in 941 and was succeeded by another Olaf, son of the Sihtric who had died as king in York in 927. In the following year Edmund recovered the lands he had conceded to the Northumbrians, an achievement that was celebrated in the *Chronicle* in an annal that, like the account of *Brunanburh*, is in poetic form.

> In this year King Edmund, lord of the English, protector of men, the beloved performer of mighty deeds, overran Mercia, as bounded by Dore, Whitwell gate and the broad stream, the river Humber; and five boroughs, Leicester and Lincoln, Nottingham and likewise Stamford, and also Derby. The Danes were previously subjected by force under the Norsemen, for a long time in bonds of captivity to the heathens, until the defender of warriors, the son of Edward, King Edmund, redeemed them.

There is no hint here or elsewhere of any military action; indeed, the use of the verb *gebycgan*, 'to buy, redeem', implies that it was recovered by payment rather than force. The claim that the Danes who had settled in this area welcomed Edmund as a liberator should not be taken literally. It is consistent with the general attitude of the Chronicler that the Mercians welcomed the West Saxons, while the Northumbrians did not. The contrast between the heathen Norsemen and their Danish victims is also exaggerated. It was probably true that Olaf Guthfrithsson was not a Christian – he adopted some overtly pagan symbols on his coins – but if the archbishop of York was prepared to collaborate with him, the Danes of the East Midlands can hardly have objected on religious grounds.

LINCOLNSHIRE UNDER ENGLISH RULE

In 944 Edmund was recognized as king in Northumbria, but in 946 he was killed and succeeded by his younger brother Eadred who was soon accepted as king by the Northumbrians. However, a year or two later they rebelled and in succession recognized as kings of York Olaf Sihtricsson and an exiled Norwegian king, Erik known as 'Bloodaxe'.[17] The expulsion and death of Erik in 954 (or possibly 952) marked the end of Northumbrian independence. One effect of the chaotic political situation in Northumbria in these years was that Eadred attempted to strengthen his authority in Lindsey and on the other side of the Trent. The fort at Newark may have been built at this time to hinder attack from the north, whether by land or river; the name means 'new work' in the sense of fort. It is, moreover, probably no accident that Eadred is the first English king to have a coin struck naming the Lincoln mint. This is the more remarkable because in his reign only three other mints are named on coins.[18] It cannot be claimed that the naming of mints on coins is a measure of the effectivenenss of royal authority, but the spread of the practice to Lincoln at this time would be consistent with increased royal interest in the area. It may also be significant that the type of coin struck at Lincoln for Eadred displayed the king in profile with a crown. Most of Eadred's coins only had inscriptions.

Fig. 7.3 Penny of King Eadred (946–55). The reverse inscription is blundered but there is no doubt that it names Are as the moneyer and Lincoln as the mint (SCBI 34, no. 686; Blunt, Lyon, and Stewart 1989, pp. 192, 313).

The crowned bust was used for Athelstan at York and in East Anglia as well as in southern England, but under his brothers it seems only to have been used in Danish areas, including Norwich and Lincoln, plausibly as a visual reminder of royal power.[19]

Northumbria never recovered its independence. When the English kingdom was divided, as happened in 957, 1016, and in 1035, the boundary was the Thames, not the Humber. The division of 957 was between the two sons of Edmund. The elder, Eadwig, who succeeded his uncle Eadred in 955, retained Wessex while his younger brother, Edgar, became king of the Mercians and Northumbrians with a separate court. The bishops, ealdormen, and thegns who attended Edgar's council were mostly Mercians, but this was hardly a triumph of Mercian separatism, and was certainly not the result of rebellion. The relatively abundant charter witness lists of the period give no hint of any extraordinary tensions other than those that were to be expected in any royal court, especially when the king was young; Edgar was only 16 in 959. Eadwig's superiority was acknowledged, and the fundamental unity of the kingdom was reflected in the coinage; Mercian mints continued to issue coins in Eadwig's name until his death in 959. Only then, when Edgar succeeded as sole king, were coins issued in his name.[20]

Within three or four years of becoming king of the English, Edgar clearly stated his attitude to the Danish areas of England; they were in most respects to be left to govern themselves. In 962 or 963 he addressed a set of legal instructions to Oslac, earl of Northumbria, in which he declared, 'It is my will that secular rights be in force among the Danes according to as good laws as they can best decide on'. There is a similar clause later with the addition, 'I have ever allowed them this and will allow it as long as my life lasts, because of your loyalty, which you have always shown me'. One exception was specified: procedures to deal with theft, the local application of which is discussed below, were imposed on 'all the nation, whether Englishmen, Danes or Britons, in every province of my dominion'.[21] His claim that he had always allowed the Danes such freedom was one that could have equally been made by his predecessors. There is nothing to suggest that Athelstan and his brothers had attempted to install agents from other parts of the kingdom, or to interfere with the procedures of local courts in the areas recovered from the Danes. The coin of Eadred naming the Lincoln mint, mentioned as a possible sign of increased royal interest in the region, was struck by Are, a moneyer whose career began before Athelstan's conquest.[22]

Edgar's reign was longer than that of any king since Edward. He achieved a remarkable degree of authority, symbolically demonstrated in 973 by his coronation at Bath and by a ceremony at Chester in which six or more British rulers recognized him as overlord. It was almost certainly in the same year that there was another, more material, manifestation of royal authority, the reform of the coinage. A new type of penny was introduced and struck in all mints. This replaced the several different types that were current earlier in his reign, and these old coins disappeared from circulation very quickly. The dies for the new coins were distributed from Winchester, and were probably made there. The new coins have a stylized bust of the king on the obverse, surrounded by his name and title, and the reverse consists of a small cross placed centrally and surrounded by the names of the moneyer and mint. 347 of these coins were known in 1987, 50 of them found in Lincolnshire; 14 were made by four moneyers at Lincoln, and 36 by seven moneyers at Stamford. Within a few years of Edgar's death in 975 coins were also being struck at Caistor, Grantham, Horncastle and Torksey.[23]

After 942 the area between the Welland and the Humber was firmly part of the English kingdom, but it continued to be governed by local men. They were supervised by royal agents, some of whom were also recruited locally, and these gradually made royal authority more effective. The men principally responsible for this extension of royal authority in the tenth century were the ealdormen, or earls, as they came to be called thanks to Scandinavian influence. In tenth- and eleventh-century Latin texts both ealdorman and earl were rendered as *dux*, 'leader', an appropriate translation, for one of their main duties was to lead the military forces drawn from the districts for which they were responsible. Ealdormen were advisers as well as agents. Many of them regularly attended meetings of the royal council and one of their main functions was to implement that council's decisions. They did this through local courts or assemblies, the most important of which were normally held in the boroughs that served as the centres of the districts for which the ealdormen were responsible. Within these districts there were other regular assemblies of freemen, called wapentakes in Danish areas. By the eleventh century the area from which the members of a wapentake were drawn was itself called a wapentake, and the term for a local assembly was thus transferred to a locality.

The procedures in these local assemblies, both boroughs and wapentakes, were regulated by custom but gradually local customs were modified by the new laws and procedures ordained by the king and his councillors.[24]

In ninth-century Wessex ealdormen's districts were called 'shires', and these survived, with some boundary changes, as modern counties until 1974, but in tenth-century Mercia there were normally only three ealdormen, each of whom was responsible for a very large area. During that century smaller districts, also called shires, were formed within the large ealdormanries. Each of these shires was associated with, and most were named after, one of the boroughs that the English built or took over from the Danes. There were also subordinate officials some of whom were assigned to particular districts and ranked as ealdormen; others were called reeves, a word with a very wide range of meanings from the steward of a small estate, to men who, in rank and responsibility, were hardly distinguishable from the ealdormen themselves and were sometimes called high reeves. By the eleventh century reeves who were responsible for shires began to be known as shire-reeves, hence the modern word sheriff.

Very little is known about the men who acted as royal agents in Lincolnshire. Two of the the *duces* with Scandinavian names who witnessed charters after 928 appear to have come from south of the Humber, but they cannot be located more closely. Orm, who was a witness from 930 to 958, was probably the man who, according to Roger of Wendover, encouraged Olaf Guthfrithsson to seize the Five Boroughs after Athelstan's death.[25] The other, Morcar, witnessed a charter concerning land in Northamptonshire in 946, and another concerning Nottinghamshire granted in 958 by Edgar when he was king of Mercia and Northumbria.[26] No link can be proved between that Morcar and the 'chief thegn of the Seven Boroughs' who was killed in 1015, but the coincidence of names and, apparently, of their area of interest, makes some connection likely.[27]

The success of Edmund in recovering the Five Boroughs and of Eadred in at last making Northumbria a permanent part of the English kingdom does not mean that they had more authority north of the Welland than Athelstan had towards the end of his reign. They were at best little more than overlords in the area. This impression is reinforced by the fact that the only laymen with Scandinavian names who appear in any witness list before Edgar's reign were *duces*, not thegns or *ministri*. It is, of course, possible if unlikely that one or two of the thegns with English names in these lists came from Lincolnshire. The contacts that Athelstan and his brothers had with Lincolnshire appear to have been exclusively, and infrequently, with the local leaders, the *duces*. Even under Edgar the people of Lincolnshire and other Danish areas, were allowed great freedom in determining their own laws and legal procedures. Edgar did, however, make one exception. He decreed measures to combat theft that were 'to be common to all the nation, whether Englishmen, Danes or Britons'.[28] These included the appointment in every borough, hundred, and wapentake of a standing group of men to act as witnesses of all sales and purchases; no transaction was to be made without the witness of two or three of them. He further provided that anyone setting out to make a purchase must first tell his neighbours of his intention and on his return report 'in whose witness he bought the goods'. Unexpected purchases made on a journey had to be announced 'and if it is livestock, he is to bring it to the common pasture with the witness of his village'. If he did not do so, within five days the villagers had to inform the man in charge of the hundred (or wapentake) and so free themselves from any penalty. If they did not, 'each herdsman is to be flogged' and the cattle forfeited, even if acquired legally, 'because he would not announce it to his neighbours'. The confiscated cattle were to be divided between the lord of the estate and the hundred, which must have been an additional incentive to the villagers to report offences.

These arrangements were closely connected with the development of the system of tithings, that is, groups of ten or twelve men who were mutually responsible for their good behaviour and, if necessary, for accusing, arresting, and producing any of their number guilty of a crime.[29] These arrangements are first explicitly described in the laws of Cnut, but tithings already existed in Athelstan's reign. They may, indeed, have been developed in Wessex by Alfred, and introduced into Mercia by his children or grandsons, but it was probably Edgar who attempted to impose it on Danish areas.[30] Post-Conquest evidence reveals in more detail how the system, then called frankpledge, worked. The sheriff checked twice a year to ensure that all men over the age of twelve were in tithings. Edgar's attempt to impose the system of tithings throughout all his kingdom was, however, not completely successful for it never extended north of the Humber, and we cannot assume that it was effectively operating in Lincolnshire in his reign.

THE DANES RETURN

After Edgar's death in 975 there was a succession dispute between his sons, the half-brothers Edward and Æthelred. The faction supporting Edward won, but he was murdered three years later and Æthelred then became king. It was in his reign that Viking raiders once again caused widespread disruption in England. There had been sporadic attacks throughout the tenth century, especially on the the western parts of Britain by raiders from Ireland, the Isle of Man and the Scottish islands, but in the 990s east England suffered several large-scale attacks by raiders from Scandinavia.

Most of the raids reported in the *Chronicle* were on southern England and East Anglia. Indeed, the only attack on Lincolnshire before Swein's invasion in 1013 was in 993. Some other raids may have escaped notice but there seems little doubt that the Vikings concentrated their attention elsewhere. Their purpose was to intimidate the English into buying peace, and that was most effectively done by attacking the estates of the king himself, and of his leading counsellors, clerical as well as lay. Many of the most valuable of these were in the south and, what is more, they were more accessible to raiders than estates, for example, in the heart of Mercia.

The attack in 993 began with the sacking of Bamburgh. The fleet then sailed to the Humber and raided both the Northumbrian and the Lindsey shores. The English assembled what the *Chronicle* described as 'a very large army', apparently with the intention of confronting the invaders in Lindsey. That is suggested by the local connections of two of the three leaders, Fræna, Frithegyst, and Godwine. Fræna was once described as 'of Rockingham', an important royal estate in Northamptonshire, and he also gave land in Leicestershire to Peterborough Abbey, and Godwine can with little hesitation be identified as the ealdorman of Lindsey who died in 1016.[31] The English army was defeated. The Chronicler blamed the three leaders who, he claimed, 'first started the flight'. He was writing after Æthelred's death, and tended to explain defeats by such acts of cowardice or betrayal, but here, as elsewhere, he was probably mistaken. Fræna and Frithegyst were not disgraced; they still attended meetings of the royal council a decade later. Godwine had a very common name and cannot therefore be identified with any confidence among the witnesses in Æthelred's charters, which include at least two Godwines.

It was probably the failure of the defences in the Humber region in 993 that led Æthelred to make two important changes. First, he appointed Ælfhelm, a member of one of the leading Mercian families, as ealdorman of Northumbria.[32] This was a break with former practice; previous ealdormen in south Northumbria had either been chosen from the the house of Bamburgh or had close connections in the Danelaw. The king may have hoped that Ælfhelm would strengthen royal authority north of the Humber and be an effective leader in defending the whole region. The experiment was not a success. He was killed and his sons blinded in 1006, apparently on the king's orders, and Uhtred, a member of the house of Bamburgh, chosen in his place. No reason was given for Ælfhelm's removal. He may, as Dorothy Whitelock suggested, have been suspected of pro-Danish sympathies.

A second innovation was to combine the boroughs of north-east Mercia with their districts in a single region with a common council under its own ealdorman. The first reference to this newly created district is in a code of law agreed at a council held at Wantage, probably in 997. This provided specifically for the maintenance of order by the king's agents in the district known as the Five Boroughs. The boroughs are not named but there is general agreement that they were Lincoln, Stamford, Leicester, Nottingham, and Derby.[33]

The so-called Wantage code begins by prescribing penalties for breach of the peace. Peace given by the king in person is declared to be unemendable, meaning that the life and property of anyone guilty of that offence would be literally in the king's mercy. It continues:

> And the peace which the ealdorman and the king's reeve give in the meeting (*geþincðo*) of the Five Boroughs, that is to be atoned for with twelve hundred. And the peace which is given in the meeting of one borough is to be atoned for with six hundred; and that which is given in a wapentake, is to be atoned for with a hundred, if it is broken; and that which given in an alehouse is to be atoned for, if a man is killed, with six half marks, and if no-one is killed, with twelve ores.

The figures are sums of money expressed in terms of long hundreds, that is 120, of ores. An ore was a Scandinavian accounting unit of 16 pence. In more familiar terms, the penalties listed in the Wantage Code were therefore £144, £48, £8, £2, and 16 shillings. These give some indication of the relative status of the various assemblies. Nothing more is known about the least important of them, the 'alehouse'. It is unlikely to have been an ordinary tavern. As the equivalent word was used in Scandinavia for guilds, especially burial guilds, it may be another instance of Scandinavian influence.[34]

As Patrick Wormald has pointed out, 'no West Saxon king or council could have produced a code so thoroughly Scandinavian in form and content', and he draws the reasonable conclusion that it must have been compiled by 'men completely familiar with Danelaw usage', one of whom may have been Sigeferth, the bishop of Lindsey.[35] It was compiled in the same year as another code, explicitly stated to be English law, issued from a council at Woodstock. Æthelred did not, however, simply accept the Danelaw practices as Edgar had done. The close similarity between some provisions in the Wantage and the Woodstock codes implies that Æthelred and his councillors introduced some English legal rules and practices into the Danelaw. The penalties prescribed are very much heavier than in areas under English law. This suggests that following the Viking raid on Northumbria and Lindsey in 993, Æthelred was trying to strengthen his authority in the area and ensure loyalty.

Although no attack is reported on either Lindsey or Kesteven during the next twenty years, the area was indirectly affected by having to contribute to the tributes exacted by the raiders or to pay the wages of Scandinavians who were recruited to help the defence. Lincolnshire was prosperous, with relatively large quantities of money in circulation. Much of this was gathered by tax collectors and the Lincolnshire mints produced a large proportion of the coins paid to the Scandinavians. Caistor, Horncastle, Grantham, and Torksey ceased to be mints early in Æthelred's reign, but Lincoln and Stamford continued to produce very large quantities of coin.

The raids culminated in 1013 when the Danish king, Swein Forkbeard, who had led several earlier raids, came determined to conquer the kingdom. Lindsey was the base from which he launched his campaign. He reached the coast of Kent in the summer and immediately proceeded to the Humber and up the Trent to Gainsborough. The Northumbrians and the people of Lindsey submitted to him 'at once', according to the *Chronicle*. Then, apparently with little delay, he was recognized in the rest of the Five Boroughs district and in the area of Danish settlement north of Watling Street. His army was provided with horses and he then went south, leaving his ships and the hostages that had been delivered to him in charge of his son Cnut. By Christmas Swein had been accepted as king throughout the country, and shortly afterwards Æthelred went into exile in Normandy. Swein returned to Gainsborough, but did not enjoy his triumph long; he died on 3 February 1014.

The Danish army promptly chose Cnut as his successor, but most of the English did not. He stayed until the end of April, but the only area to offer him support was Lindsey. Æthelred returned in the spring, promising to be a better king, and immediately took the initiative. He gathered an army and went north, reaching Lindsey before Cnut and his English allies were ready. Cnut withdrew and sailed back to Denmark leaving the 'wretched people' of Lindsey to Æthelred's revenge. The *Chronicle* says that Lindsey 'was ravaged and burnt, and all the men who could be got at were killed'.

In the following year there was an assembly at Oxford in which Eadric, the ealdorman of Mercia, betrayed Sigeferth and Morcar, described as 'the chief thegns of the Seven Boroughs'. They were certainly associated with the district otherwise known as the Five Boroughs and this unique reference has been taken to imply some extension of the district; it has, for example, been suggested that the additional boroughs were York and Boroughbridge. It is more likely that they were Newark and Torksey, two boroughs that had by then developed within the district of the original five. Sigeferth and Morcar were both killed, apparently with the king's approval for he imprisoned Sigeferth's widow at Malmesbury, and claimed the estates of the dead men. The nature of the accusation against them is unknown; it may have been connected with the reception of Swein in their area, although, as Pauline Stafford has suggested, it might possibly have been because they supported the ambitions of Edmund, the king's only surviving son by his first wife.[36] The murder of Sigeferth and Morcar was hardly calculated to strengthen the loyalty of the Five Boroughs to Æthelred and the area quickly transferred its allegiance to the king's son, Edmund. In defiance of his father he rescued Sigeferth's widow from Malmesbury, married her, and took over the estates of the dead men. He then formed an alliance with Uhtred, earl of Northumbria.

When Cnut returned in the summer of 1015 to claim his inheritance, the English were, therefore, deeply divided. To make matters worse, before the end of the year Ealdorman Eadric abandoned Æthelred and joined forces with Cnut. After unsuccessfully attempting to organize opposition to Cnut, Edmund and Uhtred began to devastate Eadric's territory in western Mercia. In the early part of 1016 Cnut advanced north to Northamptonshire and then through the territory of the Five Boroughs to York apparently by-passing Lindsey where he may have reasonably expected some hostility. The *Chronicle* describes his progress 'along the fen to Stamford, and then into Lincolnshire; then from there to Nottinghamshire and so into Northumbria towards York'. This induced Uhtred to hurry north and submit to Cnut 'out of necessity, and with him all the Northumbrians'. He was, however, killed before long and a Norwegian, Eric, was appointed earl of Northumbria in his place.

Æthelred spent the winter in London, where he was joined by Edmund, and when the old king died on 23 April 1016, Edmund was recognized as king in both London and Wessex. He struggled for a while against Cnut but after his defeat at *Assandun*, a battle in which Godwine, ealdorman of Lindsey was killed, the two kings came to terms, and divided the kingdom. Mercia was conceded to Cnut and Edmund retained Wessex until his death later that year, on 30 November. Cnut was then accepted as king and at an assembly held in 1018 he agreed to uphold King Edgar's laws, implying a willingness to allow local assemblies a greater degree of freedom in regulating their own affairs. Such an 'imperial' policy was all the more appropriate after Cnut was also recognized as king in Denmark.

Cnut had some time earlier, perhaps during his father's campaign, married Ealdorman Ælfhelm's daughter, Ælfgifu. This alliance with one of the most important Mercian families, a family that Æthelred had done so much to harm, was a shrewd political move that ensured him significant support in his dealings with the Mercians, especially in the Five Boroughs. They had two sons, named Swein and Harald after Cnut's father and grandfather. In 1017 Cnut also married Æthelred's widow Emma. Churchmen, in particular the archbishop of Canterbury, considered this the only legitimate marriage and therefore supported the claims of their son Harthacnut. Cnut clearly considered all his sons legitimate. Harthacnut was associated in the government of Denmark from an early age, and succeeded his father there. In 1030 Swein was made king of Norway, under the tutelage of his mother, but the Norwegians drove him out, possibly even before Cnut's death. Harald remained in England and was, after some delay, accepted as Cnut's successor in England.

Cnut also completed the dramatic reduction of the Old English aristocracy that had begun in Æthelred's time. By the end of his reign almost all the families that had provided the tenth-century ealdormen had lost power. In their place Cnut promoted two earls of obscure background but whose descendants played a prominent role in subsequent politics.[37] One of them, Godwine, was English. His daughter married Edward the Confessor, his son became king in 1066 and three other sons were earls. The other of Cnut's creations, Siward, was a Dane who married the daughter of Uhtred of Bamburgh, the earl of Northumbria killed early in Cnut's reign. Their son, Waltheof, was made earl of Northumbria by William the Conqueror. The one leading family with roots in Æthelred's time was represented by Leofric who was made earl of Mercia by Cnut. His father had been one of Æthelred's ealdormen. Despite the efforts of Æthelred to weaken Ælfhelm's family, it remained very influential, especially in Mercia and the North, as events proved after Cnut's death. Its network of connections probably included Earl Leofric's family. The evidence, although falling short of proof, strongly suggests that Ælfgifu's cousin married the Morcar who was killed in 1015, and that their daughter married Earl Leofric's son Ælfgar.[38]

Some Scandinavians may have settled in Lincolnshire during Cnut's reign, but the only recent immigrant who can be identified among the shire's landowners on the eve of the Conquest, Ulf *Fenisc*, probably arrived after Cnut's death. His byname has been interpreted as meaning 'Fenman', but the Old English word for fen is *fenn*, with a double final consonant. The only satisfactory interpretation is that it described Ulf as coming from the Danish island of Fyn.[39] Such a description implies that he was a newcomer. The fact that in 1065 Ulf *Fenisc* ranked third in England among the lay landowners below the earls and that only three of Edward the Confessor's charters were attested by a thegn called Ulf, the earliest dated 1059, suggests that he arrived towards the end of Edward's reign.[40]

After Cnut's death in 1035 the succession was claimed by Harald, but Emma, supported by the archbishop of Canterbury and Earl Godwine, pressed the claim of Harthacnut. Harald was strongly backed in Mercia, not only by his mother but also by Earl Leofric, almost all the thegns north of the Thames and most of the fleet in London. To avert civil war the kingdom was divided but, as Harthacnut remained in Denmark, in 1037 Harald was recognized as full king, and consecrated. It was not until 1040, after Harald's death, that Harthacnut took up his inheritance in England, but he too had a short reign. When he died in 1042 the English chose Edward, Æthelred's only surviving son by Emma.

THE CREATION OF THE SHIRE

Cnut's conquest of England removed the need for the Five Boroughs as a defensive zone and the district was broken up into separate shires, each with its own assembly or court held in its main borough. Boroughs needed fairly frequent courts to regulate their internal affairs, in particular to settle trade disputes. Larger areas, shires, similarly needed courts but these met less frequently, two or three times a year, in the boroughs that served as the administrative centres. To judge by the scale of penalties in the Wantage Code, the borough courts mentioned in it were the equivalent of shire courts. Leicester had a court of this kind, and so too did Derby and Nottingham but they met together in Nottingham and the two shires continued to have a common sheriff until the sixteenth century. The association between Lincoln and Stamford was even closer; by 1066 they both belonged to one shire, with a court held in Lincoln. In 918 they had separate districts, for the people of Stamford submitted to Edward in that

Fig. 7.4 10th- to 11th-century Anglo-Scandinavian metalwork from Lincolnshire. While locally made, this material has Scandinavian affinities and uses Viking-style decorative motifs. The two objects on the left are stirrup mounts and on the right is a strap end decorated with animal interlace. The function of the mount (centre) is unknown. Photo by K. Leahy. Reproduced with permission.

year while those of Lincoln did not. But if numismatists are right in supposing that Stamford and Lincoln produced the same type of coins for Athelstan and his brothers, these boroughs may have been placed under the same royal agent after 927. It is therefore possible that the link between Lincoln and Stamford, like that between Derby and Nottingham, was already established in the time of Athelstan, and persisted after the break up of the Five Boroughs.

Domesday Book shows that by 1066 Kesteven, together with Holland, had been combined with Lindsey to form a single shire. This unification of Lindsey with the 'shire' of Stamford probably happened early in Cnut's reign when, as will be argued below, the area was reassessed in carucates. The change had not been made in 1016, for in that year the *Chronicle* reports the death of Godwine, ealdorman of Lindsey. The chronicler has, however, generated some confusion by referring to Lincolnshire in the same annal. This passage has been quoted above, where it was suggested that Cnut avoided Lindsey. The most likely explanation is that Lincolnshire had been formed when that section of the *Chronicle* was compiled, but not in 1016. Simon Keynes has shown that 'the main account of Æthelred's reign was written at one time, between 1016 and 1023'.[41] Kesteven was not, however, completely absorbed. Long after the Norman Conquest, business concerning it that was normally a matter for the shire court at Lincoln was occasionally dealt with in Kesteven. Lincolnshire was, in fact, inconveniently large and even Lindsey was divided into three ridings, each with its own court. These courts seem to have functioned much as shire courts and in the section of Domesday Book that deals with disputes there are many more references to the witness of the ridings than to that of the whole shire. Kesteven is itself once referred to, incongruously, as a riding and there are also some references to the 'men of Holland' as well as to its constituent wapentakes.[42]

Most of the routine business of the shire was done not in regional assemblies, whether of the whole shire, the ridings of Lindsey, Kesteven or Holland, but in the wapentakes. These were assemblies of free men drawn from smaller areas. The word was Scandinavian but the institution was not. Most of the 33 wapentakes in the Lincolnshire Domesday have English names, including Bolingbroke, Hill, and Horncastle in an area with a relatively large number of Scandinavian place-names; the sixteen that are Scandinavian in whole or part were presumably renamed, a process that continued after 1086 when the Domesday wapentakes Epworth and Wolmersty were given the Scandinavianized names Axholme and Skirbeck.[43] The Domesday wapentakes had roots in the distant past but they were not necessarily the same as they had always been. Some were later altered by division, combination or boundary changes and similar changes must have occurred earlier.

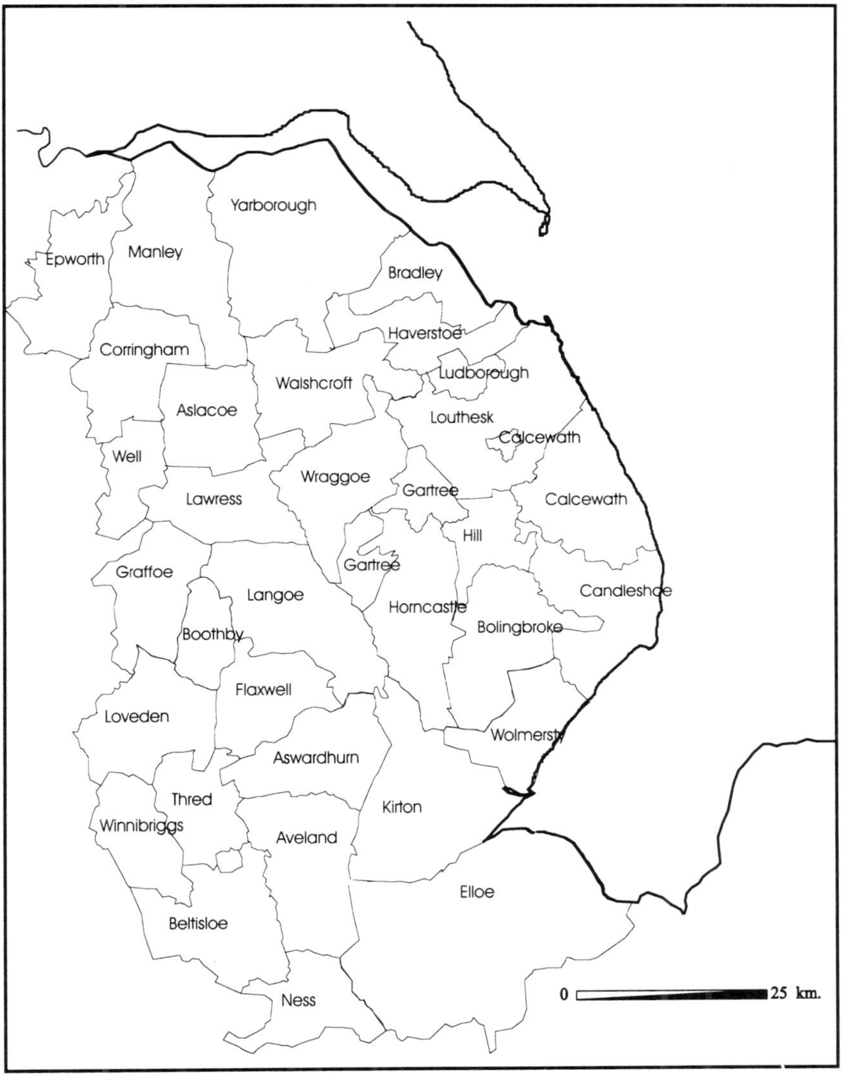

Fig. 7.5 Wapentakes in Lincolnshire.
Map prepared by and © A. Vince.

They were probably in origin assemblies of the freemen who belonged to the lordships or royal estates some of which survived as eleventh-century sokes. Several sokes are coextensive with a wapentake but some extended into several wapentakes. Sometimes, especially when several sokes overlapped in a wapentake, this may have been because sokes had been enlarged or wapentakes reorganized. It does, however, seem likely that some lordships were originally so large that they comprised several separate assemblies of freemen. These were not normally held in the vills that served as the centres of those estates, but at some convenient meeting place accessible from the whole area. Most Lincolnshire wapentakes are named after features that presumably marked the meeting places. Calcewath was a ford, Lovedon a hill, Louthesk and Aswardhurn refer to particular trees, an ash and a thorn, and several were named after hills or, perhaps, burial mounds: Aslacoe, Haverstoe, Candleshoe, Wraggoe, Beltisloe, Langoe, Threo. In the tenth century there was a tendency to bring wapentakes, and their equivalents in English England, the hundreds, under closer royal control and to link them more closely with royal vills.[44] This led to some renaming, but there is little trace of this in Lincolnshire; only three wapentakes are named after settlements: Corringham, Kirton, and Boothby, all royal estates in 1086 that were held by the earls before the Conquest.

The dues and services owed to the lords of sokes were rendered at the soke centres. It was in the wapentake assemblies that the freemen did their public business, one important part of which was to witness land transfers. In the disputes reported in the Lincolnshire Domesday it is normally the witness of the wapentakes that is recorded, occasionally with a riding or the whole shire concurring. There are, in fact, only nine references to the witness of the shire and eight of them concerned the king or the property of important churches (the archbishop of York, the bishops of Lincoln and Durham, and the abbeys of Peterborough and Westminster). The witness of wapentakes is recorded in many entries in the Lincolnshire Domesday concerning disputes over the ownership of, or rights over, land. Some record the witness of wapentakes to the purchase, exchange, gift, or pledging of land. These assemblies were involved not simply because their witness was a valuable guarantee, but also because the land was liable to pay dues and render service and it was important to know who was responsible. Many of these transactions were between members of the local community, but there were also gifts of land and of privileges by the king. In the tenth century such grants were normally the subject of charters that served as title deeds, but in the eleventh century simpler documents, called writs, authenticated by the king's seal, began to be used, and became very popular. They were in the vernacular and were addressed to the ealdorman, bishop, and thegns of the relevant shire or shires. No pre-Conquest writ addressed specifically to the shire of Lincoln has been preserved, but one that certainly concerned Lincolnshire and must have been displayed in its court is Edward the Confessor's announcement following the appointment of Ealdred as archbishop of York in 1061: 'King Edward sends friendly greetings to my bishops and my earls and all my thegns in the shires in which Archbishop Ealdred has land. And I inform you that my will is that he be entitled to his sake and his soke, over his lands and over all his men, to toll and to team, within town and without.'[45] Royal grants could also be declared orally by royal agents. Both processes are mentioned in Domesday Book in entries that show that although writs were formally addressed to the shire they could be received by the courts of the ridings. That is implied by several entries in Domesday Book, for example: 'In Willoughby in the Marsh hundred the bishop of Durham claims the land of Alnot the priest against Gilbert of Ghent; and the men of the riding say that they never saw the bishop's predecessor seized of it, either by writ or deputy; and they testify in Gilbert's favour.'[46]

RIDINGS, HUNDREDS, AND CARUCATES

Apart from the preservation of order, the most important functions of royal government concerned the collection of renders and services due to the king, in particular the raising of the military forces needed for defence.[47] In the ninth century, in Lincolnshire as in most other parts of England, these obligations were levied on the basis of assessments in terms of hides, but by 1066 throughout the district of the Five Boroughs and Yorkshire the units of assessment had been changed to *carucata* and *bovata*, Latin translations of words introduced by the Danes, *plogesland*, 'ploughland', and its eighth part, an 'oxgang'. Post-Conquest evidence from other parts of England, including Domesday Book, suggests that although many different fractions of hides did occur their normal subdivisions were halves and quarters, the latter called *virgata* in Latin. There are no pre-Conquest references to carucates or bovates in Lincolnshire but late tenth-century texts from Peterborough and York show that although hides were still the normal units at that date, oxgang had begun to be used as a subdivision, yet another example of Scandinavian linguistic influence. In the Peterborough text the word oxgang occurs once along with several references to hides and acres.[48] The York text, a charter dated 963 granting land at Sherburn, describes it in terms of whole and half hides as well as pairs of oxgangs, the latter apparently representing virgates.[49]

The carucates and bovates of the Lincolnshire Domesday were, however, not simply the old assessment in hides translated into Danish terms; their regularity and artificiality shows that they were the result of a complete reassessment. The new arrangements can be seen most clearly in Lindsey, thanks to the Lindsey Survey of about 1115 which shows that the non-royal land in Lindsey was assessed at 1800 carucates, equally divided between the three ridings. Each riding seems originally to have had six wapentakes, although these were of unequal size, ranging from Yarborough with 168 carucates, to Ludborough with 36. To make up the six in the North Riding, Gartree and Bolingbroke wapentakes were included in it, although geographically they lay within the South Riding. The contrast between the equality of the ridings (achieved by such extraordinary means) and the inequality of the wapentakes implies that the latter already existed when the assessment was distributed, while the ridings were probably newly created; if not, they must have been greatly modified as a result of the reassessment.

The assessment was distributed in units of twelve carucates, called hundreds, 50 in each riding.[50] There is nothing like the Lindsey Survey to provide clues to the way in which the new assessments were distributed in Kesteven and Holland. In particular, it is difficult to determine what land was not assessed because it was royal. It does, however, seem likely that the total number of carucates assigned to Kesteven and Holland was 1800, the same as Lindsey. These were similarly distributed in twelve-carucate hundreds and there were therefore 150 of them in each half of the shire. Domesday Book does not systematically record the hundreds, but it does name 98 of them, and others are mentioned in later texts. Some were identical with manors assessed at twelve carucates and a few manors were reckoned as double hundreds, but most hundreds comprised components in different settlements. Some of these scattered hundreds can be reconstructed, but that is rarely possible.

There is no doubt that the organization of hundreds and ridings was closely linked with the imposition of the new assessment in carucates. The total was not the result of adding together the assessments of the component parts, it was rather the reverse; the process began at the top with the allocation of 1800 carucates to Lindsey and the same to Kesteven and Holland. These were then distributed among the existing wapentakes. In Lindsey each riding was allocated the same amount, 600 carucates, and there were, therefore, by definition 50 twelve-carucate hundreds in each riding. It is likely that each wapentake was originally given a round number of hundreds; according to the Lindsey Survey only five wapentakes had fractions of hundreds. The hundreds were consequently formed as territorial units in the process of distributing the assessment of each wapentake. Representatives from the resulting hundreds were probably involved in the final stage, when the assessment of each piece of property was determined.

Whatever role the hundreds had in the original reassessment, there is no doubt that they continued to have some function, probably connected with the collection of the geld and the rendering of other services or dues that were based on the same assessment. Domesday Book proves that they could give testimony and hundreds occasionally attested documents as corporate groups. That some still had corporate functions in the early thirteenth-century is demonstrated by a document recording an agreement between two double hundreds in Holland concerning the boundary of the marsh between them.[51]

It is not known when the reassessment in carucates was made. Various dates in the tenth century have been suggested. The most extreme is the claim that the Danes were responsible, and that hides were reintroduced by the English in some areas.[52] One of the many objections to this was put very bluntly by Jolliffe when he remarked that 'the carucate has never been nearer Denmark than 400 miles'.[53] Edgar's charter of 963 describes Sherburn in Yorkshire in terms of hides, and shortly after the year 1000 Wulfric Spot bequeathed hides of land in areas that were carucated sixty years later. The date of the change is narrowed by surveys compiled in Cnut's reign describing some Yorkshire estates in terms of ploughlands and bovates, implying that the reassessment had happened by then. It has been objected that hides continued to be used to describe units of property long after ploughs had been adopted as the basis of taxation assessments, but I am not aware of any evidence for this.[54] The reassessment was probably made necessary by the *heregeld*, an annual tax introduced in 1012 to pay a mercenary fleet, but Cnut, as a conqueror, was better placed to enforce such a major change than Æthelred in the last years of his reign. It may well have been accomplished in connection with the exceptionally heavy tax levied by Cnut in 1018, as suggested by Stenton in 1910.[55]

EARLS AND SHERIFFS

This reassessment was a crucially important stage in the extension of royal authority in Lincolnshire, a development that deprived the aristocracy of the shire of the freedom to make their own laws that they had enjoyed in the tenth century. Until the middle of the eleventh century the maintenance of royal authority in Lincolnshire was the responsibility of the Mercian ealdormen, or earls as they began to be called under Cnut, except for a short period at the end of Æthelred's reign when Lindsey had its own ealdorman, Godwine, the first royal official in the shire whose name is known. Godwine was a common name and it is therefore not possible to be certain that he was the thegn who witnessed numerous charters of Æthelred between 996 and 1014, although that is likely.[56] Godwine, who was killed in the battle of *Assandun* in 1016, may have been promoted by Edmund after his seizure of the Five Boroughs in 1015.

It is uncertain what arrangements Cnut made to govern Mercia before Leofric was made earl in 1032, a position he retained until his death in 1057.[57] Lincolnshire was presumably in his earldom although the only evidence for his interest in the shire is his benefaction to Stow Minster in 1054. He was succeeded by his son Ælfgar, who last appeared as earl in 1062; he probably died soon after that date. It is likely that he was succeeded by his son Edwin but there are indications that Tostig, who had been made earl of Northumbria in 1055, also acted as earl in Lindsey. According to Domesday Book he had the comital estate of Kirton in Lindsey before Edwin, who held it in 1066, and in the rebellion against him in 1065 his men in Lincoln as well as in York were killed.[58] It is possible that Tostig extended his authority south of the Humber when Ælfgar was temporarily banished in 1058.

The rebellion against Tostig succeeded. He was driven into exile and Ælfgar's other son, Morcar, was made earl of Northumbria. It is curious that although Domesday Book records him as an important landowner in Yorkshire, he is never described as earl in that county, while Edwin, who held a number of major royal estates there, is frequently called earl in the Yorkshire Domesday. What is more, Morcar was entitled to the earl's third penny from Torksey, which shows that he must have acted as earl in Lindsey. The succession to the Mercian and Northumbrian earldoms was, therefore, rather more complicated than has generally been realized. Edwin and Morcar seem in fact to have been jointly earls of both Mercia and Northumbria. This is also implied by the best, contemporary, version of the *Chronicle* which refers to the large force that 'Earl Edwin and Earl Morcar assembled from their earldom' (in the singular) in 1066. Earlier in that year they together repelled an attack on Lindsey by Tostig. They are also referred to jointly in the Yorkshire Domesday, and one entry in the Cheshire Domesday refers to 'the reeves of the Earls Edwin and Morcar'.[59] They were sons of Ælfgar but apparently had different mothers; the references in Domesday Book and elsewhere to the mother of Morcar, but not to the mother of Edwin, suggests that they were half-brothers.[60] Morcar's mother was almost certainly the daughter of the Morcar, chief thegn of the Seven Boroughs, who was killed in 1015. As sons of Ælfgar they inherited estates in most parts of Mercia but it was Morcar's family connections in the Five Boroughs that made him a natural choice to succeed Tostig in the northern Danelaw.

Earls held official estates and enjoyed great privileges, including the right to a third of many royal revenues. They necessarily depended on subordinate agents to whom many duties were delegated. The most important were the sheriffs, most of whom were probably local magnates. The only pre-Conquest sheriff of Lincolnshire who can be identified is Merleswein, who held that office immediately before and after the Conquest. He not only had an Anglo-Scandinavian name, he was also an important landowner in both Lincolnshire and Yorkshire.[61] The sheriff presided over the shire court in the absence of the earl, and probably reviewed the operation of the tithing system in the eleventh century as he did in the twelfth. Sheriffs had a great range of other duties which they performed with the help of subordinate officials. They were responsible for raising military levies when necessary, controlling the mint, collecting taxes, and they also exacted legal penalties, for example by confiscating property that was forfeit.

The submission of Stamford to King Edward in 918 was the first stage in the absorption of Lincolnshire in a united English kingdom. It was, however, not until 942 that both Kesteven and Lindsey were permanently incorporated in the kingdom, and royal authority remained relatively weak in that area for many years. This was partly because Lincolnshire was for much of the time a backwater, remote from the centres of power. The local Anglo-Danish aristocracy was firmly entrenched and did not readily make way for newcomers. Its links were with Northumbria and the areas of Danish settlement in Leicestershire and Nottinghamshire, not with the heart of Mercia or Wessex. Apart from short periods when the see of Lindsey was revived, the church was supervised by a bishop whose see, and main estates, were in Oxfordshire. The monastic reformation, that was made possible by, and at the same time enhanced, the power of kings, did not much affect Lincolnshire; the great abbeys of the Fens, even Crowland, had little property north of the Welland. This was however a period of remarkable economic growth in that part of England, reflected most obviously in the development of Lincoln into one of England's greatest cities. There were many other signs of economic vitality, in the countryside and along the coast as well as in the smaller towns.

By the middle of the eleventh century, however, royal government was felt in many ways throughout the shire. Most people contributed to the geld and all adult males were supposed to be in tithings and many were expected to perform military service. Royal officials supervised a hierarchy of courts, from wapentakes to the shire, in which land transactions were publicly witnessed, and accusations of crime were made and judged. It was in the towns that royal government can be most clearly seen in action, in the mints, the markets, and in meetings of the shire court. The organization of these towns will best be considered separately in connection with their role in the economy of the shire. First some attention must be given to another key factor in the growth of government and the increasingly effective royal control, the church.

NOTES TO CHAPTER VII

1 The campaigns mentioned in this chapter are mapped in Hill, D. 1981, pp. 56–60, 65–71 and in Hooper and Bennet 1996, pp. 26–30, 36–9.

2 Thacker 1992, pp. 203–6, 209.

3 Smyth 1975, pp. 102–7, argues that Ragnald was recognized as king in York soon after the battle of Tettenhall. Reasons for rejecting this claim are given by Blunt, Stewart and Lyon 1989, p. 6 n. 4 (quoting Dorothy Whitelock), and pp. 98–9, 265.

4 Blunt, Stewart, and Lyon 1989, p. 105.

5 Blunt, Stewart, and Lyon 1989, pp. 103–5.

6 S 396, trans. *EHD* I, no. 103, pp. 546–7, S 97.

7 *Liber Eliensis* ii.25, ed. Blake, pp. 98–9.

8 Smyth 1975, p. 109.

9 Stewart 1967; Stewart 1982; Blunt, Stewart, and Lyon 1989, pp. 106–7.

10 Chadwick 1905, pp. 184–6; Stenton 1971, p. 351.

11 Blunt 1974, summarized with additions and corrections in Blunt, Stewart and Lyon 1989, pp. 108–13.

12 Blunt 1974, pp. 90–1.

13 Wood, M. 1980.

14 S 392.

15 Smyth 1979, pp. 90–1.

16 Blunt, Stewart and Lyon 1989, pp. 216–19.

17 For this interpretation of events in Northumbria in Eadred's reign, see Sawyer 1995.

18 Blunt, Stewart, and Lyon 1989, pp. 256–7.

19 Blunt, Stewart, and Lyon 1989, pp. 191–4, 198.

20 Blunt, Stewart, and Lyon 1989, pp. 278–80.

21 IV Edgar, 2, 12, text and trans. Robertson 1925, pp. 28–39, trans. *EHD* I, no. 41, pp. 434–7.

22 Blunt, Stewart and Lyon 1989, p. 285.

23 Jonsson 1987a, Caistor: pp. 125–6, Horncastle: p. 138, Lincoln pp. 142–4, Louth: pp. 146–7, Stamford: pp. 164–6. For Grantham, Jonsson 1987b, see Fig. 9.8a.

24 Loyn 1984 is a good general account of pre-Conquest government.

25 *EHD* I, no. 4, p. 283.

26 S 520, 679. He also witnessed S 550 and 552a in the company of several *duces* with Scandinavian names.

27 See below p. 140.

28 IV Edgar, see note 21 above.

29 Morris, W. 1910; Pollock and Maitland 1898 i, pp. 568–71.

30 William of Malmesbury, *Gesta Regum*, II. 4, ed. Stubbs.

31 Keynes 1980, pp. 205–6; Hugh Candidus, pp. 69–70; Robertson 1939, no. 40, pp. 74–83. For Frithegyst see Appendix 7.

32 Whitelock 1959, pp. 80–1.

33 See above, pp. 4, 123.

34 Blom 1960, col. 309.

35 Wormald 1978, pp. 61–2.

36 Stafford 1978, p. 36.

37 Keynes 1994a.

38 Sawyer 1979, pp. xlii–xliii.

39 Sawyer 1994, p. 22.

40 Clarke 1994, pp. 34–5, 352–4; S 1028, 1029, KCD no. 815.

41 Keynes 1978, p. 231. He does, though, think that 1016–17 would be the most likely date, n. 19 on p. 245.

42 DB i. 376b, 377b = *LD* 72/1, 73/3, 4, 6.

43 Fellows-Jensen 1978, pp. 342–4.

44 Cam 1932.

45 S 1159.

46 DB i. 375a = *LD* 69/19.

47 Assessments, ridings, and hundreds are discussed by Roffe 1992, especially pp. 32–42. On some points we reach different conclusions.

48 Robertson 1939, no. 40.

49 S 712.

50 The hundreds of Lincolnshire were very different from the hundreds of Wessex and English Mercia which were the equivalent of wapentakes.

51 Stenton 1927, pp. lxviii–lxix.

52 Hart 1992, chapter 10.

53 Jolliffe 1934, p. 21.

54 Phythian-Adams 1978, p. 20, claims that the *cassati* of S 1014 dated 1046 concerning Rutland were hides. The use of that word was, rather, due to conservatism. Cnut's charter of 1033, S 968, equates *cassati* with ploughlands. The suggestion that 'carucates' only described the arable is unacceptable, cf. Stenton 1927, no. 163

55 Stenton 1910, p. 90.

56 S 935, dated 1016, witnessed by Godwine is spurious.

57 Keynes 1994a, pp. 77–8.

58 In Nottinghamshire Tostig is named as the pre-Conquest tenant of sokeland of Kirton in Misson, DB i. 281b, cf. 293a; *Vita Ædwardi Regis*, ed. Barlow, p. 51.

59 DB i. 264b.

60 DB ii. 286b; Sawyer 1979, p. xlvi.

61 He also held land in Somerset, Devon and Cornwall, Clarke 1994, pp. 322–4.

CHAPTER VIII

THE CHURCH IN THE TENTH AND ELEVENTH CENTURIES

The Danes who conquered and settled in Lincolnshire were pagans but they soon recognized the truth or at least the advantages of Christianity. Their leaders, like those in East Anglia and Northumbria, were probably converted before the end of the ninth century and by the beginning of the tenth most of the Danish settlers were as Christian as their English predecessors had ever been.[1] It is true that early in the eleventh century Wulfstan, archbishop of York, expressed concern about the prevalence of pagan rituals. He prescribed penalties for anyone who 'carries on any heathen practice, either by sacrifice or divination, or practises witchcraft by any means or worship of idols', and ordered the punishment of anyone responsible for making on his land 'a sanctuary round a stone or a tree or a well or any such nonsense'.[2] A set of decrees, probably issued by a northern synod, and certainly composed by Wulfstan, is more explicit. One clause orders priests to 'entirely extinguish every heathen practice; and forbid worship of wells, and necromancy, and auguries and incantations, and worship of trees and worship of stones, and that devil's craft which is performed when children are drawn through the earth, and the nonsense which is performed on New Year's day in various kinds of sorcery, and in heathen sanctuaries and elder trees, and in many various delusions in which men carry on much that they should not'.[3] Such heathen habits cannot be blamed on the Scandinavian immigrants; throughout Europe, and long after this period, churchmen complained about similar non-Christian practices and superstitions.[4]

The Viking raids and conquest had, however, caused great changes in the institutions and organization of the church in Lincolnshire. None of the abbeys and nunneries founded before the early ninth century survived, there were no longer bishops of Lindsey, and the bishopric of Leicester had been removed to Dorchester on the river Thames near Oxford. Despite the disruption of the dioceses, episcopal authority was maintained by the archbishops of York who assumed responsibility for the parts of Mercia conquered by the Danes. It must have been largely thanks to them that many churches in both Lindsey and Kesteven continued to function much as they had done before the ninth-century turmoil.

ANCIENT SHRINES AND MONASTIC REVIVAL: CROWLAND

Although the early religious communities had disappeared, some of the shrines they had housed were still remembered in the tenth century as holy places. In 909 an English army took the relics of St Oswald from Bardney.[5] This suggests that the shrine survived, although it had presumably been stripped of the gold, silver, and jewels that Offa and others had given it. Similarly, in the 970s a party from the newly established abbey of Thorney in Cambridgeshire raided Louth to seize the body of St Herefrith.[6]

There is no evidence that Partney or Threekingham were known to have relics of saints in the tenth century; those of St Werburga were removed from Threekingham to Hanbury in Staffordshire soon after her death. It is, however, significant that Partney and Threekingham (as well as Louth) were among the seven places in which the Lincolnshire Domesday records the existence of markets.[7] This implies that long after these monasteries had disappeared their sites continued to be locally important as places where people gathered from time to time to buy and sell, an activity that had earlier been closely linked to the festivals celebrated in those religious communities.

Only one of Lincolnshire's early shrines, Crowland, was revived as a monastery before the Norman Conquest, but the fact that several of the religious houses founded after 1066 were on the sites of early monasteries, suggests that the spiritual significance of those places was still remembered. At Bardney this was thanks to Bede who was explicitly acknowledged as the authority for the early importance of the place by Gilbert of Ghent when he founded a Benedictine priory there in 1087.[8] Bede, who provides the only evidence for the existence of a monastery at Partney, is likely also to have been responsible for its choice as the site of a hospital in 1115. Knowledge of some other early religious houses is more likely to have depended on local tradition. An Augustinian house was founded at South Kyme before 1169, a cell of Bridlington Priory was founded at Edenham by Walter of Ghent soon after 1100, and the Gilbertine priory of Tunstall, founded before 1164 may have owed its location to its proximity to Hibaldstow, which was itself acquired by Peterborough after the Norman Conquest.[9]

The only monastery in Lincolnshire on the eve of the Norman Conquest, Crowland, was the northernmost of a group of Fenland houses that were revived or refounded in the reign of King Edgar. The monasteries that survived the ninth-century Viking invasions, most of them in southern England or western Mercia, were thought by some leading churchmen to be too worldly. This view was already expressed in King Alfred's reign by his biographer, Bishop Asser, who complained that 'although there still remain many monasteries founded in that land, but none properly observing the rule of this way of life'.[10] Existing communities with their

Fig. 8.1 Fragments of two late 10th-century grave covers in the wall of the tower of Aisthorpe church. Photo P. Everson and D. A. Stocker. © Department of Archaeology, Durham University.

well-established traditions and close links with local aristocracies were unlikely to reform themselves; external pressure was needed, and that was best exerted by kings. Royal support was also required to protect the endowment of newly established monasteries. Kings had been taught that their power depended on divine favour and since the seventh century they had patronized religious communities in which prayers were regularly offered on their behalf, but in the tenth century proponents of reform encouraged them to believe that only the intercession of monks who lived a regular life were of any value. Both Edmund and his brother Eadred regarded the new ideas favourably, but it was Edmund's young son Edgar who took them up with enthusiasm. He promoted three of the leading monastic reformers to important bishoprics. Dunstan who, as abbot of Glastonbury, had trained many of the men who later developed the reform movement, was made archbishop of Canterbury, Æthelwold, later remembered as 'the father of the monks', was chosen as bishop of Winchester, and Oswald, considered to be the third leader of the movement, was chosen first as bishop of Worcester and later archbishop of York. Supported by Edgar, these men reformed some old communities and founded new ones, often on the sites of earlier monasteries. Several of the most important were in the Fenland, immediately south of Lincolnshire; between 969 and 973 Ely, Peterborough, and Thorney were refounded by Æthelwold, and Ramsey by Oswald.[11]

There is no doubt that Edgar encouraged monastic reform for genuine religious motives but there were also worldly considerations. Monastic communities dependent on royal patronage were centres from which royal influence could be disseminated. This function was especially important in districts recovered from the Danes, and the area dominated by the Fenland houses founded by Æthelwold and Oswald formed, in effect, a barrier between two areas of Danish colonization in East Mercia and East Anglia. Æthelwold tried to extend the influence of Peterborough in Lincolnshire by endowing it with the site of the seventh-century monastery of Barrow, which he obtained from King Edgar in 971.[12] The imposing stone church of St Peter in Barton-on-Humber, in the Barrow estate, was presumably built when it was owned by the abbey.[13] Peterborough lost Barrow in or soon after 1014 and in 1066 Barrow itself was held by Earl Morcar and Barton by Ulf *Fenisc*.[14] This loss, which was later explained as a confiscation following the abbey's failure to pay geld, is a reminder that even major monasteries could lose land in the early eleventh century and that Domesday Book may give a misleading impression of their original endowments. There is, however, no reason to believe that any monastery acquired much land north of the Welland in the 100 years before 1066.[15] At that date neither Ely nor Thorney had any, Crowland and Ramsey had five and three manors respectively, and each lost one in the aftermath of the Conquest. The largest monastic estate before the Conquest was Peterborough's. It had six manors with a total assessment of 40 carucates. Only one of these manors, Fiskerton, was in Lindsey. All the Fenland abbeys, except Ely, claimed that they had lost land in Lincolnshire before the Conquest but, apart from Barrow, these losses did not amount to much even if all the claims were sound. There was, clearly, little enthusiasm for monasticism in pre-Conquest Lincolnshire. Few of the donors who can be identified were closely connected with the shire and most of the donations that can be dated were made in the eleventh century, many of them after 1040.

Crowland was in many respects very different from its Fenland neighbours.[16] Thurketel, who founded or revived the monastery, had been a member of (or was in confraternity with) St Paul's in London, a college of secular canons, which suggests that he was not an enthusiastic supporter of monastic reform. The abbey seems to have been an old-fashioned community with little influence in the church at large; there is, at least, no evidence that any Crowland monk was chosen as a bishop before the Norman Conquest. Its early history is bedevilled by the efforts made in the twelfth century to make good the losses sustained in a fire in 1091 which destroyed the monastery. At least 15 charters were forged after that disaster to provide documentary evidence for its privileges and possessions. Many of these charters were later included in a fantastic history of the abbey attributed to Ingulf, who was abbot at the time of the fire. At least two of these spurious charters, supposedly grants by Æthelbald and Edgar, were apparently seen by Orderic Vitalis when he spent five weeks at Crowland in the early twelfth century, probably in 1114 when the rebuilt church was consecrated. During his stay he 'abbreviated and clarified' the *Life of Guthlac* by Felix and added an account of Crowland's history after Guthlac's death, which he included in his *Ecclesiastical History*. The senior members of the community, who were Orderic's main source of information, believed that from Guthlac's time the island of Crowland had never been without monks despite the depredations of the Vikings, and that its revival began with King Eadred's grant of the abbey to Thurketel, described as a wealthy clerk, and kinsman of both the king and Archbishop Osketel.

This dated the revival of Crowland at least 30 years too early, for in 971 Thurketel was abbot of Bedford. One version of the *Chronicle* reports that when Archbishop Osketel died at Thame in 971, his kinsman, Thurketel conveyed the body for burial in Bedford, explaining that Thurketel 'was abbot there at that time', implying that he was no longer abbot when the annal was written, which Dorothy Whitelock judged to be 'probably in 978 at the latest'. The revival of Crowland can, therefore, be dated between 971 and Thurketel's death, which the *Liber Eliensis* implies was before Bishop Æthelwold's in 984.[17] Orderic listed six estates that Thurketel gave to Crowland from his patrimony: Wellingborough, Wothorpe, and Elmington in Northamptonshire, Beeby in Leicestershire and Oakington and Cottenham in Cambridgeshire. For one of them, Beeby, there is independent evidence in the *Liber Eliensis* to the effect that it was bequeathed by Archbishop Osketel (who died in 971) to Bishop Æthelwold who granted it to Thurketel in exchange for land in Cambridgeshire. The location of these estates suggests that Thurketel did not belong to a family based in Lincolnshire.

The earliest evidence for the benefactors of Crowland is provided by the *Guthlac Roll*, an illuminated history of the abbey made in the twelfth century. One of the drawings shows thirteen donors pressing their gifts on the saint (Fig. 8.2). The artist tried to arrange them in chronological order with King Æthelbald in front closely followed by Thurketel, and with the post-Conquest donors at the back. Thurketel's own gifts to the abbey named in this picture are the same as those noted by Orderic. The roll suggests that most of Crowland's small Lincolnshire property was given in the eleventh century, not the tenth. It is noteworthy that, with the exception

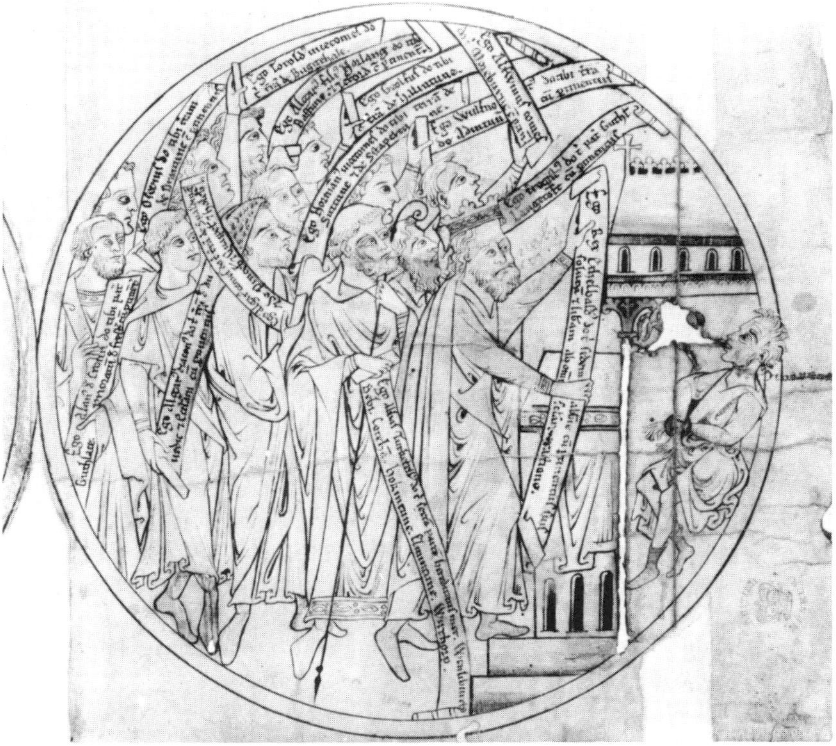

Fig. 8.2 The benefactors of Crowland Abbey in the Guthlac Roll, British Library, MS Harley Y 6. Reproduced with permission of the British Library.

of Thurketel, none of the pre-Conquest benefactors of Crowland had a Scandinavian name. In the eleventh and early twelfth centuries Crowland's links were with Bernicia. Earl Waltheof was a benefactor and was buried there, and in about 1126 one of his kinsmen, a Crowland monk with the same name, was elected abbot.[18]

BISHOPS AND THEIR CHANGING DIOCESES

Episcopal authority weathered the Viking storm better than the monasteries. The disappearance of the bishopric of Lindsey and the removal of the bishopric of Leicester to Dorchester meant that the Christians of Lincolnshire had to rely on the archbishop of York for the ordination of priests, the consecration of churches, and other episcopal functions. This period of Danish rule therefore gave the archbishops of York an opportunity to extend their authority, not only over Lindsey, which had once belonged to their see, but also over parts of the sees of Leicester and Lichfield that were under Danish lordship. The submission of Stamford in 918 enabled the bishop of Dorchester to extend his diocese and, in effect, recover an area that had been the responsibility of his predecessor at Leicester. The archbishops of York were, however, reluctant to abandon their claim to Lindsey. It remained part of their diocese, certainly until 927, when Athelstan was acknowledged as king in York, and probably until Archbishop Wulfstan was imprisoned in 950 or 951.

It is possible that the see of Lindsey was revived during the period of Danish domination.[19] There is no direct evidence for this but charters of Athelstan after he was acknowledged as king in Northumbria are witnessed by otherwise unknown bishops, at least some of whom were apparently from the northern province. Between 929 and 934 Wigred of Chester-le-Street appears towards the end of the episcopal subscriptions in eight charters, all but one of which were also witnessed by the archbishop of York.[20] In these charters nine bishops who are not named in any episcopal lists appear among the last episcopal subscriptions, most of them immediately above or below Wigred. As Dorothy Whitelock remarked, 'They may have been assistant bishops only, but it seems possible that an attempt was made to revive more sees in Northumbria at this time.'[21] If so, it is very likely that one or more of these nine bishops occupied the see of Lindsey.

The first bishop of Lindsey who can be identified with any confidence in the tenth century is Leofwine, whose first charter subscription was in 953. When he was made bishop of Dorchester in 971 his two dioceses were united. This promotion shows that he was considered trustworthy by the English royal government, which is consistent with the assumption that he was appointed by Eadred after Archbishop Wulfstan's imprisonment to strengthen English royal authority south of the Humber.

Wulfstan was released by 953. It is unlikely that he was allowed to return to Northumbria, although he attests as archbishop immediately after the archbishop of Canterbury in one charter of 953 (S 900) and several in 955; there are no charters for 954. We know that the expulsion and death of Erik Bloodaxe marked the end of Northumbrian independence, but contemporaries did not; Eadred had good reason to fear that Wulfstan might once again oppose him. It is likely that Wulfstan regained episcopal authority in the diocese of Dorchester, alongside Osketel, who had been bishop of that see since 950 at the latest. After Eadred regained control of Northumbria in 954 (or 952) Osketel was given responsibility for the York diocese, although he was not consecrated archbishop until 959, three years after Wulfstan's death and shortly before the kingdom was reunited under Edgar. Osketel's Danish ancestry may well have made him more acceptable to the Anglo-Danish aristocracy of Northumbria than a West

Saxon or Mercian bishop would have been. Dorothy Whitelock drew attention to the curious fact that as long as Archbishop Wulfstan was alive, Osketel and Leofwine do not appear together as witnesses.[22] It may be that when one of them attended a royal council in southern England, the other remained in the Humber region to guard against, and give early warning of, any trouble.

In 956 Osketel, as bishop of Dorchester, was given Southwell and its extensive sokeland.[23] This not only restored another part of the former diocese of Leicester that had fallen under the control of York, it also provided Osketel with a conveniently located base for his activity in the York diocese. Two years later Edgar granted him another estate near the boundary of Northumbria, at Sutton near Retford, which had probably also originally been in Leicester diocese.[24] When he became archbishop he retained both Southwell and Sutton, which were thereafter treated as belonging to the archbishopric. This was presumably a factor in the extension of the diocese of York to include the whole of Nottinghamshire, in which the archbishopric had two other extensive sokes in 1066. The incorporation of Lindsey in the diocese of Dorchester when Leofwine was promoted to that see in 971 after Osketel's death was some compensation for the loss of Nottinghamshire.

Dorchester was a huge diocese. The bishop, whose cathedral was well over a hundred miles from Lincoln, cannot have had much effective authority in either Kesteven or Lindsey. His main demesne estates were in Oxfordshire and Buckinghamshire, and Wulfwig, the last bishop before the Norman Conquest, had no demesne manors in Kesteven, although he did lease land in Drayton in Holland (between Bicker and Swineshead, the centre of a very important soke) from Ramsey Abbey.[25] This was a source of weakness for royal as well as ecclesiastical government. Bishops were royal councillors, transmitting and enforcing royal authority alongside secular agents; in the eleventh century bishops and ealdormen presided jointly over shire courts. It is, therefore, not surprising that when the Humber region's defences proved ineffective in 993 the bishopric of Lindsey was once again revived, in effect as the ecclesiastical counterpart of the district of the Five Boroughs.[26] Indeed, it has been suggested that Sigeferth, bishop of Lindsey, was responsible for drafting the law code promulgated at Wantage for the Five Boroughs.[27] Lindsey did not survive as a separate see after the break-up of that district. The last subscription of a Lindsey bishop was in 1011.

It is not known when Lindsey was reincorporated in the diocese of Dorchester. This certainly happened before the death of Cnut. It was in his reign that Æthelric, bishop of Dorchester (1016–34) received food rent from Stow minster. His successor, Eadnoth II, also did so, and the right of the bishop of Dorchester to this render was confirmed when Earl Leofric and Godgifu enriched Stow in 1054.[28] Stow then became an important outpost for the Dorchester bishops. The bishops of Dorchester must also have taken over the cathedral in Lincoln, and Wulfwig obtained another base in Lindsey by obtaining Louth for the bishopric at the cost of £160.[29] His active interest in Lindsey was in part a reaction to the persistence of the archbishops of York in claiming that it belonged to their see. On 3 May 1061 Pope Nicholas II ruled in favour of the bishopric of Dorchester in response to a complaint by Wulfwig that Ælfric, archbishop of York (1023–51), had invaded the diocese of Lindsey in general and the church of Stow specifically.[30] Wulfwig, who became bishop of Dorchester in 1053, must have made his complaint in the time of Ælfric's successor, Cynesige, or possibly, assuming an unusually rapid process in Rome, after Cynesige's death on 22 December 1060. Wulfwig's appeal shows that he considered York's claim to be a serious threat to his rights in Lindsey, and in particular concerning Stow minster. He may have judged it politic to lay the blame on a previous archbishop.

The enrichment of Stow by Leofric and Godgifu in 1054 and the confirmation on the same occasion that it was under the authority of the bishop of Dorchester was obviously an attempt to counter the archbishops'

Fig. 8.3 Stow: St Mary's Church.
View from the south-east.
Photo and © P. Dixon.

claim. Cynesige consented to the arrangement and declaration made in 1054, although he claimed a special relationship with Stow by giving it a bell, as he also did to Beverley and Southwell, that were unquestionably archiepiscopal minsters.[31] Despite the decision of Pope Nicholas, the question of Lindsey's ecclesiastical affiliation remained uncertain. After Remigius had been appointed bishop of Dorchester, but before the see was removed to Lincoln, William I accepted that Stow was his legitimate concern, but nevertheless treated Thomas, who was consecrated archbishop of York on 25 December 1070, as the episcopal authority in Nottinghamshire and Lincolnshire.[32] It was not until 1072 that it was decided, in the Council of Winchester, that the province of York was bounded on the south by the Humber. That was, however, not the end of the dispute, which was not settled until 1093 when the archbishopric's claims were finally 'redeemed' by King William II. According to the York historian, Hugh the Chanter, the king paid the archbishop £3000. Dorothy Owen has suggested that the area disputed between the archbishops of York and the bishops of Dorchester/Lincoln was the West Riding of Lindsey, which became a separate archdeaconry in the twelfth century.[33] Contemporary evidence, however, makes it clear that the dispute concerned the whole of Lindsey. In the charter in which William II declares that he has bought out York's claim, that claim is explicitly said to have been 'upon Lincoln and upon Lindsey and upon the manors of Stow and Louth'.[34]

The archbishop of York not only claimed ecclesiastical authority in Lindsey, in 1086 he also had a large amount of property in all parts of Lincolnshire, as he did in Yorkshire. Elsewhere in England south of the Humber he had very little. Two manors in Kesteven and one in Lindsey were post-Conquest acquisitions.[35] It is possible that Archbishop Thomas had obtained other manors to strengthen his claims south of the Humber, but in the absence of any evidence to that effect we cannot rule out the possibility that some of his property in Lincolnshire had been held by his pre-Conquest predecessors. It is most improbable that the pre-Conquest tenants of all the archbishop's manors who are named in Domesday Book were independent landowners with full rights of disposal. Some are more likely to have been tenants of Archbishop Ealdred. Nothing is known about how or when the archbishop(s) obtained most of their Lincolnshire property; much of it may well have been acquired when the area was under their ecclesiastical authority in the late ninth and early tenth centuries.[36] The large Lincolnshire fief of the bishop of Durham in 1086 poses a similar problem. There is no evidence about its acquisition in Durham sources. Neither the bishop nor the community of St Cuthbert is named as the pre-Conquest tenant of any manor, but that may only mean that they held none in demesne in 1066. The fact that one manor is called Biscathorpe,

'Bishop's thorp', implies that it was held by a pre-Conquest bishop, presumably of St Cuthbert's.[37]

Insecurity in the Humber region, whether caused by rebellion, invasion, or both, had led to the revival of the see of Lindsey twice in the tenth century. After the Norman Conquest, when William was faced by very serious opposition in Northumbria he took more decisive action by removing the see from Dorchester to Lincoln.[38] Remigius did not take over the old cathedral in Lincoln, but began to build a new church in the highest part of the city, close to the castle. In planning this building Remigius emphasized the political, even military, significance of the move and took precautions against possible attack. Richard Gem has drawn attention to some features of this church that made it defensible, confirming the comment of Henry of Huntingdon that it was 'a strong church with very strong projecting towers, and, as befitted the times, invincible to enemies'.[39] Remigius did not, however, break with the past completely. Early in his pontificate, before moving the see to Lincoln, William I confirmed to St Mary at Stow and to the monks the endowment that had been given by Godgifu.[40] The reference in this writ to monks of St Mary's may be taken together with an entry in Domesday concerning Ralph, formerly priest in Haugham, who had become a monk at Stow.[41] The implication is that the secular canons of Stow had been replaced by monks, probably by Remigius, although he kept the church in his own hands, as he did with the religious community at Eynsham in Oxfordshire until 1091 when he transferred it to Stow and appointed an abbot for the joint community. He also retained Louth as a demesne manor, and secured for the bishopric three churches that had apparently once been episcopal minsters, whatever their status in 1066. They were well placed to serve as bases from which episcopal authority could be reasserted; Wellingore in Kesteven, Kirton in Lindsey, and Caistor in the North Riding.[42] By 1072 he had also obtained Sleaford. There is no evidence to show whether there was any form of collegiate life in these churches in the eleventh century, as there was apparently at Castle Bytham.[43] The most remarkable survivals were Grantham and Horncastle, which had exceptionally large parishes in the twelfth century, that almost certainly derived from an early period in the history of the church in Lincolnshire when episcopal minsters provided the main framework of church organization.[44]

MINSTERS AND PARISHES

Church dues were originally paid to an episcopal minster from the whole of its *parochia*; any churches established by landowners on their property within the *parochia* of a minster were considered to be dependent chapels.

It was from the minsters that chrism, the consecrated oil used in baptism, was distributed, and the minsters were entitled to soul-scot, a sort of ecclesiastical death-duty, even when burial took place elsewhere. In the law of the church as it was being defined in the eleventh and twelfth centuries, parish churches were distinguished from others by the right to administer the rites of baptism and burial; they were also entitled to a share of the tithes. These were originally voluntary renders but by the tenth century they had become compulsory and were supposed to be rendered to the bishop's minsters. A law of Edgar allowed a landowner who had a church with a cemetery to retain a third of the tithe.[45] This was the decisive stage in creating new parishes around local churches. Our knowledge of this process depends on evidence from other parts of England, but there is no doubt that it happened in Lincolnshire; by the end of the twelfth century the county was divided into a large number of parishes.

This fragmentation of ancient minster *parochiae* must have been hastened by the disruption caused by the Danish conquest. It was also facilitated by the relative weakness of ecclesiastical authority in the area during the tenth century. The enforcement of church law depended partly on spiritual sanctions, but secular support was also needed and that was best provided by kings and their agents. It has recently been shown that in Hampshire and Surrey, and probably elsewhere in southern England, minsters were relatively successful in retaining their rights, in particular their entitlement to a major share of the tithes within their *parochiae*.[46] The law of Edgar, mentioned above, should be seen as a restriction in conformity with Canon Law, anticipating what was to become the general rule in twelfth-century England, that a local church was only entitled to a third of the tithe from its parish. This was a remarkable demonstration of the effectiveness of tenth-century English kings in supporting their bishops, at least in southern England. In Lincolnshire, which was not so firmly controlled by kings or bishops, minsters were less fortunate. Long after it was brought under the rule of English kings in the tenth century, their local agents tended to be drawn from the local aristocracy, the very people who were then beginning to build and endow their own churches. Most of the minsters that survived until the Conquest were in the centre of royal or comital sokes. Comparison with Yorkshire, where a relatively large number of extensive parishes with many dependent chapels survived into the twelfth century and later, is instructive.[47] The contrast with Lincolnshire reflects the greater effectiveness of episcopal authority in the archdiocese, which from the time of Osketel was in the charge of a succession of able and politically influential archbishops. In Lincolnshire owners of churches were better able to usurp ancient rights, and create *de facto* parishes, most of which were much smaller than parishes in many other parts of England. This implies that the units of lordship for which

Fig. 8.4 Cumberworth Cross. This small lead cross, measuring c. 10.5 cm in height, was found by F. J. Green during excavation at St Helen's church, Cumberworth. It was located above burials which were cut through timber buildings, both predating the first stone phase of the church.
The text incised on the cross is in Latin and reads:
\+ xp̄i ex hoc signo [—] expiatum [—] exiguum squalorem m[..t]
[u]olutum qu[i] in uirt[ute] [cr]ucis mundum de morte red[em]it
ta[r]tara disrupit aut celestia pandit
With the exception of three or four words lost from the lacunae, this can be translated, '+ through this sign of Christ [—] the small foulness [accusative] [—], he who by the power of the cross redeemed the world from death, shattered hell or threw open heaven'.

(caption continues opposite)

these parishes were formed were themselves small, a result of the break-up of estates during the tenth century.[48]

CHURCHES

In many parts of England landowners expressed their religious devotion by making gifts to monasteries, but as we have seen this rarely happened in pre-Conquest Lincolnshire. The landowners of the region apparently preferred to demonstrate their piety and wealth by building and adorning their own churches. By 1066 there were churches in all parts of the shire, although the exact number is unknown. Domesday Book records over 250 but there were certainly many more than that. The compilers of the survey made no attempt to record churches systematically; in Buckinghamshire, for example, only four are mentioned. Apart from the few that were themselves independent landowners, most churches were considered to be private property and are recorded among the assets of manors along with mills, meadows, and fisheries. Information about these manorial appurtenances was supplied by the landowners or their stewards, but not all did so. Nine complete churches were divided between two or three owners. The failure of some to report that they owned part of a church has resulted in the 22 incomplete fractions of churches in the Lincolnshire Domesday. For example, in 1086 Norman de Arcis had half a church at Stallingborough, but the other half is not accounted for; it may have belonged to one of the other manors in Stallingborough, but it may well have been owned by someone who held no land there.[49]

There is occasionally independent evidence for the existence of churches that are not recorded in Domesday. The most obvious is the survival of physical traces of a pre-Conquest church. In at least fifteen Lincolnshire churches there are pre-Conquest details that have survived later rebuilding. At Edenham, for example, two large carved roundels and a string course about fifteen feet above the floor can be seen in the wall above the Early English arcade between the nave and the south aisle.[50] These

(Fig. 8.4 continued)
Similar wording occurs in some sacramentaries: see for example Concordances et Tableaux pour l'Étude des Grandes Sacramentaires *(Fribourg, 1983), nos. 1219, 3585, 4160. A lead cross from Bath, now illegible, may also have contained a similar text (Okasha 1971, pp. 51–2). There is no personal name on the cross. If it was indeed a funerary cross, the deceased may have been a well-known person or, perhaps more likely, a second cross, now lost, may have contained further text including the personal name. There is no evidence for dating the text except for the script. This minuscule script resembles 10th/11th-century manuscript hands and is probably of a similar date. I am indebted to Elisabeth Okasha for providing this caption. Photo and © David Stephens, Downland Partnership.*

features, which are probably earlier than the Danish invasion, show that there was a fairly large stone church at Edenham that is not mentioned in Domesday Book. Eight of the churches with traces of pre-Conquest structure do, however, appear in Domesday Book, including the three with substantial remains of pre-Conquest fabric. A large part of the late tenth-century church of St Peter in Barton-upon-Humber has survived successive enlargements from the eleventh to the nineteenth centuries.[51] At Hough-on-the-Hill the tower and upper part of the nave walls are also of the late tenth century,[52] and at Stow the transepts and the piers of the crossing were constructed in the mid eleventh century. According to Henry of Huntingdon, Stow was built by Godgifu, but the arches of the crossing were certainly made after the Conquest, as were the choir and nave.[53]

Most surviving Lincolnshire churches were not built in stone until after the Conquest, but there is good evidence that many of them stand in pre-Conquest churchyards, implying the existence of an earlier church. A few of these early churchyards have been found by excavation. At Holton-le-Clay, for example, the first stone church was built shortly after

Fig. 8.5

Stow church, showing the piers at the crossing. Photo and © P. Dixon.

the Norman Conquest in a graveyard that had been in use for at least a hundred years.[54] A similar sequence has been uncovered on the site of St Mark's in the Lincoln suburb of Wigford where a stone church was first built in the middle of the eleventh century in a churchyard that began to be used a hundred years earlier.[55] There was an earlier graveyard, in use in the ninth century at the latest, under the tenth-century church of St Peter's at Barton-upon-Humber. About 30 graves were carefully emptied before that church was built.[56]

Many more early churches can be identified by means of Anglo-Saxon stone sculpture in the form of architectural details, as at Edenham, or grave monuments, whole or broken. Much of this sculpture is embedded in the later fabric of churches, but some pieces are free standing in churches or churchyards. Although such stones could be moved, and the original location of some is not known, it is likely that most belonged to a predecessor of the church in which they have been found. There is, for example, no reason to suppose that the sections of two Anglo-Saxon cross shafts at Creeton have not always been there, and the fragments of two late Anglo-Saxon grave covers mounted in the tower of Aisthorpe church in 1867 (see Fig. 8.1) suggest that it was on the site of a pre-Conquest church. Most of these fragments of sculpture come from free-standing monuments and therefore cannot prove the existence of stone churches. They are, however, good evidence for the existence of churchyards and, as many can be dated, if only within broad limits, they not only supplement the evidence of Domesday Book, but also show that some of the churches that are mentioned in Domesday already existed a century or more before it was compiled.

Some of Lincolnshire's pre-Conquest carved stones are well known.[57] Eighty-nine pieces, mostly fragments, found in or near 47 churches were described or noted by D. S. Davies in 1926, and in 1964 Lawrence Butler was able to describe eighteen more. Since then some grave monuments have been found by excavation, notably at St Mark's, Wigford, where some 70 stone covers or markers of graves were discovered, twenty of them judged to be of the tenth or eleventh century. The corpus of early sculpture in the shire has been greatly enlarged by Paul Everson and David Stocker who have systematically looked for fragments embedded in the walls of Lincolnshire's churches. With their new discoveries they have been able to catalogue over 350 stone sculptures of the tenth and eleventh centuries from nearly 150 sites. Some are post-Conquest, but early Norman grave monuments almost certainly indicate churchyards that were established before 1066. This comprehensive survey has not been published, but one group of tenth and eleventh century, locally-produced, grave covers, known as 'Lindsey Slabs', has been discussed in the report on the excavation of St Mark's, Wigford, where two were found. Thirteen similar grave covers have been found elsewhere in Lindsey, eight of them in or near churches that are not mentioned in Domesday Book. Stone sculptures make it possible to identify more than 30 other churches that are not in Domesday Book. One other place where no church is mentioned in Domesday, Kirton in Lindsey, is shown by its name to have had a church, probably an important one, in the ninth century when the Scandinavians invaded, and there is no reason to suppose that it had disappeared 200 years

Fig. 8.6 One of the two grave covers known as Lindsey Slabs found, broken into seven fragments, in the excavation of St Mark's, Wigford. It is dated mid 10th to 11th century. Scale 1:10.

Stones drawn by R. Sutton. © CLAU. Reproduced with permission.

later.[58] Domesday Book itself indirectly revealed the existence of a church at Gosberton in Holland by calling the place *Gosebertechirche* or *Gozeberdecherca*.[59]

Before the eleventh century most churches were built of wood. There was, therefore, no tradition of building in stone and some features in tenth-century stone churches suggest that they were built by carpenters. In St Peter at Barton-upon-Humber, for example, stone slabs were used as though they were wooden beams in apparent ignorance of the different properties of the two materials. More remarkably, in two of the belfry openings, wooden boards were used in place of stone slabs to form the inner arches. Warwick Rodwell, who was responsible for the detailed investigation of this church, commented that 'gritstone slabs were evidently in short supply by the time the builders reached the uppermost levels of the tower, and the substitution of timber in places where it would not be noticed was a natural solution. Such a compromise would be unthinkable to a true mason, emphasizing that the builders of the Barton tower were carpenters at heart.' He has also pointed out that many of the joints used at Barton are those of carpenters not masons. Indeed, the external decoration of Barton church appears to be an attempt to reproduce in stone forms that were familiar in contemporary timber structures.[60]

Most traces of early timber churches have been destroyed by later rebuildings or by grave diggers, but some have survived such disturbances. At Burnham post-holes that presumably belonged to an earlier church building were found under the floor of the chancel of the first stone church, built in the late tenth century.[61] At St Mark's in Lincoln the first stone church was built in the late eleventh century alongside, and in the graveyard of, the earlier timber church, of which only the bottom of some post-holes survived grave digging.

It seems likely that the most important churches – cathedrals, minsters and churches belonging to monastic communities – were the first to be built or rebuilt in stone. It is likely that the stone church of St Peter at Barton-upon-Humber was built when that place was held by Peterborough Abbey. The foundations of a stone church have also been found at Barrow. This may have been on or near the site of the earlier monastery and may reflect the continued importance of that place as a religious centre. It had an apse, a common feature after the Norman Conquest but otherwise unknown in the Anglo-Saxon churches of Lincolnshire and the surrounding region. It does therefore seem likely that it was built after, not before, 1066. It has been claimed that the church at Burnham, about four miles south of Barrow, was rebuilt in stone in the late tenth century. If so, it suggests that the fashion of building churches in stone began earlier in this part of Lincolnshire than elsewhere, possibly stimulated by the example of Barton.

Fig. 8.7 St Peter's Church, Barton-upon-Humber.
Photo and © Warwick Rodwell.

Nothing is known about the early history of the tenth-century church at Hough-on-the-Hill. It may have been a minster, but by 1066 it was, like Barton, in secular ownership. One minster church that did remain in church ownership was at Stow. The earliest part of the present building was erected in the mid-eleventh century, on the eve of the Conquest, after the community had been enriched by Leofric and Godgifu in 1054. There was certainly a church there earlier, associated with burials found close to the north wall of the nave, but nothing is yet known about its size or structure.

Fig. 8.8 Detail of St Peter's Church, Barton-upon-Humber, showing 'timber' forms used by the stonemasons.
Photo and © Warwick Rodwell.

Fig. 8.9 Western tower and external stair-turret of All Saints, Hough-on-the Hill, c. 1000 A.D. Photo and © P. Everson and D. Stocker.

There were probably minster churches at Caistor and Castle Bytham and there are traces of possibly Anglo-Saxon fabric in the walls of both, but those features cannot be closely dated, and may be post-Conquest.[62]

In 1050 almost all Lincolnshire churches were still timber buildings, but in the following decades there was a dramatic change as dozens of them were rebuilt in stone. The imposing new building at Stow may have encouraged some landowners to reconstruct their churches, and before long there was a lively competition as others followed their example. This surge of activity continued into the next century but many churches cannot be more closely dated than 'mid-eleventh to early twelfth century', and some wooden churches were not rebuilt in stone until somewhat later; at Long Sutton in Holland, for example, this did not happen until about 1180.[63] There was no sudden change in the styles and techniques of building after 1066. The new styles favoured by the Norman conquerors were gradually adopted alongside the old. This was not a sign of Lincolnshire conservatism, rather it is evidence of a living tradition in which old and new elements were combined. Some details, such as the Romanesque decoration of the arches at Broughton and the carving on the head-stone of a window at Barnetby-le-Wold, clearly indicate a post-Conquest date, while at Glentham the use of a late Saxon grave slab as one of the jambs in a belfry opening, suggests that that tower was built after the Conquest.

The men who built these churches eagerly used any dressed stones that were available; grave covers, crosses and even stones from ruined Roman buildings, including some massive blocks of Millstone Grit that must have been first quarried in the Pennines. In Lincolnshire they are only found in the north, near the Humber, and presumably came from York. It is not surprising that they are never found very far from a waterway. Stones of this kind are to be seen in the walls of churches at Alkborough, Broughton, Burton upon Stather, Whitton, and Winteringham. Smaller, more easily managed stones were preferred by later builders but eleventh-century masons were willing to use these massive blocks that needed no dressing and whose weight could give stability.

Most tenth-century churches were very small. Apart from such exceptional buildings as cathedrals and minsters, few English churches built before 1050 had a nave of more than 36 sq. yards, and some were half that size.[64] It is not possible to determine the total area of the timber churches at Burnham and St Mark's in Lincoln but both were less than thirteen feet wide. The first stone church at Burnham was larger, but its nave was only 54 sq. yards and the tower nave of St Peter's at Barton was little more than 30 sq. yards. Churches on this scale were clearly not intended to accommodate large numbers of people. They were not built to serve communities, but were rather chapels built and maintained by landowners for their own purposes. Some were probably private chapels, but many, including those in berewicks and on sokeland, seem to have been built so that owners could keep some of the tithes. The land needed for churches and graveyards was best provided by landowners. Some churches were founded by churchmen or monastic communities, but most were built by laymen whose priests served them as well as the Lord God.

These privately owned churches could be bought and sold, exchanged, given away and even used as pledges. They could also be divided. This might happen when the estate to which they belonged was partitioned among heirs. So, for example, sometime before 1066 Withcall was divided between two lords, one of whom had a third of both the mill and the church, while the other had the remainder of both these assets.[65] Thirty-one of the churches recorded in Domesday Book were in divided ownership but 225 were undivided. Even if many fractions of churches are omitted, it is remarkable that so many had only one owner in 1086.

In some places Domesday Book records more than one church. Some of these may have been in different settlements that were grouped together under one name in the survey. There must, however, have been settlements with two or more churches built by different landowners. Church reformers of the eleventh and twelfth centuries thoroughly disapproved of the private ownership of churches but they were unable to abolish it entirely. They did, however, succeed in reducing lay ownership to the right to present, or nominate, the priest. The churches themselves, and the priests, were increasingly subjected to church law and a regular parochial system was organized. In the process many private churches disappeared and by the end of the twelfth century, when documentary evidence for churches becomes more abundant, there was little duplication of churches in rural communities. Nevertheless a few pairs survived in the medieval period, at Bilsby, Binbrook, and Swaby; there are still two churches in the churchyard at Alvingham, one of them serving the neighbouring parish of North Cockerington. When churches were merged the owners and their heirs may have retained a right of presentation to the surviving church; and such shared rights may therefore be a sign that a church has disappeared, but not necessarily, for they may be due to the partition of a single church. It has been suggested that some churches were divided into fractions because they were founded by a number of landowners.[66] That may have been so, but was unusual; relatively few of the churches recorded in Domesday Book were shared. Some of the church foundations or churchyards that have been found by excavation may have belonged to churches that were later removed to new sites – such shifts did occur – but they may equally represent second churches that have disappeared. The graveyard found 230 yards west of the present church at Fillingham is a good example.[67] The church foundations and graveyard found at Barrow is not, for Barrow only had one lord in 1066; the abandoned church was probably the short-lived predecessor of the present church of Holy Trinity, about 430 yards away.[68]

One aspect of the lay ownership of churches that particularly exercised reformers in the eleventh century was the retention of tithe by laymen. Although the reformers were not able to stop laymen nominating priests, they did succeed in gaining general acceptance of the rule that tithe had to be devoted to religious purposes. A third was reserved for the parish church, but the remainder could be allocated by the owner to whatever religious corporation he chose, normally a monastic community, but cathedrals also benefited.[69]

The rule that parish churches were entitled to a share of tithe may have contributed to the building boom that began in the second half of the eleventh century. Many churches were then not only rebuilt in stone, but also enlarged.[70] Towers may have been built for the sake of prestige, but the larger naves had the practical purpose of accommodating larger numbers of parishioners than the earlier churches. Willingly or not parishioners now began to have responsibility for their church, and in the thirteenth century that responsibility was institutionalized by the creation of churchwardens. This later communal responsibility has tended to conceal the seigneurial origin of most parish churches. Even in the twelfth century some landowners appear to have coerced their tenants to make contributions to 'their' churches in addition to tithe. The church of St Margaret of Keddington was endowed with land not only by the lord from his own demesne, but also with an acre given by each of his tenants. This has been cited as an example of communal endowment, but such uniformity seems rather to imply compulsion than the voluntary generosity of many individuals.[71] The evidence of Domesday Book underlines the seigneurial character of most Lincolnshire churches. It is possible that some urban churches may have been founded by groups of burgesses, but neither Domesday nor the early twelfth-century evidence give any hint that many churches in Lincoln or Stamford were in joint ownership; those that are mentioned all appear to have been held by individuals, with the exception of half a church in Lincoln held by Toki son of Outi.[72]

Some of the tenth- and eleventh-century stone monuments that have been found in or near many Lincolnshire churches may have marked the graves of the owners of those churches or members of their families. They not only displayed the status of the dead, but also ensured that they were left in peace longer than others, whose graves were either unmarked or had a simple wooden cross, and were likely to be disturbed after 20 or 30 years. Other people than church owners may well have commissioned similar stone memorials; it is unlikely that all fifteen grave covers of the period found at St Mark's, Lincoln belonged to one family. Some probably marked the graves of relatively wealthy people who lived in that quarter of the city. None of these Lincolnshire grave monuments are of very high quality, but they cannot have been cheap. They are therefore evidence for what may be called a middle class, to which most church owners apparently belonged, wealthy enough to spend some money on relatively ostentatious memorials to themselves or their relatives.

Despite weaknesses of organization in the century before the Norman Conquest the church flourished in Lincolnshire, but in an old-fashioned mode. There were many churches, but they were tiny and few were built in stone. Most were privately owned by men who probably demanded tithe from their tenants, but retained much of it. Pre-Conquest Lincolnshire was, at least ecclesiastically, a backwater. Merchants and landowners must have been aware of the new ideas that were current elsewhere in England, if not abroad, but there is little sign that they had much effect in Lincolnshire until the middle of the eleventh century, or even later. The enrichment of Stow, which must have been encouraged and welcomed by Bishop Wulfwig, may indicate a growing awareness that the northern part of the diocese needed closer attention, but it was Wulfwig's successor, Remigius, who imposed effective episcopal authority there.[73] By moving the cathedral from Dorchester to the thriving city of Lincoln and, with the support of the Conqueror, acquiring estates and churches in the shire, this active and determined prelate broke Lincolnshire's ecclesiastical isolation, opening it to the new ideas, intellectual and liturgical as well as architectural and legal, that were then being shaped in Western Christendom.

NOTES TO CHAPTER VIII

1 Whitelock 1941.

2 The Northumbrian Priests' Law, cc. 48, 54 in *Councils and Synods*, pp. 461–3.

3 The so-called Canons of Edgar, c. 16 in *Councils and Synods*, p. 320.

4 Popular religion in nineteenth-century Lincolnshire has some parallels to the practices condemned by Wulfstan, see Obelkevich 1976, pp. 258–312.

5 *Chronicle* s.a. 909.

6 Owen, A. 1980.

7 See below, pp. 174–6.

8 Dugdale, *Monasticon Anglicanum* i. 628–30.

9 These religious houses are listed in Owen, D. 1971, pp. 146–53. See also Stocker 1993. Peterborough's manor in Hibaldstow (DB i.346a = *LD* 8/22) was acquired after the Conquest according to Hugh Candidus, p. 71.

10 Asser, c. 93, ed. Stevenson, pp. 81–2, trans. *EHD* I, no. 7, p. 300.

11 Stenton 1971, pp. 445–56.

12 S 782.

13 Rodwell and Rodwell 1982

14 Hugh Candidus, pp. 64–5; DB i. 360a, 354b = *LD* 30/1–4, 24/13–15.

15 The Lincolnshire landholdings of pre-Conquest religious communities are discussed in detail in Appendix 7.

16 Page, F. 1934.

17 *Liber Eliensis* ii.31, ed. Blake, p. 105; St Paul's, London, exchanged land obtained after Thurketel's death while Æthelwold was alive.

18 Orderic, pp. 324–5, 344–5, 350–1.

19 For the bishops of Lindsey see Appendix 6.

20 The exception, S 412, dated 23 March 931, may have been issued between the death of Hrothweard and the accession of Wulfstan.

21 *EHD* I, p. 93.

22 Whitelock 1959, p. 74.

23 S 659.

24 S 679.

25 DB i. 348a = *LD* 12/59.

26 See pp. 128–9.

27 Wormald 1978, p. 61.

28 Appendix 8.

29 DB i. 345a, 375a = *LD* 7/56, 69/5.

30 *RA* i, no. 247, pp. 186–8.

31 Raine 1888, p. 344.

32 See the writ quoted in Appendix 8.

33 Owen, D. 1971, pp. 21–2, citing *RA* ix, Appendix I, pp. 256–62, 'The Archdeacons of Stow'.

34 RA i, no. 4, pp. 11–13. Pope Nicholas confirmed to Wulfwig's church *maxime parrochiam Lindissi ecclesiamque Stou cum Newerca*, *RA* i, no. 247, pp. 186–8. Newark was given to the church of Stow by Leofric and Godgifu, see Appendix 8.

35 Lavington and Skillington were obtained from Ulf son of Topi, DB i. 376b = *LD* 72/10; Benniworth had been owned by Godric, who had sake and soke, DB i. 339b, 375b = *LD* 2/16, 69/27.

36 The tendency of Domesday Book to name occupiers rather than owners, discussed in Appendix 3, means that the archbishop might only be named as tenant if he had demesne estates.

37 DB i. 341a. = *LD* 3/41. See also the bishop of Durham's claim in Grantham, DB i. 337b = *LD* 1/9, and Fig. 1.1.

38 *RA* i, no. 2, pp. 2–4; Owen, D. 1994.

39 Gem 1986; Henry of Huntingdon, *Historia Anglorum*, p. 212.

40 See Appendix 8.

41 DB i. 345a = *LD* 7/55.

42 *RA* i, no. 2, pp. 2–4; Fig. 10.1; cf. DB i. 337b–338b =*LD* 1/6, 38–80.

43 Owen, D. 1971, p. 8.

44 See above p. 63. It has been suggested, Morris, R. 1988, p. 197, that such large parishes may have been relatively recent creations. That is most unlikely in

Lincolnshire where episcopal and royal authority was relatively weak during the tenth century.

45 Edgar II, cc. 1–2; text and trans. in Robertson 1925, pp. 20–21; trans. in *EHD* I, no. 40, p. 431.

46 Hase 1988; Blair 1991, pp. 105–7.

47 Morris, R. 1989 pp. 133–8.

48 See above, pp. 111–14.

49 DB i. 361b = *LD* 32/1.

50 Taylor and Taylor 1965, p. 227. See Fig. 5.2.

51 Rodwell and Rodwell 1982.

52 Taylor and Taylor 1965, pp. 320–4. See Fig. 8.9.

53 Gem 1988, p. 26. See also Appendix 8.

54 Sills 1982.

55 Gilmour and Stocker 1986.

56 Rodwell and Rodwell 1982. Two undated burials have been found under the foundation of the nave wall of the earliest church at Rand, Field 1983b.

57 I am indebted to Paul Everson and David Stocker for advice on these stone sculptures.

58 See above, p. 63.

59 DB i. 344b, 348b = *LD* 7/36, 12/76.

60 Rodwell 1986, pp. 171–4.

61 Coppack 1987.

62 Taylor and Taylor 1965, pp. 127–9, 716.

63 Owen, D. 1971, p. 5.

64 Morris, R. 1989, pp. 287–9.

65 DB i. 343b, 364a, 375a = *LD* 4/72, 40/26, 69/4.

66 Owen, D. 1971, p. 4.

67 Field 1983a. She also states that there were two churches in each of the parishes of Waddingham, South Kelsey, and Spridlington.

68 Boden and Whitwell 1979, *Med. Arch.* 22 (1978), p. 147, cf. Rodwell and Rodwell 1982, p. 308 and n. 51.

69 Hill, F. 1948, pp. 69–70, notes that Lincoln Cathedral was entitled to two-thirds of the tithe from numerous parishes. His argument that these renders can be traced back to the pre-Conquest rights of the episcopal minster in Lincoln is unconvincing.

70 Morris, R. 1989, pp. 165–7.

71 Stenton 1927, pp. lxx–lxxi.

72 DB i. 336a = *LD* p. 3/2. Toki also had two whole churches.

73 For Remigius, see Bates 1992.

CHAPTER IX

MARKETS, TOWNS, AND THE ECONOMY OF THE REGION

For some 300 years after the end of Roman rule the people of Lincolnshire had to manage their affairs without the benefit of coins. After the first decade of the fifth century Roman coins ceased to be imported into Britain, and within a short period those remaining were used not as money but as ornaments or as a source of metal, the gold and silver being reworked into objects such as rings or jewellery, or used to adorn the weapons and clothing of people of high status. Gold was especially associated with power; it was given to win the favour of kings or to reward their followers. The Anglo-Saxons also defined compensations and penalties in terms of gold. The earliest English law code, produced in Kent soon after the year 600, specified such payments in terms of shillings (*scillingas*) that were the equivalent of twenty *sceattas*. At that time these were weights of gold, not coins. A *sceat* (the word is related to 'scatter' and 'shatter') was a tiny piece of gold, the weight of a grain of barley, 0.065g, and the shilling (deriving from a word meaning 'to cut') weighed 1.3 g, the weight of the gold coins that began to be struck in England in the second quarter of the seventh century. The earliest coins were produced in Kent and London, but in the middle years of the century some were also made in north-eastern England, possibly York.[1] Only six of these 'York' coins are known, one of which was found in 1991 at Burton-by-Lincoln. Several other seventh-century gold coins have been found in Lincolnshire, all but one from Frankia. One, struck in Lieusaint-en-Brie, near Paris, was found in the nineteenth century near Lincoln, the other, from Quentovic, near Boulogne, was found in 1994 near Caistor.[2] The very rich site identified as

Fig. 9.1
The 7th-century gold 'York' shilling (thrymsa) found in 1991 at Burton-by-Lincoln. Private collection. Photo and © Mark Blackburn.

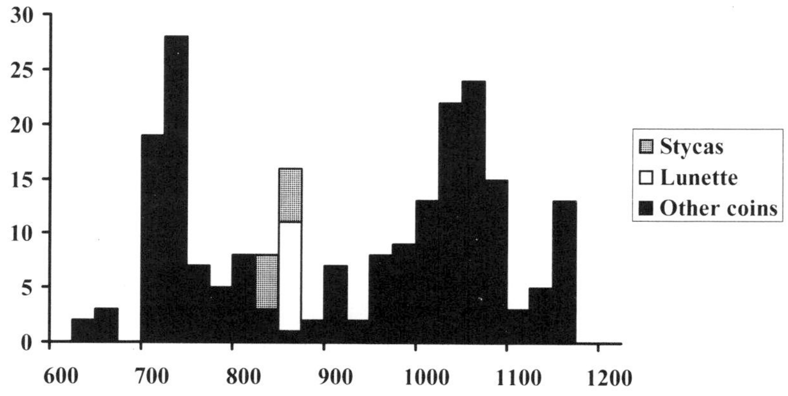

Fig. 9.2 Single coin-finds from Lincolnshire excluding productive sites (228 coins).
© Mark Blackburn.

'South Lincs' has yielded an Anglo-Saxon thrymsa, five Merovingian tremisses, a plated imitation and a blank gold flan.[3]

By the end of the century in both England and Frankia this gold coinage had been replaced by one of silver. Only two of the earliest silver coins have so far been found in Lincolnshire,[4] but by about 700 very large numbers of later issues, most of them from Frisia, began to reach Lindsey and for several decades there was as much coin in circulation there as at any time before the Norman Conquest. That, possibly surprising, assertion is based on the rate of coin loss indicated by the coins found singly by excavation or metal detectors. Fig. 9.2, prepared by Mark Blackburn on the basis of the 228 coins struck before AD 1175 that were found singly in Lindsey (excluding Flixborough, near Grimsby, South Lincs and Torksey) before 1994, is an attempt to show when they were lost within periods of 25 years.[5] Comparison with Fig. 9.3, which is based on the 378 coins found singly and recorded between 1984 and 1992 in the whole of England (excluding productive sites like Flixborough), shows that the Lincolnshire pattern is generally consistent with that for the whole country although, with the exception of the rich 'South Lincs' site, fewer coins reached Kesteven than Lindsey in the eighth century.[6] Similar evidence from south Lincolnshire suggests that far fewer coins reached that part of the region in the eighth century. These diagrams show that the number of coins in circulation dropped dramatically after about 750. This change, which occurred elsewhere in southern England and in western Europe, and the fact that after about 720 coins were lighter and contained smaller proportions of silver suggest that the source of silver that made this

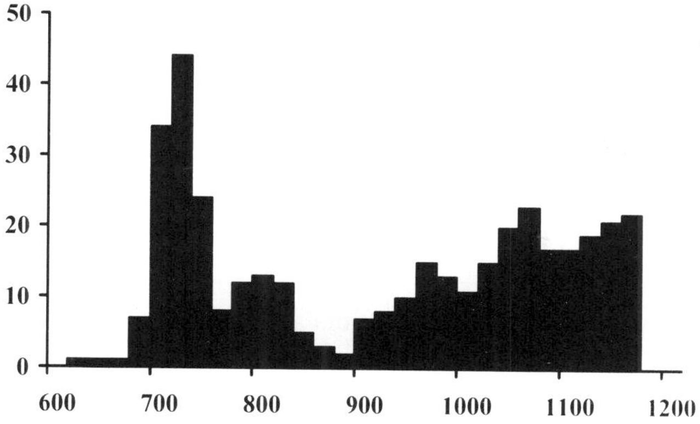

Fig. 9.3 *English single coin-finds (excluding productive sites) recorded by M. Blackburn and M. Bonser 1984–92 (378 coins).* © *Mark Blackburn.*

abundant coinage possible was exhausted by about 750.[7]

After that date most people must have relied on barter or credit to obtain what they needed and could not themselves produce or gather. Payments for land or privileges recorded in charters were nevertheless generally expressed in terms of money, although they were sometimes, perhaps often, rendered in kind. An unusually revealing example is a memorandum recording the purchase of land by the abbot of Breedon, in Leicestershire, from King Æthelred between 675 and 692 when coins were very scarce in that part of England. The payment is described as '500 *solidi*, that is twelve beds, namely feather mattresses and elaborate pillows together with muslin and linen sheets as is customary in Britain, also a slave with a slave girl; also a gold brooch and two horses with two wagons'.[8] This text, besides showing that sums of money could mean goods, also shows what varied forms of wealth could be accumulated and used in exchanges in the highest strata of early English society. Many things changed hands not by way of trade but as gifts, rent, or tax. Large numbers of animals and huge quantities of food and raw materials were despatched to other parts of Mercia as renders to the king or to landowners such as the abbey of *Medeshamstede*. Producers and landowners based in Lincolnshire nevertheless retained a surplus large enough to justify holding markets or fairs in many parts of the shire.

The huge increase in the number of coins circulating in north-west Europe in the late seventh century was accompanied by the development of trading places on or near the coasts of the English Channel and the North Sea. These appear to have been created by merchants in collaboration with local rulers who provided protection and gained benefits by exercising the right of pre-emption and by collecting tolls.[9] The English called them *wic* (singular and plural) and used that word to name them. The English *wic* were *Hamwic* (the precursor of Southampton), Fordwich and possibly Sandwich in Kent, Aldwych ('the old wic') adjacent to Roman London, Ipswich, and outside Roman York, which was called *Eoforwicceaster*, 'the fort of *Eoforwic*', by the English.[10] There is no evidence of a *wic* in Lincolnshire. It has been suggested that the name Wigford commemorates one associated with Lincoln, but no trace of any settlement or significant activity has been found there between the Roman period and the tenth century.[11] What is more, Lincoln does not appear to have had much contact with the coastal region in the seventh and eighth centuries. Lindsey is, therefore, the one east coast kingdom without a *wic*, probably because at the time these emporia were being created Lindsey was subject to Mercian kings who were more interested in winning control of those that had been established in London and Kent than in encouraging the development of one in that part of their empire.

FAIRS AND MARKETS

Lindsey was, nevertheless, prosperous. The coins and ornamental metalwork found there suggest that it was one of the wealthiest regions of England in the eighth and ninth centuries; numerous brooches, buckles, strap-ends and other pieces of metalwork of that period have been found at over 40 widely scattered sites. Fewer coins have been found in south Lincolnshire but relatively large quantities of ornamental metalwork have been found in Kesteven, especially in the neighbourhood of Sleaford. The prosperity of Lincolnshire depended on the ability of people to exchange their surplus produce. There were, doubtless, then as later itinerant craftsmen and pedlars, but there was also a need for regular markets. The earliest were probably annual fairs but by the tenth century there were also weekly markets in some, perhaps many, places. Patronal and other festivals celebrated in churches provided ideal opportunities for buying and selling. Some fairs lasted several days and attracted people from far afield. It was, therefore, appropriate that the Old English word *stow*, meaning a place where people assembled, was used to name some important churches, including Stow St Mary, where a yearly market was held in the eleventh century, and probably long before that. Three markets recorded in Domesday Book, Louth, Partney, and Threekingham, presumably originated as annual fairs associated with the monasteries that were in those places in the eighth century, although there may also have been weekly markets at Louth and Partney in the eleventh century as there were later.[12] The Threekingham fair was in fact two miles away from Threekingham at

Fig. 9.4 *Range of mid to late Saxon axes and adzes for woodworking, forming part of a hoard from Flixborough.*
Photo courtesy of Humber Archaeology Partnership.

Fig 9.5 *Lead tank from Flixborough which contained the hoard of mid to late Saxon carpentry tools.*
Photo courtesy of Humber Archaeology Partnership.

Stow Green.[13] These fairs must have been very well established to survive the disappearance of the religious communities. Domesday Book is not a complete record of markets and fairs; it did not, for example, mention the yearly market at Stow St Mary.[14] It is, therefore, likely that fairs were held in connection with festivals in most, perhaps all, the major churches of the region, including the cathedral in Lincoln.

Churches were also natural centres for weekly markets held in connection with worship on Sundays, when people were not obliged to work. Many were held in or near churchyards, and as late as 1285 Edward I legislated against the practice. Sunday markets were flourishing in the early tenth century when Athelstan acknowledged the failure of his attempt to prohibit them. A century later Æthelred and Cnut tried to forbid them, but with no more success.[15] It was in the thirteenth century that many markets were, at last, moved to other days of the week, but a few were still held on Sundays in the fourteenth and fifteenth centuries.[16] At the end of the twelfth century there were Sunday markets in Lincolnshire at Bardney, Bolingbroke, Burton upon Stather, Edenham, Fleet, Sleaford, Spalding, Stamford, and Wainfleet.[17] Only one of these, Burton upon Stather, appears in Domesday Book, but it is likely that several others already existed in the eleventh century, or even earlier.[18] The fact that Domesday Book lists bread and fish among the commodities traded at South Ferriby and Barton-upon-Humber and, by implication, at Caistor, suggests that these markets were weekly.[19] Ferry landings were natural locations for markets. Domesday Book records a market together with a ferry at Barton-upon-Humber.[20] The reference to tolls at Grimsby implies that there was a market there as well as a ferry.[21] Domesday also lists a market near the confluence of the Trent and the Humber, at Burton upon Stather, a significant name; its second element derives from a Scandinavian word meaning 'landing places'.[22]

The sites of some other markets or fairs are indicated by exceptional concentrations of ornamental metalwork, some of high quality, and coins that have been found with the help of metal detectors. Some of these finds may come from the residences of wealthy people, but when the sequence of coins begins in the eighth century and continues until the twelfth or even later it seems more likely that they were places where people traditionally gathered and traded. As the finders and landowners, naturally, try to keep their sites secret from other searchers, the exact locations cannot be disclosed even when known to numismatists or archaeologists. One site, near Grimsby, has yielded numerous sceattas as well as coins of Edgar and Cnut.[23] From the intervening period, when coins were relatively scarce, there is one ninth-century Northumbrian styca and a quantity of ninth-century metal objects. Another site that has produced a large amount of ornamental metalwork, much of it of the ninth century, is near Louth and

a. b. c. d. e. f.

Fig. 9.6 Coins of the 7th and 8th centuries from a productive site near Grimsby, found in 1997. a. Merovingian gold tremissis, mid 7th century, from the Netherlands; b. English silver sceat, series B, London?, c. 690; c. and d. English silver sceattas, series J, York?, c. 720; e. Continental silver sceat, series E (porcupine type), Lower Rhineland, c. 700; f. Continental silver sceat, series X (woden/monster type), Ribe, c. 720. (Private collection.) Photo and © Mark Blackburn.

is distinguished from other sites in that vicinity as Louth A. One sceat and an early tenth-century York coin have been found there, together with numerous coins of the eleventh century and, surprisingly, three late medieval continental coins. Further south, near Alford, Anglo-Saxon ornaments have been discovered in a small area of 100 yards square together with eight coins: three sceattas, two coins of Offa, and one each of Coenwulf, king of Mercia 796-805, Æthelred II, and William I. It is, unfortunately, not possible to say whether medieval markets or fairs were held in these places, although that does seem likely. Even without such confirmation the evidence of these metal-detector finds suggests that in eastern Lindsey some eleventh-century markets or fairs were already in existence in the early eighth century.

Much of the produce that changed hands in these and similar places, such as animals, food, clothing, leather goods, wooden objects, basket work and salt, has left few traces. With the help of modern methods of analysis those traces can yield valuable information and will, in time, make possible a much more comprehensive study of the economy of Anglo-Saxon Lincolnshire and the standard of living of its inhabitants than can be attempted at present. Fortunately, one important product for which there was a universal and continuous demand, pottery, has been recovered from most parts of the region in sufficient quantities to provide a basis for some preliminary conclusions about its manufacture, distribution, and use.

Pots were used for a great variety of purposes: as tableware, in kitchens and workshops, and for storage. They were easily broken, but in most conditions fragments survive and even small pieces can enable experts, in many cases, to determine the size and shape of the complete vessel and how it was made. They can, for example, assert that none of the pottery used in Lincolnshire before the mid ninth century was made on a fast wheel.[24] Microscopic fragments of rock occurring naturally in the clay or added to improve its quality can sometimes indicate the region in which a pot was made. Such evidence has shown that some of the cremation urns used in sixth- and seventh-century Lincolnshire came from the area of Charnwood Forest, while others were made locally.[25]

In addition to pottery produced locally there were also imports, notably from Ipswich which was already in the seventh century a centre for the production of excellent pots that were distributed along the east coast of England. Pieces of Ipswich ware are found in the Fens and in eastern and northern parts of Lindsey, but not more than about 15 miles inland.[26] If this East Anglian pottery was imported by way of trade, its distribution suggests that before the Danish conquest in the ninth century traders did not need to go far inland to obtain what they wanted. It is significant that most of the concentrations of ornamental metal work and coins, including those that have been mentioned above as probable sites of markets or fairs, are in this coastal region.[27]

THE EFFECTS OF THE DANISH CONQUEST: THE REVIVAL OF LINCOLN

The economy was transformed by the Vikings. As raiders they caused much destruction, but as settlers they brought great benefits to the surviving inhabitants and began the process that made eleventh-century Lincoln one of the major cities not just of England, but of western Europe. They stimulated the economy in three ways. First, by redistributing the treasure they had acquired in various parts of western Europe as plunder, tribute or ransoms. Their loot included gold and gems but the bulk was silver in the form of coins, jewellery and plate. The Viking leaders probably retained the most valuable items for themselves and used the silver to reward their men. Viking hoards of silver containing coins, rings, ingots, and occasionally pieces of jewellery have been found in many parts of the British Isles. Although most of these hoards are small, their owners had greater purchasing power than most of the English inhabitants of Lincolnshire. The settlement of a large number of relatively wealthy people must have stimulated the local economy and contributed to the revival of Lincoln. So far the only evidence for the activity of craftsmen in the city in the late ninth century is pottery fired in the complex of kilns on Silver Street. The three tenth-century kilns that have been excavated there produced pottery of a type that was being made before the year 900, presumably in nearby kilns that have not been located.[28] Although the workshops found at Flaxengate and in Wigford were established after the middle of the tenth century, when Lincoln was rapidly expanding, it is likely that specialists in various crafts were already working in the city soon after the Danish conquest when it was once again a centre of secular authority. In the period of Mercian hegemony any significance that Lincoln had as a regional centre was due to the church, but for the Danish conquerors the upper part of the city was an ideal base, and coins struck in Lincoln towards the end of the ninth century are a sign of its new status.[29] People who were drawn to Lincoln for political, legal, or social reasons when it was under Danish control were potential customers for craftsmen and traders.

Finds of pottery in various parts of Lincoln, especially in the south-east quarter of the lower city, show that there was increased activity towards the end of the ninth century, and it was apparently at that time that Silver Street was created, joining the south and east gates. Flaxengate was another new development about the turn of the century and Grantham Street may also

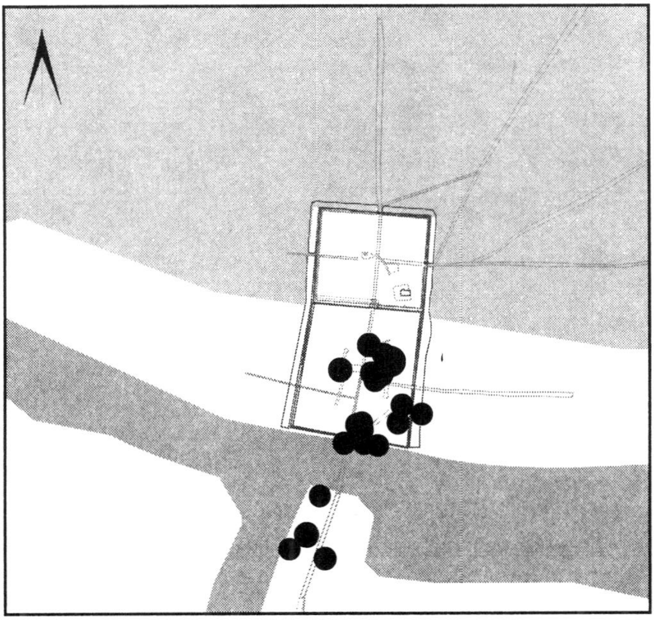

Fig. 9.7 Lincoln in the late 9th to early 10th centuries. The city consisted of an ecclesiastical/aristocratic centre within the walls of the Roman fortress and a commercial settlement in the lower city. The black dots represent finds of Lincoln Gritty ware, used during the earliest phase of the Anglo-Scandinavian occupation. The Witham at this time was a wide river, bounded by marsh/fen and the finds of Lincoln Gritty ware in the Wigford suburb to the south may indicate an early bridgehead settlement but are more likely to have been brought on to the site with refuse used to reclaim the south bank of the Witham in the mid 10th century when a suburb grew up there. Map prepared by A. Vince. © A. Vince.

have been established then.[30] Little is known about developments in the upper city. Coins found scattered near the site of St Paul-in-the-Bail together with a strap end and a belt slider may indicate that a market was held there from the late ninth century, the date of coin fragments that may have been Viking loot.[31]

The Danes also influenced the local economy by introducing skilled potters from northern France. These craftsmen used various sophisticated techniques, including the fast wheel, to produce pottery of higher quality than had been made in England earlier. These potters, who must have been under the protection and control of the leaders of the Danish armies, began working in England even before the Danes began to settle. The earliest known kilns were in Lincoln, Stamford, Torksey, and York, the invaders' bases, and these places continued to be important centres for the production of this improved pottery until shortly before the Norman Conquest; at Stamford and Torksey even longer. It is surprising that the techniques of these potters, which had long been widely practised on the Continent, were not introduced into England before the ninth century and that this was then done by the Danes. Having become familiar with this high quality pottery during their campaigns in Frankia, they apparently preferred it to English pottery and ensured a supply by importing potters who could make it. As conquerors they were better able to overcome the conservatism of the established pottery industry than their English counterparts. It was from the Danelaw centres that knowledge of the new techniques was gradually spread, first to Northampton by a Stamford potter, and then to other parts of England.[32]

Another consequence of the Danish conquest was that more produce remained in the hands of Lincolnshire's inhabitants than when the area was under Mercian rule; *feorm* and other forms of tribute were no longer paid to Mercian kings and their agents. The new rulers, of course, made demands and some produce may have been sent to York, but it is unlikely that they exacted as much as their English predecessors. The disappearance of the monasteries that had consumed a great deal of local produce had a similar effect. The people of the region were, therefore, able to profit from the greatly increased demand for English produce on the Continent in the late tenth century.

EXPORTS

One of the main causes for this increased demand was the discovery, shortly before 970, of a large source of silver in Germany at Rammelsberg in the Harz mountains.[33] This enabled the Germans to import cloth and other goods on a much larger scale than previously and contributed to the rapid growth of various industries in the towns of the Rhineland, Lorraine, and Flanders. These in turn needed food and raw materials that England was well placed to supply. As a result large quantities of silver were imported into England, enabling King Edgar and his successors to produce an enormous number of coins of good quality, and to maintain the currency despite the large sums paid to Scandinavians from the 980s to 1051. This flow of silver into England, beginning in the late tenth century, suggests that Henry of Huntingdon's description of Anglo-German trade in his own time, the 1140s, is relevant earlier. According to Henry, 'although little silver was mined in England, much was brought from Germany by the Rhine on account of England's wonderful fertility in fish and meat, in most precious wool, and in cattle without number. As a result, a larger supply of silver is found in England than in Germany.'[34]

Lincolnshire was a good source for the exports mentioned by Henry. One of its main products later was wool of good quality that fetched high prices. In the 1280s Boston exported an annual average of about 10,000 sacks, containing some 3,000,000 fleeces.[35] They did not all come from Lincolnshire, but a large proportion did. Sheep farming may not have been on that scale two centuries earlier but there are some indications that the sheep population was already very large in the eleventh century. The animal bones found at Flaxengate in Lincoln suggest that there was a significant increase in the sheep population in the late tenth century.[36]

Domesday Book does not record livestock in Lincolnshire as it did in Norfolk where there were over 46,000 sheep on demesnes in 1086, including some exceptionally large flocks on the salt marshes of the Fenlands.[37] There is no reason to suppose that the demesne flocks of Lincolnshire were smaller; the high values given for many manors in Holland were probably due in large measure to sheep. In other parts of England, when comparison is possible, the demesne flocks of 1086 were commonly as large as they were on the same demesnes in the twelfth century. Domesday gives no information about the size of peasant flocks and later medieval sources rarely do so either, but the few descriptions of peasant flocks in the twelfth and thirteenth centuries show that the peasants sometimes had very many more sheep than their lords. As the area of grazing land was reduced under the pressure of increasing population, landowners had the advantage in the competition for the available resources and peasants found it difficult to maintain such large flocks as they did formerly.[38] It is, therefore, possible that there were as many sheep in some parts of Lincolnshire in the eleventh century as there were two centuries later. Archaeological evidence suggests that they were reared for their wool. Apart from a short period in the second half of the eleventh century, probably after the Norman Conquest, most of the sheep bones found at Flaxengate were from animals that were three or more years old, implying that they were kept for their wool rather than meat, although the mutton was welcome and was consumed in large quantities.[39] There are, therefore, grounds for supposing that 'most precious wool' made an important contribution to the wealth of Lincolnshire long before Henry of Huntingdon's time.

Cloth may already have been an important product and export in the eleventh century as it was later. The discovery of over 600 spindle whorls at Flixborough suggests that cloth making was one of the main activities there in the eighth century. Rough cloth was made in most communities, perhaps in most households, but the demand for better quality fabrics led to larger-scale production by specialist weavers, fullers and dyers. It is likely that Lincoln and Stamford were centres for these activities before the Norman Conquest. Lincoln was later renowned for high-quality cloth dyed scarlet. Although there is evidence that yarn was dyed in Wigford in the tenth century there is nothing to show that 'scarlet' was made in the city before the Conquest. Simple fabrics called *haberget* that were particularly associated with Stamford were certainly produced in pre-Conquest Lindsey and it is likely that cloth of that kind was exported from Lincoln in the eleventh century.[40]

Other exports from Lincolnshire probably included meat and fish, as mentioned by Henry of Huntingdon, and cheese; a list of tolls levied at Arras in 1036 includes English cheeses.[41] The inhabitants of the rapidly growing towns across the North Sea consumed a large amount of food and had an acute need for preserved food that could be eaten in the late winter and spring. As salt was a good preservative, it is likely that Lincolnshire produced and exported salted meat and fish.

The earliest explicit reference to Lincolnshire's overseas trade concerns Norwegians, not Germans. Henry II issued a writ ordering Norwegians who come to Grimsby and other ports of Lincolnshire to pay toll and other dues as they had done in the time of his grandfather at the beginning of the twelfth century.[42] This trade can be traced back at least to 1069 when Turgot, who was a hostage imprisoned by William I in Lincoln castle, escaped on a Norwegian merchant ship from Grimsby.[43] The only Norwegian exports mentioned in twelfth-century records are falcons and hawks, but they probably also brought furs and walrus ivory, which was certainly being worked in Lincoln before the Conquest.[44] By the thirteenth century Norway's main export was dried cod, known as stockfish, an important form of preserved food. It was probably already being supplied to Lincoln and other English towns before the Norman Conquest. Norway's imports are likely to have been much the same then as they were a century later, cloth, wheat, flour and honey.

There was a demand for Lincolnshire's produce in southern England as well as in other parts of north-west Europe. London was probably the largest city in eleventh-century Europe and needed huge quantities of food and raw materials that could most conveniently and cheaply be transported by boat. Complaints in Domesday Book about the imposition of new tolls in havens on the coast of Lindsey suggest that coastal traffic was on a fairly large scale. One witness said that he had seen toll taken from 24 ships from Hastings.[45] Such a specific count is unlikely to have been taken over a protracted period. The ships were presumably not plying directly between Lindsey and Hastings; they are more likely to have discharged cargo in intermediate ports, including London, or possibly across the Channel.

THE CONTROL OF TRADE

This commercial expansion happened after Lincolnshire was firmly under the control of English kings, who benefited greatly from it. The merchants paid toll and kings also profited when foreign coin and bullion was exchanged for English coins, the only legal tender. Kings were, therefore, eager to encourage merchants and offer them protection. When, late in Edgar's reign, merchants from York were imprisoned and robbed by the inhabitants of Thanet, the king 'was so furious with these villagers that he despoiled all of them of their possessions and even deprived some of life'.[46] Such an example must have deterred others from interfering with traders and no similar punitive action is reported before the Conquest. Light is cast on relations between English kings and foreign merchants by an incident in 1095. The rebellious earl of Northumberland attacked and robbed four large ships bringing Norwegian merchants to England. The merchants appealed to the king and, when the earl refused to restore the stolen goods, full compensation was paid from the royal treasury. This episode suggests that the goodwill of these merchants was worth keeping.[47]

Toll was originally a royal prerogative. In the eighth century it was levied on ships arriving in coastal *wic*, and later, in the form of 'waggon-shillings' and 'load-pennies', inland at Droitwich, which was an important source of salt. By the end of the ninth century similar tolls were being gathered by royal agents in markets held in the newly fortified *burhs* that were key centres of expanding royal government.[48] When English kings gained control of Lincolnshire in the tenth century its *burhs*, Lincoln, Stamford, and Torksey, were included in this system. The tolls paid by foreign merchants visiting Lincolnshire in the twelfth century were probably first imposed by Athelstan, if not by his Scandinavian predecessors. Tolls were also levied on goods brought for sale by the English; Domesday Book reports that the Torksey burgesses holding messuages there were exempt from tolls on goods entering or leaving the town in return for conducting royal agents to York.[49] A list of tolls levied in London early in the eleventh century shows that its trade was mainly in such things as wool and cloth, timber, fish, wine, pigs, dairy produce, eggs and hens. Lincoln's must have been very similar, if on a smaller scale.[50]

Early in the tenth century Edward the Elder and Athelstan made an unsuccessful attempt to limit buying and selling to markets that were supervised by royal agents in the *burhs*. By the end of his reign Athelstan explicitly admitted that buying and selling could take place elsewhere, and a century later many landowners had markets on their estates in which they were entitled to collect toll on some goods, but not on foodstuffs.[51] English kings were more successful in requiring that purchases should take place before witnesses who could testify that they were legal transactions, a process known as vouching to warranty, in Old English *team*.[52] Landowners who had the right to collect toll also had the right to hold the process of *team* for their own markets. Domesday lists 35 Lincolnshire landowners who had these rights on the eve of the Conquest.[53] Most of the markets mentioned in Domesday Book were held by landowners named in that list, but two, Burton upon Stather and Caistor, were on royal estates.[54]

LINCOLN

The produce that was exported from Lincolnshire came from all parts of the region, but much of the resulting wealth was concentrated in Lincoln, with the result that the city expanded rapidly in the tenth century. By the middle of that century the northern part of Wigford, a Roman suburb that was abandoned by the fifth century, had been reoccupied; in the absence of excavations south of the site of St Mary's Guildhall, it is not possible to say how far this development extended. Evidence from the several sites that have been excavated suggests that the reoccupation of the land either side of Ermine Street did not begin near the city and gradually progress south. Nor was it ribbon development. It has been argued that initially there were groups of buildings, including churches, scattered along the road, separated from each other by open ground, and that the first church of St Mark, constructed in the mid tenth century, was 'relatively late in the order of parish foundation in Wigford', apparently in a gap between earlier developments.[55] The infilling continued and when, a century later, St Mark's churchyard was enlarged, itself a sign of growing population, the extension was on to marginal land between the church and the river Witham, presumably because the street frontage was built up on both sides of the church.[56] Another pre-Conquest suburb was Butwerk, a name meaning 'outside the fortification', an area that began to be occupied before the end of the tenth century. It appears to have reached its full extent by the Norman Conquest; that is the implication of the report in Domesday Book that Colswein built two churches outside the city on waste land that William I gave him 'that was never built upon before'. They have been identified as St Peter at Well and St Augustine's, both at the eastern edge of

Butwerk.[57] After about 950 there are also clear signs of increased activity inside the lower city.

The development of Lincoln was largely due to the fact that it was the main centre for royal government in the region. It was the site of one of the largest mints in England and, after the creation of Lincolnshire, it was the base from which the sheriff supervised the king's business. If the earl was absent it was the sheriff, together with the bishop, who presided over the shire court that normally met twice a year in the city. The main landowners of the shire were, consequently, regular visitors and Domesday Book shows that some had houses in the city. Foreign merchants were required to pay toll and other dues to the king's agents in Lincoln. They did not have to visit Lincoln to do this – there must have been royal agents in Grimsby and other main ports – but we can assume that many did so in order to trade in the city's markets.

Some indication of the prosperity of the region in this period of economic expansion is given by the activity of the mints of Lincoln and Stamford. The productivity of a mint depended on the amount of silver available. There were two main sources. First, coins in circulation that had to be reminted when the type was changed. After the coinage reform of *c.* 973 this happened at intervals of approximately six years until the end of Cnut's reign, and then more frequently, every two or three years. The second source, foreign coin or bullion, was obviously more important in ports of entry like Lincoln than in mints inland. It has been estimated that in the eleventh century, at least until 1066, Lincoln produced over 10% of England's coins and that Stamford's share ranged from 2.5 to 7%. In the two decades before the Norman Conquest they jointly issued a quarter of the coinage, even more than London.[58] These figures suggest that there was a very large amount of silver circulating in the region or being imported through it. Comparison of Figs. 9.2 and 9.3 suggests that on the eve of the Conquest coins were more plentiful in Lincolnshire than in other parts of England, reflecting the relative prosperity of the region at that time.

As the main centre of this prosperous region Lincoln continued to expand throughout the eleventh century; the set-back after the Norman Conquest was short lived. This growth is reflected by the provision of churches. At the beginning of the twelfth century there were at least 32. Most of them were founded between the Danish and Norman Conquests, but at least two, built by Colswein, were more recent. Sir Francis Hill argued that the other two churches in Butwerk nearer the walls, St Bavo and St Rumbold, were also post-Conquest foundations because their dedications to the patron saints of Ghent and Malines respectively suggests 'Flemish post-Conquest piety'.[59] That is possible, but there may well have been fairly close links between Lincoln and Ghent earlier in the eleventh century, and the medieval spellings of Rumbold imply that he was the

a. b. c. d. e.

Fig. 9.8 Coins from five Lincolnshire mints in the reigns of Æthelred II and Cnut. Horncastle, with only three known coins, is omitted. For Louth see p. 197.

	mint	*king*	*type*	*date*	*no. in SCBI 27*
a.	Grantham	Æthelred II	First Hand	c. 979–85	
b.	Lincoln	Æthelred II	Crux	c. 989–96	38
c.	Stamford	Æthelred II	Long Cross	c. 996–1003	1152
d.	Caistor?	Cnut	Pointed Helmet	c. 1025–30	1
e.	Torksey	Cnut	Pointed Helmet	c. 1025–30	1537

The moneyer of the Lincoln coin was Colgrim, the same as in the coin-die from Flaxengate, Fig. 9.9. Dates from Stewart 1990. The Grantham coin, the only one known, is from Kungliga Myntkabinettet, Stockholm, see Jonsson 1987b.

English saint Rumwold.[60]

By 1066 there were at least 1270 tenements within the walls and in suburbs. Of these, 1150 were held by burgesses who each paid a penny a year as a symbolic annual rent, called 'landgable', to the king. There were also 120 tenements that did not. Many tenements were probably much the same size as the property excavated on Flaxengate, which measured about 96 by 61ft.[61] Some of the tenements fronting on the main thoroughfares were larger than that and those held by great magnates such as Harald Godwinsson, Earl Morcar and Ulf *Fenisc* must have been much bigger in order to accommodate their retinues, servants, and horses when they visited the city.

The development of the city must have been regulated by agreement among the burgesses or by some superior authority. The allocation of space and the determination of property boundaries cannot have been done in a free-for-all. Some streets in the medieval city roughly followed the line of Roman streets, but most were newly laid out in the ninth or tenth centuries. Some may have originated as footpaths through the Roman structures that remained above ground, but their width had to be agreed and

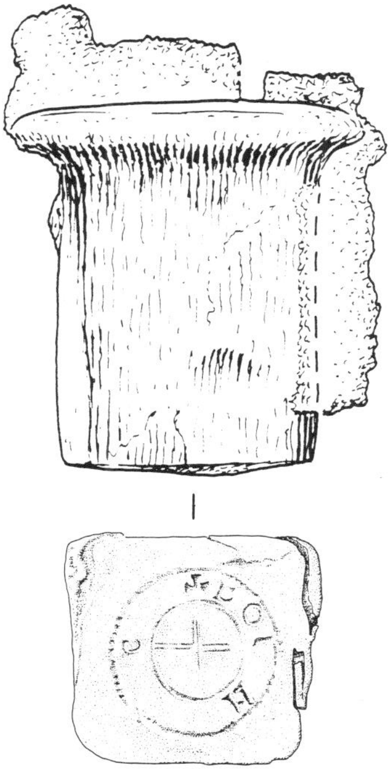

Fig. 9.9 An encrusted coin die, partially cleaned, found in the excavation of Flaxengate. It is the upper (reverse) die for pennies of King Æthelred II of the Crux type (current c. 991–7) produced in the Lincoln mint by the moneyer Colgrim. It suggests that Flaxengate was the site of a die-cutter's workshop (Blackburn and Mann 1995).

Drawn by D. Watt, © CLAU.

encroachments prevented. The process began under Scandinavian rule but after 927, apart from the short period of Olaf Guthfrithsson's success, it was supervised by reeves of English kings.

Very little is known about the role of the burgesses in the government of the city before the Conquest. The *Motstow* in High Street, meaning 'the meeting place', certainly existed at the end of the twelfth century when the nearby church of St Peter was distinguished from others with the same patron as *ad Placita*, or Peter at Pleas.[62] It was, doubtless, the meeting place of the borough court before the Conquest. According to Domesday Book in a dispute about ownership 'all the burgesses' declared the law and in 1054 the endowment of Stow St Mary was done 'with the witness of all *burhware* of Lincoln'.[63] An assembly of over 1000 is improbable, whether held in the street or in the church. It is more likely that a small group including, or perhaps consisting of, the lawmen acted on behalf of the rest, with larger meetings occasionally.

The account of Lincoln in Domesday Book begins with the names of the twelve lawmen in the time of King Edward and their successors in 1086. It says nothing about their functions, which must have been much the same as in York where a lawman was described in 1106 as *legislator vel iudex*.[64] It has been assumed that lawmen were a Scandinavian innovation, and that

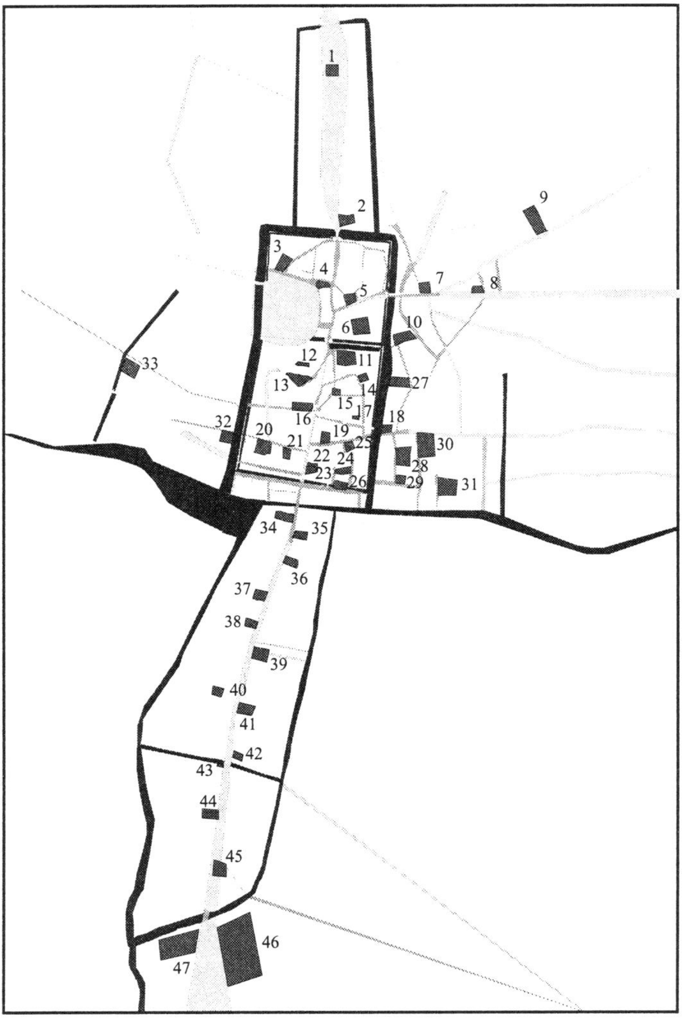

Fig. 9.10 Churches and religious houses in Lincoln before 1107. Lincoln had 46 parish churches in the medieval period of which some, such as St Giles (no. 9) and Holy Innocents (no. 46) seem to have early lost their independence and survived as parochial rights attached to hospitals. Five were mentioned in the Domesday Book: St Laurence (no. 19), St Mary (no. 6), All Saints (no. 5), St Michael (no. 11) and St Peter at Pleas (no. 22). Although not recorded by name, the churches of St Peter at Arches (no. 23), St Peter ad Fontem (no. 30) and St Clement in Butwerk (no. 31) are also almost certainly referred to in Domesday Book, whilst St Martin (no. 16) is the subject of a writ of William the Conqueror. St Benedict (no. 34) was granted to St Mary of Lincoln between 1100 and 1107. The churches of St Mary le Wigford (no. 36) and St Peter at Gowts (no. 41) are normally ascribed to the Anglo-Saxon period on architectural grounds whilst the

they expounded the law, as the lawmen of Scandinavia are supposed to have done, but this is most unlikely. Urban development was in its infancy in ninth-century Scandinavia and there is no evidence that Scandinavian towns ever had similar groups of lawmen. The fact that the name was Scandinavian does not prove that the institution was, any more than the adoption of the Scandinavian word 'law' means that the English were unfamiliar with law before the ninth century. The name and its Latin translation implies some legal function. The *judices* of Chester were obliged to attend the borough court but they were chosen or selected and therefore did not have the same status as the hereditary and privileged lawmen of Lincoln and Stamford, who may once have constituted the court or council of those towns, and had a similar role to the *witan* of some Devonshire towns early in the eleventh century.[65] The lawmen of Lincoln all had sake and soke. One of them, Ulf, son of Svartbrand, had the additional right described as toll and team that together with sake and soke amounted to what can be called full ownership, and he is the only lawman in the list of such privileged landowners in the Lincolnshire Domesday. It may be significant that while other lawmen had some property near the city, Ulf's son Svartbrand, who held a manor in Candlesby, was the only one to have any near the coast.[66]

The lawmen were certainly an urban élite. Their possession of sake and soke gave them a privileged status, and one of them was ranked with the aristocracy of the shire. The office, or title, was hereditary. Five of those listed in 1066 had been replaced by their sons twenty years later and three still lived. The fact that one is described as 'Godric son of Eadgifu' suggests that the inheritance could be through women as well as men. Three of them held a relatively large share of the town fields which were assessed at twelve and a half carucates; two lawmen each had one carucate and a third had half a carucate. Some were wealthy enough to lend money against the security of rural estates, but nothing is known about their property in the city, apart from the house that one of them held as a pledge. As at Stamford, some probably held a great deal more than others. A few of them held land near the city as tenants or owners, or as pledges for loans.[67]

Fig. 9.10 caption continued

churches of St Mark (no. 37) and St Peter Stanthaket (no. 13) have been dated to the 11th century through excavation, as has the nave of St Paul-in-the-Bail (no. 4). The church of St Margaret in Pottergate (no. 10) was recorded in 1115 and that of All Saints Hungate (no. 21) is first recorded at the same time. The churches granted by Henry I in 1100–7 seem to have been St Michael (no. 11), St Peter Stanthaket (no. 13), St George (no. 17), Holy Trinity (no. 25), St Edmund (no. 24), St Swithin (no. 26), Holy Trinity on the Hill (no. 27), St Rumbold (no. 18), St Bavon (no. 28), St Augustine (no. 29), St Peter in Eastgate (no. 7) and the churches of St John (no. 35), Holy Trinity (no. 43), St Michael (no. 42), St Margaret (no. 44) and St Mark (no. 37). © *A. Vince.*

It has been suggested that some lawmen acted as moneyers.[68] It is true that the names of seven of the 1066 lawmen were also the names of pre-Conquest Lincoln moneyers. Some are so common that they could well be coincidental, but Sverting and Walrafn were not common names. The moneyers with those names, however, were active well before the Conquest (Sverting 1023–46; Walrafn 1029–44).[69] This does not necessarily rule out the possibility that some of the other lawmen were moneyers.

On the eve of the Norman Conquest there may have been as many as 12,000 people living in Lincoln. Most previous estimates of the population have been much lower and were based on the assumptions that there was only one household on each tenement and that the average size of a household was five. Both assumptions are questionable. In towns expanding as rapidly as Lincoln was in the eleventh century, households tended to be larger than in times of depression or in the countryside. In such circumstances many tenements had more than one household. That was the situation in twelfth-century Winchester and in some parts of London in the thirteenth century.[70] In an exceptional entry, Domesday Book reports that in Nottingham Roger de Busli had three tenements on which there were 11 houses.[71] The Flaxengate excavation suggests that there was a similar density of occupation in Lincoln even in the tenth century. There were at least three buildings on the Flaxengate property before the Conquest, with more in the eleventh century when the Grantham Street frontage was developed. The permanent inhabitants of Lincoln were not only burgesses and their families. There were servants, apprentices, craftsmen, labourers, clergy, and royal officials. In addition, the magnates and local landowners needed stewards to take care of their property in the city. It does, therefore, seem reasonable to assume that in 1066 the average number of people per tenement was about ten, giving a total population of over 12,000, more than in the early nineteenth century.

Traces of pre-Conquest buildings found in several parts of Lincoln give some indication of their size and wall construction. At Flaxengate during the tenth and eleventh centuries most structures had walls made of planks set directly in the earth. As the buried parts decayed the buildings could be shored up for a while but after about 30 years they were beyond repair. The property was then cleared and new buildings were erected. These rebuildings provided opportunities to alter the lay-out. The buildings only had one storey and most were about 16 ft wide and from 32 to 52 ft long. One exceptional tenth-century structure had walls resting on stone footings, possibly to provide dry storage space.[72]

The little that can be said about the internal arrangements of the buildings depends mainly on the distribution of the finds recovered during the excavation. These show that in the second half of the tenth century there

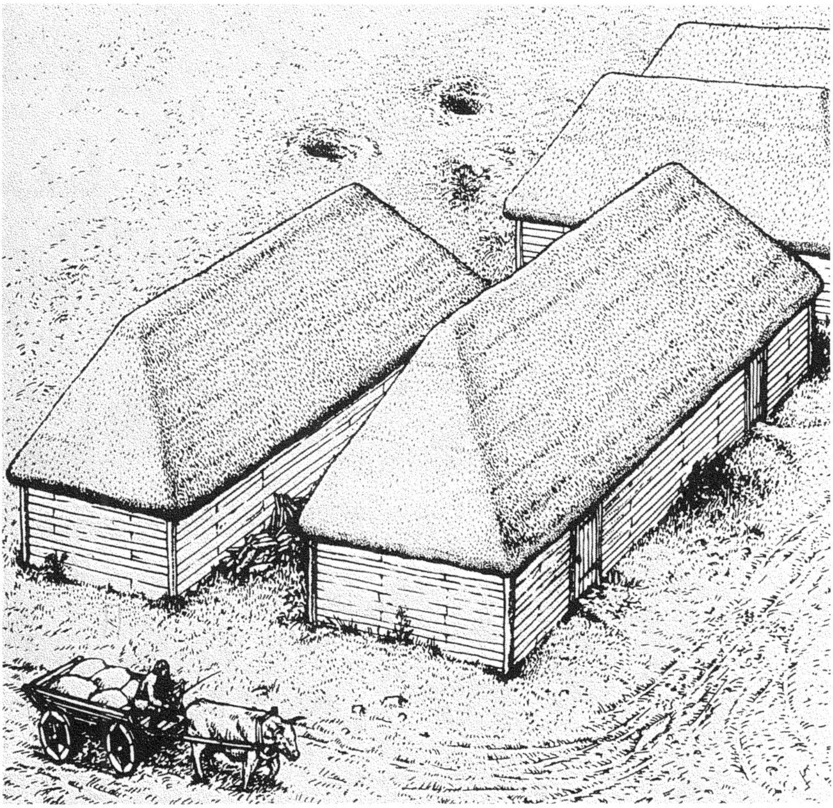

Fig. 9.11 Reconstruction drawing of 11th-century houses in Flaxengate, Lincoln. Drawn by R. Sutton. © CLAU.

were some buildings in which workshops were combined with living quarters. Metal was worked in the vicinity earlier but it was only then that craftsmen began to work on this property. The materials used were glass, iron, silver, brass, copper, bone, and antler. Small quantities of partly worked jet, slate, and Norwegian ragstone were also found. Spindle whorls and weaving tools show that yarn was spun and cloth made, too. Some houses, including the succession built on the corner of Flaxengate and Grantham Street, were residences without workshops. The corner site may have been occupied by the owners of the tenement, while the other buildings were let to tenants.

Lauren Adams Gilmour's analysis of the early medieval pottery from Flaxengate has allowed her to draw some conclusions about the way of life in these houses.

> We have no direct evidence of any ceramic tablewares designed for individual servings of food in the earliest periods; unless there were tablewares in other materials, for instance treen, meals must have been eaten straight out of the cooking-pot. This would have been most convenient if meals were taken on low seats round the hearth. The earliest purpose-made tablewares from Flaxengate are the little tenth-century drinking pots of local ware; the only other vessels probably exclusively used as tableware were the later tenth-century identically glazed Stamford ware shallow bowl and cup, perhaps made as a set, and unparalleled at Stamford itself. From the mid-eleventh century, glazed pitchers and jugs begin to appear. If meals in the late Saxon household were taken on low seats around the hearth, participants may have tipped water or ale from the spouted pots, pitchers, and large containers standing against the walls into medium sized wooden bowls or their sloping-sided ceramic counterparts. Beginning in the later tenth century...meals appear to have been more commonly taken at a board, with drink standing on the table for pouring into cups in the course of the meal.
>
> The only evidence throughout the period for household lighting were the small ceramic lamps; their relative proportion in the assemblage changed little over the ninth to the early thirteenth centuries and was never more than 2 per cent. Suspension lamps, the commonest type from the late ninth to the early eleventh century, gradually lost popularity and, like the deep-banded pedestal lamps without a saucer, gave way to shallow-bowled, saucered pedestal lamps, perhaps accompanying a change in the type of fat used.[73]

The animal bones found in the excavation provide some information about diet.[74] It has been estimated that the average annual meat consumption of adults was about 55 lbs. In the mid eleventh century cattle seem to have provided about 80% of the total meat weight, pigs about 13% and sheep about 7%. The pigs may have been kept on the tenement along with geese and domestic fowl. Small quantities of wildfowl, mostly caught in the winter, and fish were also eaten. Some fish were from fresh water, presumably the Witham or Trent, but cod, haddock, and flatfish came from coastal fisheries or from more northerly parts of the North Sea. Cereals were a cheaper and, for many people, a more important food, but the quantities consumed cannot be estimated archaeologically. Latrine pits of the eleventh century on the north bank of the Witham show that, as might be expected, diet could be varied with fruit and nuts.[75]

Lincoln depended on a regular supply of huge quantities of timber for buildings, other raw materials, food, and fuel. Some measure of the scale of the demand for food can be based on the evidence of the animal bones found in the Flaxengate excavation. In his discussion of this material, Terry O'Connor calculated that on the assumption that there were some 4,000 adults in the city, flocks totalling 5,000 sheep would be needed to supply

Fig. 9.12 Pottery manufactured in Lincoln dating from the late 9th to early 11th centuries. From left: dish, pedestal lamp, three cooking pots. Photo by J. O'Neill. © CLAU.

the amount of mutton consumed, and that these required between 5,000 and 10,000 acres of grazing which, as he comments, was a very considerable area of farmland to produce only 7% of the meat supply.[76] If, as suggested above, the population of the city was 12,000, these estimates should be doubled. Lincoln's needs could only be met by drawing on the surplus of a very large area, and it was this more than anything else that united Lindsey and north Kesteven in the eleventh century.

The Lincolnshire Domesday records burgesses in three other places before the Conquest. The most important were the royal boroughs of Stamford and Torksey, which is described as both a *villa* and *suburbium*, and was held by the queen before the Conquest. These are described immediately after Lincoln. In the royal manor of Grantham, which had also been held by the queen, there were 111 burgesses and 77 'tofts of sokemen of the thanes' in 1066 and also twenty years later.[77] The bishop of Lincoln's manor of Louth had 80 burgesses in 1086 but not, apparently, before the Conquest.[78] The only indication that Louth had special status on the eve of the Conquest, apart from its market, is a fragment of a single coin with mint-signature beginning LV. Its identification as Louth is rendered more likely by the fact that the coin is in the distinctive style of Lincoln.[79]

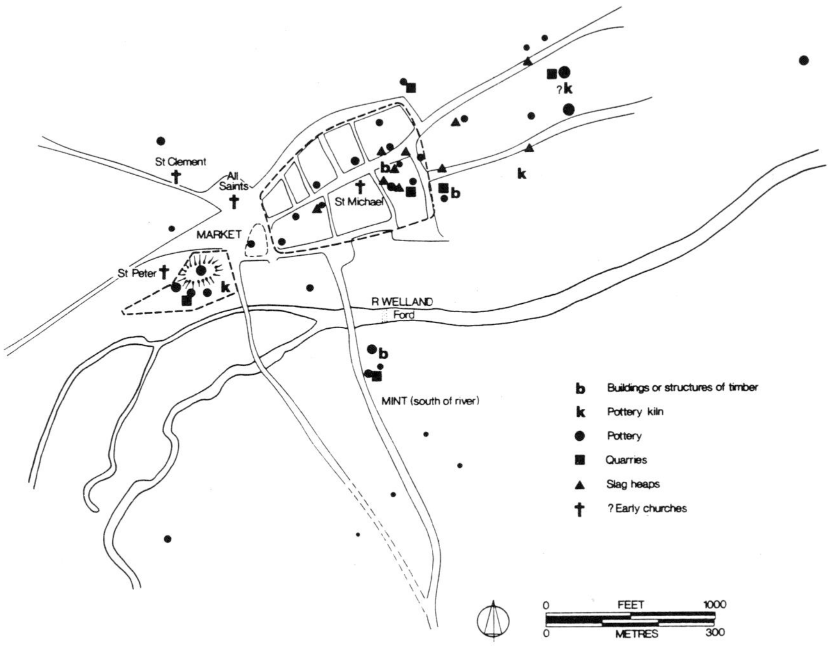

Fig. 9.13 Plan of Saxo-Norman Stamford.
From Mahany, Burchard, and Simpson 1982, fig. 5, with permission of the Society for Medieval Archaeology.

STAMFORD AND TORKSEY

The urban history of Stamford began with the Danish occupation of the site overlooking the ford by which the Jurassic Way crossed the Welland.[80] The north and south limits of the Danish fort are roughly indicated by Broad Street and St Mary's Street, with Red Lion Square in the west and Star Lane and St George's Street in the east. The fort built by King Edward in 918 to confront the Danes became the nucleus of the southern extension of the town across the river, later known as Stamford Baron. The line of the ramparts of Edward's fort may be represented by Park Lane, Pinfold Lane, and Church Street, with High Street St Martin's as its central axis. It must have been this *burh* that was referred to in the nearby place-name Burghley.

To the west of the Danish fort, immediately north of the keep of the Norman castle, the well-endowed church of St Peter was probably associated with a major estate centre before the Danes arrived and that was represented on the eve of the Norman Conquest by Queen Edith's extra-burghal manor. Traces of a palisade inside two parallel ditches have been found south of the castle site. As the outer ditch cuts through a layer including red-painted Stamford ware it must have been made after the potters introduced by the Danes had begun to work nearby.[81] This suggests that this site was fortified by the Danes before they constructed the larger fort.

Very little is known about the development of Stamford before it reached the stage described in Domesday Book. It was then a flourishing town with well over 400 tenements, implying that it had more than 4000 inhabitants, and was about a third the size of Lincoln. Few traces of pre-Conquest buildings have been found, but there is abundant evidence of industrial activity. During the tenth century iron was made at several places in the area that had been occupied by the Danish fort, and three pottery kilns have been found outside it. It was probably a mint from the time of Athelstan and after the coinage reform of *c*. 973 in some issues it produced more coins than either Chester or Norwich. Domesday records the existence of at least four churches, but explicitly names only one of them, St Peter's, although it implies that one was dedicated to All Saints. Later evidence has made it possible to identify another as St Clement's in Scotgate, whch suggests that the town had expanded to the west well beyond the bounds of the Danish fort. There were also 70 tenements in Queen Edith's extra-burghal manor which was also west of the fort.

Stamford was unusual in that it was divided between three shires. Five wards were in Lincolnshire, one was south of the river in Northamptonshire, and the queen's manor 'belonged to Rutland'. As the ward south of the river, which was held by Peterborough Abbey, is not described in Domesday Book, the number of tenements in it is unknown. North of the river there were 170 tenements rendering all customs to the king, but there were 241 that did not. This includes 77 that were held by sokemen 'who have their lands in demesne, and seek lords where they will', over whom the king had limited rights. They are not explictly said to have been there in 1066, but their privileged position makes it most unlikely that they were a new element in the town. Fifty-one and a half tenements were held in 1086 by nine lawmen who had limited jurisdiction 'over their own houses and over their own men'. There were twelve lawmen in 1066 but Domesday does not say how many tenements they had. The queen had 70 tenements free of everything except 'baker's custom', a payment made by women who baked and sold bread. There were also 42 tenements that were held by five other landowners and were occupied by burgesses whose rents were counted as income in manors outside Stamford. For example, nine were held by the lord of a manor in Uffington in which there were, according to Domesday Book, nine burgesses of Stamford who rendered four shillings.[82]

Pottery and iron-working figure prominently in the archaeology of pre-Conquest Stamford, and in the eleventh century stone was quarried in and around the town, but its prosperity cannot have been based on such products. Stamford was well placed to serve as a regional centre not only for local exchanges but also for the collection and shipment of wool, dairy produce, and other goods that were in demand elsewhere in England and across the North Sea. It was probably also engaged in the cloth trade before the Conquest. Stamford was later famed for a type of woollen fabric called *haberget*, that was made on vertical, warp-weighted looms.[83] Some of this cloth was made in the town, but most was produced in the surrounding countryside. Cloth of this type was made on such looms in most parts of Anglo-Saxon England and there is no reason to doubt that some was already being exported through Stamford in the eleventh century, if not before.

The third royal borough described at the beginning of the Lincolnshire Domesday, Torksey, was on the eve of the Conquest about half the size of Stamford, with 211 burgesses.[84] It was held by the queen together with the

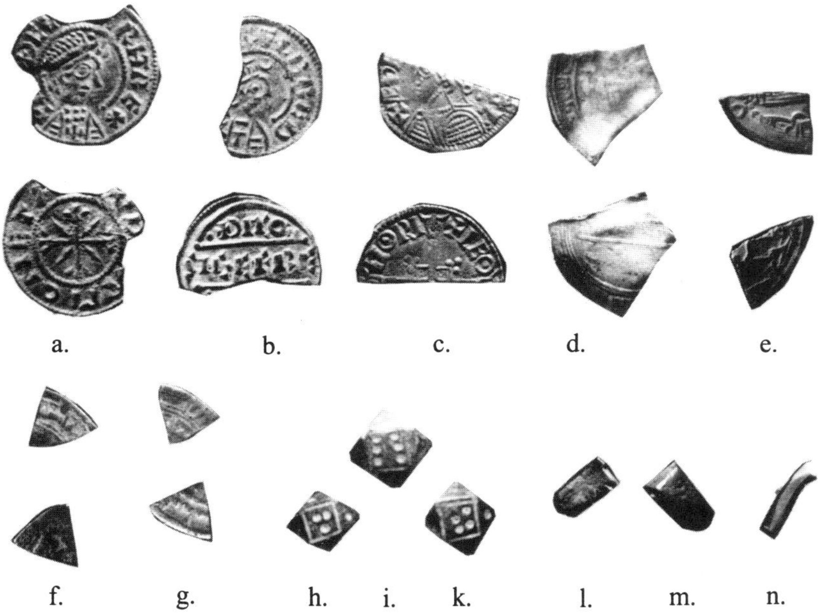

Fig. 9.14 Finds from Torksey, 9th–11th century. a. Æthelberht of Wessex (860–5), silver penny, floriate Cross type, Canterbury, moneyer Dudda; b. Alfred of Wessex (871–99), silver penny, Lunettes type, 871–c. 875, Canterbury, moneyer Sigeferth; c. Vikings of Dublin, Sihrtic III, silver cut halfpenny, imitating Æthelred II's Helmet type, c. 1005; d.–g. 'Abbasids', cut fragments of silver dirhems, 9th century; h.–k. Anglo-Scandinavian? polyhedral copper alloy weights, units 6 (i), 4 (k), and 3 (h). Similar weights have been found in Scandinavia, Russia, and the Near East; l.–n. Hacksilver and hackgold of the late 9th/early 10th century?; l. and m. Cut terminals from silver rods; n. Cut piece of a gold *rod. (Fitzwilliam Museum, Cambridge.) Photos and © Mark Blackburn.*

nearby manor of Hardwick. Torksey is first mentioned in 872 when the Viking army wintered there. It was then, or soon afterwards, that potters who were brought by the Danes from Frankia set up kilns there and began producing a distinctive type of pottery known as Torksey ware. Long before the Danes arrived it was one of the most important landing places on the Trent. Its great advantage was the Foss Dyke that enabled boats to travel between the Trent and the Witham. The exceptionally large number of coins that have been found in and near Torksey together with ornamental metalwork suggest that fairs or markets were held there in the eighth and ninth centuries, although some of the ninth-century coins were probably brought by Vikings.[85] Fewer tenth- and eleventh-century coins have been found, possibly because the dyke was then blocked. It needed cleaning from time to time; in the thirteenth and fourteenth centuries there were frequent complaints that it was silted up. That may well be the reason that very little tenth-century Torksey pottery has been found in Lincoln. If so, the substantial quantities that began to reach the city early in the eleventh century could indicate that the dyke had been cleared.[86] The economic expansion at that time would have made the effort worthwhile. After the Conquest Torksey pottery was once again scarce in Lincoln – very little has been found on the site of the castle – suggesting that in the confusion of the Conquest the dyke was not kept free of silt. It was not re-opened until 1121.[87] The blockage of the dyke probably explains why Torksey, unlike Lincoln and Stamford, declined after the Conquest. In 1086 there were only 102 burgesses and 111 tenements were waste. Domesday Book emphasizes Torksey's close relationship with Lincoln. Its burgesses had the same customs as those of Lincoln, it is described as a *suburbium* and, together with Hardwick, contributed a fifth of the geld paid by the city.

When the dyke was open, Torksey was Lincoln's outport on the Trent, giving access to the heart of Mercia and to Northumbria. By the twelfth century Lincoln had an even more important outport at Boston, near the mouth of the Witham. It is not mentioned in Domesday Book, but during the twelfth century it rapidly grew to become a town of great importance. Sea-going ships could unload their cargoes for sale there or to be shipped to Lincoln on river boats that returned with goods for export. Boston was connected to the Wolds by the slight ridge, or chain of islands, called 'the stick' by the English, that provided a route across the Fens. It was, therefore, a convenient port for the export of wool and other produce from east Lindsey. The site of Boston lay in what is described in Domesday Book as Skirbeck Hundred.[88] All but two bovates of that hundred belonged to the huge soke of Drayton that was held before the Conquest by Ralf the Staller and was given by William I to Alan, Count of Brittany. There were, according to Domesday Book, two churches in the hundred. One can confidently be identified as St Botolph's, that gave its name to the town.

This church was the focus of a fair that when first mentioned, between 1125 and 1135, was clearly well established. Thanks to its good communications by river and land the site must have been one of the most important landing places on the Lincolnshire coast, at least from the tenth century when Lincoln was rapidly expanding, and the demand for Lincolnshire's produce overseas began to grow.

The rapid growth of Boston in the twelfth century demonstrates the vitality of the region's economy. The Norman Conquest, discussed in the next chapter, caused much disruption but recovery was quick. Within ten years order was restored and the resources were being exploited with greater efficiency to the benefit of the people of Lincolnshire as well as of their new lords.

NOTES TO CHAPTER IX

1 Grierson and Blackburn 1986, pp. 15, 157, 163. A sixth 'York' coin appeared at a recent (1987) auction.

2 Blackburn 1994. A plated forgery of a gold coin, probably made in the seventh century but of uncertain origin, has been found near Louth, Blackburn 1993.

3 See Appendix 9.

4 Series B sceattas from the 'South Lincs' site, see Appendix 9. Another was found near Grimsby in 1997, see Fig. 9.6.

5 He explained that 'in order to reflect the probable date of loss of the coins, rather than their date of striking, an adjustment has been made assuming that approximately one third of the coins struck in each twenty-five year period were not lost until the next period, and that there were effective recoinages *c.* 765, *c.* 792 and *c.* 875 which removed earlier issues from circulation'. Blackburn 1993, pp. 80–1.

6 The columns in the histogram in this previously unpublished diagram are for periods of 20 years, unlike the 25-year periods of Fig. 9.2. I am indebted to Mark Blackburn for allowing me to publish these diagrams.

7 Grierson and Blackburn 1986, pp. 150–4, 168–72.

8 S 1804, trans. Campbell, J. 1989b, p. 27.

9 Wood, I. 1994, pp. 301–2.

10 Sawyer 1978, pp. 223–5.

11 Reynolds 1977; p. 26; Bassett 1989a, pp. 16–7. For Wigford, see Steane 1990.

12 DB i. 345a, 355a, 356a = *LD* 7/56, 24/45, 91. The medieval markets and fairs are listed in Platts 1985, pp. 296–304.

13 Roffe 1986. An annual fair, but no weekly market, was held at Stow Green until modern times; see p. 66 above.

14 S 1478. In Domesday Book the word *mercatus* seems to have been used for both weekly markets and annual fairs. A fraction of a *feria* in Suffolk is the only explicit reference to a fair in the whole survey, DB ii. 418a.

15 Sawyer 1986b, pp. 65–6.

16 Owen, D. 1971, p. 110.

17 Cate 1937 and for Bardney, Platts 1985, p. 296.

18 See below, note 20.

19 DB i. 375b = *LD* 70/1, 2.

20 DB i. 354b = *LD* 24/13.

21 DB i. 376a = *LD* 70/14. For the ferry see above, p. 30, n. 23.

22 Ekwall 1960, *s.n.*. Domesday describes this as a half market pertaining to Kirton in Lindsey, held in Thealby, Derby and Burton (DB i. 338b = *LD* 1/64). These three places are named because they constituted a hundred, see Appendix 3. The implication of this entry is that there was also a market at Kirton.

23 The coins found on this, and other sites, are listed in Appendix 9. For information about finds of ornamental metal work I am indebted to Kevin Leahy. See also Fig. 9.6.

24 Vince 1993d, p. 154.

25 Vince 1993b, p. 4.

26 Vince 1993b, p. 5. For additional information on this point I am indebted to Alan Vince.

27 The concentration of church dedications to Sts Helen and Margaret in Lindsey is another indication of close links between Lindsey and other coastal regions of eastern England: the focus of Helen's cult was York and there was a special devotion to St Margaret in East Anglia, Owen, A. 1988.

28 Miles, Young, and Wacher 1989.

29 See above, p. 102.

30 Perring 1981, pp. 43–4; Vince 1993c, pp. 163–5.

31 Vince and Young 1991, p. 26. The coins are listed in Appendix 9.

32 Kilmurry 1980, pp. 176–95; Vince 1993d.

33 Sawyer 1965, p. 160.

34 *Historia Anglorum*, pp. 5–6, quoted in Campbell, J. 1989a, p. 15.

35 Carus-Wilson 1964, p. 189.

36 O'Connor 1982, p. 47.

37 The only reference to sheep in the Lincolnshire Domesday is the report that Gilbert of Ghent had a flock at Great Sturton in the Wolds (DB i. 354b = *LD* 24/21). For Norfolk see Darby 1952, pp. 144–6.

38 Sawyer 1965, pp. 162–3.

39 O'Connor 1982, pp. 23–4, 48.

40 See below p. 196.

41 Loyn 1962, p. 96.

42 *EHD* II, pp. 1039–40.

43 Historia Regum, pp. 202–3.

44 Sawyer 1986a. Alan Vince tells me that a waste piece of walrus ivory, identified by James Rackham, has been found in a pit of the late tenth or early eleventh century on Micklegate, now part of High Street, *PNL* 1, pp. 72–3.

45 DB i. 375b = *LD* 69/39, 40.

46 *EHD* I, no. 4, *s.a.* 974, p. 284.

47 Sawyer 1986a, p. 186.

48 Sawyer 1986b, pp. 62–3.
49 DB i. 337a = *LD* p. 11/1.
50 IV Æthelred, cl. 1-2, ed. and trans. Robertson 1925, pp. 70–3.
51 Sawyer 1986b, pp. 62–3.
52 Harmer 1952, pp. 76–7.
53 DB i. 337a = *LD* p. 13.
54 They were held in 1065 by Earls Edwin and Morcar respectively (DB i. 338ab = *LD* 1/38, 64, 65). The fact that Edwin is not listed as having toll and team implies that he held Burton upon Stather, in the soke of Kirton in Lindsey, in his capacity as earl.
55 Gilmour and Stocker 1986, pp. 6, 83. The argument that St Mark's is later than St Edward's, its neighbour to the south, poses a problem. The dedication to St Edward cannot be earlier than 978, when he was martyred, some time after the date proposed for the first St Mark's church. The explanation could be that St Edward's originally had another dedication; such changes were not uncommon.
56 Gilmour and Stocker 1986, pp. 90–1.
57 DB i. 336b = *LD* pp. 6–7; Hill, F. 1948, pp. 133–4.
58 Metcalf 1981, pp. 74–7.
59 Hill, F. 1948, p. 36.
60 Most early forms are *Rum(w)old, -(w)ald, or Romald.* The first with a *b* is *c.* 1270; *PNL* 1. 134. It was possibly through Lincoln that knowledge of this Buckinghamshire saint reached Scandinavia in the twelfth century, Toy 1983, p. 100.
61 Perring 1981, p. 43.
62 PNL 1, p. 132. *Motstow* was later converted into *motston,* and interpreted as the 'mootstone', Hill 1948, pp. 61, 289.
63 DB i. 336a = *LD* p. 5/15, S 1478.
64 Leach 1891, p. 192.
65 Tait 1936, pp. 42, 124.
66 DB i. 370b = *LD* 68/8. For the land held by lawmen, see Hill, F. 1948, pp. 39–40.
67 DB i. 376a, 377a = *LD* 71/3, 72/18.
68 Hill, F. 1948, p. 40.
69 Jonsson and van der Meer 1990, p. 83. The dates of the coin types in North 1963 need some, but not much, revision, cf. Stewart 1990.
70 Biddle and Keene 1976, pp. 343–4, 440–1; Keene, D. 1984.
71 DB i. 280a.
72 Perring 1981, pp. 36–40.
73 Gilmour, L. 1988, p. 178.
74 O'Connor 1982, pp. 47–8.
75 Greig 1989.
76 O'Connor 1982, p. 48.
77 DB i. 337b = *LD* 1/9. 77 tenements in Stamford were also held by sokemen. This is either an extraordinary coincidence or the reference to sokemen's tofts in Grantham is a mistake.
78 DB i. 345a = *LD* 7/56.

79 Jonsson 1987a, pp. 146–7, with a description of another possible Louth coin. See above, pp. 51, 81, for indications that Louth had a long history as an important centre.

80 The following account of Stamford is largely based on Mahany and Roffe 1983, and Mahany, Burchard, and Simpson 1982. See also Hall 1989, pp. 193–201.

81 Kilmurry 1980, p. 32, where it is suggested that the palisade and inner ditch may have been a little later than the outer ditch. Hall 1989, p. 195, citing Kilmurry, suggests the opposite.

82 Roffe 1977; DB i. 358a = *LD* 27/35.

83 Carus-Wilson 1969.

84 For Torksey, see Hill, F. 1948, pp. 307–13.

85 See Appendix 9.

86 For information about Torksey pottery I am indebted to Alan Vince.

87 Hill, F. 1948, p. 308.

88 For this paragraph see Owen, D. 1984.

CHAPTER X

THE NORMAN CONQUEST

Edward the Confessor died, childless, on 5 January 1066. The only surviving male representative of the English dynasty was Edgar the Ætheling, grandson of King Edmund Ironside, but there were two foreign claimants, Harald Hardrada, king of Norway, and William, duke of Normandy. Edgar was too young to provide the leadership needed at that critical time and the English council quickly chose an experienced warrior, Harold Godwinsson, as king. The Norwegian king was the first to arrive, accompanied by Tostig who had earlier in the year attacked Lindsey with a force of 60 ships and been driven off by the local militia under the leadership of Edwin and Morcar. The Norwegian fleet sailed up the Humber and landed at Riccall on the Yorkshire Ouse on 18 September. Edwin and Morcar had ample warning and summoned levies from both Mercia and Northumbria. On 20 September, when Harald approached York, they attempted to stop him at Fulford, a mile from the city wall, but were defeated. He was welcomed in York and might reasonably have expected that the Northumbrians would rally to him as they had to Swein in 1013. On Monday, 25 September, probably in the hope of receiving submissions, he was seven miles east of York, at Stamford Bridge where roads from many parts of the East Riding converged. He was surprised there by Harold Godwinsson, who had hurried north. The invaders were decisively defeated, and the Norwegian king was killed. William of Normandy landed in Pevensey Bay three days later. King Harold quickly returned south and was killed in battle against the Normans near Hastings on 14 October. After this disaster many thought that Edgar the Ætheling should be king, but when Ealdred, archbishop of York, the earls Edwin and Morcar, and other English leaders realized that they could not effectively resist the Norman invaders, they submitted to William, who was crowned in Westminster Abbey on Christmas Day 1066.[1]

William then seized the land of all those who had fought against him. The main confiscation in Lincolnshire at that stage was of Harold Godwinsson's estates, all but one of which were held in 1086 by Hugh of Avranches, Earl of Chester. It is unlikely that there were many other forfeitures in Lincolnshire immediately after William's coronation; few local men who survived the battles of Fulford and Stamford Bridge can have taken part in the Hastings campaign.[2]

People who had supported Edgar's claim were able to secure their property and status, at least temporarily, by submitting to William, although some, including the monks of Peterborough, were required to pay for their misjudgement. The monks' offence was that on the death of their abbot, Leofric, on 1 November 1066, they elected their provost Brand who sought confirmation of his appointment from Edgar the Ætheling 'because the local people expected that he would be king'. This angered William, but after the intervention of 'distinguished men' and the payment of 40 marks of gold, the king was reconciled.[3] As Stenton suggested, William was probably also influenced 'by a sense that it would be indiscreet at that moment to indulge his anger against an abbot with powerful kinsmen in the unquiet Danelaw'.[4] Brand belonged to an important Lincolnshire family which, to judge by their names, was of Scandinavian descent.[5] William could not be sure that men of this kind who had loyally fought for King Harold against the Norwegians would be so ready to support him if the Danes invaded, as they did three years later.

REBELLIONS AND CONFISCATIONS

In March William went back to Normandy to celebrate his triumph. He took with him as hostages the potential leaders of English opposition, Edgar the Ætheling, Edwin, Morcar and Waltheof, who had recently been made earl of several shires, including Huntingdon, by Edward the Confessor. There was, nevertheless, some resistance during his absence, partly provoked by the heavy-handed actions of the men he left in charge. When, early in December, William returned to England one of his first tasks was to reduce Exeter and the south-west into submission. This and other revolts provided new opportunities for confiscations, but the need to reward his warriors led William to begin to seize land without just cause. The Peterborough version of the *Chronicle* complained that after his return 'he gave away every man's land' and Orderic explained: 'The king, with so much fighting on his hands, was most anxious to keep all his knights about him, and made them a friendly offer of lands and revenues and great authority, promising them more when he had completely rid the kingdom of all his enemies.'[6] Such confiscations must have increased the willingness of some men to resist the Conqueror and may have been the reason Merleswein, sheriff of Lincoln, who had estates in Somerset, Devon, and Cornwall, as well as in Lincolnshire and Yorkshire, accompanied Edgar the Ætheling into exile in Scotland in the summer of 1068.

Edwin, Morcar, and Waltheof remained in William's court and

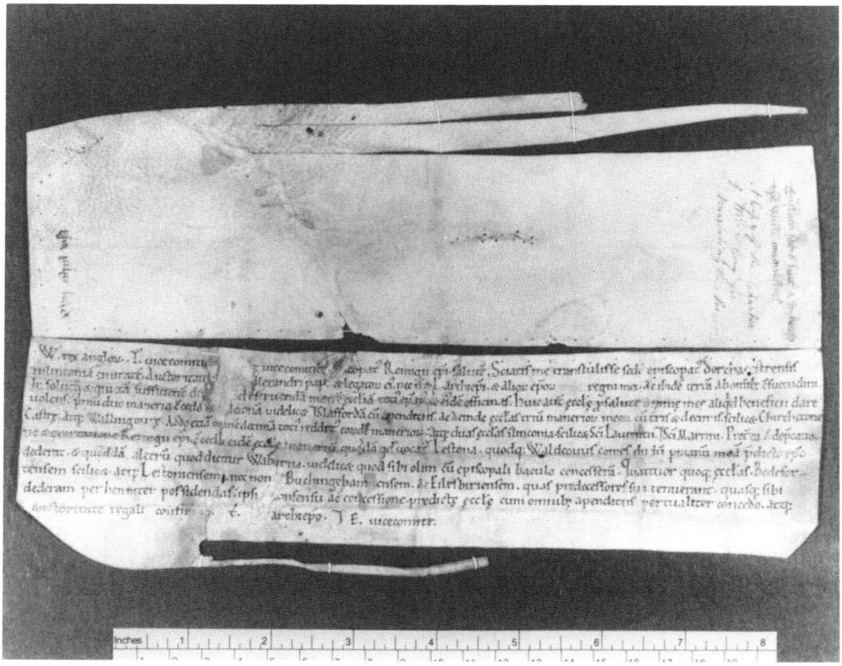

Fig. 10.1 Writ of William I, issued in 1072, addressed to all the sheriffs in Remigius's diocese informing them that his see was to be removed from Dorchester in Oxfordshire to Lincoln and that the bishop had been granted, inter alia, the manors of Welton and Sleaford, the churches and tithes of the royal manors of Kirton, Caistor, and Wellingore, and the churches of St Lawrence and St Martin in Lincoln. This type of document declaring royal grants, authenticated by the royal seal (which has in this case been lost), was used by English kings in the first half of the 11th century and adopted by the Norman conquerors.
© Dean and Chapter of Lincoln Cathedral.

witnessed charters he issued during the celebration of Whitsun (11 May) at Westminster.[7] Soon after that they left for the north. William reacted quickly to this display of independence with a campaign in which he built castles at Warwick, Nottingham, York, Lincoln, Huntingdon, and Cambridge, and put them in charge of reliable vassals. Edwin and Morcar submitted and do not appear to have taken part in the rebellions that occurred in the next two years. These began early in 1069 when the newly appointed earl of Northumbria and his men were killed in Durham. This insurrection encouraged Edgar, Merleswein, and others to attack York. The city was taken but not the castle and after a very rapid march William raised the siege and built a second castle on the opposite bank of the Ouse. Edgar returned to Scotland.[8]

These measures to control York were severely tested later in the year when a Danish fleet, said to number 240 ships or more, arrived in the Humber. It had been sent by Swein Estrithson but was led by his brother and three of his sons. This was the signal for a general rising in Northumbria led by, among others, Edgar the Ætheling, Waltheof, and Merleswein. The English and Danish armies joined forces and on 20 September took the city of York and both its castles. According to Orderic, before the attack on York Edgar raided Lindsey but was surprised by the king's garrison in Lincoln. Edgar escaped, but most of his party was captured and their ship destroyed.[9] William reacted to the loss of York without delay. As his army approached the city the Danes withdrew to the Isle of Axholme where they were sheltered by extensive marshes. Nevertheless, William forced them to return to the north bank of the Humber.

The success of the Northumbrian rising encouraged rebellions in other parts of England. Most were suppressed without much difficulty by local Norman forces, but the revolt in Mercia was a serious challenge that required William's personal intervention. He left the counts of Mortain and Eu to contain the Danes and their allies north of the Humber, and marched to Stafford where he defeated one of the main concentrations of rebels. The Danes took advantage of William's absence to reoccupy York, but when, after some delay in crossing the River Aire, William and his army advanced on the city, the Danes once again returned to their ships. William regained control of the city and celebrated Christmas there. The submission of Waltheof and other leaders early in the New Year marked the end of the end of the Northumbrian rebellion.[10] In January William made a difficult winter march across the Pennines to Cheshire, where he surprised the remaining Mercian rebels, who were quickly defeated. He then returned south to celebrate Easter in Winchester.

The Danish fleet was still in the Humber 'where the king could not get at them'.[11] Its leader had, however, promised to leave England at the end of the winter in return for tribute and licence to take provisions from the neighbourhood.[12] This presumably meant Lindsey, for there can have been little worth having in east Yorkshire thanks to the systematic devastation of the region during that winter by William's troops. Orderic may have referred to this when he reported that when the Danes 'judged it safe they came out of the marshes to share the feasts of the country people which are colloquially known as farms'. The Old English word *feorm* could mean either a feast or the tribute rendered to a ruler or lord. It is, therefore, possible, and more likely, that Orderic misunderstood what happened, and that the Danes took tribute in Lindsey.[13] It was probably at this time that William granted the Isle of Axholme to Geoffrey of La Guerche in the hope that he would prevent the Danes using it in future.[14]

The Danish fleet did not leave in the spring, but moved to a new base in Ely, 'and the English people from all the Fenlands came to them and expected that they were going to conquer all the country'.[15] According to the *Peterborough Chronicle*, the move to Ely happened after the Danish king Swein joined the fleet in the Humber. There is no other evidence for such a visit and Swein is not mentioned in connection with the move to Ely. The same chronicle reports that later in the year William and Swein came to an agreement, but that does not prove that Swein was in England.

In the early summer the Danes were joined by a band of English outlaws, led by Hereward, a tenant of Peterborough Abbey, which they had sacked. The *Peterborough Chronicle* reports that Hereward's band handed over their loot from the abbey to the Danes, who then left with it.[16] Hereward's band remained at Ely and were later joined by the outlawed bishop of Durham, Earl Morcar, and a major, but obscure, English magnate called

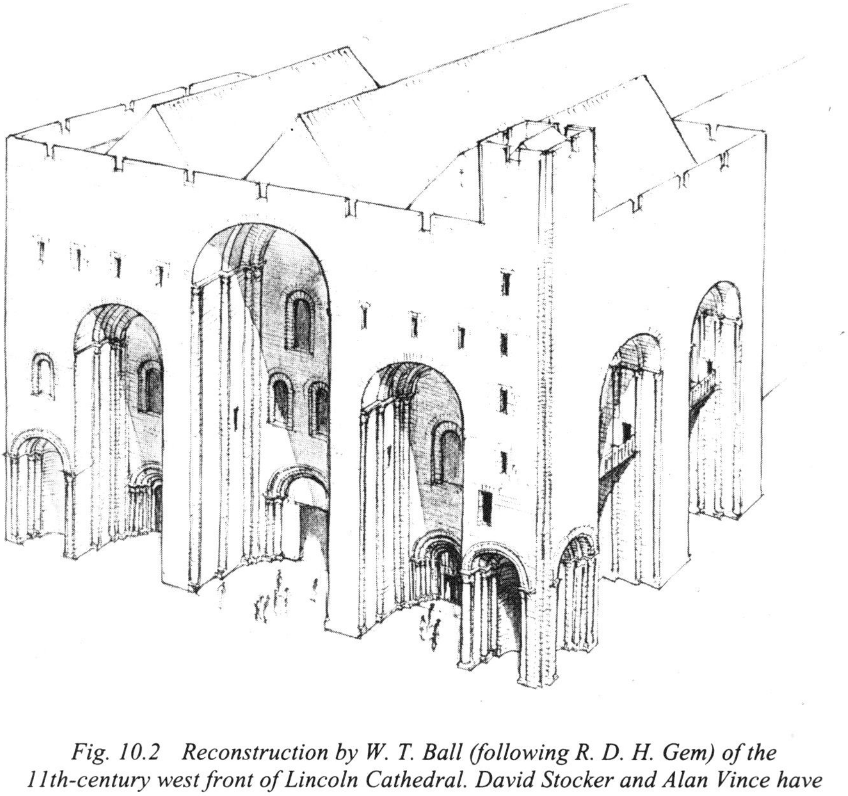

Fig. 10.2 Reconstruction by W. T. Ball (following R. D. H. Gem) of the 11th-century west front of Lincoln Cathedral. David Stocker and Alan Vince have suggested that it was originally a free-standing fortification built before the see was transferred to Lincoln. © R. D. H. Gem.

Siward Barn, together with hundreds of their men.[17] In 1071 William besieged Ely and after forcing most of the rebels to surrender, Morcar and Siward Barn were imprisoned. A few escaped under the leadership of Hereward who 'passed out of history into legend'.[18]

William's response to these widespread risings was not only to defeat the insurgents by force and devastate areas that persistently rebelled. He also took hostages, some of whom were held in Lincoln castle.[19] His most effective means of reducing the danger of future opposition was to extend the process begun in 1068 and confiscate the estates of many of the surviving English landowners and grant them to his own men. The results can be seen in Domesday Book which shows that by 1086 the native aristocracy had been completely replaced. Most of the new lords were Normans, but some, including Gilbert of Ghent and Drogo de la Beuvrière, were from Flanders, and others, notably Count Alan of Richmond, were Bretons. In 1086 there was only one Englishman, Colswein, with a substantial fief in Lincolnshire, but he is not recorded as holding any land there before the Conquest.

OLD LORDSHIPS: NEW LORDS

Apart from Colswein the only English people who appear as tenants of the king in Lincolnshire were minor thegns and women who had small properties and posed no threat to William. Some of them owned land before the Conquest but it was not always the same land as in 1086. It is likely that in 1066 there were many similar people whose land was obtained, legally or not, after the Conquest by the invaders. We cannot, however, assume that all those named in Domesday Book as holding land on the eve of the Conquest were independent owners. Domesday can sometimes be shown to name pre-Conquest sub-tenants rather than the owners of the land, and may possibly have done so often. Consequently it is impossible to determine how many such minor independent landowners there were in pre-Conquest Lincolnshire. There is certainly no justification for assuming that the Conquest was followed by a tenurial revolution in which huge numbers of free men and women of no more than local importance were replaced by a small group of William's supporters, some of whom held vast estates.[20]

It is, however, clear that William often granted all or most of the estates confiscated from an individual to a single beneficiary. This was administratively convenient; the transaction could be effected simply by writs addressed to the relevant shire courts. In this way the land of Ulf *Fenisc* was granted to Gilbert of Ghent, not only in Lincolnshire but in all the other eight shires in which Ulf held land. In the terminology of Domesday, Ulf was Gilbert's *antecessor*, his predecessor. Similarly, most

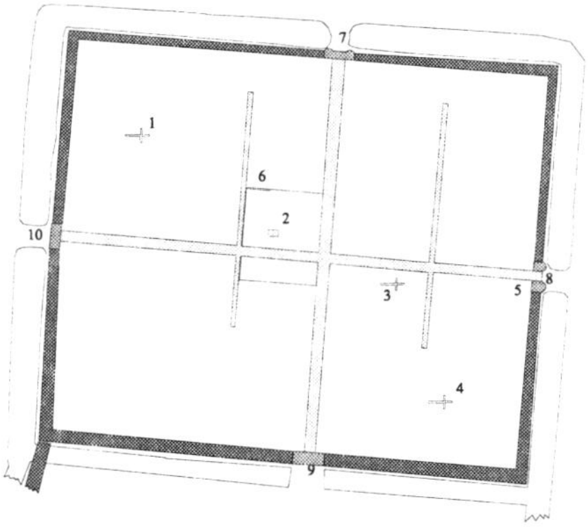

Fig. 10.3a In the mid 11th century much of the Roman street pattern and probably traces of many Roman structures would have been visible, such as the gates (7, 8, 9, 10) and remains of the forum (6). Four churches were present: (1) St Clement, (2) St Paul, (3) All Saints, and (4) St Mary.

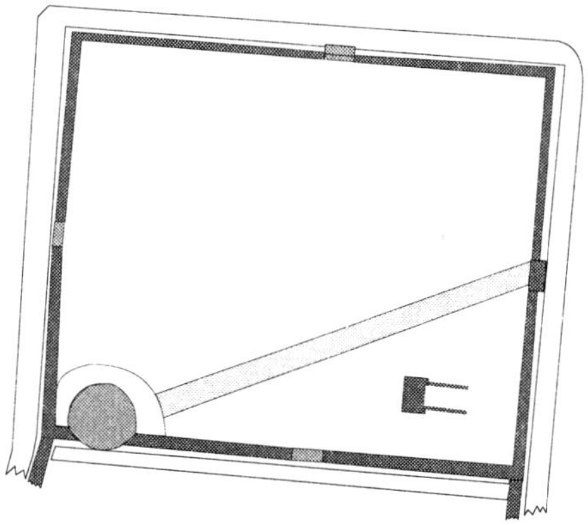

Fig. 10.3b Late 11th century. The first Norman developments in the upper city were the construction of a motte in the south-west corner of the Roman walls and the fortified west end of the cathedral. A new road, Eastgate, was constructed leading to the motte from a rebuilt east gate.

Fig. 10.3 The development of the upper city of Lincoln from before the Norman Conquest to the mid 12th century, as interpreted by David Stocker and Alan Vince. Maps drawn by A. Vince. © A. Vince.

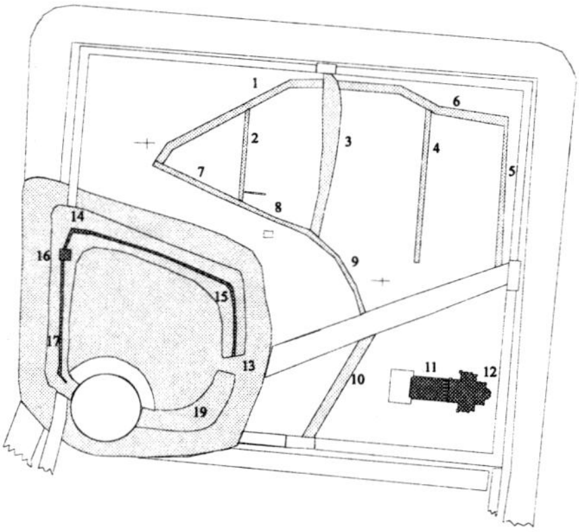

Fig. 10.3c *Early 12th century. The inner bailey was constructed, blocking off the west end of Eastgate (13), and the cathedral was completed (11, 12). A lane (7, 8, 9, 10) ran parallel with the inner bailey ditch and it may be that part of the medieval street pattern in the north of the bail was laid out.*

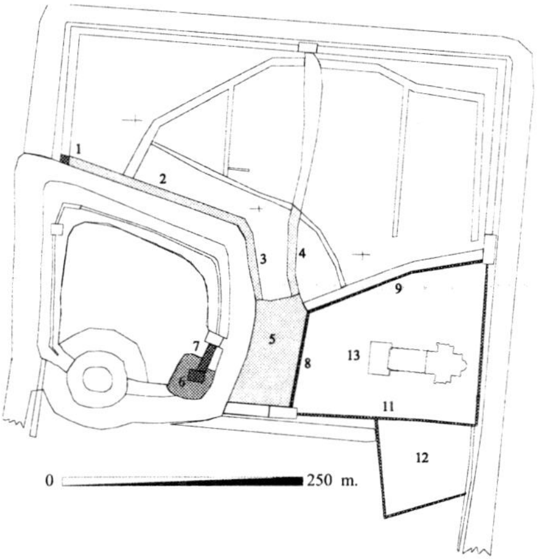

Fig. 10.3d *Early to mid 12th century. Two stone towers (7, 8) were built in the inner bailey, one the work of Earl Ranulph and the other of his mother Countess Lucy. The cathedral is surrounded by a continuous precinct wall (8, 9, 11) and the Bishop's Palace (12) is constructed over part of the Bail ditch.*

a. b. c.

Fig. 10.4 One of the five Lincoln moneyers who operated both before and after the Norman Conquest appears on most of his coins as Ouðgrim or Oðgrim, common English forms of the Scandinavian name Auðgrímr. He apparently began work under Harold I (1035–40) and regularly produced coins until the second type of William I, current 1068–71. Three of his coins are illustrated here: a. Edward the Confessor's last type, current 1065–6; b. Harold II; c. William I, the last type he produced. The Lincoln moneyer with the same name who was active in Æthelred's reign, but not in Cnut's, may have been a relative. (SCBI 27 nos. 789, 800, 818.)

of Merleswein's lands were acquired by Ralf Paganel and Gilbert Alselin's *antecessor* was Toki, son of Outi. These, and many other post-Conquest lords had, in effect, stepped into the shoes of one or more pre-Conquest landowners, for some were given the land of more than one *antecessor*; Remigius, for example, had the land of both Halfdan, son of Topi, and Barthi, as well as that belonging to the bishopric before the Conquest. All large fiefs in Domesday Book included manors that were held before 1066 by people other than the *antecessores*. Some were obtained by marriage, purchase, exchange, or by special grant, but there is reason to think that many of these manors were in fact part of the *antecessor*'s estate and that the people named were close kinsmen or sub-tenants. In other words, many 1086 fiefs had much the same composition, and in some case a very similar structure of demesne and tenanted land, as pre-Conquest lordships.

William could alternatively give all the land in a particular wapentake or other district to one person, with the exception of any that had already been granted to someone else. A good example of such a grant in Lincolnshire early in William's reign is the Isle of Axholme which was entirely held by Geoffrey of La Guerche. As Robin Fleming has shown, there were many territorial grants of this kind in other parts of England that must have been made after so-called *antecessorial* transfers were made.[21] The grant of

Axholme, is, however, shown to be early by the fact that Geoffrey held a manor there that had belonged to Ulf *Fenisc*, the *antecessor* of Gilbert of Ghent, who claimed it.[22]

There is little direct evidence to show when the tenants-in-chief of 1086 obtained their land in Lincolnshire, but many transfers were probably made in the troubled years 1069–70 or very soon afterwards.[23] The land of Halfdan, son of Topi, must have been confiscated and given to Bishop Remigius before the death of Abbot Brand on 27 November 1069, for Brand compensated Halfdan, his kinsman, for this loss by allowing him to rent one of Peterborough's manors, Dunsby, near Bourne.[24] This early grant of land in Lincolnshire to Remigius shows that he was already building up the endowment of the bishopric well before the see was moved to Lincoln. The land of Halfdan's brother Ulf in Lincolnshire and in Holderness was probably confiscated at much the same time and given to Drogo de la Beuvrière. Robin Fleming has argued that because Drogo held a great deal of land in Holderness that had belonged to William Malet, he must have been granted Holderness after William Malet's death in about 1071. It is, however, possible that Drogo was given Ulf's land before he acquired the whole of the three hundreds of Holderness.[25]

These confiscations and the endowment of faithful vassals consolidated William's hold on England. By the spring of 1070 there was little risk of serious opposition by the English and although the Danes were still in the Humber they had not dared to fight William. Before Easter he dismissed his mercenaries.[26] The rebels who held out for a while in Ely were a nuisance, but not a serious threat. After the imprisonment of Morcar and the death of Edwin, who was murdered by his own men as he fled to Scotland in 1071, the only member of the Old English aristocracy who retained any power was Waltheof. It was a measure of William's confidence that in 1072 Waltheof married the king's niece, Judith, and was made earl of Northumbria, as his father Siward had been.

The effectiveness of the measures William took after the crisis of 1069–70 was demonstrated in 1075 when Waltheof together with Ralf, earl of Norfolk and Roger, earl of Hereford, rebelled. William was in Normandy at the time and stayed there, relying on his representatives in England to restore order. They did so with little difficulty. Ralf fled to Brittany and Roger was imprisoned; both lost their lands. Waltheof once again submitted to William, but this time he was not pardoned. He was beheaded at Winchester in May 1076, and buried at Crowland where he was soon regarded as a martyr.[27] The earls had appealed to the Danes for help but their fleet arrived after the rebellion had been crushed and they had to content themselves with plundering York.

Although Lincolnshire was by 1075 firmly under the control of William's government, and the native magnates had been replaced by William's men, in many respects little had changed in the previous ten years. The destruction wrought by English rebels, Danish seamen, and Norman troops must have still been apparent, but Domesday Book shows that there was a remarkable recovery in the next ten years.[28] The expansion of Lincoln and Stamford, interrupted by the Conquest, had been resumed and the economy of the shire was, at least by 1086, once again flourishing. Old English lordships formed the basis of many Domesday fiefs, including several of the most extensive, and the men and women who worked the land were, with few exceptions, natives. So, too, were the craftsmen who provided most of the tools, clothing, and other goods that were needed locally. The one group that can be studied in detail, the moneyers, showed remarkable continuity. Five of the nine Lincoln moneyers who struck Edward the Confessor's last issue also struck William's early coins. The crisis of 1069–70 may have disrupted the mint; only one moneyer struck coins before and after 1071, but for the rest of William's reign the moneyers were, to judge by their names, with one possible exception, all natives.[29]

Most of the landowners and their vassals spoke Norman French but this had very little influence on the language of the majority, in contrast to the ways Danish speech had earlier affected the local dialects. The king's principal agents were foreigners, but they relied on English assistants. The institutions of government, the courts of wapentakes, ridings and the shire, had all been formed before the Conquest. The king made his wishes known to these courts and to his agents by sealed writs, a device developed by the Anglo-Saxons. The coinage was controlled and taxes collected as in the time of King Edward. There were a few legal innovations, but the law and the means of administering it in William's reign were largely the same as in his predecessor's. Remigius's cathedral and William's castle in Lincoln were massive symbols of the new order and the many church towers that were built in stone after the Conquest reflected new fashions, but in 1086 and for some time afterwards Lincolnshire was much the same as it had been when King Edward was alive and dead.

NOTES TO CHAPTER X

1 *Chronicle* C, D, E, *s.a.* 1066; Florence, *s.a.* 1066. There are general accounts of these and subsequent events in Barlow 1955, pp. 77–99, Douglas 1964, pp. 181–244, and Stenton 1971, pp. 580–621.

2 The only forfeiture in 1066 recorded in the Lincolnshire Domesday was by Grimkell who gave his land 'to Merleswein the sheriff for his offence against the king and made him his heir', wording that suggests this forfeiture happened before the Norman invasion (DB i. 376b = *LD* 71/11; cf. DB i. 362b–363a = *LD* 35/2, 16).

3 *Chronicle* E, *s.a.* 1066. Obits added at about the time of the Norman Conquest in a

psalter of Crowland Abbey suggest that the English royal family was held in special regard there, Keynes 1985.

4 *LD*, p. xliv.

5 For this family see Appendix 10.

6 Orderic, pp. 220–1.

7 Davis, *Regesta*, nos 22, 23.

8 *Chronicle* D, E, *s.a.* 1068.

9 Orderic, pp. 226–7.

10 Orderic, 232–3.

11 Chronicle D, *s.a.* 1069

12 Florence, *s.a.* 1069.

13 Orderic, pp. 230–1.

14 DB i. 369 ab = *LD* 63. Fleming 1991, p. 176n, doubts that the grant of Axholme was so early. For indications that it was see below n. 22 and p. 225.

15 *Chronicle* E, *s.a.* 1070.

16 This interpretation of the *Peterborough Chronicle* is based on the commentary by Cecily Clark 1970, p. 64.

17 *Chronicle* E, *s.a.* 1071.

18 Douglas 1964, p. 222.

19 See p. 182.

20 This controversial question is discussed in Appendix 3.

21 Fleming 1991, pp. 160–82.

22 Another Axholme manor, Haxey, had belonged to the *antecessor* of Henry of Ferrières, Siward Barn, who must have lost his land in 1071 at the latest: DB i. 369 ab; 376b = *LD* 63/, 7, 12, 16, 21, 26; 71/16.

23 This question is discussed in detail by Fleming 1991, chapter 5, although some of her conclusions are questionable; see Appendix 3.

24 Hugh Candidus, p. 69.

25 Fleming 1991, pp. 160, 177. There is some doubt about the date of William's death.

26 Orderic, pp. 236–7.

27 Orderic, pp. 346–51.

28 Darby 1977, pp. 248–52.

29 Mossop 1970, end table.

Appendix 1

PAGAN ANGLO-SAXON BURIALS

This appendix is based on Leahy 1993, pp. 39–42, with the addition of burials in Kesteven that are not included in his list. Cemeteries outside the county at Newark, Great Casterton and near Stamford are also included. In making the additions I have followed Leahy in excluding single finds of metalwork or pottery unless there are indications that they were associated with burials. In entries based on Leahy's list (indicated by an asterisk *) many details and references are not repeated, but a few additional references are given. For advice on dating I am indebted to Kevin Leahy. Where possible dates or date-ranges are indicated, normally in terms of centuries in Roman numerals; e.g. late VI/early VII means late sixth or early seventh century.

*Ancaster. Graves and at least 40 cremations: early VI.

*Asgarby. A female grave (VI) found in 1811. In 1915 a rich warrior grave (late VI/ early VII) was found in an inhumation cemetery that may also have included some cremations.

*Barton-on-Humber, Castledyke. *c.* 200 graves and 1 cremation: VI–VII. Two hanging-bowls were found. The earlier without associated finds, the later (VII) was in a warrior-grave (Bruce-Mitford 1993, nos 1–2; Drinkall and Foreman forthcoming).

*Barton-on-Humber, West. Traces of an inhumation cemetery: VI.

Baston. 10 cremation urns found *c.* 1863. Two graves and evidence of over 50 cremations excavated in 1966, presumably including those found earlier (Meaney 1964, pp. 151–2, Mayes and Deane 1976): late V– late VI.

Belton, Old Rectory. ?Inhumation cemetery. 'at least 5 very fragmentary iron knives and ?part of a spearhead' found ?1903 (Meaney 1964, p. 152).

Benniworth. An enamelled escutcheon of a hanging-bowl found in 1933 probably came from a rich grave of VII (Bruce-Mitford 1993, no. 3).

*Bottesford. Evidence of a cremation and perhaps of inhumations.

*Brocklesby. An inhumation cemetery is indicated by finds of metalwork: VI–VII.

*Burgh-le-Marsh, Cock Hill. A grave (late VI/early VII) found in 1933 was in a barrow that may be post-medieval (*LHA* 12(1977), p. 73).
*Burton upon Stather, Bagmoor. Cemetery with 'many urns' and inhumations, destroyed by mining *c.* 1928: late V–VI.
*Caenby. High-status grave in a large barrow, excavated 1850 (East and Webster, forthcoming): early VII.
*Candlesby. ?Inhumation cemetery.
*Carlton Scroop. Inhumation cemetery: late V–VI.
Castle Bytham. A grave found in 1850 contained a silver-gilt ring brooch, glass and terracotta beads, jet, and 'the lower jaw of a large beaver with one end set in metal' (Meaney 1964, p. 153).
*Caythorpe. Mixed cemetery of unknown size destroyed *c.* 1899.
*Cleatham, in Manton parish (often misleadingly referred to as in Kirton-in-Lindsey). About 60 urns found in 1856. 1014 cremations and 64 graves excavated 1984–89: V–VII. A hanging-bowl of *c.* 600 was found (Bruce-Mitford 1993, no. 5).
*Cleethorpes, Beacon Hill. ?Inhumation in a Bronze-Age barrow.
*Coleby. Inhumation cemetery. 80 skeletons found in 1833 with broken pots that could have been cremation urns or accessory vessels.
Denton. 2 graves in an abandoned villa were excavated in 1950. An urn found in1948 implies a cremation (Meaney 1964, pp. 153–4).
*Elkington, South. 290 urns were found in 1946–47 when an estimated quarter of the cemetery was excavated: late V–VI.
*Elsham. 625 cremations and 5 graves excavated 1975–6: V–VI.
*Farforth. Inhumation cemetery: VI.
*Ferriby, South. Inhumation cemetery.
*Fillingham. Indications of an inhumation cemetery.
* Fonaby, Caistor. At least 49 graves and some 17 cremation urns found 1956–7: late V–VI.
Grantham, Spittlegate. Inhumation cemetery (Meaney 1964, p. 163).
*Grayingham. Single female grave found *c.* 1888.
Great Casterton. Graves and cremations in the counterscarp of the Roman ditch (Fennell 1974, p. 287): late V–VI.
*Heckington. Graves found in 1815 and 1821.
*Horncastle. Graves found in and around the town: VI.
*Ingham. ?An inhumation cemetery. A hanging-bowl (VI–VII) has been found in the parish (Bruce-Mitford 1993, no. 6).
*Irby upon Humber, Welbeck Hill. 72 graves and 5 cremations excavated 1962–79: VI.
*Keal, West (Hall Hill). Large cremation cemetery, possibly with some inhumations: V–VI.
*Keelby. Mixed cemetery: late V–VI.
*Kirton in Lindsey. Burial of a warrior found *c.* 1920: VII.

*Laceby. Inhumation cemetery: VI.

*Louth. Inhumation cemetery: VI.

*Loveden Hill in Hough-on-the-Hill parish. Nearly 2000 cremations and more than 40 graves, some with high status goods, including three hanging bowls (VI and two of VII, Bruce-Mitford 1993, nos 8–10):V–VII.

*Manton Warren. Hanging bowl (VI–VII) probably from a grave (Bruce-Mitford 1993, no. 11).

*Market Rasen. Indications of an inhumation cemetery. Parts of a hanging bowl (VII) have been found there, but not necessarily on the same site (Bruce-Mitford 1993, no. 12).

*Nettleton, near Caistor. Inhumation cemetery found *c.* 1855 with hanging-bowl (VI; Bruce-Mitford 1993, no. 4). A grave found in 1972 may be from the same cemetery.

*Newark, Millgate, Nottinghamshire. Large cremation cemetery: V–VI.

*Northorpe. Inhumation cemetery: VI.

*Partney. Barrow with at least four burials, found in 1950.

*Quarrington. Predominantly cremations, found *c.* 1826: V–VII.

*Riby. Small inhumation cemetery found in 1915: VII.

Roxby. Small inhumation cemetery with one cremation: VI; and ten metres to the south, a late cemetery: VII.

*Ruskington. 180 identifiable burials and a small number of cremations from what must have been a much larger cemetery: VI–VII.

Saltersford. Single inhumation (Meaney 1964, p. 162).

Scotter. Inhumations (Meaney 1964, p. 162; Eagles 1979, pp. 389–90).

*Searby. Inhumation cemetery found 1849–64.

*Sleaford Large inhumation cemetery with six cremations. 241 graves recorded in 1882 from an estimated 600: late V–VI.

Sleaford, Old. Burial: late VI/ early VII (White 1988).

Sleaford, Old Place. Single inhumation found in 1959 (Meaney 1964, p. 163).

Spridlington. Grave (Eagles 1979, p. 394).

*Stenigot. Barrow with at least three 7th-century burials found in 1954.

Near Stamford, in Rutland. Inhumation cemetery found 1854, 1879 (Meaney 1964, pp. 163–4).

Swaby. ?Inhumation cemetery (*LHA* 27 (1992), pp. 45–6).

Tallington. Inhumation cemetery (inf. R. H. Healey).

*Tetford. 11 graves from a larger cemetery found 1958: VII.

*Thimbleby. Metalwork probably indicate an inhumation cemetery.

Threekingham. Many skeletons found 1780–1826 indicate a large inhumation cemetery (Meaney 1964, p. 165).

Uffington. Inhumations, 3 graves found (*LHA* 28 (1993), p. 72) (inf. H. H. Healey).

*Waddington. 11 graves recorded in 1947.

*Walesby. 23 inhumations excavated in 1990: VI–VII.

*Welbourn. Inhumation cemetery found before 1915: *c.* A.D. 600.

*Welton-by-Lincoln. 11 graves found in 1971.

*Willingham, South. Cremation cemetery. This may have been in Benniworth (Eagles 1979, p. 394).

Willoughton. Hanging-bowl of VII, possibly from a grave (Bruce-Mitford 1993, no. 14).

*Winceby. ?Inhumation cemetery found in 1931.

Witham Common. Inhumation cemetery found 1740–46.

*Wold Newton. Cremation cemetery; 20 urns found in 1828.

Woolsthorpe. Mixed cemetery.

*Worlaby. 12 graves and one disturbed cremation excavated 1965–6, other burials had been ploughed out: VI.

Appendix 2

THE TRIBAL HIDAGE

The purpose of this appendix is to amplify the brief comments on the Tribal Hidage in the text and to give reasons for doubting the identification of the *Bilmiga* of one version with the *Billingas* who are apparently represented by several place-names in Kesteven on the Fen Edge (see p. 49).

The Tribal Hidage is a list of over thirty peoples in England each with a number of hides, i.e. assessment units used before the Conquest to determine the renders or tribute due to a superior. There are three Recensions in seven medieval manuscripts and one printed version published in 1626: A is in Old English, B is apparently in Latin and C is a Latin translation of an Old English text (Dumville 1989). The earliest manuscript, British Library, MS. Harley 3271, a miscellaneous compilation written in several hands of the first half of the eleventh century, is the only evidence for Recension A, which is reproduced and printed in tabular form by Dumville, pp. 226–7 (see Fig. 5.1). The only evidence for Recension B is the printed version which is reproduced by Dumville, pp. 228–9. It is very close to Recension A, but with some small differences, one of which, *Belmiga* for *Bilmiga* in Recension A, is relevant here. Recension C is represented by six manuscripts of the thirteenth and fourteenth centuries, listed by Dumville, p. 230. There is no satisfactory edition of this Recension, but the variant forms of the names are listed by Wendy Davies who showed that they all derived from one Old English text that is different from and is in some respects superior to that of Recension A (Davies and Vierck 1974, pp. 288–92; Dumville 1989, p. 230).

It is generally accepted that the Tribal Hidage derives from a list of peoples subject to the Mercians with their assessments for the purpose of collecting tribute. It was certainly made before the ninth-century Scandinavian conquests, and most scholars accept that the original list was made in the late seventh or early eighth century. It begins with the land of the Mercians, assigning 30,000 hides to the area ‘first called Mercia’ and continues with groups of very different sizes, ranging from 300 hides (five groups) to the Mercians and East Angles, each with 30,000 hides, and Recensions A and B end with the West Saxons who are assessed at 100,000 hides. The large figures appear to be symbolic, expressing the status of the groups, some of whom were at some time, like Lindsey, independent kingdoms (see above, p. 76). The exceptionally large figure given for the West Saxons, which apparently reflects the superior status of their kingdom, suggests that the Tribal Hidage in its present form was compiled in the ninth or tenth century by a West Saxon. It was, however, based on an earlier list of assessments that must have been Mercian (Sawyer 1978, pp. 110–11; cf. Dumville 1989, note 10).

Some groups, including most of those with large assessments, can be identified but there is more uncertainty about the location of many of the smaller groups (Davies and Vierck 1974; Hart 1971). In Recension A the list is in two parts, with the total assessment of the first 19 groups being correctly given as 66,100 hides. The groups that can be identified in this first part are listed in an approximately clockwise order, beginning with the 'Wrekin-dwellers'. The people of Lindsey with the land of Hatfield are the sixth group, followed by the South and North *Gyrwe*, who were associated with the district in which Peterborough lay, and whose Fen extended into Huntingdonshire and as far as Crowland (see above, p. 47). The next groups are the East and West *Wixna* and the *Spalda*. The *Wixna* have been identified with the *Wissa*, who are named in the *Life of St Guthlac* (Colgrave 1956, p. 168), and apparently lived on the River Wissey in Norfolk and gave their name to Wisbech in Cambridgeshire. This identification is consistent with the apparently topographical arrangement of this part of the list, but Wendy Davies has questioned it on the ground that these names have no hint of the *x* of the *Wixna* (Davies and Vierck 1974, p. 232). The fact that several names in the Tribal Hidage are undoubtedly corrupt reduces the force of that objection. The case for associating the *Spalda* with Spalding has been strengthened by the Fenland Survey (above, pp. 47–9), although that would break the clockwise order. Wendy Davies has objected that the place-name Spalding derives 'from the group-name *Spaldingas*, rather than from *Spalda*' (Davies and Vierck, p. 232). It is, therefore, possible that when the Tribal Hidage was compiled the *Spalda* were located further south, and that some of them, called the *Spaldingas*, had already settled on the silt on which Spalding lies. The clockwise order of the first part of the Tribal Hidage is maintained by the three other groups in it, the 14th to the 16th, that can be located with any confidence; namely in the shires of Huntingdon, Buckingham, and Hertford, in that order (Davies and Vierck 1974, pp. 232, 234).

The order of the identifiable groups in the second part of the Tribal Hidage is not so consistent, but the *Bilmiga*, the 26th group named, come immediately after the *Arosætna* who occupied the Arrow valley in Warwickshire and *Færpinga* who have been identified with the *Feppingas* whose territory included Charlbury in Oxfordshire. Davies has also questioned that identification of the *Færpinga*, but did not take account of the marginal note in Recension A placing the *Færpinga* in *Middelenglum*. This makes it likely that the *Bilmiga* were found in that part of England, rather than on the edge of the Fens.

Another reason for questioning the identity of the *Bilmiga* with the *Billingas* is the variation in the spelling of the name. In Recension B it is *Belmiga*, and the manuscripts of Recension C all have an extra syllable: *Bilmiliga* or *Bilimliga* (two manuscripts), *Birmiliga*, *Biliniliga* (two manuscripts), and *Silimliga* (Davies and Vierck 1974, p. 292).

Appendix 3

DOMESDAY BOOK

This appendix has two purposes: to note some publications that are helpful guides in the interpretation of the information about Lincolnshire in DB, and secondly to consider whether or not the changes in land-ownership after the Conquest amounted to a 'tenurial revolution'.

Anyone interested in the early history of Lincolnshire has been fortunate to have the translation of the Lincolnshire Domesday by C. W. Foster and T. Longley, published in 1924, and reprinted in 1976 (*LD*) in which most of the over 2000 place-names were correctly identified. They were less successful in resolving the problems posed by the Domesday treatment of some pre-Conquest personal names (Fellows-Jensen 1985).

It was almost twenty years later that the modern discussion of the reasons for and the methods of the Domesday Survey were, after an understandable delay, initiated by V. H. Galbraith's remarkable article on 'The Making of Domesday Book' (1942). Since the 1950s there has been a succession of articles and books on this topic (listed by Bates 1986) culminating in the spate of publications in connection with the millennium of the Domesday Enquiry in 1986 (e.g. Forde 1986, Holt 1987, Sawyer 1985). The most important of these 'millennium' publications is the superb facsimile of DB, the Lincolnshire section of which has an introduction by David Roffe (1992) whose painstaking study of the northern counties in DB has cast much new light on both the methods of the enquiry and the way its results should be interpreted (Roffe 1990).

Roffe has underlined the need to take account of the layout of DB, the space between entries, differences in the form of rubrics and even of the initial letters of entries, all of which he has shown to be significant. He has also shown in some detail how, in the course of the writing of DB itself, the main scribe and any others responsible for its production, made changes in the information that was recorded, and the way it was presented, thus complicating comparison between counties (Roffe 1990, pp. 315–25; cf. Sawyer and Thacker 1987, pp. 293–5). There are, for example, no slaves (*servi* or *ancillae*) in the Lincolnshire Domesday, but that does not mean that there were not any in the shire. This is one of the characteristics shared by Yorkshire and Huntingdonshire, two of the five northern counties that for the purposes of the enquiry were grouped together to form what is known as Circuit VI. The others were Derbyshire and Nottinghamshire with, respectively, 20 and 24 slaves. It was with this group of counties that the compilation of the final form of DB began, Lincolnshire being second after Yorkshire. It appears that the compilers only began to note slaves as the work progressed; in the neighbouring shires of Cambridge and Northampton there are 541 and 737 respectively (Darby 1977, p. 338). Similarly, the fact that commendation is noted regularly in only two circuits, III and VII (i.e. the counties of Middlesex, Hertford, Buckingham, Cambridge, and Bedford in circuit III, and Essex, Suffolk, and Norfolk in circuit VII) does not mean that there was no commendation in Lincolnshire. The DB descriptions of Lincolnshire, Yorkshire, and Huntingdonshire are also different from other shires in having separate sections describing disputes (*clamores*). The Lincolnshire *clamores*, with the verdicts of jurors from wapentakes, ridings, and the shire, are the last contemporary item in DB i (fos 375a–377b). Roffe has argued convincingly that the text of these county surveys was being written before the verdicts on points of dispute had been obtained. Elsewhere such evidence was incorporated in the text (1990, pp. 325–8; 1992, p. 8).

One point of particular importance for the interpretation of the Lincolnshire Domesday is Roffe's demonstration that the twelve-carucate hundreds not only provided the survey's raw material concerning geld-assessments (whether in the form of existing assessment lists or evidence collected from hundredal juries), but that these hundredal returns also affected the arrangement of the final result in which the evidence of manorial resources provided by landowners or their agents was incorporated (Roffe 1992, pp. 4–7). Roffe's work is, therefore, an indispensable guide for any future analysis of the Domesday evidence, although his arguments are complex and demanding.

Two other works should be mentioned in this context. First, the major endeavour by H. C. Darby to map the Domesday statistics for every county. Lincolnshire was among the first to be dealt with (Darby 1952, pp. 26–96), and his survey of the results of the whole project (Darby 1977) included some important revisions, especially concerning values (Darby 1977, pp. 208–31, 380–1). Secondly, Reginald Lennard's refreshingly lucid and careful discussion of the evidence of DB (1959) would be a good starting point for anyone wishing to plunge into this subject. By drawing on other evidence from the period Lennard was able to give a fuller and less distorted picture than can be based on DB alone.

Differences between circuits and counties obviously affect the evidence of DB for pre-Conquest society and the changes brought about by the Conquest. William used two main methods of distributing land to his followers. One was to grant an individual all the land in a district, for example a wapentake. There is only one example of this in Lincolnshire, the grant of Axholme to Geoffrey de la Guerche (DB i. 369a-b = *LD* 63/1–27). The other was to grant an individual all the lands of a pre-Conquest landowner, called in DB the *antecessor*. Gilbert de Ghent, for example, was given the lands of Ulf *Fenisc* throughout England, including Lincolnshire (Clarke 1994, pp. 34–5). The tenants-in-chief of 1086, who held the land of one or more *antecessores* also had land that, according to DB had not been held by their *antecessores*. In Lincolnshire, for example, Gilbert de Ghent had 13 manors that had been Ulf's, but another 10 were held TRE by three other men.

It has been generally assumed that all the pre-Conquest tenants named in DB, some of whom had very little land, were landowners, and that William I, by granting the land held by such people to a few of his followers, wrought a tenurial revolution. In 1985 I argued that many of the people named as pre-Conquest tenants in DB were sub-tenants of lords who were the *antecessores* from whom William's tenants-in-chief derived their legal title. In other words, that the structure of estates in 1086 was not very different from what it had been on the eve of the Conquest.

This interpretation of the evidence was vigorously challenged in 1987 by Robin Fleming, who elaborated her discussion of the tenurial changes following the Conquest in a book published in 1991. The difference between us is not so great as might at first sight appear; I had already taken account of much of the evidence that she cites against me. There are, it is true, only a few instances where there is no doubt that the pre-Conquest tenant named in DB was the sub-tenant of an identifiable *antecessor*, in most cases thanks to the evidence of the *clamores*. There are, however, indications that many other pre-Conquest tenants named in DB were sub-tenants (Sawyer 1985b). It is, for example, likely that parts, perhaps large parts, of the 1086 estates of the archbishop of York and the bishop of Durham in Lincolnshire were held by their pre-Conquest predecessors, although they are not named as pre-Conquest tenants. One of the manors held in 1086 by the bishop of Durham was, indeed, called *Biscopetorp* now Biscathorpe (Bishop's thorp; DB i. 341a = *LD* 3/41). It is significant that one of the privileged pre-Conquest landowners listed towards the beginning of the Lincolnshire Domesday was Fyach who is not named as the tenant of any land in Lincolnshire, implying that he was the superior lord of one or more of those who are named (DB i. 337a = *LD* p. 13).

Fleming claims that when compact blocks of land were granted to individual Normans, for example the land held in Nottinghamshire by Roger de Bully and William Peverel, the pre-Conquest tenants named in DB must have been independent, minor thegns. Her argument is that although 'Circuit VI is silent on pre-Conquest lordships ... the men most likely to have been the lords of Nottinghamshire's minor landholders were powerful thegns ... who held major interests in the region. Yet the lands of these great thegns devolved on to Norman lords through strict adherence to antecessorial inheritance. Therefore, the men most likely to have been lords of Nottinghamshire's lesser landholders are found with well-defined successors, but the lands of the county's minor thegns were appropriated into one of the shire's two territorial fees' (Fleming 1991, pp. 148–9). The force of this argument is weakened by the example of Axholme in Lincolnshire. The whole wapentake (then called Epworth) was held in 1086 by Geoffrey de la Guerche despite the claims of Gilbert de Ghent and Henry de Ferrières to succeed to parts of it by right of their *antecessores* Ulf Fenisc and Siward Barn (DB i. 369 a–b, 376b = *LD* 63/5–27, 71/16).

This is not the place to rehearse the arguments advanced in 1985 but I hope that the evidence that has been cited here is enough to show that, despite exchanges, sales, usurpations, and other transfers that happened between 1066 and 1086, the Lincolnshire estates held by the tenants-in-chief in 1086 were to a large extent based on those held on the eve of the Conquest by the privileged landowners listed towards the beginning of the Lincolnshire Domesday (DB i. 337a = *LD* p. 13). The transfer of land in Lincolnshire after the Conquest was less than revolutionary.This conclusion is not inconsistent with the argument advanced above (pp. 111–14, 155–7) that many small, independent estates or 'manors' were created in the ninth and tenth centuries by the breakup of large estates or sokes. In the confusion of political unification, rebellions, Viking invasions and Danish conquests many minor landowners must have submitted to powerful lords in the hope of gaining protection. Land could also be lost by failure to pay geld; Peterborough Abbey lost Barrow (and Howden in Yorkshire) in this way (see pp. 147, 242). The precariousness of landownership is well illustrated by the example of the abbey of Burton upon Trent; by 1066 it had lost over half of its original endowment by Wulfric Spot *c.* 1004 (Sawyer 1979, pp. xliv–xlv).

Appendix 4

THE FIRST CHURCH ON THE SITE OF ST PAUL-IN-THE-BAIL

After the Victorian church of St Paul-in-the-Bail was demolished in 1971 excavation of its site revealed traces of a complex sequence of graves, churches, and other structures, beginning with an apsidal building superimposed on a rectangular one in the courtyard of the forum (F igs. 4.1, App. 4.1). That these buildings have been the subject of much discussion and disagreement is hardly surprising; the dating evidence, discussed below, can only show that the apsidal structure was built sometime between the fourth century and the seventh. The purpose of this appendix is to give reasons for thinking that it was a church built early in the seventh century, possibly by Paulinus before 631. The full report on this very difficult excavation has not yet been published. The most up-to-date account is by Michael Jones (1994) who gives a well-balanced review of the possible interpretations with a most useful survey of evidence for churches elsewhere in these centuries (see also Steane 1991 and 1992).

The shape of the building, its orientation with the apse in the east, and the continued use of its site for graves and churches leave little room for doubt that it was a church. Internally the nave was *c.* 8 m wide and at least 15 m long, and the apse was 7 m wide and 6 m deep. It has been conjectured that the nave was originally about 20 m long with a western entrance reached by a flight of steps from the west porticus of the forum, which was *c.* 75 cm above the level of the courtyard. The foundations were cut through the courtyard paving, which probably served as the floor of the church. As no trace of mortar was found in the wall trenches it is most unlikely that they were made of stone; there are, in fact, indications that they rested on horizontal wooden sills. The only post-holes found, five of them, were in the north–south trench separating the apse from the nave, apparently for posts that served as a screen.

The main dating evidence is provided by the analysis of radiocarbon in bones from graves found on the site. That method is not always reliable and at best can only indicate the period within which the person whose bone is analysed probably died. Specialists in this dating technique claim that if the period includes two so-called standard deviations before and after the central date determined by the analysis there is a 94.5% probability that the death occurred within those limits. It is certainly misleading to treat the central date as most probably the right one. The central date for grave 34, for example, is AD 441 but the death could, with varying degrees of probability, be any time between 250 and 650, and there is a small chance (5.5%) that it was before or after that period. (See Fig. App. 4.2.)

In the following table the periods include two standard deviations. The numbers of the graves are indicated on the plan.

Grave no.	*Probable date range (AD except no. 32)*
3	890–1170
4	880–160
5	880–1160
7	880–1160
14	890–1210
16	400–670
17	550–855
19	540–890
21	550–860
23	650–960
24	770–1030
25	30–380
26	390–680
27	780–1180
28	650–960
29	450–770
30	420–690
31	630–950
32	370 BC–220
34	250–650
37	990–1280
38	550–890

Grave 25 is apparently aberrant and can be ignored. Grave 32 is also too early to be a primary burial but as it was found in the foundation of the screen between apse and nave it is possible, even likely, that it was a relic. The same applies to 34 which was also found in the screen foundation. As the other dates are reasonably consistent and those of the control sample (37) fit the context in which it was found, the following discussion assumes that most are correct.

After the apsidal church was demolished its site was used for burials. Those from the foundation trenches are the most important guide to the date of demolition. According to 30 this could have happened between the beginning of the fifth century and the end of the seventh. Similar limits are suggested by 26 from what had been the interior of the church. Little weight should be put on these results for there are indications, discussed

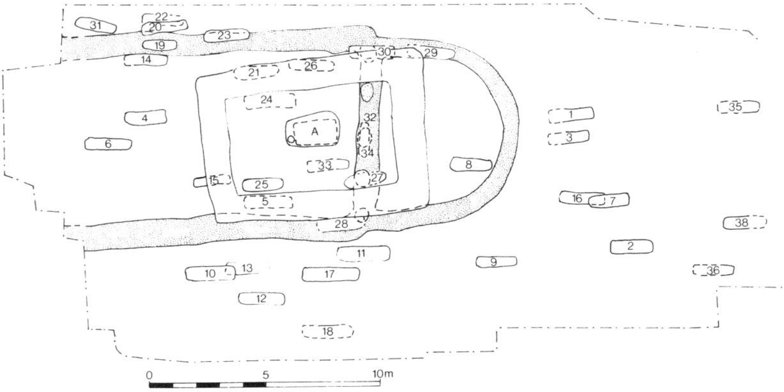

Fig. App. 4.1 Plan of graves excavated at St Paul-in-the-Bail.

© CLAU.

below, that these end dates are too early. Grave 29 gives more realistic limits for the demolition, 450–770. The next burials were not before the middle of the sixth century; one in a foundation trench (19), and four elsewhere (17, 21, 31, 38). Two, both from foundation trenches, were after the middle of the seventh century, and the rest were all after the mid eighth century. If there were any burials before the seventh century, they were few and infrequent and most of them were after the middle of the sixth century. It is more significant that all these post-demolition burials could be after 630, and many of them certainly were.

Reexamination of the stratigraphy has led to the suggestion that the stone-lined pit marked A in Fig. App. 4.1, was also made after the demolition of the apsidal church (Vince 1993c, p. 156). It was empty apart from a seventh-century hanging bowl which suggests that it was originally a high-status grave from which the remains were removed at some stage, perhaps to be translated to another shrine or for safety in time of trouble, for example, the period of Viking attacks. The fact that no bones were found suggests that the remains were removed while the skeleton was still articulated (Gilmour 1979, p. 217). This grave was in the centre of a single-cell stone structure that can reasonably be interpreted as a mausoleum (R. Morris 1983, p. 38). Traces of post-holes found under the foundation of the stone wall suggest that the grave may originally have been enclosed by a timber structure that was replaced by a stone one, probably in the eighth century.[1] Graves 24 and 27 were placed in the mausoleum close to its wall in or after the late eighth century. This structure later formed the west end of a church, the east wall of which cut grave 3 (890–1170) showing that this extension was not built before the tenth century.

This evidence makes it possible that the apsidal church was built in the fourth century. It cannot have stood for much more than a century, if so long. This would mean that the religious significance of the site was remembered through the fifth and sixth centuries although few, if any, burials were made in that time. Such continuity makes it much more likely that the apsidal church was built in the seventh century and that it collapsed, or was demolished, in the eighth century. This would make the placing of the mausoleum in the seventh or eighth century exactly where the altar of the apsidal church once stood less remarkable.

It is, therefore, possible that the apsidal church was built by Paulinus as, in effect, the twin of Edwin's church in York. Both were built on a similar site, the main monumental square of each city. The dedication to St Paul, if original, would also be appropriate in the Roman mission to Edwin's kingdom; the York church was dedicated to St Peter. The difference between them was that St Peter's continued to be the cathedral of the York diocese, but when Bede wrote his *History* St Paul's had been abandoned, and had, perhaps, been replaced by the new cathedral built by Bishop Cyneberht which, it is suggested above, may be identified as the church later known as St Peter at Pleas (see pp. 63, 79).

This interpretation offers a possible explanation for the building that preceded the apsidal church. They were both constructed in the same way, and the east end of the earlier one, although not apsidal, was separated from the rest by a screen of posts. It could have been the first church on the site, built quickly for, or soon after, the baptism of Blæcca probably in 628, which was soon replaced by a finer building which provided a suitable setting for the consecration of Honorius as archbishop of Canterbury in 631. This would be another parallel with York, where the original wooden church in which Edwin was baptised was being replaced by a stone one before Edwin's death (above, p. 58).

The main objection to this identification is that Bede reports that Paulinus built in Lincoln 'a magnificent church of stone'. It is, however, unlikely that Lincoln had a stone church before York. Bede never saw the building and was presumably told about it by Bishop Cyneberht. There is no need to suspect Cyneberht of deliberately giving false information. If

1 On the original plan of the excavation grave 5 (dated 880–1160) is shown under the mausoleum wall, but a more recent analysis of the material shows that this burial was in a wooden coffin south of the single-cell structure.

the walls were plastered, Cyneberht could, perhaps, have said that it was marvellously built to look like stone, and been misunderstood.

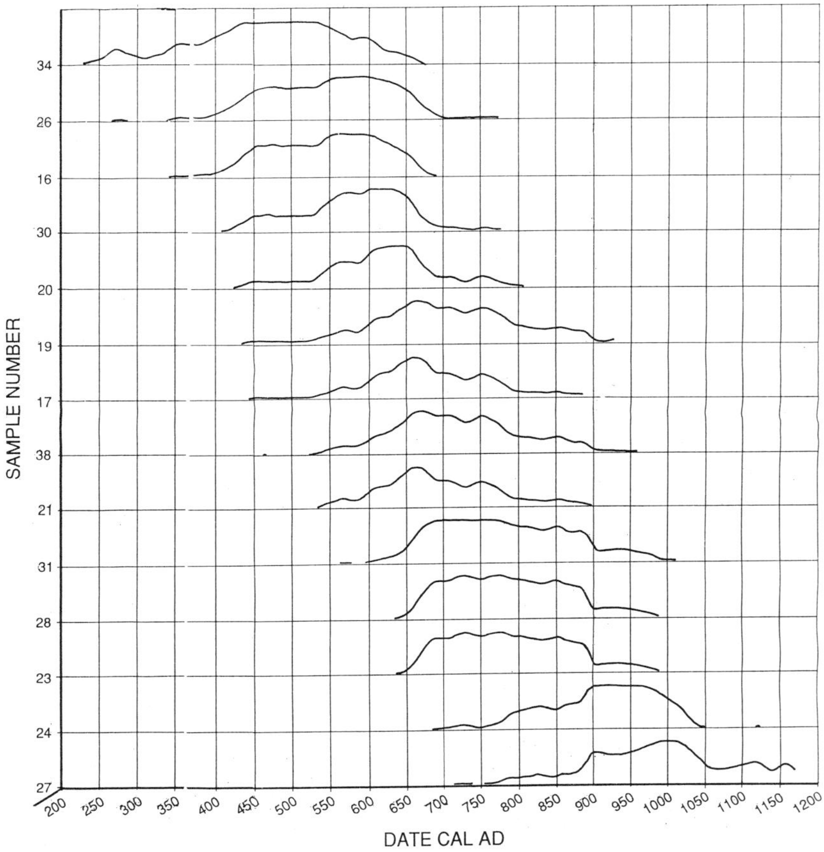

Fig. App. 4.2 Carbon-14 determination for selected burals at St Paul-in-the-Bail. Sample numbers refer to graves as illustrated in Fig. app. 4.1.
© CLAU.

Appendix 5

CHARTERS

Charters, wills and other documents concerning Lincolnshire that are generally judged to be authentic and have been used in this book are here listed briefly. References are given to the best or most accessible edition and, if possible, to a translation. Fuller information about the pre-Conquest texts are given in S, a revised edition of which is being prepared. Memoranda or notes about grants of land in Lincolnshire to *Medeshamstede* (later Peterborough) and to Ramsey are discussed in Appendix 7.

S 782 AD 971. King Edgar to Æthelwold, bishop; grant of land at Barrow-upon-Humber for Peterborough Abbey, in return for 40 pounds of silver and a golden cross. *Latin with English bounds*. Printed BCS 1270. For the bounds see *PNL* 2, pp. 29-30; Everson and Knowles 1993.

S 1412 AD 786 x 796. Beonna, abbot of *Medeshamstede*, to Cuthbert, *princeps*; lease of 10 hides (*manentes*) at Swineshead, in return for 1000 shillings and annual hospitality, with ultimate reversion to *Medeshamstede*. *Latin*. Printed BCS 271.

S 1440 AD 852. Agreement between Abbot Ceolred and the community at *Medeshamstede*, and Wulfred, concerning land at Sempringham, Sleaford and Cheal in Lincolnshire and at *Forde* and *Lehcotum*. *English*. Printed Robertson 1939, no. 7, with translation.

S 1478 AD 1054. Agreement between Bishop Wulfwig, and Earl Leofric and Godgifu, his wife, concerning the endowment of the monastery at Stow St Mary. *English*. Printed Roberston 1939, no. 115, with translation. See below, Appendix 8.

S 1536 AD 1002 x 1004. Will of Wulfric, including a bequest of land at Tathwell. *English*. Printed Whitelock 1930, no. 17, with translation, and Sawyer 1979, no. 29, with translation on pp. xv–xix. It was confirmed by King Æthelred, S 906.

Whitelock 1930, no. 39, with translation. Between November 1066 and about 1068. Will of Ulf and his wife Madselin making various arrangements for their land, mostly in Lincolnshire, in preparation for their pilgrimage to Jerusalem. Ulf himself disposed of land in Claxby, Keelby Cotes, Kettleby, Kirmington, Limber, Manthorpe, North

Ormsby (Lincs.), and in Wilby (probably Northants.). His mother exchanged land in Kettleby and Messingham (Lincs.) with him. Madselin's property was in North Stoke, Stroxton (which she exchanged for land in Winterton, all in Lincs.), and at *Lohtun*. Their other property was in Castle Bytham, Carlton-le-Moorland, Lavington (now Lenton), Cold Overton, and Skillington (Lincs.), and in Hardwick (Northants.), Hoby (Leics.), and *Mortune* (possibly in N. Yorks.). The beneficiaries included the abbeys of Crowland, Peterborough, Ramsey and Thorney; Stow St Mary; Ulf's brother Halfdan, his servants (*cnihtas*), and his kinsman, Abbot Brand (see Appendix 10). Some was bought or mortgaged by Ealdred, archbishop of York. *English.*

Davis, *Regesta*, no. 8 Soon after November 1066, probably at Christmas. William I to Peterborough Abbey, confirming at the request of Abbot Brand land in Scotter, Scotton, Manton, Raventhorpe, Messingham, Cleatham, Hibaldstow, Walcot on Trent (Lincs.). *Latin*. Printed Dugdale, *Monasticon Anglicanum* i. 383. See Appendix 10.

Davis, *Regesta*, no. 333 AD 1070 x 1072. Writ of William I addressed to Thomas, archbishop of York, and the sheriffs of Nottinghamshire and Lincolnshire, informing them that he has given to St Mary at Stow Newark and Fledborough (Notts.) and Brampton and Well Wapentake (Lincs.). *English*. Printed in Appendix 8, with translation.

S 1498, the will of Ealdorman Æthelmær has not been included because there is good reason to think that it does not refer to Lincolnshire. It includes a bequest of money to *Burnan*, apparently a church. Dorothy Whitelock (1930, p. 127) suggested that it was possibly Bourne in Lincolnshire because Æthelmær also bequeathed land at *Cottesmore*, which she identified as Cottesmore in Rutland, about ten miles from Bourne. Margaret Gelling (1954, p. 308) has identified *Cottesmore* as a lost place in Broadwell in Oxfordshire and has argued that *Burnan* is therefore probably not in Lincolnshire (Gelling 1979, p. 189). There seems to be no good reason for assuming that *Cottesmore* was in Oxfordshire; Barrie Cox (1994a, p. 16) has identified it as in Rutland. Gelling (1979, p. 189) has, however, given a better reason for doubting that *Burnan* was the Lincolnshire Bourne by pointing out that the other spellings of the Lincolnshire place-name suggest that it derives from *brunnr* not OE *burna* (cf. Fellows-Jensen 1978, p. 152).

The following pre-Conquest charters are certainly spurious or of doubtful authenticity, although some may be based on early records:

S 68 AD 664. Wulfhere, king of Mercia, to St Peter's, *Medeshamstede*; confirmation and grant of lands in many places. The Lincs. names include several found in memoranda and charters from the abbey's archive discussed in Appendix 7, and most of the Abbey's manors listed in DB. *Latin with bounds*. Printed BCS 22.

S 72 AD 680. King Æthelred to St Peter's, *Medeshamstede*; grant of land at Swineshead and Bardney, Lincs., and elsewhere. *English*. Printed BCS 49. The list of names is probably based on an early record. It has been suggested that several of the unidentified places were in Lincolnshire, i.e. *Hrepingas*, *Cedenac*, and *Lodeshale*. This is doubtful. See Appendix 7.

S 82 AD 716. Æthelbald, king of Mercia, founds a monastery at Crowland. *Latin with bounds*. Printed BCS 135.

S 135 AD 793. Offa, king of Mercia, to Crowland Abbey; grant of privileges. *Latin*. Printed BCS 268.

S 162 AD 806. Coenwulf, king of Mercia, to Crowland Abbey; grant of privileges and confirmation of grants of alms in Bucknall, Hallington, Langtoft, Baston and Rippingale, Lincs. *Latin*. Printed BCS 325.

S 189 AD 833. Wiglaf, king of Mercia, to Siward, abbot of Crowland, and Crowland Abbey; confirmation and grant of privileges and grant of land at Bucknall, Hallington, *Gernthorp*, Langtoft, Deeping, Baston, Rippingale, Holbeach, Whaplode, Spalding, Drayton, Laythorpe and Kirkby, Lincs., and elsewhere. *Latin*. Printed BCS 409.

S 200 AD 851. Berhtwulf, king of Mercia, to Siward, abbot of Crowland; confirmation of marshes at Crowland, Spalding, and elsewhere, and of land at Langtoft, Deeping, Thetford, Baston, Rippingale, Whaplode, Holbeach, Pinchbeck, Spalding, Sutterton, Algarkirk, Drayton, Kirby, Bucknall, Hallington, and *Germuthorp*, Lincs., and elsewhere. *Latin*. Printed BCS 461.

S 213 AD 868. Burgred, king of Mercia, to Crowland Abbey; confirmation of privileges and land etc.. The Lincolnshire places named are the same as in S 200 but without Holbeach and with the addition of Laythorpe. *Latin*. Printed BCS 521.

S 538 AD 948. King Eadred to Crowland Abbey; confirmation of privileges and of land. The Lincolnshire places named are the same as in S 213 but without Sutterton and with the addition of Dowdike. *Latin*. Printed BCS 872.

S 741 AD 966. King Edgar to Crowland Abbey; grant of privileges and confirmation of the lands named in S 538 with the addition of Burtoft and Sutterton, Lincs. *Latin*. Printed BCS 1178.

S 787 AD 972. King Edgar to Peterborough Abbey, with later confirmations; includes a confirmation of land at Barrow-upon-Humber and of a mint at Stamford. *Latin*. Printed BCS 1258, 1280.

S 792 AD 973. King Edgar to Thorney Abbey; grant of privileges and confirmation of land at Barrow-upon-Humber and in Holland at Gedney, Lutton, *Angarhala*, and Tydd St Mary, and in Cambs., Hunts., and Northants. *Latin*. Printed Hart 1966, pp. 165–72.

S 965 AD 1032. King Cnut to Crowland Abbey; confirmation of privileges and lands including Crowland itself and the marshes of *Alderlound* and *Goggislound*. *Latin*. Printed KCD 748.

S 1029 AD 1060 King Edward to Peterborough Abbey; confirmation of land at Fiskerton, Lincs. *Latin*. Printed KCD 808. This text, together with S 1059 and 1060, is discussed by Hart 1966, pp. 105–6.

S 1030 AD 1060. King Edward to Ramsey Abbey; confirmation of land at many places, including *Offerton* or *Orfyridtune* in Holland, Wispington, Martin, Marham on the Hill, and Quarrington, Lincs. *Latin*. Printed KCD 809.

S 1049 AD 1045 x 1050. King Edward to Crowland Abbey; confirmation of lands and privileges. *Latin*. Printed KCD 794.

S 1059 AD 1061 x 1066. King Edward to Peterborough Abbey; confirmation of an agreement concerning land at Scotton, Scotter, Manton and Northorpe, Lincs. *Latin*. Printed KCD 819.

S 1060 AD 1055 x 1060. King Edward to Peterborough Abbey; confirmation of land at Walcot on Trent, Lincs. *Latin*. Printed KCD 806.

S 1189 AD 810. Ælfgar, *comes*, to Siward, abbot of Crowland and the Abbey; grant of land at Holbeach, Whaplode, Spalding, Pinchbeck, Algarkirk, Dowdike, Drayton, and Burtoft, Lincs. *Latin*. BCS 331.

S 1190 AD 819. Fregist, *miles*, to Siward, abbot of Crowland and his Abbey; grant of land at Langtoft, Lincs. *Latin*. BCS 365.

S 1191 AD 825. Ælfgar, *miles*, to Siward, abbot of Crowland; grant of land at Baston, Lincs. *Latin*. Printed BCS 383.

S 1230 AD 1051. Thorold of Bucknall to Crowland Abbey; grant of land at Spalding, Lincs., for the foundation of a cell there. *Latin*. Printed KCD 795.

S 1233 AD 1054 x 1057. Godgifu, wife of Leofric, to St Mary's Stow; grant of land at Newark and Fledborough, Notts., and at Brampton in Torksey and Marton in Well Wapentake, Lincs., with papal confirmation. *Latin*. Printed KCD 818.

S 1294 AD 966. Dunstan, archbishop of Canterbury, Osketel, archbishop of York, and others, to Crowland Abbey; confirmation of lands and privileges. *Latin*. Printed BCS 1179.

Appendix 6

BISHOPS

In HE iii. 24 Bede described Diuma, Ceollach, and Trumhere as successively the first bishops of the kingdom of the Mercians, of the people of Lindsey and of the Middle Angles. In HE iii. 21, however, he records Diuma's consecration after the death of Penda in November 655 as 'bishop of the Middle Angles and the Mercians since a shortage of bishops made it necessary for one bishop to be set over *both peoples'*. This suggests that initially, while Oswiu ruled Lindsey, it may have been considered to be under the Northumbrian bishop as it had been under Paulinus.

Diuma was consecrated by Finan, bishop of Lindisfarne, probably before Peada was murdered in April 656. He died 'after a short space of time' and was succeeded by Ceollach who was also consecrated by Finan, but 'not long after' he returned to Iona. Plummer suggested that this was 'probably connected with the successful rebellion of Wulfhere against Oswiu in 658' (1896a ii. 186). Bede lists Wulfhere's bishops as Trumhere, Jaruman, Chad, and Winfrith (HE iii. 24). Trumhere, a kinsman of the Deiran king Oswine who was murdered by Oswiu, would have been a suitable choice after Oswiu lost control of Mercia (HE iii. 14, 24). By 664 Jaruman had succeeded Trumhere (HE iii. 30), but after his death, generally assumed to have been in 667, Wulfhere invited Wilfrid to visit Mercia 'to perform episcopal duties' (Eddius Stephanus, c. 14). In 669 Archbishop Theodore installed Chad as 'bishop of the Mercian race and of the people of Lindsey'. He established his see at Lichfield, where he died 2 March 672 (HE iv. 3). His successor Winfrith was deposed by Theodore (HE iv. 6; cf. Plummer 1986a ii. 215). This must have been before Wulfhere's death in 675 because the next bishop, Seaxwulf, was driven from Lindsey when Wulfhere lost control of it after his unsuccessful invasion of Northumbria in 674 (HE iv. 12; Stenton 1971, p. 85). For a while Lindsey was apparently treated as part of the diocese of York, which was then held by Wilfrid. When Wilfrid was expelled from Northumbria in 678 Eadhæd was consecrated as the first bishop of the separate diocese of Lindsey, but when the Mercians recovered Lindsey he returned to Northumbria and was made bishop of Ripon (HE iv. 12). Lindsey continued as a separate, but Mercian, diocese, see below.

After Seaxwulf's death the diocese of Lichfield was divided and a separate bishopric was created for the Middle Angles (Page, R. 1966, p. 5). This happened by July 692 at the latest; Wilfrid, who was expelled from Northumbria in 691, as bishop of the Middle Angles consecrated Oftfor as bishop of the Hwicce during the vacancy after the death of Theodore in September 690 and the election of his successor (HE iv. 23; v. 8). Wilfrid may have continued as bishop of the Middle Angles until he became bishop of Hexham in 706 (Eddius Stephanus, cc. 48, 60), but according to the earliest (early ninth-century) episcopal lists (Page, R. 1966, p. 5) Wilfrid was expelled and the Middle Anglian bishopric was reunited with Lichfield under Headda, who had been bishop of Lichfield after Seaxwulf. The date of Headda's death is not known, but by 731 he had been succeeded by Aldwine, who was also called Uuor (HE v. 23). It was after his death in 737 (*Historia Regum*, ii. 32, trans. *EHD* I, p. 264) that the Middle Anglian bishopric was again, and permanently, separated from Lichfield. The earliest reference to Leicester as the see of the Middle Anglian bishopric is from 803 (Stenton 1971, p. 134 n) but it was probably established there long before that, perhaps even in Wilfrid's time (Bailey 1980).

The following list of the bishops of Leicester and Dorchester is based on Keynes 1986.

Bishop	*Accession*	*Death or translation unless otherwise stated*
LEICESTER		
Torhthelm (Totta)	737	764
Eadberht	764	781 x 785
Unwona	781 x 785	801 x 803
Wernberht	801 x 803	814 x 816
Ræthhun	814 x 816	839 x Dec. 840
Ealdred	839 x Dec. 840	Dec. 840 x 844
Ceolred	Dec. 840 x 844	869 x 888
DORCHESTER		
Alhheard	869 x 888	893 x 896
Wigmund or Wilferth	893 x 900	903 x 909
Cenwulf	*c.* 909	909 x 925
Wynsige	909 x 925	934 x 945
Æthelwald	934 x 945	949 x 950
Osketel (abp of York 959)[1]	949 x 950	1 Nov. 971

1 Osketel first appears as archbishop in a trustworthy charter in S 681, dated 959. S 659, dated 958 for 956, is a grant to Osketel as bishop; his attestation as archbishop is probably due to the York copyist (*EHD* I, pp. 556–7)

Leofwine, bp of Lindsey by 953	united Lindsey and Dorchester 971	971 x 975
Ælfnoth	971 x 975	975 x 979
Æscwig	975 x 979	23 Apr. 1002
Ælfhelm	1002	1007 x 1009
Eadnoth I	1007 x 1009	18 Oct. 1016
Æthelric	1016	8 Dec. 1034
Eadnoth II	1034	18 or 19 Sept. 1049
Ulf	1049	expelled 14 Sept. 1052
Wulfwig	1053	1067

LINDSEY

The earliest bishops of Lindsey named by Bede were Eadhæd, Æthelwine, Edgar and Cyneberht (HE iv. 12). Edgar appears as *electus* in S 1248, dated June 693, in a witness list that was partly based on a Mercian charter of that date (Hart 1966, pp. 135-41). This means that Æthelwine was bishop of Lindsey for at most 14 years, which Bede calls 'a long time' (HE iii. 27); it was certainly much longer than previous Mercian episcopates. Edgar's was even longer. He is the last bishop in a witness list that may have been derived from an authentic record of a local council held *c.* 716 (S 22; cf. Brooks 1984, pp. 191–7; Keynes 1993b, pp. 10–11).

The dates of accession and death of the next four bishops depend on annals in *Historia Regum* ii. 30–58, trans. *EHD* I, pp. 264–74.

Bishop	*Accession*	*Death*
Cyneberht	?	731
Aluwioh	733	750
Aldwulf	750	765
Ceolwulf	765	796

The dates of most of the later bishops depend on their appearance in witness lists.

Eadwulf	796 (*electus* in S 148)	836 x 839 (S 190)
Beorhtræd	836 x 839 (S 1438)	862 x 866 (S 309)

Beorhtræd is the last ninth-century bishop of Lindsey in the episcopal lists (Page, R. 1966, pp. 11, 16). Some bishops who witness later Mercian charters may have been of Lindsey (O'Donovan 1973, pp. 91–4).

Eadbald in S 212 dated 866
Burgheard in S 215 dated 869.

Eadberht, whom O'Donovan considers a possible Lindsey bishop, is in the same list of witnesses, but is first of the five and is therefore more probably of Lichfield. Burgheard is fourth. Eadberht is also in S 216 dated 875 but this is most probably a forgery. The succession of Lindsey bishops is unlikely to have continued after 872 when the Danish army wintered in Torksey. Arthur Owen has suggested that St Herefrith of Louth, whose feast day was 27 February, may have been the last bishop of Lindsey in the ninth century 'whose name did not become known to national chroniclers though remembered locally' (1980, see also Owen, A. 1997).

The bishopric was revived in the mid tenth century. Leofwine, who is named as the successor of Beorhtræd in the late tenth-century episcopal list in MS Cotton Tiberius B v (Page, R. 1966, p. 16), first appears as a witness in 953 (S 560, 561). He appears fairly frequently among the last bishops witnessing charters of Eadred and of Edgar as king of Mercia and Northumbria, but only one of Edgar's after he became king of England (S 735 dated 965; S 1294 dated 966 is a Crowland forgery). After the death of Osketel, 1 Nov. 971, Leofwine succeeded him as bishop of Dorchester, uniting that see with Lindsey (Whitelock 1959, pp. 74–5). He was dead by 975 when his successor at Dorchester, Ælfnoth, witnessed S 803.

Lindsey was revived as a separate bishopric under Æthelred (above, p. 115). Sigeferth appears in five charters between 996 (S 878) and 1004 (S 906), in one of which he appears as *Lindissi aecclesiae episcopus* (S 891 dated 997). He was probably succeeded as bishop of Lindsey by Ælfstan (see Keynes 1980, p. 264) who witnessed two charters, S 922 dated 1009 and S 924 dated 1011.

Appendix 7

LAND HELD BY RELIGIOUS COMMUNITIES BEFORE THE CONQUEST[1]

With the exception of Barrow which, according to Bede, was founded by Chad with an endowment of 50 hides given by King Wulfhere (HE iv. 3) nothing is known about the land held by the religious communities of Lincolnshire before the tenth century. There is, however, a little information about the Lincolnshire properties of *Medeshamstede* before the Scandinavian conquest.

ST PETER'S, *MEDESHAMSTEDE*, LATER PETERBOROUGH

Two charters preserved in the Peterborough cartulary known as the Black Book (London, Society of Antiquaries, MS 60) show that *Medeshamstede* had ten hides in Swineshead at the end of the eighth century and land at Sempringham, Sleaford, Cheal, *Forde*, and *Lehcotum* fifty years later (S 1412, 1440). Lennard's suggestion (1944, p. 57) that *Forde* was Greatford in Kesteven, about 16 km north-west of the abbey, is probably correct.

The same cartulary contains four memoranda recording early grants of land to *Medeshamstede*, translated and discussed by Stenton (1933, cited here in the reprint 1970, pp. 179–92), who argued that there is 'no reason to doubt that they represent, with substantial accuracy, transactions which occurred in the late seventh century' (1970, p. 183). They are:

S 1803 Friduric, *princeps* of King Æthelred, to St Peter's, *Medeshamstede*; grant of 20 hides (*manentes*) at Breedon-on-the-Hill, Leics. (*Bredun*) to found a monastery there. The brethren of *Medeshamstede* chose one of their number, Hedda, as abbot (of Breedon).

[1] Much of the evidence on which this appendix is based has been discussed thoroughly by Cyril Hart 1966.

S 1805 The same *princeps* Friduric, to abbot Hædda; grant of 31 hides (*manentes*) called *Hrepingas*.

S 1804 After this, King Æthelred, to Hedda, abbot of Breedon; grant of 15 hides (*manentes*) called *Cedenan ác*, in return for 500 *solidi* (see above p. 173).

S 1806 Æthelred, king of the Mercians, to the brethren of *Medeshamstede*; grant of 30 hides (manentes) at *Leugttricdun*.

Three of the names in these memoranda, *Bredun*, *Hrepingas*, and *Ceden ác*, also occur in a list of the possessions of *Medeshamstede* supposedly confirmed by Æthelred, king of the Mercians, in a forged charter dated 680 (S 72). Stenton argued convincingly that the list of names in this charter (which included *Barþanig* (Bardney) and *Lodeshalh*) was 'an attempt to set out, concisely, the possessions mentioned in documents descending from the pre-Danish monastery of Medeshamstede' (1970, p. 181). S 1803 and S 1805 show that Breedon was a daughter house of *Medeshamstede* and Stenton argued that Bardney was probably another (1970, p. 181; see also p. 65 above). These were colonies of *Medeshamstede's* monastic empire that extended to distant parts of the Mercian empire.

It has been suggested that several other names in these *Medeshamstede* texts as well as Bardney and Swineshead were of places in Lincolnshire. The proposed identifications are, however, very doubtful. They are:

Hrepingas – Rippingale. (Ekwall 1960, *s.n.*) tentatively suggested that this name was connected with Rippingale in Kesteven. Stenton pointed out that Breedon is unlikely to have been endowed with land 40 miles away (1970, p. 185 n).[2] Rumble 1977 has given good reasons for thinking that it is more likely to have been, or been associated with, Repton in Derbyshire.

Ceden ác. – Cadney. This identification which was made, with a query, by Hart 1966, p. 97, is rejected in *PNL* 2, p. 75. Cadney was even further from Breedon (60 miles) than Rippingale.

Leuttricdun – Laughterton. Ekwall (1960 *s.n.*) comments that if the early form was a misspelling of *Leagttricdun* 'it may belong here, and the OE form was *Leahtric-dun* "hill where lettuce (OE *leahtric*) grew". Only it would be remarkable to find this Latin loan-word (Lat. *lactuca*) so early in a place-name.' Laughterton is south of Torksey, about 45 miles from Peterborough.

2 In the eleventh century Peterborough had land in north Lindsey (see below), but conditions then were very different.

Lodeshale, Lodeshac (S 68, 72) – Louth. Hart 1966, p. 97 suggests this as a probable identification. This is not likely. Louth is named from the river-name Lud which derives from OE *hlud*. The earliest forms of Louth all have *-u-*, not *-o-* (Ekwall 1960 *s.n.*).

According to DB on the eve of the Conquest Peterborough Abbey held almost 40 carucates of land in Lincolnshire in the following places: Fiskerton with sokeland in Scothorne, Holme and Sudbrook and a berewick in Reepham; *Adewelle* (either Bowthorpe or a lost settlement in Careby; *LD* pp. l–li) with berewicks in Witham on the Hill, Manthorpe and Toft with Lound and in Little Bytham; Osgodby; Walcot near Folkingham with sokeland in Haythby; and Donington (DB i. 345b = *LD* 8/1–11).[3] With the exception of Fiskerton and its sokeland, which was in Lawress wapentake, and Donington in Kirton wapentake, all were in south-west Kesteven. The donors of some of these estates (and of others that the abbey lost) are named by Hugh Candidus who compiled a list of benefactions made after its revival, excluding those acquired by Bishop Æthelwold (d. 984) and Ealdwulf, abbot until 992 (Hugh Candidus, pp. 67–71) A version of that list, in some respects fuller than that in Hugh's *Chronicle*, is in the Black Book, fo. 71v, written by the same scribe as the annals 1132–54 in the Peterborough Chronicle (Clark, C. 1970, pp. xvii–xviii; some variants in the Black Book are printed by Mellows as footnotes in his edition). Although some information in this list was drawn from spurious documents (e.g. S 1029 concerning Fiskerton) these had been confected to serve as title-deeds and it is likely that those concerning recent donations contain reliable information about the transactions.

Fiskerton was bequeathed to the abbey by Leofgifu of London who died on pilgrimage to Jerusalem. Queen Edith claimed that Leofgifu had given it to her and Leofric (abbot 1052–1066) bought it from the queen (S 1029; Hugh Candidus, p. 40).

Thurlby. According to Hugh Candidus it was given by *Elfsi cild* but the Black Book shows that the donor was *Fredegist filius Kate* (Hugh Candidus, p. 71, n. 1). He was probably the man who gave Langtoft to Crowland Abbey (see above, p. 128). Hart (1966, p. 244) suggests that he may have been the Frithegyst who was defeated by Vikings in 993. It is, however, more likely that he was the *Fredgist* named as the pre-Conquest tenant of a manor in Deeping St James (*Estdepinge*) where Peterborough Abbey claimed to have sokemen (DB i. 366a = *LD* 51/2). It is close to both Crowland and Langtoft.

3 The endowment of Peterborough Abbey is discussed by King 1973.

Osgodby in Lavington. According to the Black Book it was given by *Elfsi infans filius Outi*, probably representing *Ælfsige cild filius Auti* (Hugh Candidus, p. 71, n. 1). Auti was a fairly common Scandinavian name in the Danelaw (von Feilitzen 1937, p. 169; Fellows-Jensen 1968, pp. 43–4). He was possibly the man who was the privileged holder of two hides of land in Bluntisham, Hunts., in the late tenth century (*Liber Eliensis*, ed. Blake, p. 99). According to Hugh Candidus, p. 40, it was, like Fiskerton, recovered from Queen Edith by Abbot Leofric.

Walcot near Folkingham was given, together with Birthorpe in Sempringham by Halfdan son of Brenting. Hart (1966, p. 245) suggests that Brenting was a surety when Maxey was bought for Peterborough Abbey *c.* 984 (Robertson 1939, p. 76) and that this gift was made during the abbacy of Ælfsige (1006–1042). For the later history of other estates Halfdan gave to the abbey see S 1481.

The abbey also held Stamford Baron, south of the Welland in Northants, and ten tenements (*mansiones*) and a mill on the Lincolnshire side of the river (DB i. 336b = *LD* p. 9/1, p. 11/10; cf. Hugh Candidus, p. 70). Its property in Lincoln was apparently acquired after the Conquest (DB i. 336a–b = *LD* p. 5/15, p. 7/19, 20). It also had property in Grantham (DB does not specify how much) but that also appears to have been acquired after the Conquest from a nun with the very rare name Alswið (DB i. 337b = *LD* 1/9; von Feilitzen 1937, p. 153).

The abbey was also given land in the following places before the Conquest that it did not hold in 1066:

Barrow, given by King Edgar to Bishop Æthelwold for the abbey (S 782). It was forfeited, together with Howden in Yorkshire in connection with the payment of geld when Abbot Ælfsige was in exile with Queen Emma, i.e. late 1013 to mid 1017 (Hugh Candidus, pp. 64–5; Lawson 1984, esp. pp. 724, 730).

Quadring, cf. Thurlby above.

Birthorpe, cf. Walcot near Folkingham above.

Hough on the Hill, Leadenham and Washingborough were given by Godgifu *domina* , probably the widow of Siward, earl of Northumbria (d. 1055) (Hugh Candidus p. 70, cf. S 1481).

Dunsby, near Hacconby in Aveland Wapentake, was given by Ælfgar of Dunsby (Hugh Candidus, p. 69). It was claimed by the abbey in 1086 but the wapentake said it did not belong to the abbey TRE (DB i. 377a; = *LD* 72/45; cf. Appendix 10).

CROWLAND ABBEY[4]

On the eve of the Conquest Crowland held six carucates and five bovates of land in Holland in Holbeach and Whaplode with a berewick in Spalding; Dowdike with berewicks in Drayton, Algarkirk and Burtoft; and ten carucates in Ness wapentake in Langtoft and Baston (DB i. 346b = *LD* 11/1–8). The donors of this property are named in the Guthlac Roll (Fig. 8.2) as follows:

Algar comes, presumably Earl Ælfgar who died in or soon after 1062, is represented as giving Holbeach, Whaplode, Spalding and Pinchbeck. TRE he held nine carucates in Spalding with ten carucates of sokeland in Pinchbeck that were in 1086 held by Ivo Taillebois (DB i. 351b = *LD* 14/96, 98).

Algarus filius Norland, donor of Baston and Thetford, cannot be identified.

Fregistus, who was probably the *Fredgist* who held Deeping St James TRE (above, under Peterborough), gave Langtoft.

Algar diaconus who gave Dowdike with its church may have been the *Ælger diaconus* who held land in Heckington TRE (*LD* 72/31 = DB i. 377a).

These donations are all represented in the spurious Crowland charters as if they were made in the early ninth century (S 1189–91). S 1189 attributes the gift of Dowdike to Ælfgar *comes*.

Crowland also had three carucates in Rippingale that were let to Hereward by Abbot Wulfketel who 'repossessed this land before Hereward left the country because he had not kept the agreement'. It was, nevertheless, confiscated and in 1086 was held by Oger the Breton (DB i. 364b, 377a = *LD* 42/13, 72/48). The soke of three carucates in Dowsby belonged to the abbey's manor of Rippingale TRE, but it was held by Guy de Craon in 1086 (DB i. 367a, 377b = *LD* 57/12, 72/49).

RAMSEY ABBEY

DB records that on the eve of the Conquest Ramsey Abbey had ten carucates and two bovates of land in Kesteven in the following places: Quarrington with sokeland in Old Sleaford, Dunby St Andrew (near Brauncewell) and Morton (unjustly held by Oger the Breton in 1086); Threekingham; and meadow in Coteland that was assessed for the geld in Cranwell (DB i. 346b, 364b = *LD* 10/1–5, 72/43). It also had one carucate in Drayton in Holland which was held TRE by Wulfwig, bishop of Dorchester and was claimed by Bishop Remigius in 1086 (DB i. 348a,

4 The endowment of Crowland Abbey is discussed by Page, F. 1934.

377b = *LD* 12/59, 73/1). Hart 1966, p. 103 identifies this as the land at *Offerthun* in Holland which, according to the Ramsey Chronicle was given to the abbey by Æthelric, bishop of Dorchester (1016–34). This property, with different spellings, was supposedly confirmed to the abbey in spurious charters of Edward the Confessor and William I (S 1030; Davis, *Regesta*, no. 95). The thirteenth-century Ramsey Chronicle provides information about the abbey's acquisition of land in many other places, apparently on the basis of lost documents, and a little additional information is given by lists of benefactions in the Ramsey Cartulary. The Lincolnshire references in these texts are as follows:

Æthelstan Mannesson (d. *c.* 986) bequeathed land at Hackthorn to his youngest daughter with ultimate reversion to Ramsey Abbey (Hart 1966, pp. 101–2; his attempt to identify this land is unconvincing).

Leofsige the deacon gave land at Langton by Horncastle, Wispington, Martin, and Waddingworth in the reign of Harthacnut (1040–42) (Hart 1966, pp. 102–3).

Leofsige, nephew of Leofsige the deacon, gave land at Threekingham and Mareham on the Hill (Hart 1966, pp. 241–2).

In 1051 Iól (a Scandinavian name) of Lincoln gave land in Quarrington, Sleaford and Cranwell (possibly the meadowland in Coteland) (Hart 1966, p. 242).

See also the spurious confirmation charter S 1030 listed in Appendix 5.

THORNEY ABBEY

According to DB Thorney Abbey did not hold any land in Lincs., but it may have been endowed with some by Bishop Æthelwold. Although its foundation charter (S 792) is spurious it contains some information about the abbey's endowment that may derive from reliable sources. It claims that Bishop Æthelwold gave it land in Gedney, Lutton, Tydd St Mary, and *Angarhala* that he had bought from Ealdorman Æthelwine. There is no other evidence that Thorney had land in these places and TRE Earl Ælfgar had land in the first three (DB i. 338a, 351b = *LD* 1/28–31, 14/97). It is possible that these places were given to the abbey but were taken back by Æthelwine (d. 992) or one of his successors as ealdorman/earl of East Anglia. The claim in the same charter that Thorney was also endowed with Barrow is far less credible; that passage is copied from S 782, an authentic charter (see above under Peterborough Abbey).

STOW MINSTER, SEE APPENDIX 8

WESTMINSTER ABBEY

In 1086 Westminster held the manor of Donnington Pigot with a berewick in Thorpe on the Hill that had been held TRE by Æðelric son of Mæregeat who gave it to the abbey, presumably after the Conquest at the same time as he gave it Kelvedon Hatch in Essex (DB ii. 14b).[5] William I confirmed this Lincolnshire land to the abbey in the time Abbot Vitalis, i.e. 1076–85 (Davis *Regesta*, no. 212). It also claimed land that had belonged to Doddington Pigot but was held by Baldwin (DB i. 370a, 377a = *LD* 65/1–5, 72/27).

5 Fleming 1991, pp. 136–7 assumes that Doddington was given to the abbey before 1066.

Appendix 8

STOW MINSTER

In Florence of Worcester's annal for 1057 Eadnoth, anachronistically called bishop of Lincoln, is named in connection with St Mary's, Stow, but the verb is missing from the relevant clause. It is also missing in Roger of Hoveden's *Chronica* (ed. W. Stubbs, i. 103) which in this passage is based on Florence, but in the copy of the same annal in the *Historia Regum* attributed to Symeon of Durham (ed. Arnold, ii.173) the word *construxit* is supplied. There were two bishops of Dorchester called Eadnoth, the first died in 1016, the other held the see 1034–49. The first Eadnoth cannot have claimed Lindsey as part of his diocese before 1011 at the earliest, if indeed he ever did. If, as suggested in Chapter VI, Lindsey ceased to be a separate diocese when the Five Boroughs ceased to be an administrative district, the restoration of Lindsey to the diocese of Dorchester probably happened after the death of bishop Eadnoth I. The period 1011–16 was hardly a suitable time for building a minster in Lindsey; Gainsborough was Sven's base when he conquered England in 1013, the area was ravaged by Æthelred's forces after Cnut withdrew in 1014, it was involved in Edmund's rebellion against his father and it was on the route of Cnut's campaign in 1016. It is therefore likely that the bishop named by Florence was Eadnoth II. The fact that he and his immediate predecessor, Æthelric, both received food rents from St Mary's, Stow (S 1478, discussed below) suggests that the minster existed when Æthelric was bishop. It was, presumably founded before the Danish conquest and, like Grantham, survived the ninth-century disruptions.

There is evidence that Stow was a church, probably an important one, long before the eleventh century. A small excavation in the angle between the north transept, built shortly before the Conquest, and the nave, built soon after it, revealed foundations of what was, presumably, a *porticus*, or enclosed aisle, attached to the nave of an earlier church which may have been contemporary with the transept or part of the church that Eadnoth built earlier in the century. These foundations cut into 17 graves. If the foundations were of the church built in the 1050s, the cemetery must have been in use long before the time of Eadnoth II to have such a concentration of burials. The excavator, Naomi Field, also reported that 'a substantial spread of burnt daub and charcoal were also found which may have come

Fig. App. 8.1 Stow Minster.
Foundations of a porticus north of the ?11th-century church excavated in 1983 by Naomi Field, on the north side of the standing church, looking west. This porticus cut through an earlier graveyard. The western jamb of the Romanesque north doorway can be seen in the top left-hand corner.
Photo and © Naomi Field.

from a timber building beyond the limits of the excavation. Beneath the burnt levels and also cut by the *porticus* foundations was part of a limestone rubble path which contained many fragments of re-used Roman tile. A burial lay sealed beneath this path suggesting that even at this early date the site was ecclesiastical' (Field 1984, p. 106).

This evidence strengthens the probability that the name Stow here refers to a church of some importance. The basic meaning of the word was 'place', and often had the particular sense of 'a place where people assembled'. It was, therefore, an appropriate name for churches that attracted large numbers of people at festivals, and was sometimes combined with the name of a saint, as in Hibaldstow and Edwinstow (Smith 1970, ii. 158–61; Gelling 1982).

Apart from the building itself, the main evidence for Stow minster in the eleventh century comes from the chartulary of the abbey of Eynsham, near Oxford, close to the south-western limit of Dorchester diocese. In 1091 monks were transferred from Eynsham to Stow and the communities were combined under Columban, who was then appointed abbot (Bates 1992, pp. 30–32). When, three years later, Robert Bloet, Remigius's successor as bishop of Lincoln, returned the combined community to Eynsham, it kept documents concerning Stow before the merger. Some, possibly all, of these records were copied in the chartulary compiled at the end of the twelfth century (Salter 1907). These included two in Old English that are important for the history of Stow before the Conquest.

The first (S 1478; the best edition and translation is in *Councils and Synods* i. 538–43) is a record of a meeting which confirmed arrangements concerning Stow made by Wulfwig soon after he became bishop of Dorchester in 1053, with Leofric, earl of Mercia, and his wife, Godgifu. The numerous witnesses include Leofwine who was chosen as bishop of Lichfield after the death of Wulfsige in October 1053 (*Chronicle* D) and Earl Siweard who, according to the *Chronicle*, died early in 1055, shortly before a council held 'a week before mid-Lent', i.e. in the middle of March (Mid-Lent Sunday in 1055 was on 26 March). It can, therefore, safely be assumed that the meeting was held in 1054, very probably on one of the festivals of St Mary in August or September (see below). The text relates that Leofric and Godgifu endowed the minster (*þæt mynster godian*, which may mean 'repair the minster', *Councils and Synods*, p. 539), and settled it with priests who were to follow the forms of service used at St Paul's, London.The lands they gave were 'to provide food and clothes to the brethren who are therein' but the bishop was to have food-rent (*feorm*) from the minster as Æthelric and Eadnoth (successive bishops of Dorchester 1016–49) had before him, (literally 'the bishop is to have in his food-rent each of the things which Bishop Æthelric and Bishop Eadnoth had before him, from those which belong by rights to his bishopric'). This is specified as 'two parts of each of the things which comes into the minster, and the priests are to have the third part, except at the two festivals'. The bishop was to have 'all that comes there for eight days' at each festival, but only two thirds of the food, one third being reserved for the priests. As Dorothy Whitelock pointed out the feasts were 'presumably the Assumption, 15 Aug., and the Nativity, 8 Sept., when food would be more plentiful than at Candlemas, 2 Feb. or at the Annunciation 25 Mar.' (*Councils and Synods*, p. 541, n.1).

The lands given by Leofric and Godgifu are not named in the record of the 1054 meeting, but some are specified in a writ issued by William I early in his reign. As this writ is neither well known nor readily accessible, it is given here with a translation.[1]

1 I should like to thank Professor Joyce Hill of Leeds University for her help in revising the translation.

Will'm king gret Þomas arce-biscop 7 Þurold 7 Earnwig his scyrgerefan 7 ealle þa þegnas on Snotingeham scyre 7 on Lincolscyre frencisce 7 englisce freon[d]lice 7 ic kyðe eow þæt ic an Sce Marian æt Stowe 7 þan munecan Niweweorce 7 Fladburh 7 Brantune 7 Wylle Wepentæc, mid sace 7 mid soce 7 tolle 7 teame swaforforð swa Godgyfe on Eadweardes dæge kynges fyrmest hæfde on eallan þingan 7 þa Remig. biscop gesweotelian mæg þæt rihtlice þær to gebyrige 7 ic beode þæt cume in ongean swa hwæt swa is ut gedon 7 non oðer.

King William sends friendly greetings to Archbishop Thomas and Thurold and Earnwig his sheriffs and all the thegns in Nottinghamshire and in Lincolnshire, French and English. And I inform you that I give to St Mary at Stow and the monks, Newark and Fledborough (in Nottinghamshire) and Brampton and Well Wapentake (in Lincolnshire) with sake and soke and toll and team as fully and as completely as Godgifu first had [them] in all things in the time of King Edward and those [things] that Bishop Remigius is able to testify rightly belong thereto. And I require that there shall come back in whatever has been taken away and nothing else.

This writ was obviously issued between the accession of Thomas as archbishop of York in 1070 and the death of Remigius in 1092. In the edition of the chartulary W. H. Stevenson supplied a very thorough note on the date of this writ in which he argued that it clearly showed that 'Remigius was already concerned with Stow, but had not yet succeeded in establishing himself as diocesan'. He suggested that it was 'perhaps anterior' to the transfer of the see to Lincoln, which he believed happened in 1075. This suggestion was disregarded by the editor, H. E. Salter, who gave the date limits 1075–1092 in the margin, a dating that was adopted by H. W. C. Davis in the *Regesta*, no. 333. It is, however, clear that the decision to move the see was made by 1073 at the latest (Bates 1992, pp. 11–12; Bishop and Chaplais 1957, no. 13 date the writ authorizing the move 1072, before Whitsun). The language of the writ strengthens the likelihood that it was issued early in William's reign for, as Bishop and Chaplais (1957, p. xiii) observed 'from about 1070 these documents ceased almost completely to be written in the vernacular'. The fact that the writ was addressed to Archbishop Thomas although it concerned land in Lincolnshire and Nottinghamshire, implies that he was considered at the time to be the diocesan in those shires. Nottinghamshire was then, and continued to be, in York diocese, but it was not until April 1072 that the Council of Winchester determined that the Humber formed the southern boundary of York province (*Councils and Synods*, pp. 601–3). The writ is unlikely to be later than that.

Stevenson accepted this text as a copy of a genuine writ. There are only two variants from the normal formulas of eleventh-century writs. First, it was addressed to 'his' rather than to 'my sheriffs'. This may well have been due to the copyist; Harmer 1952, p. 123 draws attention to an example of such a change in a thirteenth-century Abingdon chartulary. Secondly, the use of *án*, the first person present of *unnan* 'to give' instead of the normal past tense 'have given'. The present tense is, however, used in some authentic writs of William I both in English (*Regesta* no. 12 = Douglas 1932, p. 6) and Latin (e.g. *Regesta* no. 236 = Bishop and Chaplais 1957, no. 26).[2]

In 1086 the places named in the writ as well as Stow itself were held by Remigius. Domesday Book confirms that before the Conquest St Mary of Stow held Brampton and, with some stated exceptions, two-thirds of the forfeitures in Well wapentake (DB i. 344a, 376a = *LD* 7/10, 71/9–10). In the Nottinghamshire Domesday Godgifu is named as the pre-Conquest tenant of Newark and Fledborough (DB i. 283b–84a). It is possible that here, as occasionally elsewhere, Domesday named the owner (or tenant) sometime before the Conquest, but it may be that Godgifu retained a life interest in these places, whether or not she paid any rent to Stow. The letter of Nicholas II is good evidence that by 1061 Stow claimed to possess Newark (*RA*, i. no. 247, pp. 186–88; *Councils and Synods*, pp. 550–2). The writ implies that the minster had suffered losses and later Remigius complained of the negligence of its leaders (Salter 1907, no. 5, pp. 32–5).

Leofric and Godgifu were renowned for their generosity to several important churches in Mercia, giving valuable ornaments as well as land (Florence of Worcester, ed. Thorpe, i. 216). It was their gifts that made possible the rebuilding of Stow church on a large scale. Henry of Huntingdon even claims that Godgifu built it (*Historia Anglorum*, ed. Arnold, p. 196. It has generally been assumed that Henry meant Leofric, but that is not what he says: *Lefricus...defunctus est eo tempore: cujus uxor Godiva...abbatiam apud Coventre construxit, et auro et argento incomparabiliter ditavit. Construxit etiam ecclesiam Stow sub promontorio Lincolniæ, et multas alias.* Commentators have apparently been influenced by the passage in Florence mentioned above. The writ quoted above implies that Godgifu was the main donor). The work was, however, not complete before the Conquest. The transepts and the piers of

2 The Latin writ that immediately precedes the Old English writ concerning Stow in the chartulary (Salter 1907, no. 26; *Regesta*, no. 334) cannot be accepted as genuine. It purports to be a writ of a King William granting the abbacy of Stow to Columban. He was appointed abbot in 1090 or 1091, but the addressees are exactly the same as in the Old English writ issued some 20 years earlier, on which it was obviously modelled.

the crossing were constructed by then, but the arches of the crossing were completed after the Conquest, presumably by Remigius in preparation for the establishment of the abbey there in 1091. Remigius presumably also rebuilt or altered the nave and choir but they were completely rebuilt in the twelfth century (Gem 1988, p. 26).[3]

The community certainly existed on the eve of the Conquest and immediately after it. In Domesday Book there is a report that the whole county witnessed that land of Ulf of Ormsby was sold to St Mary of Stow and was held by that church on the day King Edward died. They also confirmed that Remigius held it later, although by 1086 it was in the hands of Drogo de la Beuvrière (DB i. 360b, 376a = *LD* 30/20, 70/27). Ulf, who can be identified as the son of Topi, made a will between November 1066 and 1069 in which he noted that he had 'granted' Ormsby to St Mary's, Stow (Whitelock, *Wills*, no. 39).

Remigius planned to transfer the monks of Eynsham and their property to Stow even before the see was moved to Lincoln. A charter of William I granting Eynsham to Stow is certainly much earlier that the date, 1080x1087, given in the edition of the chartulary (Salter 1907, no. 3; *Regesta*, no. 266 dates it 1070x1087). In the same charter William granted Sleaford to Remigius *pro commutatione altaris de Stou et quatuor carucarum terrœ quœ pertinent ad episcopium* (Remigius's manor of Stow was assessed at 4 carucates, DB i. 344a = *LD* 7/1). As Sleaford was part of the endowment of the bishopric listed in the writ authorizing the removal of the see to Lincoln, dated 1072 by Bishop and Chaplais (1957, no. 13), the grant of Sleaford in compensation for the bishop's loss of income from Stow must have been earlier than that. Remigius postponed the merger of Eynsham with Stow for almost 20 years during which he kept both communities in his own hands, apparently treating them as old-fashioned episcopal minsters. (Bates 1992, pp. 30–2, advances good reasons for dating *Regesta*, no. 266 before the mid 1070s, although his assertion that its addressees are identical with those of the Old English writ is a mistake.) Remigius retained Sleaford despite the delay in transferring the Eynsham monks to Stow. Distinguished as New Sleaford, it remained in the hands of the bishops of Lincoln until the sixteenth century (Trollope 1872, pp. 123–34).

The reference in Domesday Book to Ralph, priest of Haugham, who became a monk (*monachus*) in St Mary's, Stow, illegally transferring a carucate of land to it (DB i. 344a = *LD* 7/5), does not say when that happened, but it is consistent with the continued existence of the

3 I should like to thank Dr Richard Gem for his advice on the architectural history of the church.

community there throughout the reign of William I. It also suggests that Remigius installed monks in Stow, perhaps replacing the secular canons, before 1086. If so, Stow resembled Eynsham, which Domesday Book shows was a community of monks without an abbot and under the authority of Remigius (DB i. 155a; Eynsham Church appears as a tenant-in-chief in Gloucestershire, DB i. 166a).

A good measure of the importance of St Mary's at Stow in the minds of contemporary churchmen is the attention paid to it by Eadnoth II, by both Wulfwig and Remigius very early in their pontificates, and by the archbishops of York. This interest in Stow implies that it had a special place in the traditions of the church in Lindsey. It is tempting to think that it was one of the two communities mentioned in the 830s by Bishop Beorhtred in his profession of obedience to Archbishop Ceolnoth (see p. 79), but that can be no more than speculation.

Appendix 9

COINS FOUND IN LINCOLNSHIRE BEFORE 1994

Single finds and hoards of Anglo-Saxon coins found in Lincolnshire before the end of 1994 are here listed topographically. Some later coins found in the same places are also listed. For coins discovered after 1994 reference may, in due course, be made to the data-base of single-finds of coins from the British Isles from the period 410–1180 and of hoards from that period being prepared in the Fitzwilliam Museum, Cambridge.

For coins earlier than the reform of *c.* 973 the following details are given, as far as possible: the authority issuing it, the type, the region or mint in which it was produced, and the date. More recent coins are not listed individually; only the number of each king is noted. Further information may be found in the references cited. Where no reference is given, the information has been generously provided by Dr Mark Blackburn.

Alford. a. sceat, series H, type 48, origin uncertain, *c.* 725–40?; b. sceat, series J, type 27b, origin uncertain, *c.* 715–25; c. sceat, series –, type 51, English?, *c.* 710–20?; d. Offa of Mercia, light issue, Canterbury, *c.* 765–92; Offa of Mercia, light issue, London or Canterbury, *c.* 765–92; f. Coenwulf of Mercia, *Tribrach* type, London, *c.* 798–804; one each of Æthelred II and William I. Most of these coins have been found, together with various small Anglo-Saxon artefacts, within an area 100 yards square (Bispham 1986; *Single Finds* 2, no. 2).

Alkborough. Sceat, series X related, type 30/51 var., English, *c.* 720–30? (Blackburn 1993).

Ancaster, near. One of Edward the Confessor (Blackburn, Colyer, and Dolley 1983, table 2.28).

Appleby. Æthelred II of Northumbria, first reign, styca, York, 840–4? (Blackburn, Colyer, and Dolley 1983, table 2.8).

Bardney. a. sceat, series D, type 2c, Lower Rhineland, *c.* 700–10; b. sceat, series E, Metcalf var. G2, Lower Rhineland, *c.* 700-710; c. sceat, series E, secondary var., *c.* 715–30, Lower Rhineland or Frisia; d. sceat, series F, type 24b, English, uncertain region, *c.* 700–10; Athelstan,

Circumscription Cross type, York, 927–39; one of William I; one of Stephen (*Single Finds* 4).

Barrow upon Humber (St Chad's church). a. Burgred of Mercia, *Lunette* type, London, *c.* 865–74; b. Alfred of Wessex, *Lunette* type, London?, *c.* 871–5 (Blackburn, Colyer, and Dolley, table 2.12–13).

Barton upon Humber. Alfred of Wessex, *Lunette* type, London?, *c.* 871–5 (Blackburn 1993).

Billinghay, near. One of Æthelred II.

Binbrook. Sceat, series G, type 3a, origin uncertain, *c.* 715–25 (*Single Finds* 2, no. 10).

Binbrook (possibly a different site from the last). a. sceat, series E, variety unspecified, Lower Rhineland or Frisia, *c.* 700–50?; b. sceat, series J, type 37, English, uncertain origin, *c.* 715–25 (Blackburn 1993).

Bitchfield. Offa of Mercia, East Anglia, late phase?

Boston region. Æthelwulf of Wessex, Saxoniorum type, Canterbury; and one each of Cnut, William I, and Henry I (*Coin Register* 1994, nos 191, 215, 241, 253).

Brigg. Sceat, series E, 'VICO' var., Lower Rhineland, *c.* 695–710 (*Single Finds* 2, no. 15).

Brocklesby. Aldfrith of Northumbria, sceat, series Y, York, *c.* 700 (*Coin Register* 1988, no. 138).

Burgh le Marsh. a. sceat, series E, 'plumed bird' var., Lower Rhineland or Frisia, *c.* 710–25?; b. sceat, series E, secondary var., Lower Rhineland or Frisia, *c.* 715–30? (Rigold and Metcalf 1984, p. 248).

Burton-by-Lincoln. Anglo-Saxon gold shilling, 'York' type, mid 7th cent. (Blackburn 1994).

Caistor-on-the-Wolds (Grammar School boarding house). Eadberht of Northumbria, sceat, series Y, York, 737–58 (Rigold and Metcalf 1984, p. 248).

Caistor-on-the-Wolds, near (various locations). a. Merovingian tremissis, Quentovic; b. sceat, series F, English, origin uncertain, *c.* 700–15; c. Coenwulf of Mercia, *Cross fourchée* type, Canterbury, *c.* 810–21; one each of Æthelred II and Cnut (Blackburn 1993; *Single Finds* 1, no. 2; *Single Finds* 3, no. 84).

Claxby-by-Alford. Sceat, series E, Metcalf var. D, Lower Rhineland, *c.* 700–10; one of Cnut (*Single Finds* 1, nos. 4–5).

Cleethorpes. One of Æthelred II.

Coningsby, near. One of Edward the Confessor (*Coin Register* 1988, number 183).

Crosby. Sceat, series E, 'plumed bird' var., Lower Rhineland or Frisia, *c.* 710–20 (Rigold and Metcalf 1984, p. 250).

Donington, near. One of William I (Blackburn, Colyer, and Dolley, table 2. 31).

Epworth. Eadberht of Northumbria, sceat, series Y, York, 737–58 (Rigold and Metcalf 1984, p. 251).

Ferriby, South. a. sceat, series J, type 85, English, *c.* 715–25; b. 'sceat', series G, type 3a, origin uncertain, *c.* 715–25 (Blackburn 1993).

Ferriby, South. Eadwig, *Two-Line* type, York, 955–9 (*Single Finds* 4).

Fiskerton (Short Ferry Bridge). One of Edward the Confessor (Blackburn, Colyer, and Dolley 1983, table 2. 27).

Flixborough, excavations 1990–91. A productive site with 53 Anglo-Saxon coins all of the 8th or 9th century. These comprise 23 sceattas: one series C, two series D (types 2c and 8), eleven series E (including two 'plumed bird'), two series G (types 3a and 36), two series J (types 27b and 37), one series N (type 41b), one series O (type 57), one series R, one series U (type 23b), one series Y (Eadberht, class B); eight broad flan pennies: one Offa of Mercia (light coinage), one Ceolnoth, archbishop of Canterbury (Portrait/*Dorovernia Ca* monogram type, North 241), one Berhtwulf of Mercia (Portrait type), one Æthelwulf of Wessex (*Open Cross* type), two Æthelberht of Wessex (*Open Cross* type), two Alfred of Wessex (*Lunette* type); 22 Northumbrian stycas (Blackburn 1993).

Gainsborough, near (site A). Æthelred II of Northumbria, base 'styca', York, 840–8? (*Single Finds* 4).

Gainsborough, near (site B). Æthelred I of Wessex, *Lunette* type, 866–71 (Blackburn 1993).

Gainsborough, near. Uncertain fragment, probably late 9th or 10th cent., possibly a Viking issue; one of Stephen (*Single Finds* 4).

Glentham. One of William II (Blackburn, Colyer, and Dolley 1983, table 2. 32).

'Goltho' (excavation). Edgar, *Two-line* type, Lincoln?, 959–73; two of Cnut (Blackburn, Colyer, and Dolley 1983, table 2.18, 22–3).

Grantham, near. Archbishop Æthelheard, *Three-line* type, Canterbury, 793–6 (Blackburn, Colyer, and Dolley, table 2.2).

Grimsby, near (a moderately productive site on the Wolds with later medieval finds, including two tumbrels for weighing 14th-century coins). a. sceat, series D, type 2c, Lower Rhineland, *c.* 700–10; b. sceat, series E, Metcalf var. D, Lower Rhineland, *c.* 700–10; c. sceat, series E, Metcalf var. A, Lower Rhineland or Frisia, *c.* 710–30; d. sceat, series E,

Metcalf var. A, Lower Rhineland or Frisia, *c.* 710–30; e. sceat, series E, uncertain variety, probably Lower Rhineland or Frisia, *c.* 700–40; f. sceat, series K, type 32a, Kent or Thames valley, *c.* 720–30; g. sceat, series L, type 18, south-east England, *c.* 725–40; h. sceat, series W, type 54, England, uncertain region, *c.* 700–15; i. Northumbrian styca, irregular series, copying names of Æthelred I and of the moneyer Tidwulf, York?, *c.* 845–65; Edgar, *Two-Line* type, 959–73; two of Æthelred II and one of Stephen (*Single Finds* 1, nos 9–10; Blackburn and Bonser 1984; *Single Finds* 3, nos 103–6; *Single Finds* 4).

Grimsby, near. Merovingian tremissis, Sion (Switzerland).

Grimsby area. One of Cnut and two of Henry II (*Single Finds* 4).

Grimsthorpe. Æthelred II of Northumbria, first reign, styca, York, 840–4? (Blackburn, Colyer, and Dolley 1983, table 2.9).

Horncastle. One of William I (Blackburn, Colyer, and Dolley 1983, table 2. 30).

Horncastle, near. Two of Æthelred II (Blackburn, Colyer, and Dolley 1983, table 2.19, 21).

Irby upon Humber, near Grimsby. Æthelred II of Northumbria, first reign, styca, York, 840–4? (Blackburn 1993).

Keelby, near (site A). a. sceat, series E, Metcalf var. A, Lower Rhineland or Frisia, *c.* 710–20; b. sceat, series R, Blackburn class H, East Anglia, *c.* 720–35?; c. Æthelred II of Northumbria, second reign, styca, York, 844-8?; d. Northumbrian base styca, irregular series, York?, *c.* 845–65 (Blackburn 1993).

Keelby, near (site B, apparently different from site A). Ecgberht of Wessex, *Dorob C* type, Canterbury, *c.* 828–39; one of Æthelred II; one of Edward the Confessor; one of William I and one of Henry of Northumberland (1136–52) (*Single Finds* 3, no. 108; *Coin Register* 1987, nos 173, 199; Blackburn 1993).

Kelsey, South. Sceat, series E, Lower Rhineland or Frisia, *c.* 700–40 (Blackburn 1993).

Kingerby. Sceat, series K, type 32a, East Kent, *c.* 720–30 (*Coin Register* 1991, no. 107).

Kirkby, East. *St Edmund,* East Anglia, *c.* 900 (Blackburn, Colyer, and Dolley 1983, table 2.16).

Kirmington. a. Eanred of Northumbria, styca, earlier phase, York, *c.* 830; b. Ceolnoth, archbishop of Canterbury, *Lunette* type, Canterbury, *c.* 866–70 (Blackburn, Colyer, and Dolley 1983, table 2.7; *Coin Register* 1987, no. 104).

Limber (Great?), near. Wulfred, archbishop of Canterbury, *Monogram* type, Canterbury, *c.* 810–22 (Blackburn, Colyer, and Dolley 1983, table 2.4).

Lincoln (Danes Terrace). One of Æthelred II, and one of Edward the Confessor (Blackburn, Colyer, and Dolley, table 1. 15, 26).

Lincoln (Flaxengate). a. Vikings of the southern Danelaw, *Two-line* type copying the names of Alfred and of his moneyer Ludig, *c.* 885–95; b. *St Edmund*, *c.* 905, East Anglia; c. *St Edmund,* East Anglia, *c.* 910; e. *Two-line* type, *c.* 890–973; f. Edgar, *Two-line* type, Newark?, 959–73; two of Cnut; six of Edward the Confessor; one of William I and one of William I or II (Blackburn, Colyer, and Dolley 1983, table 1, nos 5–7, 9–11, 19–20, 23–4, 28–31, 35, 38). See also Blackburn and Mann 1995 for a coin die found here.

Lincoln (St Paul's church). a. 'Æthelred of Wessex' (probably posthumous), *Lunette* type, London?, *c.* 870–5; b. Alfred of Wessex, *Lunette* type, Canterbury, *c.* 871–5; c. Æthelred I or Alfred of Wessex, *Lunette* type, Canterbury or London?, *c.* 870–5; d. Burgred of Mercia, Æthelred II or Alfred of Wessex, *Lunette* type, Canterbury or London?, *c.* 864–75; e. *St Peter*, York, *c.* 912; four of Æthelred II, one of Harthacnut (Blackburn, Colyer, and Dolley 1983, table 1.1–4, 8, 12–14, 16, 22).

Lincoln (Usher Gallery grounds). One of Edward the Confessor and one of Olaf Kyrre, king of Norway (1066–93) (Blackburn, Colyer, and Dolley 1983, table 1.27, 32).

Lincoln (West Parade). One Danish from the time of Magnus the Good (Blackburn, Colyer, and Dolley 1983, table 1.25).

Lincoln (various locations). One of Æthelred II, two of Cnut, four of William I (Blackburn, Colyer, and Dolley 1983, table 1.17–8, 21, 33–4, 36–7). Ten coins found in excavations after that publication are described in Blackburn, forthcoming.

Lincoln, near. Merovingian gold tremissis, Lieusaint-en-Brie (dep. Seine-et Marne), mid 7th cent. (Blackburn 1993).

Lincoln, near. One of Edward the Confessor and one of Olaf Kyrre, king of Norway (1066–93) (*Coin Register* 1987, nos. 159, 168).

Lincoln region?, Vikings of the southern Danelaw, *Two-line* type copying the name of Alfred, *c.* 885–95 (Blackburn, Colyer, and Dolley 1983, table 2.15).

Lincoln, 'just north of'. Sceat, series D, type 2c, Lower Rhineland, *c.* 700–10 (Blackburn 1993).

Lincolnshire, north. Ceolwulf I of Mercia, East Anglian mint, 821–3.

Lincolnshire, north-east (site unknown). Æthelred II of Northumbria, first reign, styca, York, 840–4? (*Single Finds* 1, no. 17).

Lincolnshire, south. Merovingian tremissis, Blangy-sur-Ternoise (Pas-de-Calais), moneyer Ansoaldus. Other coins from the same, very productive, site found by 1997 are listed by Bonser 1997, pp. 41–2, as follows: One thrymsa, Two emperors type; five Merovingian tremisses, from Canac, Quentovic (moneyer Anglus), Maastricht (moneyer Domaricus), and two unrecognized types; one plated imitation and a gold blank flan, *c.* 37% Au; 49 sceattas: two series B, two series C (one of them type 2), four series D (type 8), 23 series E, one series F, two series G (type 3a), three series J (two type 37, one type 85), one series K (type 32a),, one series N, one series R imitative, one series U, seven series X, one series 70 imitative; one Merovingian denier, ?Paris region; a fragment of a ninth-century Lunette type. In addition this site has yielded two Ancient British gold staters; one of Stephen, cut half; and one of Henry II, 'Tealby' type.

Lincolnshire. One of Æthelred II (*Coin Register* 1993, no. 214).

Long Sutton? One of Æthelred II (Blackburn, Colyer, and Dolley 1983, table 2.20).

Louth, near (site A). Sceat, series E, secondary var., Lower Rhineland or Frisia, *c.* 720–30?; *St Peter*, *Sword/Cross* type, York, 920–27; three of Harold I and one of Harthacnut, three of Edward the Confessor, one of William I, two of Stephen, three of Henry II, and several later medieval coins (*Single Finds* 2, nos 36–40; *Single Finds* 3, nos 113, 114; *Coin Register* 1990, nos 229-30, 232; *Single Finds* 4).

Louth, near (site B). One of Edward the Confessor and one of Stephen (*Single Finds* 2, nos 41, 42).

Louth, near (site C). a. Merovingian or Anglo-Saxon? contemporary plated forgery of a gold tremissis?, origin uncertain, 7th cent.?; b. Alfred of Wessex, *Two-line* type, mint uncertain, *c.* 880–99; two of Henry II (*Single Finds* 2, nos 43, 44; *Coin Register* 1987, no. 34; *Single Finds* 4).

Louth, near (site F). Wulfred archbishop of Canterbury, *Transitional Monogram* type, Canterbury, *c.* 810 (*Coin Register* 1987, no. 100).

Louth, near (site G). One of Cnut and one of Henry I (*Single Finds* 4).

Louth, near (site H). a, b. Two sceattas, types unspecified, one silver, one base, *c.* 675-750; c. Offa of Mercia, heavy issue, Canterbury, *c.* 792-6 (Blackburn 1993); d. Eadred, unknown type, 946–55; e. Edgar, *Horizontal* type, York, 959–73 .

Louth, near (unknown site 'east of Louth'). Æthelheard, archbishop of Canterbury, with Offa of Mercia, Canterbury, 792–6 (Blackburn 1993).

Mablethorpe, near. Sceat, series E, secondary var., Lower Rhineland or Frisia, *c.* 720–40 (Blackburn 1993).

Market Rasen, near. Sceat, series –, type 70, English, region uncertain, *c.* 720–40?; *St Peter, without sword*, York, *c.* 905–15 (*Coin Register* 1988, no. 158; *Single Finds* 4).

Marton, near. Sceat, series J, type 72, English, *c.* 710–75 (*Coin Register* 1994, no. 152).

Nettleham. Sceat, series E, unusual style, base silver, Lower Rhineland or Frisia, *c.* 710–40? (Rigold and Metcalf 1984, p. 256).

Normanby, near Scunthorpe. a. sceat, series L, type 12/52 var., London, *c.* 725–50; b. sceat, series R, East Anglia, *c.* 730–50 (Rigold and Metcalf 1984, p. 256).

Normanby-by-Stow. One of Cnut (Blackburn, Colyer, and Dolley 1983, table 2.24).

Normanby le Wold. Burgred of Mercia, *Lunette* type, London, *c.* 865–74 (Blackburn, Colyer, and Dolley 1983, table 2.11).

Osbournby. 'Sceat', series X, type 31, Frisia, *c.* 710–35 (*Coin Register* 1987, no. 95).

Scawby. Berhtwulf of Mercia, *Portrait/Cross-crosslet* type, London, *c.* 841–3 (Blackburn, Colyer, and Dolley 1983, table 2.10).

Scunthorpe, near. a. sceat. series E, secondary var., Lower Rhineland or Frisia, *c.* 720–40; b. sceat, series L, type 23e, southern England, *c.* 725–40 (Blackburn 1993).

Sleaford, near (site 1). a. Edgar, *Two-Line* type, York; three of Æthelred II, two of Cnut, one each of Harold I, Edward the Confessor, William II and Henry II.

Sleaford, near (site 2). a. sceat, series R, East Anglia, *c.* 710–40; b. sceat, series G, type 3a, origin uncertain, *c.* 715–25; one each of William II and Stephen.

Sleaford, near (site 3). a. sceat, series G, type 3a, origin uncertain, *c.* 715–25; b. Offa of Mercia, heavy issue, *c.* 792–6; one of Cnut .

Sleaford, near (site 4). One each of Edward the Confessor and Henry II.

Stamford. Sceat, series T, type 9, East Midlands?, *c.* 715–20?

Stamford Castle. Vikings of the Southern Danelaw, *Two-line* type copying names of Alfred and of his moneyer Ludig, *c.* 885–95 (Blackburn, Colyer, and Dolley 1983, table 2.14; identification amended by Blackburn, personal communication).

Stoke Rochford. One of Edward the Confessor (Blackburn, Colyer, and Dolley 1983, table 2.29).

Stow (site A). Styca, irregular series?, York, mid 9th cent. (Blackburn 1993).

Stow (site B). a. sceat, series E, secondary var., Lower Rhineland or Frisia, *c.* 720–50; b. sceat, series G, type 3a, origin uncertain, *c.* 715–25; c. Offa of Mercia, heavy issue, London, *c.* 792–6; d. Offa of Mercia, heavy issue, London, *c.* 792–6 (Blackburn 1993).

Sturton-by-Stow. a. sceat, series D, type 2c, Lower Rhineland, *c.* 700–10; b. sceat, series S, type 47, Essex or London, *c.* 720–40 (Blackburn 1993).

Swallow, near. Sihtric 'Caoch', *Sword/Hammer* type, north-east Midlands, 921–7 (Fitwilliam Museum, *Annual Report* 1995, pp. 26–7.

Swinderby, near. a. sceat, series E, secondary var., Lower Rhineland or Frisia, *c.* 715–30; b. sceat, series G, type 3a, origin uncertain, *c.* 715–25; c. Eadberht, bishop of London, under Offa, London, *c.* 772–89; d. Ceolwulf I of Mercia, *Three-Line* type, East Anglian mint, 821–3; two of Stephen (*Single Finds* 4).

Threekingham. Sihtric 'Caoch', *Sword/Hammer* type, north-eastern Midlands, 921–7 (Blackburn, Colyer, and Dolley 1983, table 2. 17).

Torksey, 'in the Fossdyke'. Offa of Mercia, heavy issue, Canterbury, *c.* 792–6 (Blackburn, Colyer, and Dolley 1983, table 2.1).

Torksey (various locations). a–e. five sceattas, series E (one var. D?, three var. A, one secondary var.), Lower Rhineland or Frisia, *c.* 700–40; f. Offa of Mercia, heavy issue, London, *c.* 792–6; g. Coenwulf of Mercia, *Tribrach* type, London, 798–*c.* 804; h. Æthelbert of Wessex, *Floriate Cross* type, *c.* 862–5; i. Alfred of Wessex, *Lunette* type, Canterbury, *c.* 871–5; j. Northumbrian base styca, mid-9th cent.; a cut halfpenny of Sihtric III of Dublin, *c.* 1010 and one of Henry I (Blackburn 1993; *Coin Register* 1994, nos 169, 192, 236, 247); Continental imitation of Long Cross coin of Æthelred II (*Coin Register* 1988, no. 243).

Torksey (from a single field, widely distributed and not apparently a dispersed hoard). a–g. seven Northumbrian stycas: a. Æthelred II, first reign, York, *c.* 840–4?; b. Æthelred II, second reign, York, 844–8?; c-d. two of Archbishop Wigmund, York, 837-54?; e–g. irregular series, mid 9th cent.; h. Burgred of Mercia, *Lunette* type, London?, *c.* 870 (Blackburn 1993).

Torksey or Torksey region ('north-west of Lincoln, on or near the east bank of the River Trent'). Eight Northumbrian stycas: a. Archbishop Eanbald II, 796–830s?; b. Eanred, *c.* 835?; c. Archbishop Wigmund, 837–54?; d. Æthelred II, 840–8?; e. Redwulf, 844?; f–h. three of irregular series, mid 9th cent. (Blackburn 1993).

Ulceby, near. Sceat, series D, type 2c, Lower Rhineland, *c.* 700–10 (Blackburn 1993).

Washingborough. Coenwulf of Mercia, *Cross Moline* type, Rochester?, *c.* 810–20 (Blackburn, Colyer, and Dolley 1983, table 2.3).

Wellingore. One of Edward the Confessor (Blackburn, Colyer, and Dolley, table 2.26).

Willingham, near. Four of Æthelred II, one each of Cnut, Harold I, Edward the Confessor and Henry I (*Coin Register* 1988, nos. 169, 178; *Single Finds* 4).

Winteringham. a. sceat, series J, type 27, plated forgery, English, *c.* 715–30; b. sceat, series J, type 37, English, *c.* 715–30; c. Eanred of Northumbria, styca, earlier phase, York, *c.* 830 (Rigold and Metcalf 1984, p. 266; Blackburn, Colyer, and Dolley 1983, table 2.6).

Witham, River (below Lincoln?). One of Edward the Confessor (Blackburn, Colyer, and Dolley 1983, table 2.25).

Wroot. Sceat, series E, Lower Rhineland or Frisia, *c.* 700–50 (*Coin Register* 1987, no. 64).

HOARDS

Barrowby, near Grantham. Hoard deposited *c.* 1025 probably of several hundred coins of which only twelve coins of Cnut from the Stamford mint were apparently listed before it was dispersed (Blackburn, Colyer, and Dolley 1983, table 3. 4).

Owersby, North, near. Fragment of Edgar, *Two-Line* type, Five Boroughs region, found close to a group of four Edgar coins fused together (Blackburn and Bonser, 1989; *Coin Register* 1994, no. 198)

Stamford. 40+ coins deposited *c.* 900. The known coins are 15 or 16 pennies and 23 halfpennies of Alfred of Wessex, many of them imitations, and one obole of Charles the Bald (Blackburn, Colyer, and Dolley 1983, table 3. 1).

Tetney. 420 coins deposited *c.* 970. 45 of Eadred, 77 of Eadwig and 292 of Edgar, three uncertain and three of Scandinavian kings of York (Blackburn, Colyer, and Dolley 1983, table 3.2).

Walmsgate. Nine coins of *Lunette* type deposited *c.* 873, comprising two pennies of Burgred of Mercia, one of Æthelred I of Wessex, and six of Alfred of Wessex (Marshall 1987; Blackburn 1993, p. 81).

Welbourne. 20+ coins, the eight that have been listed are of Æthelred II (Blackburn 1985).

Appendix 10

THE FAMILY OF ABBOT BRAND

The fullest discussion of this family is by Stenton in his introduction to *LD*, pp. xl–xliv. Brand, prior of Peterborough Abbey, was elected abbot after the death of Abbot Leofric on 1 November 1066. He died on 27 November 1069 (*Chronicle*). Hugh Candidus names three of Brand's brothers who, together with Brand, gave or bequeathed 52 carucates of Land, almost all in Lincolnshire, to Peterborough Abbey; Askil son of Toki, Siric, and Siward (pp. 71–2). The Domesday *Clamores* (DB i. 376b = *LD* 71/15) confirm that Askil was Brand's brother. A fourth brother, Godric, was elected abbot of Peterborough after the death of Turold in 1098 (*Chronicle s.a.* 1098; Hugh Candidus, pp. 86–7, 138).

Most of the land given to the abbey by Brand and his brothers was in the wapentakes of Corringham and Manley in the north of Lindsey. A charter of William I confirming Peterborough's possession of most of that land claims that it was held by the abbey before the Conquest (Davis, *Regesta* no. 8). This is not confirmed by DB, but the fact that the charter was witnessed by Wulfwig, bishop of Dorchester, shows that the abbey had obtained them before his death in 1067. With the exception of one carucate in *Normannebi* and half a carucate in *Aletorp* (probably Normanby in Burton on Stather and Althorpe on Axholme) all the brothers' donations that are named by Hugh Candidus were still held by the abbey in 1086. DB names Askil as the TRE holder of manors in Scotton, Scotter, Raventhorpe, Risby and Walcot on Trent (DB i. 345b–346a = *LD* 8/15, 17, 23, 27, 28; DB i.376b = *LD* 71/15) as well as Muskham in Nottinghamshire (DB i. 376b = *LD* 71/15; apparently Peterborough's manor in North Muskham although according to DB i.284a the abbey already held it TRE). Askil also leased Manton from Brand (DB i. 376b = *LD* 71/15). The only other brother named as TRE tenant in any of the places in question is Siward, described as *Rufus*, who held one carucate in Northorpe (DB i. 376b = *LD* 71/15). The *Sigric* who witnessed the agreement concerning Stow minster in 1054 (S 1478, see Appendix 8) may well have been Brand's brother *Siric*. The TRE tenants named for the other places given to the abbey by Brand and his brothers were Rolft and Ælnoth; they were, presumably, sub-tenants of the brothers (see Appendix 3).

Brand's kinsmen included Ulf and Halfdan, sons of Topi. Their relationship is unknown; one possibility is that Topi and Toki were brothers. The will made by Ulf and his wife Madselin soon after the Conquest in preparation for a pilgrimage to Jerusalem (Whitelock 1930, no. 39) shows that he held a large amount of land scattered throughout Lincolnshire and some in Leicestershire, most of which was held by Drogo de la Beuvrière in 1086. As Stenton suggested (*LD* p. xliii) the Ulf who preceded Drogo as owner of the great Yorkshire manor of Aldborough and in various smaller estates in the same region was probably Ulf son of Topi. The will also names Ulf's brother as Halfdan, whose land was confiscated and given to Bishop Remigius in Brand's lifetime (Hugh Candidus, p. 69; DB i. 344a–b, 377a = *LD* 7/16, 18, 20, 22, 27). This must have happened before Brand's death in November 1069 because the abbot compensated Halfdan, his kinsman, for the loss by allowing him to rent Dunsby, near Bourne, that had been given to Peterborough by Ælfgar of Dunsby (Hugh Candidus, p. 69; DB i. 377a = *LD* 72/45). DB is, therefore wrong in naming Halfdan as the TRE tenant of Dunsby (DB i. 344b = *LD* 7/30). The will shows that Ulf was given land in Kettleby and Messingham by his mother who may be identified as the Eadgifu (*Eddeva*) named as the TRE tenant of manors in both places (DB i. 362a = *LD* 34/3, 8). She also had a manor in Grayingham, as did Halfdan who was presumably her son (DB i. 362b = *LD* 34/27). The manors held TRE by Eadgifu and Halfdan were, like those of Brand and his brothers all in the north of Lindsey. The will also names Siferth as another of Ulf's kinsmen, but nothing more is known about him.

BIBLIOGRAPHY AND ABBREVIATIONS

Abraham de la Pryme, The Diary of, Surtees Society 54 (1869)

Asser, *Life of King Alfred*, ed. W. H. Stevenson (Oxford, 1904)

Attenborough, F. L. 1922, *The Laws of the Earliest English Kings* (London)

Bailey, R. N. 1980, *The Early Christian Church in Leicester and its region*, University of Leicester, Vaughan Paper 25

Barley, M.W. 1936, 'Lincolnshire rivers in the Middle Ages', *LAAS* n.s. 1 (1938 for 1936), pp. 1–22

Barlow, F. 1955, *The Feudal Kingdom of England 1042–1216* (London)

Barrow, G. W. S. 1973, *The Kingdom of the Scots: Government, Church and Society from the eleventh to the fourteenth century* (London)

Bartholomew, P. 1984, 'Fourth-Century Saxons', *Britannia* 15, pp. 169–85

Bassett, S. 1989a, 'Lincoln and the Anglo-Saxon see of Lindsey', *Anglo-Saxon England* 18, pp. 1–32

Bassett, S. 1989b, ed., *The Origins of the Anglo-Saxon Kingdoms* (Leicester)

Bates, D. 1986, *A Bibliography of Domesday Book* (London)

Bates, D. 1992, *Bishop Remigius of Lincoln 1067–1092* (Lincoln)

BCS = W. de G. Birch, *Cartularium Saxonicum* (London, 1885–99)

Bennett, S. and N. 1993, *An Historical Atlas of Lincolnshire* (Hull)

Beresford, G. 1987, *Goltho: the development of an early medieval manor c. 850–1150* (London)

Biddle, M. and Keene, D. J. 1976, 'Winchester in the eleventh and twelfth centuries', *Winchester in the Early Middle Ages*, ed. M. Biddle (Oxford), pp. 241–448

Bishop, T. A. M. and Chaplais, P. 1957, eds, *Facsimiles of English Royal Writs to A. D. 1100* (Oxford)

Bispham, J. 1986, 'Recent metal detector finds from Essex and Lincolnshire', *BNJ* 56, pp. 183–5

Blackburn, M. A. S. 1985, 'The Welbourne (Lincs.) Hoard 1980–82 of Æthelred II coins', *BNJ* 55, pp. 79–83

Blackburn, M. A. S. 1989, 'The Ashdon (Essex) Hoard and the currency of the southern Danelaw in the late ninth century', *BNJ* 59, pp. 13–38

Blackburn, M. A.. S. 1993, 'Coin finds and coin circulation in Lindsey, *c.* 600–900', in Vince 1993a, pp. 80–90

Blackburn, M. A. S. 1994, 'A variant of the seventh-century "York" Group of shillings found in Lincolnshire', *Numismatic Chronicle* 154, pp. 204–8

Blackburn, M. A. S. 1998, 'The London Mint during the reign of King Alfred' in Blackburn and Dumville 1998, pp. 105–23

Blackburn, M. A. S. forthcoming, 'Anglo-Saxon and Anglo-Norman coin finds from Lincoln excavations 1981–94', *BNJ*

Blackburn, M. A. S. and Bonser, M. J. 1984, 'Sceattas, a styca, and other coin finds from a site in north-east Lincolnshire', in Hill and Metcalf 1984, pp. 233–9

Blackburn, M. A. S. and Bonser, M. J. 1989, 'A small fused group of coins from the reign of Edgar (959–75) found near North Owersby, Lincs.', *Numismatic Circular*, p. 225

Blackburn, M. A. S. and Dumville, D. N. 1998, eds, *Kings, Currency and Alliances: history and coinage in southern England in the ninth century* (Woodbridge)

Blackburn, M. A. S. and Mann, J. 1995, 'A late Anglo-Saxon coin die from Flaxengate, Lincoln', *Numismatic Chronicle* 155, pp. 201–8

Blackburn, M. A. S., Colyer, C., and Dolley, M. 1983, *Early Medieval Coins from Lincoln and its Shire* c. *770–1100* (The Archaeology of Lincoln VI–1)

Blair, J. 1988, ed., *Minsters and Parish Churches: The Local Church in Transition 950–1200* (Oxford)

Blair, J. 1991, *Early Medieval Surrey. Landholding, Church and Settlement before 1300* (Stroud)

Blair, J. 1995, 'Ecclesiastical organization and pastoral care in England', *Early Medieval Europe* 4, pp. 193–212

Blair, J. and Sharpe, R. 1992, eds, *Pastoral Care before the Parish* (Leicester)

Blom, G. A. 1960, 'Gilde: Norge', *Kulturhistorisk Leksikon for nordisk middelalder* (Copenhagen) 5, cols 308–13

Blunt, C. E. 1974, 'The coinage of Athelstan, King of England 924–939', *BNJ* 42, pp. 35–160

Blunt, C. E., Stewart, B. H. I. H., and Lyon, C. S. S. 1989, *Coinage in Tenth-Century England from Edward the Elder to Edgar's Reform* (Oxford)

BNJ = British Numismatic Journal

Boden, J. M. and Whitwell, J. B. 1979, 'Barrow-upon-Humber', *LHA* 14, pp. 66–7

Bonser, M. 1997, 'Fifteen years of Coin Finds from Productive Sites', *The Yorkshire Numismatist* 3, pp. 39–45

Bridbury, A.R.1955, *England and the Salt Trade in the later Middle Ages* (Oxford)

Brooks, N. 1984, *The Early History of the Church of Canterbury* (Leicester)

Brooks, N. 1989, 'The formation of the Mercian kingdom' in Bassett 1989b, pp. 159–70

Bruce-Mitford, R.1993, 'Late Celtic hanging bowls in Lincolnshire and South Humberside', in Vince 1993a, pp. 45–70

Burnett, A. 1984 'Clipped siliquae and the end of Roman Britain', *Britannia* 15, pp. 163–68

Cam, H. M. 1932, 'Manerium cum hundredo: The hundred and the hundredal manor', *EHR* 47, pp. 353–76; reprinted in H. M. Cam, *Liberties and Communities in Medieval England* (Cambridge, 1944), pp. 91–106

Cambridge, E. and Rollason, D. 1995, 'The pastoral organization of the Anglo-Saxon Church: a review of the "Minster Hypothesis"', *Early Medieval Europe* 4, pp. 86–104

Campbell, A. 1962, *The Chronicle of Æthelweard* (London etc.)

Campbell, J. 1979, 'Bede's words for places', *Names, Words and Graves: Early Medieval Settlement,* ed. P. H. Sawyer (Leeds), pp. 34–54, reprinted in Campbell, J. 1986, pp. 99–119

Campbell, J. 1986, *Essays in Anglo-Saxon History* (London and Ronceverte), pp. 99–119

Campbell, J. 1989a, 'Was it Infancy in England? Some questions of comparison', *England and her Neighbours, 1066–1453. Essays in Honour of Pierre Chaplais*, ed. M. Jones and M. Vale (London and Ronceverte), pp. 1–17

Campbell, J. 1989b, 'The sale of land and the economics of power in early England: problems and possibilities', *The Haskins Society Journal* 1, pp. 23–37

Campbell, J., John, E., and Wormald, P. 1982, *The Anglo-Saxons* (Oxford)

Carus-Wilson, E. 1964, 'The medieval trade of the ports of the Wash', *Med. Arch.* 6–7, pp. 182-201

Carus-Wilson, E. 1969, 'Haberget: a medieval textile conundrum', *Med. Arch.* 13, pp. 148–66

Cate, J.L. 1937, 'The English mission of Eustace de Flay (1200–1201)', *Études d'histoire dédiées a la mémoire de Henri Pirenne par ses anciens élèves* (Bruxelles), pp. 67–89

Chadwick, H. M. 1905, *Studies on Anglo-Saxon Institutions* (Cambridge)

Chronicle = *The Anglo-Saxon Chronicle.* The standard edition is Plummer 1892, translated by G. N. Garmonsway, *The Anglo-Saxon Chronicle*, rev. edn (London, 1954). A translation that clearly distinguishes the different versions is Whitelock, Douglas, and Tucker 1961, which is also given in *EHD* I (to 1042) and *EHD* II (1042–1154)

Clark, C. 1970, ed., *The Peterborough Chronicle 1070–1154*, 2nd edn (Oxford)

Clarke, P.A. 1994, *The English Nobility under Edward the Confessor* (Oxford)

CLAU = City of Lincoln Archaeology Unit

Cleary, A. S. E., 1989, *The Ending of Roman Britain* (London)

Coin Register 1987 – 1994 in *BNJ* 57–64 (1987–94)

Colgrave, B. 1956, *Felix's Life of Saint Guthlac* (Cambridge)

Colgrave, B. 1968, *The Earliest Life of Gregory the Great by an Anonymous Monk of Whitby* (Cambridge)

Colgrave, B. and Mynors, R.A.B. 1969, *Bede's Ecclesiastical History of the English People* (Oxford)

Cook, A. M., 1981, *The Anglo-Saxon Cemetery at Fonaby, Lincolnshire* (Sleaford)

Coppack, G. 1987, 'Saxon and early medieval pottery', in Beresford 1987, pp. 134–69

Councils and Synods, with other documents relating to the English church, 1.1 *871–1066*, eds D. Whitelock, M. Brett, and C. N. L. Brooke (Oxford, 1981)

Cox, B. 1994a, *The Place-Names of Rutland* (EPNS 67–9)

Cox, B. 1994b, 'The pattern of Old English *burh* in early Lindsey', *Anglo-Saxon England* 23, pp. 35–56.

Cox, B. H. 1973, 'The significance of the distribution of English place-names in *ham* in the Midlands and East Anglia', *EPNS Journal* 5, pp. 15–73

Darby, H. C. 1952, *The Domesday Geography of Eastern England* (Cambridge)

Darby, H. C. 1977, *Domesday England* (Cambridge)

Darling, M. and Vince, A, 1992, 'Dark Earth and the end of Roman Lincoln', *Current Archaeology* 11, pp. 364–7

Davies, W. 1977, 'Annals and the origin of Mercia', in Dornier 1977, pp. 17–29

Davies, W. and Vierck, H. 1974, 'The contexts of Tribal Hidage: social aggregates and settlement patterns', *Frühmittelalterliche Studien* 8, pp. 223–93

Davis, R.H.C. 1954, *The Kalendar of Abbot Samson of Bury St. Edmunds and Related Documents* (London)

Davis, *Regesta* = *Regesta Regum Anglo-Normannorum* vol. 1 *1066–1100*, ed. H. W. C. Davis (Oxford, 1913)

DB = Domesday Book

Dolley, M. 1983, 'The Danish descent(s) on Lindsey in 841', in Blackburn, Colyer, and Dolley 1983, pp. 40–4

Dornier, A. 1977, ed., *Mercian Studies* (Leicester)

Douglas, D. C. 1964, *William the Conqueror. The Norman Impact on England* (London)

Drinkall, G. and Foreman, M., forthcoming, *The Anglo-Saxon Cemetery at Castledyke South, Barton on Humber* (Sheffield Academic Press)

Dugdale, *Monasticon Anglicanum*, ed. J. Caley *et al.*, 6 vols (London, 1846)

Dumville, D. N. 1976, 'The Anglian collection of royal genealogies and regnal lists', *Anglo-Saxon England* 5, pp. 23–50

Dumville, D. 1989, 'The Tribal Hidage: an introduction to its texts and their history', in Bassett 1989b, pp. 225–30, 286–7

Eagles, B.N. 1979, *The Anglo-Saxon Settlement of Humberside* (Brit. Arch. Rep.; British Series 68 i and ii)

Eagles, B., 1989, 'Lindsey', in Bassett 1989b, pp. 202–12

East, K. and Webster, L. E., forthcoming, *The Taplow, Broomfield and Caenby Burials* (London)

Eddius Stephanus, *The Life of Bishop Wilfrid by Eddius Stephanus*, ed. B. Colgrave (Cambridge, 1927)

EHD I = D. Whitelock, *English Historical Documents* I *c. 500–1042*, 2nd edn (London, 1979)

EHD II = D. C. Douglas and G. W. Greenaway, *English Historical Documents 1042–1189*, 2nd edn (London, 1981)

Ekwall, E., 1960, *The Concise Oxford Dictionary of English Place-Names*, 4th edn (Oxford)

Everson, P. 1973, 'An excavated Anglo-Saxon sunken-featured building and settlement site at Salmonby, Lincolnshire', *LHA* 8, pp. 61–72

Everson, P. 1979, 'Pagan Saxon pottery from Cherry Willingham and Middle Carlton villages', *LHA* 14, pp. 79–80

Everson, P. 1988, 'What's in a name? – "Goltho", Goltho and Bullington', *LHA* 23, pp. 93–9

Everson, P. 1993, 'Pre-Viking settlement in Lindsey', in Vince 1993a, pp. 91–100

Everson, P. and Hayes, T. 1984, 'Lincolnshire from the air', in Field and White 1984, pp. 33–41

Everson, P. and Knowles, G. C. 1978, 'A tutulus brooch from Kirmington, Lincolnshire', *Med. Arch.* 22, pp. 123–7

Everson P. and Knowles, G. C. 1993, 'The Anglo-Saxon Bounds of *Æt Bearuwe*', *EPNS Journal* 25, pp. 19–37

Everson, P. L., Taylor, C. C., and Dunn, C. J. 1991, *Change and Continuity: Rural Settlement in North-West Lincolnshire* (London)

Felix = *Felix's Life of St Guthlac*, ed. B. Colgrave (Cambridge, 1956)

Fellows-Jensen, G. 1968, *Scandinavian Personal Names in Lincolnshire and Yorkshire* (Copenhagen)

Fellows-Jensen, G. 1974, 'English Field-Names and the Danish Settlement', *Festskrift til Kristian Hald* (Copenhagen), pp. 45–55

Fellows-Jensen, G. 1975, 'The Vikings in England: a review', *Anglo-Saxon England* 4, pp. 181–206

Fellows-Jensen, G. 1978, *Scandinavian Settlement Names in the East Midlands* (Copenhagen)

Fellows-Jensen, G. 1980, 'Conquests and the place-names of England, with special reference to the Viking settlements', *Ortnamn och Språkkontakt*, ed. T. Andersson *et al.* (Norna-rapporter 17, Uppsala), pp. 192–210

Fellows-Jensen, G. 1985, 'On the identification of Domesday tenants in Lincolnshire', *Nomina* 9, pp. 41–51

Fennel, K. R. 1974, 'Pagan Saxon Lincolnshire', *Archaeol. J.* 131, pp. 283–93

Field, F. N., 1981, 'Cherry Willingham', *LHA* 16, p. 70

Field, F. N. 1983a, 'Fillingham', *LHA* 18, pp. 96–7

Field, F. N. 1983b, 'Rand Church', *LHA* 18, pp. 101–3

Field, F. N. 1984, 'Stow Church', *LHA* 19, pp. 105–6

Field, N. and White, A. 1984, eds, *A Prospect of Lincolnshire...in honour of Ethel H. Rudkin* (Lincoln)

Fleming, R. 1986, 'Domesday Book and the tenurial revolution', *Anglo-Norman Studies* 9, pp. 87–102.

Fleming, R. 1991, *Kings and Lords in Conquest England* (Cambridge)

Florence = Florence of Worcester, *Chronicon ex Chronicis*, ed. B. Thorpe (London, 1848–9). A new edition and translation of the pre-Conquest part of this chronicle is now available, *The Chronicle of John of Worcester*, 2: *The Annals from 450 to 1066*, ed. R. R. Darlington and P. McGurk (Oxford, 1995). Thorpe's edition is still required for the post-Conquest annals

Foot, Sarah 1993, 'The Kingdom of Lindsey', in Vince 1993a, pp. 128–40

Forde, H. 1986, *Domesday Preserved* (London: HMSO)

Fox, H. S. A. 1981, 'Approaches to the adoption of the Midland System', in Rowley 1981, pp. 64–111

Frere, S. 1967, *Britannia: a History of Roman Britain* (London)

Galbraith, V. H. 1942, 'The Making of Domesday Book', *EHR* 57, pp. 161–77

Gelling, M. 1954, *The Place-names of Oxfordshire*, part 2 (EPNS 24)

Gelling, M., 1978, *Signposts to the Past: Place-names and the History of England* (London)

Gelling, M. 1979, *The Early Charters of the Thames Valley* (Leicester)

Gelling, M. 1982, 'Some meanings of Stow', *The Early Church in Western Britain and Ireland*, ed. S. M. Pearce (Brit. Arch. Rep., British series 102), pp. 187–96

Gem, R. 1986, 'Lincoln Minster: ecclesia pulchra, ecclesia fortis', *Medieval Art and Architecture at Lincoln Cathedral* (British Archaeological Association Conference Transactions for 1982), pp. 9–28

Gem, R. 1988, 'The English parish church in the 11th and early 12th centuries: a great rebuilding?', in Blair 1988, pp. 21–34

Gem, R. 1993, 'The episcopal churches of Lindsey in the early 8th century', in Vince 1993a, pp. 123–27

Gildas, *The Ruin of Britain and Other Works*, ed. and transl. M. Winterbottom (London and Chichester, 1978)

Gilmour, B. J. J. 1979, 'The Anglo-Saxon church at St Paul-in-the-Bail, Lincoln', *Med. Arch.* 23, pp. 214–17

Gilmour, B. J. J. and Stocker, D. A. 1986, *St Mark's Church and Cemetery* (The Archaeology of Lincoln XIII–1)

Gilmour, L. Adams 1988, *Early Medieval Pottery from Flaxengate, Lincoln* (The Archaeology of Lincoln XVII–2)

Godman, P. 1982, ed., *Alcuin. The Bishops, Kings and Saints of York* (Oxford)

Goscelin, *Life of St Werburg*, printed in *Acta Sanctorum*, Februarius I (Paris, 1863), pp. 391–4

Greig, J. 1989, 'Waterside North: plant remains – a preliminary sample', *Lincoln Archaeology 1988–9*, pp. 11–12

Grierson, P. and Blackburn, M. 1986, *Medieval European Coinage. I The Early Middle Ages (5th–10th centuries)* (Cambridge)

Hall, R. A. 1989, 'The Five Boroughs of the Danelaw: a review of present knowledge', *Anglo-Saxon England* 18, pp. 149–206

Harmer, F. E. 1952, *Anglo-Saxon Writs* (Manchester)

Hart, C. 1966, *The Early Charters of Eastern England* (Leicester)

Hart, C. 1971, 'The Tribal Hidage', *Trans. Royal Hist. Soc.* 5th ser., 21, pp. 133–71

Hart, C. 1977, 'The kingdom of Mercia', in Dornier 1977, pp. 43–61

Hart, C. 1992, *The Danelaw* (London and Rio Grande)

Hase, P. H. 1988, 'The Mother Churches of Hampshire', in Blair 1988, pp. 45–66

Hayes, P. P. 1988, 'Roman to Saxon in the South Lincolnshire Fens', *Ant.*, 62, pp. 321–6

Hayes, P. P. and Lane, T. W. 1992, *The Fenland Project, Number 5: Lincolnshire Survey, the South-West Fens* (East Anglian Archaeology Report no. 55, Sleaford)

HE = Bede, *Historia Ecclesiastica Gentis Anglorum*, ed. Plummer 1896a, i. 5–360; translation, Colgrave and Mynors 1969

Healey, R. H. 1979, 'Recent finds from South Lincolnshire', *LHA* 14, pp. 80–1

Henry of Huntingdon, *Historia Anglorum*, ed. T. Arnold (London 1879)

Hill, C. 1979, 'The archaeology of Anglo-Saxon England in the pagan period: a review', *Anglo-Saxon England* 8, pp. 297–329

Hill, D. 1978, ed., *Ethelred the Unready: Papers from the Millenary Conference* (Brit. Arch. Rep., British Series 59)

Hill, D. 1981, *An Atlas of Anglo-Saxon England* (Oxford)

Hill, D. and Metcalf, D. M. 1984, eds, *Sceattas in England and on the Continent* (Brit. Arch. Rep., British series 128)

Hill, F. 1948, *Medieval Lincoln* (Cambridge)

Historia Regum attributed to Simeon of Durham, ed. T. Arnold, *Symeonis Monachi Opera Omnia* II (London 1885), pp. 3–283. The parts used here are translated in *EHD* I, pp. 264–80

Holt, J. C. 1987, ed., *Domesday Studies* (Woodbridge)

Hooper, N. and Bennett, M. 1996, *Cambridge Illustrated Atlas. Warfare: the Middle Ages 768–1487* (Cambridge)

Hugh Candidus = *The Chronicle of Hugh Candidus, a monk of Peterborough* ed. W. T. Mellows (London, 1949)

Jarvis, E. 1850, 'Account of the discovery of ornaments and remains, supposed to be of Danish origin, in the parish of Caenby, Lincolnshire', *Archaeol. J.* 7, pp. 36–44

Jolliffe, J. E. A. 1934, 'The Era of the Folk in English history', *Oxford Essays in Medieval History*, ed. F. M. Powicke (Oxford), pp. 1–32

Jones, M. J. 1993, 'The latter days of Roman Lincoln', in Vince 1993a, pp. 14–28

Jones, M. J. 1994, 'St Paul-in-the-Bail, Lincoln; Britain in Europe?', *Churches Built in Ancient Times: Recent Studies in Early Christian Archaeology*, ed. K. Palmer (Society of Antiquaries, Occasional Paper 16), pp. 325–47

Jonsson, K. 1987a, *The New Era. The Reformation of the late Anglo-Saxon coinage* (Stockholm)

Jonsson, K. 1987b, 'Grantham – a new Anglo-Saxon mint in Lincolnshire', *BNJ* 57, pp. 104–5

Jonsson, K. 1990, ed., *Studies in Late Anglo-Saxon Coinage. In memory of Bror Emil Hildebrand* (Numismatiska Meddelanden 35, Stockholm)

Jonsson, J. and van der Meer, G. 1990, 'Mints and moneyers *c.* 973–1066', in Jonsson 1990, pp. 47–136

KCD = J. M. Kemble, *Codex Diplomaticus Aevi Saxonici*, 6 vols (1839–48)

Keene, D. 1984, 'A new study of London before the Great Fire', *Urban History Yearbook*, pp. 11–21

Keene, L. 1988, 'Coastal salt production in Norman England', *Anglo-Norman Studies* 11, pp. 133–79

Keynes, S. D. 1978, 'The declining reputation of King Æthelred the Unready' in Hill, D. 1978, pp. 227–53

Keynes, S. D. 1980, *The Diplomas of King Æthelred 'the Unready'* (Cambridge)

Keynes, S. 1985, 'The Crowland Psalter and the sons of King Edmund Ironside', *Bodleian Library Record* 11, no. 6, pp. 359–70

Keynes, S. D. 1986, 'Episcopal succession in Anglo-Saxon England', *Handbook of British Chronology*, ed. E. B. Fryde, D. E. Greenway, S. Porter, and I. Roy, 3rd edn (London: Royal Historical Society), pp. 209–24

Keynes, S. D. 1993, *An Atlas of Attestations in Anglo-Saxon Charters, c. 670–1066* (Department of Anglo-Saxon, Norse and Celtic, University of Cambridge)

Keynes, S. D. 1994a, 'Cnut's earls' in Rumble 1994, pp. 43–88

Keynes, S. D. 1994b, *The Councils of Clofesho,* University of Leicester, Vaughan Paper no. 38

Keynes, S. D. 1997, 'The Vikings in England, *c.* 790–1016', *The Oxford Illustrated History of the Vikings*, ed. P. Sawyer (Oxford), pp. 48–82

Keynes, S. D. 1998, 'King Alfred and the Mercians' in Blackburn and Dumville 1998, pp. 1–45

Keynes, S. and Lapidge, M., 1983, *Alfred the Great: Asser's Life of King Alfred and Other Contemporary Sources* (Harmondsworth)

Kilmurry, K. 1980, *The Pottery Industry of Stamford, Lincs. c. A.D. 850–1250* (Brit. Arch. Rep., British Series 84)

King, E. 1973, *Peterborough Abbey 1086–1310. A Study in the Land Market* (Cambridge)

Kristensson, G. 1967, *A Survey of Middle English Dialects 1290–1350: the Six Northern Counties and Lincolnshire* (Lund)

Lawson, M. K. 1984, 'The collection of Danegeld and Heregeld in the reigns of Aethelred II and Cnut', *EHR* 94, pp. 721–38

LD = *The Lincolnshire Domesday and the Lindsey Survey*, eds C.W. Foster and T. Longley, LRS 19 (Lincoln, 1924)

Leach, A. F. 1891, ed., *Visitations and Memorials of Southwell Minster* (Camden New Series 48, London)

Leahy, Kevin 1993, 'The Anglo-Saxon settlement of Lindsey', in Vince 1993a, pp. 29–44.

Leges Henrici Primi, ed. L. J. Downer (Oxford, 1972)

Lennard, R. 1944, 'The origin of the fiscal carucate', *EcHR* 14, pp. 51–63

Lennard, R. 1959, *Rural England 1086–1135* (Oxford)

LHA = *Lincolnshire History and Archaeology*

Liber Eliensis, ed. E. O. Blake (London, 1962)

Liebermann, F. 1889, *Die heiligen England* (Hannover)

Loveluck, C. P. 1997, 'Flixborough – the character and economy of a high-status Middle Saxon settlement in northern England', in *Rural Settlements in Medieval Europe,* Papers of the 'Medieval Europe Brugge 1997' Conference, vol. 6, pp. 179–94, eds G. De Boe and F. Verhaege, I.A.P. Rapporten 6, Zellik

Loveluck, C. P. 1998 (forthcoming), 'A high-status Anglo-Saxon settlement at Flixborough, Lincolnshire', *Antiquity* 72

Loyn, H. R. 1962, *Anglo-Saxon England and the Norman Conquest* (London)

Loyn, H. R. 1977, *The Vikings in Britain* (London)

Loyn, H. R. 1984, *The Governance of Anglo-Saxon England 500–1087* (London)

Lund, N. 1984, ed., *Two Voyagers at the Court of King Alfred* (York)

Mahany, C. 1977, 'A Saxon site at Osbournby', *South Lincolnshire* 1, pp. 267–7

Mahany, C. and Roffe, D. 1983, 'Stamford: the development of an Anglo-Scandinavian borough', *Anglo-Norman Studies* 5, pp. 197–219

Mahany, C., Burchard, A., and Simpson, G. 1982, *Excavations in Stamford Lincolnshire 1963–1969* (Soc. for Medieval Archaeology, Monograph Ser. no. 9)

Marshall, C. 1987, 'My Saxon coin hoard', *Treasure Hunting*, Jan. 1983, pp. 40–2

May, J. 1976, *Prehistoric Lincolnshire* (History of Lincolnshire 1)

Mayes, P. and Deane, M. J. 1976, *An Anglo-Saxon Cemetery at Baston, Lincolnshire* (Sleaford)

Meaney, A. 1964, *A Gazetteer of Early Anglo-Saxon Burial Sites* (London)

Med. Arch. = *Medieval Archaeology*

Metcalf, D.M. 1981, 'Continuity and change in English monetary history *c.* 973–1086, part 2', *BNJ* 51, pp. 52–89

Miles, P., Young, J., and Wacher, J. 1989, *A Late Saxon Kiln Site at Silver Street, Lincoln* (The Archaeology of Lincoln XVII–3)

Moore, J. S. 1992, 'The Anglo-Norman family: size and structure', *Anglo–Norman Studies* 14, pp. 154–96

Morris, R. 1983, *The Church in British Archaeology* (CBA Research Report 47, London)

Morris, R. 1989, *Churches in the Landscape* (London)

Morris, R. 1988, 'Churches in York and its hinterland: building patterns and stone sources in the 11th and 12th centuries', in Blair 1988, pp. 191–9

Morris, W.A. 1910, *The Frankpledge System* (London)

Mossop, H. R. 1970, *The Lincoln Mint* c. *890–1279* (Newcastle upon Tyne)

North, J. J. 1963, *English Hammered Coinage*, 1 *Early Saxon – Henry III* c. *650–1272* (London)

O'Connor, T. 1982, *Animal Bones from Flaxengate, Lincoln* c. *870–1500* (The Archaeology of Lincoln XVII–1)

O'Donovan, M. A. 1972, 1973, 'An interim revision of episcopal dates for the province of Canterbury, 850–950', *Anglo-Saxon England* 1, pp. 23–44; 2, pp. 91–113

Obelkevich, J. 1976, *Religion and Society: South Lindsey 1825–1875* (Oxford)

Okasha, E. 1971, *Hand-list of Anglo-Saxon Non-runic Inscriptions* (Cambrdige)

Okasha, E. 1992, 'A second supplement to "Hand-List of Anglo-Saxon Non-Runic Inscriptions"', *Anglo-Saxon England* 21, pp. 37–85

Orderic = *The Ecclesiastical History of Orderic Vitalis*, ed. M. Chibnall, vol. 2 (Oxford, 1969)

Owen, A. E. B. 1954, 'The Early History of Saltfleet Haven', *LAAS* n.s. 5, pp. 87–100

Owen, A. E. B. 1975, '*Hafdic*: a Lindsey name and its implications', *EPNS Journal* 7, pp. 45–56

Owen, A. E. B. 1980, 'Herefrith of Louth, Saint and Bishop: A Problem of Identities', *LHA* 15, pp. 15–9

Owen, A. E. B. 1982, 'A Fenland frontier: the establishment of the boundary between Cambridgeshire and Lincolnshire', *Landscape History* 4, pp. 41–6

Owen, A. E. B. 1984, 'Salt, sea banks and medieval settlement on the Lindsey coast', in Field and White 1984, pp. 46–9

Owen, A. E. B. 1988, 'Helen, Margaret and Andrew: some patterns of church dedications', *LHA* 23, pp. 73–5

Owen, A. E. B. 1989, 'Carlton, Reston, and Saint Michael: a reconsideration', *Nomina* 12, pp. 105–11

Owen, A. E. B. 1993, 'Beyond the sea bank: sheep on the Huttoft Outmarsh in the early thirteenth century', *LHA* 28, pp. 39–41

Owen, A. E. B. 1997, 'Roads and Romans in south-east Lindsey: the place-name evidence', *Names, Places and People. An Onomastic Miscellany in Memory of John McNeal Dodgson*, eds A. R. Rumble and D. Mills (Stamford), pp. 254–68

Owen, A. E. B. 1997, 'Louth before Domesday', *LHA* 32, pp. 60–4

Owen, D. M.1971, *Church and Society in Medieval Lincolnshire* (History of Lincolnshire 5)

Owen, D. M. 1975, 'Medieval chapels in Lincolnshire', *LHA* 10, pp. 15–22

Owen, D. M. 1984, 'The Beginnings of the Port of Boston', in Field and White 1984, pp. 42–5

Owen, D. M. 1994, 'Introduction: the English Church in eastern England, 1066–1100', *The History of Lincoln Minster*, ed. D. M. Owen (Cambridge), pp. 1–13

Page, F. M. 1934, *The Estates of Crowland Abbey* (Cambridge)

Page, R. I. 1966, 'Anglo-Saxon episcopal lists, part III', *Nottingham Mediaeval Studies* 10, pp. 2–24

Palliser, D. 1996, 'The "minster hypothesis": a case study', *Early Medieval Europe* 5, pp. 207–14

Parker, M. S. 1985, 'An Anglo-Saxon monastery in the Lower Don Valley', *Northern History* 21, pp. 19–32

Parker, M. S. 1992, 'The Province of Hatfield', *Northern History* 28, pp. 42–69.

Pawley, S. 1988, 'Grist to the mill. A new approach to the early history of Sleaford', *LHA* 23, pp. 37–41

Pedersen, B. H. 1960, 'Bebyggelsenavne på -by sammensat med personnavn', *Ti Afhandlinger* (København), pp. 10–46

Perring, D. 1981, *Early Occupation at Flaxengate Lincoln* (The Archaeology of Lincoln IX-1)

Phythian-Adams, C. 1978, *Continuity, Fields and Fission: The Making of a Midland Parish* (Leicester)

Platts, G. 1985, *Land and People in Medieval Lincolnshire* (History of Lincolnshire 4)

Plummer, C. 1892, 1896b, *Two of the Saxon Chronicles Parallel*, vol. 1 text (Oxford, 1892), vol. 2 notes etc. (Oxford,1896; reissued with a bibliographical note by D. Whitelock, 1952)

Plummer, C. 1896a, *Venerabilis Baedae Opera Historica*, 2 vols (Oxford)

PNL = K. Cameron, *The Place-Names of Lincolnshire* 1–4 (EPNS 58, 64/65, 66, 71)

Pollock, F. and Maitland, F. W. 1898, *The History of English Law before the time of Edward I*, 2 vols, 2nd edn (Cambridge)

RA = *Registrum Antiquissimum* (LRS 27–9, 32, 34, 41–2, 46, 51, 62, 67)

Rackham, O. 1976, *Trees and Woodland in the British Landscape* (London)

Raine, J. 1888, ed., *The Historians of the Church of York and its Archbishops*, vol. 2 (London)

Reynolds, S. 1977, *An Introduction to the History of English Medieval Towns* (Oxford)

Richter, M. 1973, *Canterbury Professions* (Canterbury and York Society 67)

Rigold, S. E. and Metcalf, D. M. 1984, 'A revised check-list of English finds of sceattas', in Hill and Metcalf 1984, pp. 245–68

Robertson, A. J. 1925, *The Laws of the Kings of England from Edmund to Henry I* (Cambridge)

Robertson, A. J. 1939, *Anglo-Saxon Charters* (Cambridge)

Rodwell, W. 1986, 'Anglo-Saxon church building: aspects of design and construction', *The Anglo-Saxon church. Papers on History, Architecture and Archaeology in Honour of Dr H. M. Taylor*, ed. L. A. S. Butler and R. K. Morris (CBA Research Report 60, London), pp. 156–75

Rodwell, W. and Rodwell, K. 1982, 'St Peter's church, Barton-upon-Humber: Excavation and structural study, 1978–81', *Ant. J.* 62, pp. 283–315

Roffe, D. 1986, 'The seventh century monastery of Stow Green, Lincolnshire', *LHA* 21, pp. 31–3

Roffe, D. R. 1977, 'Rural manors and Stamford', *South Lincolnshire Archaeology* 1, pp. 12–13

Roffe, D. R. 1990, 'Domesday Book and northern society', *EHR* 100, pp. 310–40

Roffe, D. R. 1992, 'An introduction to the Lincolnshire Domesday' and 'Hundreds and Wapentakes', *The Lincolnshire Domesday*, gen. eds A. Williams and G. H. Martin (London), pp. 1–31, 32–42

Roger of Wendover, *Flores Historiarum*, ed. H. O. Coxe (London, 1841). The annals quoted here are translated in *EHD* I, pp. 281–4

Rollason, D. 1978, 'Lists of saints' resting places in Anglo-Saxon England', *Anglo-Saxon England* 7, pp. 61–93

Rowley, T. 1981, *The Origins of Open Field Agriculture* (London)

Rudkin, E. H. and Owen, D. M. 1960, 'The Medieval salt industry in Lindsey marshland', *LAAS* n.s. 8, pp. 76–112

Rumble, A. 1977, '"Hrepingas" reconsidered', in Dornier 1977, pp. 169–72

Rumble, A. R. 1994, ed., *The Reign of Cnut: King of England, Denmark and Norway* (Leicester)

S = P. H. Sawyer, *Anglo-Saxon Charters: an Annotated List and Bibliography* (London, 1968)

Salter, H. E. 1907, ed., *The Cartulary of Eynsham* 1 (Oxford Historical Society 49)

Salway, P. 1981, *Roman Britain* (Oxford)

Sawyer, P. H. 1965, 'The wealth of England in the eleventh century', *Trans. Royal Hist. Soc.* 5th ser., 15, pp. 145–64

Sawyer, P. H. 1976, 'Introduction: early medieval settlement', in *Medieval Settlement: Continuity and Change*, ed. P. H. Sawyer (London), pp. 1–7

Sawyer, P. H. 1978, *From Roman Britain to Norman England* (London)

Sawyer, P. H. 1979, *Charters of Burton Abbey* (Oxford)

Sawyer, P. H. 1982, *Kings and Vikings. Scandinavia and Europe AD 700–1100* (London)

Sawyer, P. H. 1983, 'The royal *tun* in pre-Conquest England', *Ideal and Reality in Frankish and Anglo-Saxon Society,* eds P. Wormald, D. Bullough, and R. Collins (Oxford), pp. 273–99

Sawyer, P. H. 1985a, ed., *Domesday Book: a Reassessment* (London)

Sawyer, P. H. 1985b, '1066–1086: a tenurial revolution?', in Sawyer 1985a, pp. 71-85

Sawyer, P. H. 1986a, 'Anglo-Scandinavian trade in the Viking Age and after', *Anglo-Saxon Monetary History. Essays in Memory of Michael Dolley*, ed. M. A. S. Blackburn (Leicester), pp. 185–99

Sawyer, P. H. 1986b, 'Early fairs and markets in England and Scandinavia', in *The Market in History*, eds B. L. Anderson and A. J. H. Latham (London), pp. 59–77

Sawyer, P. H. 1994, *Scandinavians and the English in the Viking Age* (H. M. Chadwick Memorial Lecture 5, Cambridge)

Sawyer, P. H. 1995, 'The last Scandinavian kings of York', *Northern History* 31, pp. 39–44

Sawyer, P. H. and Thacker, A. T. 1987, 'The Cheshire Domesday', VCH *Chester* 1 (London), pp. 293–339

SCBI 27 = A. Gunstone, *Sylloge of Coins of the British Isles*, 27 *Coins in Lincolnshire Collections* (London, 1981)

SCBI 34 = M. M. Archibald and C. E. Blunt, *Sylloge of Coins of the British Isles*, 34 *British Museum. Anglo-Saxon Coins V Athelstan to the Reform of Edgar, 924–c. 973* (London, 1986)

Sills, J. 1982, 'St Peter's church, Holton-le-Clay, Lincolnshire', *LHA* 17, pp. 29–42

Sims-Williams, P. 1990, *Religion and Literature in Western England 600–800* (Cambridge)

Single Finds 1 = M. A. S. Blackburn and M. J. Bonser, 'Single finds of Anglo-Saxon and Norman coins – 1', *BNJ* 54 (1984), pp. 63–73

Single Finds 2 = M. A. S. Blackburn and M. J. Bonser, 'Single finds of Anglo-Saxon and Norman coins – 2', *BNJ* 55 (1985), pp. 55–78

Single Finds 3 = M. A. S. Blackburn and M. J. Bonser, 'Single finds of Anglo-Saxon and Norman coins – 3', *BNJ* 56 (1986), pp. 64–101

Single Finds 4 = M. A. S. Blackburn, M. J. Bonser, and D. Chick, 'Single finds of Anglo-Saxon and Norman coins – 4', in *Anglo-Saxon Productive Sites*, eds M. A. S. Blackburn and D. M. Metcalf, Brit. Arch. Rep. British series forthcoming

Smith, A. H. 1970, *English Place-Name Elements,* 2 vols (EPNS 25–6)

Smyth, A. P. 1975, 1979, *Scandinavian York and Dublin*, 2 vols (Dublin)

Stafford, P. 1978, 'The reign of Æthelred II, a study in the limitations on royal policy and action', in Hill, D. 1978, pp. 15–46

Steane, K. 1990, 'Wigford, Roman to Late Saxon', *Lincoln Archaeology 1989-90*, pp. 18–21

Steane, K. 1991, 'St Paul-in-the-Bail: a dated sequence', *Lincoln Archaeology 1990–1991*, pp. 28–31

Steane, K. 1992, 'St Paul in the Bail', *Current Archaeology* 11, pp. 376–9

Steane, K. and Vince, A. 1993, 'Post-Roman Lincoln: archaeological evidence for activity in Lincoln in the 5th–9th centuries', in Vince 1993a, pp. 71–9

Stenton, F. M. 1910, *Types of Manorial Structure in the Northern Danelaw* in *Oxford Studies in Social and Legal History*, 2, ed. P. Vinogradoff (Oxford), pp. 1–96

Stenton, F. M. 1927, *Documents illustrative of the Social and Economic History of the Danelaw from various collections* (London)

Stenton, F. M., 1970, *Preparatory to 'Anglo-Saxon England', Being the Collected Papers of Frank Merry Stenton* (Oxford)

Stenton, F. M., 1971, *Anglo-Saxon England*, 3rd edn (0xford)

Stewart, I. 1967, 'The St. Martin coins of Lincoln', *British Numismatic Journal* 36, pp. 46–54

Stewart, I. 1982, 'The anonymous Anglo-Viking issue with Sword and Hammer types and the coinage of Sitric I', *British Numismatic Journal* 52, pp. 108–16.

Stewart, I. 1990, 'Coinage and recoinage after Edgar's reform', in Jonsson 1990, pp. 455–84

Stocker, D. A. 1993, 'The early Church in Lincolnshire', in Vince 1993a, pp. 101–22

Stocker, D. A. 1997, 'Also a soldier: evidence for a Mithraeum in Lincoln', *LHA* 32, pp. 21–4

Sturman, C. J. 1984, 'Saltmaking in the Lindsey marshland in the 16th and early 17th centuries', in Field and White 1984, pp. 50–6

Tait, J. 1936, *The Medieval English Borough* (Manchester)

Taylor, H. M. and Taylor, J. 1965, *Anglo-Saxon Architecture*, 2 vols (Cambridge)

Thacker, A. T. 1985, 'Kings, saints, and monasteries in pre-Viking Mercia', *Mid. Hist.* 10, pp. 1–25

Thacker, A. T. 1992, 'Chester and Gloucester: early ecclesiastical organization in two Mercian burhs', *Northern History* 18, pp. 199–211

Thompson, E. A., 1990, 'Ammianus Marcellinus and Britain', *Nottingham Medieval Studies* 34 (1990), pp. 1–15

Toy, J. 1983, 'The commemorations of British saints in the medieval liturgical manuscripts of Scandinavia', *Kyrkohistorisk årsskrift*, pp. 91–103

Trollope, E. 1872, *Sleaford, and the Wapentakes of Flaxwell and Aswardhurn in the county of Lincoln* (London and Sleaford)

Vince, A. 1993a, ed., *Pre-Viking Lindsey* (Lincoln Archaeological Studies 1)

Vince, A. 1993b, 'Approaches to the study of Lincoln and Lindsey before the Vikings', in Vince 1993a, pp. 1–5

Vince A. 1993c, 'A tale of two cities: Lincoln and London compared', *Flatlands and Wetlands: Current Themes in East Anglian Archaeology,* ed. Julie Gardner (East Anglian Archaeology Report no. 50), pp. 152-70

Vince, A. 1993d, 'Forms, functions and manufacturing techniques of late 9th and 10th century wheelthrown pottery in England and their origins', *Travaux du Groupe de Recherches et d'Études sur la céramique dans le Nord-Pas-de-Calais, La Céramique du Vème au Xème siècle dans l'Europe du Nord-Ouest*, ed. D. Piton, pp. 151-64

Vince, A. 1994, 'Saxon urban economies: an archaeological perspective', *Environment and economy in Anglo-Saxon England*, ed. J. Rackham (CBA Research Report 89), pp. 108-19.

Vince, A. and Young, J. 1991, 'Mapping the Saxon City', *Lincoln Archaeology 1990–91*, pp. 23–8

Vita Ædwardi Regis, ed. F. Barlow (London, 1962)

von Feilitzen, O. 1937, *The Pre-Conquest Personal Names of Domesday Book* (Uppsala)

Wallace-Hadrill, J. M. 1988, *Bede's Ecclesiastical History of the English People: A Historical Commentary* (Oxford)

Wallach, L. 1975, 'The Urbana Anglo-Saxon Sylloge of Latin inscriptions', *Poetry and Poetics from Ancient Greece to the Renaissance: Studies in Honor of James Hutton,* ed. G. M. Kirkwood (Ithaca and London), pp. 134–51

Webster, L. and Backhouse, J. 1991, eds, *The Making of England. Anglo-Saxon Art and Culture AD 600–900* (London)

Whitelock, D. 1930, *Anglo-Saxon Wills* (Cambridge)

Whitelock, D. 1941, 'The Conversion of the Eastern Danelaw', *Saga-Book of the Viking Society* 12:3, pp. 159–76

Whitelock, D. 1959, 'The dealings of the kings of England with Northumbria in the tenth and eleventh centuries', *The Anglo-Saxons: Studies Presented to Bruce Dickins,* ed. P. Clemoes (London), pp. 70–88

Whitelock, D. with D. C. Douglas and S. I. Tucker 1961, *The Anglo-Saxon Chronicle* (London)

Whitwell, J. B. 1970, *Roman Lincolnshire* (History of Lincolnshire 2)

Wilkinson, L. 1980, 'Problems of analysis and interpretation of skeletal remains', *Anglo-Saxon Cemeteries 1979*, eds P. Rahtz, T. Dickinson, and L. Watts (Brit. Arch. Rep., British Series 82), pp. 221–31

William of Malmesbury, *De gestis regum Anglorum*, ed. W. Stubbs, vol. 1 (London, 1887)

Wood, I. 1984, 'The end of Roman Britain: Continental evidence and parallels', *Gildas: New Approaches,* eds M. Lapidge and D. Dumville, (Woodbridge), pp. 1–25

Wood, I. 1987, 'The fall of the Western Empire and the end of Roman Britain', *Britannia* 18, pp. 251–62

Wood, I. 1990, 'The Channel from the 4th to the 7th centuries AD', *Maritime Celts, Frisians and Saxons*, ed. S. McGrail (CBA Research Report 71, London), pp. 93–7

Wood, I. 1994, *The Merovingian Kingdoms 450–751* (London)

Wood, M. 1980, 'Brunanburh revisited', *Saga-Book of the Viking Society* 20:3, pp. 200–17

Wormald, P. 1978, 'Æthelred the lawmaker', in Hill, D. 1978, pp. 47–80

Yorke, B. 1993, 'Lindsey: the Lost Kingdom found?', in Vince 1993a, pp. 141–50

Zosimus = Zosime, *Histoire Nouvelle*, ed. Francois Paschoud, 3.ii (Paris, 1989)

INDEX

Abbreviations: abp = archbishop, bp = bishop, k. = king. Appendixes 1 and 9 are not indexed.